£3.00

D0305401

OPERA
A MODERN GUIDE

OPERA
A MODERN GUIDE

ARTHUR JACOBS
MA, HonARAM

and

STANLEY SADIE
MA, PhD, MusB

DAVID & CHARLES   NEWTON ABBOT

ISBN 0 7153 5013 7

First published 1964
by PAN BOOKS LTD
Second (revised) printing 1969
First hardback edition 1971
by DAVID & CHARLES (HOLDINGS) LIMITED
Second Impression 1973

Printed in Great Britain by
Redwood Press Limited Trowbridge Wiltshire
for David & Charles (Holdings) Limited
Newton Abbot Devon

CONTENTS

X

XI

INTRODUCTION

OPERA is a complex, strange and ever-fascinating art. In combining the form of a visual drama with that of a musical work, composers had been influenced not only by the musical means at their disposal but by theatrical practice and by the theatrical and literary tastes of their audiences. The musical scores which now delight us are the result of an encounter between the composer's genius and a variety of other factors – even, as in the case of *Rigoletto* and other Verdi operas, the hand of the political censor.

Yet the composer dominates. He dominates so strongly as to please not merely the audiences of his own time but the audiences of times to come – whose attitude to theatrical and other matters may have changed considerably. Beaumarchais's *Le Mariage de Figaro* and Sardou's *La Tosca* have retreated into the historian's cupboard: Mozart's and Puccini's operas are the continuing delight of operatic audiences from Montreal to Moscow.

Opera is fully captured only in the theatre, and normally – unless we wish to assume that composers did not know what they were doing – only when the words are fully understood, either by performance in the audience's language or by full comprehension of the original. The English words quoted in this book are taken, wherever possible, from English versions which have been used in actual performance at Covent Garden, Sadler's Wells or elsewhere; many, but not all, are available in published libretto form.

But we give the textual quotations in the original language too, not least in order to aid those who come to opera by the many fine gramophone recordings now available. For these, too, we depart from most previous books on opera in listing the characters not in order of importance in the drama but in order of singing.

As a general rule we name our characters in the language

used by the composer himself. But where the plots are classical or biblical or based on English literary sources we use the
accepted English form: and we allow certain eminent historical figures also to keep their well-known English forms,
e.g. King Philip of Spain. In the theatre, the opera-lover must
be prepared for occasional changes: for instance, as the action
of *La Traviata* takes place in France and is based on a French
play, a production of the opera in English may prefer French
names to those Italian ones which the composer, in accordance
with Italian theatrical usage, substituted.

Our synopses cover in detail sixty-six of the recognized
classics of opera by thirty-two composers from Purcell to
Britten. Many other operas and composers are mentioned in
passing. Of those operas treated in detail, each is discussed in
three parts: General introduction – Synopsis – Musical commentary. The operas are grouped under their composers, and
composers arranged in roughly chronological order within
their countries. A narrative links each composer with the one
preceding.

We are conscious, of course, of having had to restrict our
choice in order to keep the book within its bounds; and we
have excluded operetta altogether (even a work as fully a part
of the opera-house repertory as *Die Fledermaus*). We offer
our apologies to those whose favourites have had to be
omitted – as, indeed, have been some of our own! The musical
comments do not attempt the impossible task of reproducing
all the principal tunes: they are chosen with the particular
purpose of illuminating each composer's typical way of working on the intimate fusion of music and drama. In addition,
our pages provide – by means of the linking narrative, a
Prologue ('Early Opera') and an Epilogue ('The Modern
Scene') – a compressed history of opera itself. Throughout
the book, a date against an opera is, unless otherwise indicated, the date of first production, not necessarily of composition.

Our thanks are due to Mr Winton Dean, whose reading of
this book in typescript was of great help.

Permission to use copyright musical quotations was kindly

granted by the following:

Ascherberg, Hopwood & Crew Ltd (Leoncavallo, Mascagni)

Boosey & Hawkes Ltd (Richard Strauss, Stravinsky, Britten)

Durand (Debussy)

Heugel (Massenet)

G. Ricordi & Co. (London) Ltd (Verdi's *Otello* and *Falstaff* and Puccini)

Schott & Co. Ltd (Humperdinck)

Universal Edition (Janácek, Berg)

We also acknowledge our debt to the various translators mentioned, and to the following publishers of copyright translations quoted:

Ascherberg, Hopwood & Crew Ltd

Boosey & Hawkes Ltd

Breitkopf & Härtel, Wiesbaden (reproduced by permission of British & Continental Music Agencies, Ltd)

J. B. Cramer & Co. Ltd

Oxford University Press

G. Ricordi & Co. (London) Ltd

Schott & Co. Ltd

Universal Edition

ARTHER JACOBS
STANLEY SADIE
London, 1964

PROLOGUE

Early Opera

THE use of singing as an element in drama dates at least back to the Greeks, and the medieval mystery plays used it too. (One of these, *The Play of Daniel*, dating from the 12th century, has enjoyed successful modern revival.) But opera as we know it traces its birth to the Renaissance, and in particular to the period of about 1600, in Florence. It arose from such earlier dramatic forms as the madrigal comedy, the pastoral and the masque. *Daphne*, produced in 1597 with music by Jacopo Peri (1561–1633), is considered the first 'real' opera: and its employment of classical myth for its plot not only reflected the Renaissance ideal of recapturing the Greek spirit but also was prophetic of much opera to come.

These Florentine operas were the private affair of noble society. So were the early operas of Claudio Monteverdi (1567–1643), including another treatment of classical myth: *Orpheus* (in full, *La Favola d'Orfeo*, 'The Story of Orpheus'), which was produced in 1607 and is the earliest opera still to make occasional appearances in the professional theatre. But in 1637 the first public opera-house was founded, in Venice, and it was for a public audience that Monteverdi's later operas were written. The last was *The Coronation of Poppea* (L'Incoronazione di Poppea) of 1642, in which the mutual passion of the emperor Nero and Poppea triumphs over morality and justice and sends the legitimate empress Octavia into exile.

Opera is an Italian word (properly meaning simply a work, and still sometimes employed in Italian in that sense: the strict Italian word for our 'opera' is *melodramma*). The form spread elsewhere from Italy, partly in the composition of original operas in other tongues. The first great composer of French opera, significantly, was a Florentine by birth: Jean Baptiste Lully (1632–87), who entered the service of Louis XIV. Heinrich Schütz (1585–1672), who composed the first

German opera, *Daphne*, in 1627, had studied music in Italy with Giovanni Gabrieli (1557–1612).

In England, the court masques performed in the early 17th century under James I and Charles I approached the idea of opera. Then in 1656, although the public theatres were closed under the Commonwealth, a dramatic work called *The Siege of Rhodes* with music by five different composers was semi-publicly given in London: it is often reckoned the first English opera.

COMPOSERS AND THEIR OPERAS

I

HENRY PURCELL

(1659–95)

AMONG the earliest operas holding the stage in English-speaking countries is an English one: *Dido and Aeneas*. It might be imagined that this is, so to speak, the choicest flower of a whole garden of English opera cultivated by Henry Purcell and his contemporaries. This is not so. *Dido and Aeneas* is a freak growth, standing almost on its own.

Purcell's teacher, John Blow (1649–1708), had written a short, all-sung musical drama, *Venus and Adonis*, presented at court about 1684; and to some extent this served as a model for *Dido and Aeneas*. But except in this work Purcell followed the taste of the town and provided 'operas' which we should rather call spectacular plays with music. Not all the characters sang. In *King Arthur* (1691), with libretto by Dryden, King Arthur himself does not sing a note. Such works have reasonably been termed 'semi-operas' by later historians. But *Dido and Aeneas*, despite its brevity (it plays for less than an hour) is a real all-sung opera.

DIDO AND AENEAS

Libretto by Nahum Tate, after Virgil

First performed: Chelsea, London, 1689

Three Acts

Cast in order of singing:

Belinda, lady-in-waiting to Dido	*soprano*
Dido, Queen of Carthage	*soprano*
Another lady-in-waiting	*mezzo-soprano*
Aeneas, a Trojan prince	*tenor (or high baritone)*
A sorceress	*mezzo-soprano*
Two witches	*two sopranos*
A spirit	*soprano*
A sailor	*tenor*

Chorus of courtiers, people, witches and sailors

The scene is laid in ancient Carthage

JOSIAS PRIEST was a dancing-master who presumably met Purcell when both were working in the London professional theatre. Priest also ran a school for 'young gentlewomen' at Gorges House in Chelsea (which was reckoned, at that time, near London but not within London), and it was for this school that Purcell wrote *Dido and Aeneas* – perhaps for an out-of-door performance.

It is not known whether 'young gentlewomen' sang all the solo roles except that of Aeneas and the Sailor, or merely undertook the top line of the chorus, plus the dancing. Professional singers must, to a greater or lesser extent, have aided them. Aeneas's part is often sung by a baritone today, but Purcell intended a tenor. The composer himself probably directed the performance from a harpsichord, as was then customary. Strings alone form the rest of the orchestra.

The climax of the opera is Dido's farewell song, 'When I

am laid in earth'. With it, Dido, having been deserted by Aeneas (who has been tricked into his desertion by witchcraft), dies – whether of a broken heart or by suicide the text leaves in doubt. The emotional power of this song, which has become a classic of the concert-hall too, is partly responsible for the success of the opera in both professional and amateur performances.

ACT I

Belinda is endeavouring to cheer her royal mistress. The courtiers recognize that love for Aeneas (who, having fled from the sack of Troy, is a guest at the court) is making Dido unhappy; they urge her to marry him and thus to unite the thrones of Carthage and Troy. Aeneas enters and declares his love, and the music celebrates the triumph of love as the courtiers depart on a hunting party.

ACT II

In a cave, a sorceress is conjuring up her witches. They hate Dido and resolve to strike her by sending a false spirit, disguised as Mercury, to make Aeneas leave; in the meantime they will raise a storm to spoil the hunt. The spell is worked to an echo-chorus ('In our deep vaulted cell' ... '-ted cell'). A rapid dance movement, also using the echo principle, follows.

The scene changes to a grove, where the hunt is taking place. An air is sung by Belinda, and another ('Oft she visits') by the lady-in-waiting. Dido's women dance to entertain Aeneas, who displays the head of a boar he has killed. A storm arises and all flee back to town – all except Aeneas, to whom the false Mercury appears, announcing that Jove commands him to abandon the delights of love and sail away that very night. Aeneas laments but accepts the command. [Here should follow a scene and dance for the sorceress and witches: see below, pages 20–21.]

ACT III

Aeneas's sailors, at the ships, are preparing for their departure; they sing, with one of them as soloist, a song with lines immemorially suited to their trade:

> Take a boozy short leave of your nymphs on the shore,
> And silence their mourning
> With vows of returning
> Though never intending to visit them more.

The sorceress and witches observe the spectacle with glee, their vengeful chorus alluding to Dido by her alternative name of Elissa:

> Destruction's our delight,
> Delight our greatest sorrow;
> Elissa dies tonight,
> And Carthage flames tomorrow

The witches and sailors dance simultaneously.

Dido enters, heartbroken that Aeneas proposes to leave her. He says he will stay after all; but now Dido will have none of him. She dismisses him and he heads for his ships. A brief, grave chorus of courtiers leads to Dido's recitative, 'Thy hand, Belinda', leading to the air 'When I am laid in earth', in which the words 'Remember me' are instinctively repeated. Dido dies; a chorus mourns her; and the opera is over.

*   *   *   *   *

Purcell's marvellously apt musical setting of the English language shows itself particularly in recitative – and Aeneas, incidentally, has nothing but recitative to sing. The other numbers range, within one unified style, from the 'popular' idiom of the sailors' chorus to the 'learned' construction of a chaconne. Dido's first song, 'Ah, Belinda', is a chaconne, being built on a regularly repeated four-bar phrase in the bass; so, too, is 'Oft she visits' and so (even more subtly, because the repeated phrase is not four but five bars long) is 'When I am laid in earth' itself (Illus. 1).

There is a particular puzzle about the score of *Dido and Aeneas* as it has come down to us. A study of the rather complicated key structure of the opera suggests that some music is

[upper parts omitted]

missing at the end of Act II; moreover, Purcell normally ends each scene of a major work with a chorus, which is not the case here. Suspicion grows more positive with the discovery that a contemporary printed libretto shows the act ending with six more lines (for the sorceress and witches) plus a dance. The probability is that Purcell did compose music for this – music which has now been lost. The practice of many modern editors and conductors is to supply music in its place from other works by Purcell.

GEORGE FRIDERIC HANDEL

(1685–1759)

FIFTEEN years after Purcell's death Handel first set foot in England; he was naturalized there in 1726. Though his larger works later took the form of English oratorios (on religious subjects) and other (non-religious) dramatic music not intended for the stage, his first years in London were chiefly devoted to establishing himself there as a composer of Italian opera. This type of opera – all sung, without spoken dialogue, using recitative accompanied by harpsichord to link the formal numbers – had captured fashionable taste all over Europe.

Meanwhile English native opera languished. The only English work of the period to achieve lasting success was *The Beggar's Opera* (1728); it is classified by historians as a 'ballad opera' because it uses well-known tunes of the day (set to new words, by John Gay) though it is basically not an opera in the usual sense but a play, calling for actors who can manage to deliver simple, short songs. Later versions, notably Frederic Austin's (1920) and Benjamin Britten's (1948), are considerably more 'operatic' than the original.

Serious 18th-century Italian opera of Handel's type tends by our standards to seem dramatically stiff. In particular, the great majority of arias are in the *da capo* form – first part, middle part, then first part repeated, usually ornamented – which restricts development of character or situation within an aria; and, by a further convention, after each aria its singer leaves the stage. (These conventions largely served the purposes of the singers themselves, whose 'prima donna' behaviour and attitudes were notorious.) Handel, as recent revivals have strikingly shown, often transcends these limitations, sometimes by modifying the forms to suit the dramatic context, but more often by the sheer force and character of the music he writes within the accepted forms.

It has lately been suggested that his oratorios and similar works in English, to which these conventions did not apply, are dramatically more satisfactory than his operas. Several of them have been revived on the stage; the secular *Semele* (1744) and *Hercules* (1745), both on mythological plots, have had particular success.

Among his Italian operas, the most frequently revived (especially in Germany) has been *Julius Caesar* (Giulio Cesare; 1724). Others given lately include the first opera Handel wrote for London, *Rinaldo* (1711); the rather lighter *Xerxes* (Serse; 1738), an aria of which is the famous so-called Handel's Largo (actually headed *Larghetto!*); and several of the particularly fine group which includes *Tamerlane* (Tamerlano; 1724) and *Rodelinda* (1725). *Alcina* (see below) is notable for having been seen in London in three different post-war productions.

ALCINA

Libretto by an unknown author, after Antonio Marchi, based on an episode in Ariosto's 'Orlando Furioso'

First performed: London, 1735

Three Acts

Cast in order of singing:

Morgana, Alcina's sister	*soprano*
Alcina, an enchantress	*soprano*
Ruggiero, a knight, betrothed to Bradamante	*male alto*
	[see below, p. 25]
Bradamante	*contralto*
Oronte, Alcina's general	*tenor*
Melisso, Bradamante's guardian	*bass*

Chorus of Alcina's attendants and her former lovers

The scene is laid on Alcina's magic island

HANDEL's opera plots are usually derived from classical mythology or medieval legend; many of the librettos are based on the epic poetry of Tasso or (as in the case of *Alcina*) Ariosto. Spectacle and magic were an important ingredient of opera in the baroque period (1600–1750). The plots provided opportunities for such scenic display but rarely had much dramatic realism: their main function was to supply situations which could give rise to arias in a wide range of moods. This is certainly true of *Alcina*, where the modern audience is given not merely the opportunity to hear brilliant singing but the sense of universal emotions of joy and grief portrayed by subtle musical art. In cold print, however, the plot may seem dauntingly complex.

Admittedly, even in the theatre, Handel's operas are long and rather slow-moving. Being designed for audiences which listened with only intermittent concentration, they are usually heavily cut for modern performance. In *Alcina*, the unimportant character of Oberto is generally omitted, so the episodes concerning him are excluded from the following synopsis, as are a number of other sections which are conventionally cut today. The aria ending Act I ('Tornami a vagheggiar') is often, rather unsuitably, allocated in modern performances to Alcina rather than Morgana (though there is precedent for this switch in some of Handel's own performances).

Unlike most of Handel's operas, *Alcina* includes ballet – not because of any inner dramatic necessity but simply because Handel wanted to make use of a ballet company which was visiting London in 1735. It also uses a chorus, which is hardly less unusual.

The part of Ruggiero was originally designed for a male alto—a *castrato*, not a counter-tenor; today it is generally allotted to a contralto. (The problem of the *castrato* voice in early operas is discussed more fully on p. 33.)

Act I

Bradamante (in male attire, as a warrior) and her guardian Melisso have been searching for Ruggiero, Bradamante's betrothed, and are shipwrecked on an island ruled by the enchantress, Alcina. They are met by Alcina's sister, Morgana, who is attracted to Bradamante and begins to fall in love with 'him'.

Suddenly there is lightning and thunder, and the scene dissolves. Alcina is seen in her palace with Ruggiero. Her attendants sing in praise of the delights of her island; a ballet follows. Alcina welcomes the strangers and bids Ruggiero entertain them; she herself sings of her love for him: 'Tell, o tell' (Di, cor mio).*

Alcina goes, and Bradamante and Melisso try to remind Ruggiero of his duty towards his betrothed, Bradamante (Bradamante herself poses as Ricciardo, her own brother), but he says that he now loves only Alcina. Oronte, Alcina's general, enters; he loves Morgana and denounces 'Ricciardo', who seems to be his rival. Bradamante addresses Oronte and Morgana alternately in an aria: ' 'Tis jealousy' (E gelosia).

Oronte tells Ruggiero that Alcina herself is attracted by 'Ricciardo', and that he (Ruggiero) may soon join Alcina's former lovers in their various forms as wild beasts, trees and the like, to which she has transformed them. He warns Ruggiero of the fickleness of women: 'Can you a woman thus believe?' (Semplicetto! a donna credi?).

Alcina joins Ruggiero and denies his charge that she is fickle. She leaves. Bradamante tells Ruggiero of her true identity, although Melisso tries to stop her. Ruggiero, however, does not believe she is other than 'Ricciardo': 'Each look I know' (La bocca vaga).

Melisso and then Morgana try to persuade Bradamante to leave the dangerous island. But Bradamante is still determined to reclaim Ruggiero, and will not. Morgana, still believing that Bradamante is 'Ricciardo' and in love with her, promises to intercede with Alcina, who will be furious on finding that 'Ricciardo' evidently prefers another to her. Morgana sings of her love for 'Ricciardo': 'My soul is full of you alone' (Tornami a vagheggiar).

* English version by Charles Farncombe.

ACT II

In a hall of Alcina's palace, Ruggiero sings of his love for her. Melisso enters in the form of Atlante, Ruggiero's former tutor. Ruggiero is confused. Melisso puts a magic ring on Ruggiero's finger, breaking Alcina's spell. The splendid hall becomes an empty desert, and Ruggiero returns to his senses and no longer feels love for Alcina. Melisso (now also in his normal form) reminds him of his betrothed, Bradamante: 'Think of the fair' (Pensa a chi geme).

Bradamante herself enters. But still Ruggiero is not convinced of her identity, suspecting some further plot on Alcina's part. Bradamante sings angrily of Ruggiero's faithlessness: 'How shall I avenge me' (Vorrei vendicarmi). Ruggiero, alone, expresses his confusion: 'Love ever ready' (Mi lusinga).

Near her gardens, Alcina is about to transform the uncompliant 'Ricciardo' into a 'brutal shape', but Morgana interrupts her. Ruggiero enters and assures the doubting Alcina of his love (with asides making it clear that his love is really no longer for her).

Oronte comes to Alcina and tells her that Ruggiero intends to leave her. She is both heart-broken and determined on vengeance: 'Ye gentle Gods of love' (Ah! mio cor!). Oronte then tells Morgana that her 'lover' is also unfaithful. But she still rejects the love which Oronte himself offers; she goes, and he sings of his 'Ill-placed love' (E un folle).

Bradamante and Ruggiero (at last free of illusions) enter and embrace, but are seen by the jealous Morgana who angrily goes off to Alcina. Ruggiero bids farewell to the enchanted island: 'Verdant meadows' (Verdi prati).

Alcina, alone in an underground room, sings of her desertion by Ruggiero: 'Ah! still my heart' (Ah! Ruggiero crudel!). She tries to summon her evil spirits to her aid, but they do not appear: 'You hear, I know' (Ombre pallide). She goes off in a rage.

ACT III

Morgana too is now free of illusion. She realizes that 'Ricciardo', whom she loved, is a woman, Bradamante. In a court of the palace, she asks her former suitor, Oronte, to forgive her: 'Believe, dear tyrant, that I grieve' (Credete al mio dolore). She departs; before he follows, Oronte admits that he still loves her.

Alcina reproaches Ruggiero for leaving her and swears revenge: 'When you shall return again' (Ma quando tornerai). She leaves and Bradamante enters with Melisso. They talk of the danger of leaving the island: Ruggiero, having to part momentarily from Bradamante, compares his situation to that of a tigress having to leave its young: 'The Hyrcanian tigress' (Sta nell' Ircana). Bradamante determines to restore the bewitched former lovers to life: 'A faithful soul' (All'alma fedel).

Alcina learns from Oronte that Ruggiero and Bradamante are conquering the island before leaving. She expresses her grief: 'Still fears I have' (Mi restano le lagrime).

Ruggiero and Bradamante enter, intent on breaking Alcina's spell before they leave the island. Alcina tries to dissuade them by friendship, in a trio: 'Nor is this love, nor jealousy' (Non è amor, nè gelosia). Ruggiero breaks the urn in which Alcina's magical powers are vested; she, with Morgana, vanishes. Alcina's former lovers return to life. Their choruses of joy, and a ballet, end the opera.

*   *   *   *   *

One of the strongest weapons in Handel's musical and dramatic armoury was his fertile and apt melodic gift. At Ruggiero's farewell to Alcina's enchanted island, the melody in which he recalls its 'Verdant meadows' is not merely intensely beautiful in itself, but also serves to convey the mixed feelings – a twinge of nostalgic regret as well as joy and relief – which he experiences (see top of p. 29).

In a style whose musical patterns are mostly very regular, a notable dramatic effect is made by deliberately breaking

these patterns. Handel does this several times. One splendid
example is at the beginning of Act II, where Ruggiero's aria
trails off into recitative on the sudden entry of the disguised
Melisso. Another example occurs in Alcina's 'Ah! mio cor'.
In an aria of this period it is normal for the singer to enter
with the same music as has just been heard in the orchestral
introduction; here Alcina enters with an unaccompanied
'sighing' phrase ('Ah! my heart'), and then goes on with a
new counter-theme to the original introduction, heard again
in the orchestra. The effect is both arresting and moving:

One customary pattern running through all opera of this
kind is the sequence of recitative (accompanied by harpsichord) followed by aria (accompanied by orchestra). This

pattern could be broken by using 'accompanied recitative' –
recitative in which the orchestra (not just the harpsichord)
accompanies, usually in dramatic and illustrative style. There
is one such movement in *Alcina*, in the scene at the end of
Act II where Alcina tries to conjure up her evil spirits. Oddly
enough, the most striking part of this so-called 'accompanied recitative' is entirely unaccompanied. Alcina's agitation is expressed by the chromaticism and the wide 'skips' in
her music. 'I seek you, yet you hide? I command you, yet you
are silent?' she complains; and the utter emptiness and silence
around her phrases conveys her solitariness as the spirits fail
to respond:

CHRISTOPH WILLIBALD VON GLUCK

(1714–87)

GLUCK, a Bohemian-German who settled in Vienna, greatly admired Handel but rebelled against the formal conventions of the kind of Italian opera which Handel wrote. His aim – in the latter part of his career – was to make opera more truly and more naturally dramatic, more concerned with the powerful representation of emotion and less with displaying singers' virtuosity.

But because the abuses which Gluck rebelled against are largely unfamiliar today, the extent of his reforming zeal is now not too evident, and even Gluck's own operas seem sometimes a little formal and stiff. In particular the appearances and miracles of classical deities in such works as *Orpheus* (1762), *Alcestis* (1767), *Iphigenia in Aulis* (1774) and *Iphigenia in Tauris* (1779) introduce a note of artificiality. None the less all these are, from time to time, heard today – *Orpheus* in particular.

ORFEO ED EURIDICE

(Orpheus and Eurydice)

Libretto by Ranieri Calzabigi

Italian version first performed: Vienna, 1762

French version (Orphée et Euridice) first performed:
Paris, 1774

Three Acts

Cast in order of singing:

Orpheus	*male alto*
	[see below, p. 33]
Eros	*soprano*
A Blessed Spirit	*soprano*
Eurydice	*soprano*

Chorus of shepherds and shepherdesses, furies,
demons and blessed spirits

*The scene is laid in Ancient Greece, Hades
and the Elysian Fields*

THE story of Orpheus and Eurydice has appealed to many composers of opera – from Peri and Monteverdi (already mentioned) to Darius Milhaud (b. 1892), who, in. *The Sorrows of Orpheus* (1926), transposed the action to modern times. According to legend, Orpheus's magical power as a musician enabled him to regain his wife from the dead on condition that he did not look at her on the journey back from Hades – a condition he was unable to fulfil. In Gluck's opera a further miracle then happens so that Eurydice is resurrected and joins him after all.

Despite the artificiality of this resurrection, Gluck's *Orpheus* is felt as deeply expressive of real emotion – human love, the terror of hidden dark forces, the vision of unearthly bliss. Chorus and orchestra are fully used by Gluck to deepen the pathos suggested by the plight of the protagonist.

In most modern productions, the role of Orpheus is sung by a contralto. (The practice originated with the revival of the opera in 1859 by Berlioz, an ardent champion of Gluck.) This was not Gluck's intention. He wrote the role for a *castrato* male alto, Gaetano Guadagni. The *castrato* voice was, according to historical accounts, by no means effeminate-sounding, and *castrati* (not tenors!) were at the time generally allotted the heroic parts in opera.

A contralto, unless she can almost overcome the implications of womanliness in voice and demeanour, is therefore a dubious substitute. There are three other alternatives. The part could be given to a modern counter-tenor (that is, a natural male alto), singing the actual notes Gluck wrote. This has apparently never been tried on the stage; the counter-tenor voice is rather weak for a large opera house. Or a baritone can take the part, singing an octave lower. Or the part can be rewritten for a tenor – and Gluck himself re-wrote it so for the Paris production in French in 1774. This re-writing of the title-role, with some consequent shifts in the keys, was not the only change Gluck made in the French version. Modern performances generally adopt some features of the original (Italian) score, some of the French one.

The god of love appears in the original score under his Latin name, Amor; proper English usage, alongside the other Greek names, is Eros.

*   *   *   *   *

ACT I

Orpheus and his friends are weeping at the tomb of Eurydice. In answer to his cries Eros, the god of love, appears. He tells Orpheus that Zeus has had pity on him and will allow him to go down to Hades, charm its guardians by the power of his music, and bring Eurydice back – provided he does not look at her on the way. Orpheus, confident, sets out.

ACT II

At the mouth of Hades, the furies and demons at first violently resist Orpheus's coming, with repeated shouts of 'No!'.

But gradually he soothes them. Furies and demons disappear; the gates of the Elysian Fields open and the Dance of the Blessed Spirits is heard. Led by one of their number, the Spirits sing of their joyous existence.

Orpheus himself now enters the Elysian Fields: 'A purer sky' (Che puro ciel).* Eurydice is led to him, and he (not looking at her, in obedience to the command) leads her away.

Act III

Eurydice, uncomprehending, grows restive and suspicious. Can it be that Orpheus no longer loves her? He tries vainly to soothe her and does not tell her the reason for his behaviour. (He has been forbidden to do so.) At length he cannot resist Eurydice's urging and turns and embraces her. Immediately she dies.

Orpheus gives way to his grief: 'Shall no more my arms enfold her?' (Che farò senza Euridice?). He is on the point of joining his wife in death when Eros again appears, tells Orpheus that his constancy has been tested enough, and restores Eurydice to him. A chorus in praise of love formally seals the opera.

* * * * *

It is in this opera that Orpheus sings Gluck's most famous air, 'Shall no more my arms enfold her?' It is a strange air – strange because, despite its pathetic words and the sense of agonized loss which it supposedly expresses, its straightforward, major-key tune has none of the purely musical features which normally convey pathos or agony (see p. 35).

The use of the chorus as a main participant in the drama was a revolutionary step on Gluck's part. So was his dispensing with so-called 'dry recitative' (accompanied only by the harpsichord, as in Handel's operas) and having all recitative accompanied by the orchestra, thus helping to make recitative and aria sound more nearly homogenous and avoiding breaks in continuity. Equally individual is Gluck's imaginative use of the orchestra. The furies and demons call on Cerberus to

* English version by Edward J. Dent (O.U.P.).

destroy the interloper, and the terrifying barking of the monster is represented by a weird orchestral sound which sends
cellos and double-basses sliding up to repeated, emphatic high
notes:

A more familiar instrumental effect in *Orpheus* is that in the
Dance of the Blessed Spirits, often heard in the concert-hall.
The famous 'celestial' melody is often hailed as one which
could only **have** been given to the flute. But it wasn't! Gluck
gave it to a treble recorder; and though flute-players have
appropriated it, it ought to be restored.

II

WOLFGANG AMADEUS MOZART

(1756–91)

IN contrast to serious 18th-century Italian opera, with its plots concerning lofty heroes and heroines in remote times, there grew up a type of Italian comic opera which dealt with the present day and put dramatic emphasis on intrigue and absurdity. This type of opera (often referred to as *opera buffa*, which is just the Italian for 'comic opera') was originally often performed as an interlude in the performance of a serious opera (*opera seria*). Like its serious relative, *opera buffa* used recitative and not spoken dialogue to link the songs.

The centre of this type of Italian comic opera was Naples, and it was there in 1733 that the most famous example (and almost the only one still performed today) had its first performance: *The Maid as Mistress* (La Serva Padrona) by Pergolesi (1710–36). Most other works ascribed to Pergolesi, by the way, are not his but were given his name after his early death in order to win them popularity. Among these 'non-Pergolesi' works is the opera *The Music Master* (Il Maestro di Musica), which is apparently an altered version of a work by a virtually unknown composer, Auletta.

Comic opera of this type – especially in its device of putting all the characters on the stage together so that by singing 'against' each other they can represent a point of maximum dramatic complexity – is an important ingredient in the operatic style of Mozart, as in *The Marriage of Figaro*. He also used the 'lofty' style of serious Italian opera in two mature works, *Idomeneo* and *The Clemency of Titus* (La Clemenza di Tito; 1791). His German operas, *The Seraglio* and *The Magic Flute*, differ from his Italian not merely in language but in using elements of a more popular musical style and in using spoken dialogue in place of recitative. This type of German opera was of recent origin: in its simpler form it was called *singspiel* (literally, a singing play).

IDOMENEO

Idomeneo, Rè di Creta
(Idomeneus, King of Crete)

Libretto by Giambattista Varesco
First performed: Munich, 1781

Three Acts

Cast in order of singing:

Ilia, a Trojan princess, prisoner to the Cretans	*soprano*
Idamantes, son of Idomeneus	*male soprano* [see below]
Electra, a Greek princess, refugee in Crete	*soprano*
Arbaces, friend of Idamantes	*baritone*
Idomeneus, King of Crete	*tenor*
The High Priest of Neptune	*tenor*

Chorus of people, priests, soldiers and dancers

The scene is laid in ancient Crete

THIS is an 'old-fashioned' opera by the young Mozart, using a classical plot (King Idomeneus, 'Idomeneo' in Italian, is mentioned in Homer and Virgil), rather stiff action and stilted language. The original cast had an adult male *castrato* soprano as the youthful hero, Idamantes. Today the role can either be given to a female soprano or (as at Glyndebourne and Sadler's Wells) transposed down an octave for a tenor – a procedure entailing alterations of balance in the ensembles. Though lacking some of the warm humanity of Mozart's later and better-known works, the opera still justifies occasional revival. The contrast in music between the two women who are rivals for the young man's love is very effective. The quartet in the third act was considered by Edward J. Dent 'perhaps the most beautiful ensemble ever composed for the stage', and the chorus of farewell in the preceding act has enjoyed fame even when the opera has remained unperformed. The two arias for Arbaces, a subordinate role, are usually omitted in the theatre so as to tauten the action and reduce the opera's excessive length.

*   *   *   *   *

ACT I

Ilia, a Trojan princess, gives vent to her torn feelings. The Cretans, to whom she is prisoner, are her enemies – but how can she hate them when she has fallen in love with Idamantes, the king's son? She fears he loves Electra. Idamantes enters and declares his admiration for her. The Cretan people and their Trojan prisoners sing together in praise of peace, for King Idomeneus's returning fleet has been sighted.

Electra, as a refugee from Greece, is outraged at the mercy shown to the Trojans, her people's enemies. But she is interrupted by Arbaces with the news that Idomeneus's ship has been wrecked. Electra rages: if the king dies, what can stop Idamantes from marrying her rival, Ilia?

Electra's aria of rage merges into the rage of a storm on a deserted beach, where the people implore the god's mercy for the shipwrecked sailors (who are heard in the distance). Eventually Idomeneus himself lands, dismisses his attendants and reveals that he vowed, if he were saved from the storm, to sacrifice to Neptune the first person he met.

The first person he meets is Idamantes, his son. They have not seen one another for many years and do not recognize each other: when he discovers who Idamantes is, Idomeneus turns away in horror, leaving his son alone to express his puzzlement. The people enter, rejoicing at the king's safety and honouring Neptune.

Act II

Idomeneus discloses his terrible secret to his friend, Arbaces, who advises him to send Idamantes away to avoid his fate. Idomeneus decides to let Idamantes escort Electra back to Greece. Arbaces, after an aria, departs; Ilia enters and tells Idomeneus of her gratitude in finding a second homeland in Crete and a second father in him: 'Deprived of my father' (Se il padre perdei).* As she leaves, Idomeneus realizes that she loves his son: alas, it seems that Neptune will claim as victims not only Idamantes but Ilia and Idomeneus too. He sings of the disquiet in his heart: 'Though from storm at sea delivered' (Fuor del mar ho un mar in seno).

Electra sings happily of the prospect of being accompanied by Idamantes. A march calls her to the harbour to embark, where a chorus bids her a gentle farewell: 'Calm is the sea, before us now' (Placido è il mar, andiamo). As Idamantes and Electra take leave of Idomeneus, a fearful storm breaks and a monster arises from the sea, indicating the gods' anger. While the people flee in terror Idomeneus declares he is the guilty one.

Act III

Ilia sings of her love for Idamantes: 'Gentle zephyrs soft caressing' (Zeffiretti lusinghieri). Idamantes enters; the two declare their love. Idomeneus and Electra enter. Idomeneus has still not told his son about his vow, and now simply bids him go and never return. Ilia is in despair and Electra furious and vengeful over Idamantes's impending departure. A quartet follows, begun by Idamantes: 'Alone I go to wander' (Andrò ramingo e solo); then there is an aria for Arbaces.

The sea-monster has ravaged the city and killed thousands. At last in the temple, the king discloses to the people the vow he made. To avert further disaster, the High Priest and the people call on him to fulfil it. King and priests utter a prayer to Neptune. A shout arises from outside: Idamantes has killed the monster. Now, having learnt about his father's vow,

* English version by the Misses M. and E. Radford.

Idamantes presents himself for slaughter. Ilia wishes to take his place. But at the last moment Neptune's oracle intervenes, decreeing that Idomeneus is deposed, and Idamantes is to be king with Ilia as his bride. After expressing her fury, Electra leaves. Idomeneus presents to the people their new king and a chorus of rejoicing ends the opera.

*   *   *   *   *

Mozart wrote *Idomeneo* not long after his return from Paris. During his stay in the French capital a paper 'war' had been afoot between the supporters of Gluck's reform operas and those who preferred the traditional style (represented by Piccinni). Mozart – by instinct rather than conscious intention – steered a middle course in *Idomeneo*. Neither he, his singers nor his public wanted to break down, as Gluck was aiming to do, the conventional structure of recitatives and 'set-piece' arias. In this, and in his use of the chorus, Mozart followed Piccinni's example.

None the less, Mozart's use of accompanied recitative for particularly dramatic passages is much indebted to Gluck in *Orpheus* and *Alcestis*. A good example is the moment where Idomeneus and Idamantes recognize one another. It must be remembered that Idomeneus – and the audience – realize the consequences of the situation but Idamantes does not. Idomeneus' exclamation 'oh ye pitiless gods!' is thus greeted by his son with puzzlement: 'Do you join with me in lamenting my father's fate?' (we translate literally). Only when Idomeneus lets fall the word 'figlio' (son) does Idamantes know that the father he has lost stands before him.

The musical language of the opera is in general rather formal. But when, for special effect, Mozart breaks with this formality, powerful emotional stress results. Thus, notably, the phrase with which Idamantes opens the great quartet in Act III is repeated towards the end; but instead of leading, as before, to an ensemble, it breaks off and the orchestra takes over, and concludes, the music: Idamantes is evidently overcome, and words fail him (Illus. 2).

To emphasize the solemnity of the utterance of the oracle, Mozart brings trombones into the score – as similarly in *Don Giovanni* and *The Magic Flute*.

2

DIE ENTFÜHRUNG AUS DEM SERAIL
(The Seraglio)

Libretto by G. Stephanie, after a libretto by C. F. Bretzner
First performed: Vienna, 1782

Three Acts

Cast in order of singing or speaking:

Belmont, a Spanish nobleman	*tenor*
Osmin, overseer of the Pasha's harem	*bass*
Pedrillo, servant to Belmont	*tenor*
The Pasha Selim	*speaking part*
Constanze, a Spanish noblewoman	*soprano*
Blonde, Constanze's English maid	*soprano*

Chorus of janissaries, Turkish women, etc.

The scene is laid in Turkey

WHY Seraglio? This Italian term (in modern Italian spelt *serraglio*) is apparently taken from the Latin word for a door-bar in confusion with the Turkish word for a palace. The Italian term has long been used in English. But this is not an Italian opera: English references to the work with the Italian article (*Il Seraglio*) have their origin in the fact that virtually all non-Italian operas (even *The Flying Dutchman*) were, from alleged convenience to singers, mounted in Italian in 19th-century London. Normal modern English usage is to call the opera *The Seraglio*, but *The Harem* or *Escape from the Harem* would do as well. It is a German opera with spoken dialogue, written for the company that had been specially established for such works by the Emperor Joseph II in Vienna.

It is a comedy about Europeans in a Turkish Pasha's harem, and its chief ingredients are conventional: a well-to-do hero and heroine who are serious characters, and the hero's man-servant and the heroine's maid-servant who are comic. The most memorable character, however, is none of these but the overseer of the harem, Osmin – a comic villain and one of the great comic characters of opera. But there is the musical appeal of one of the most famous of all coloratura arias (in which the heroine defies the threat of torture) to add in this opera to the appeal of the comedy, which includes a 'drunk' scene with appropriately rib-tickling music. An oddity of the work is that the Pasha (who in the end is magnanimous enough to let his captives go of his own free will) does not sing at all. There are other inconsistencies of style in the work, but Mozart's felicitous contribution outweights all defects.

The Spanish names of Belmonte and Constancia are Germanized in Mozart's libretto as Belmont and Constanze.

*   *   *   *   *

ACT I

Finding himself outside a big country house, Belmont wonders whether it belongs to the Pasha Selim and if he will find his lost love, Constanze, there. But he gets no satisfaction when he inquires of the Pasha's overseer, Osmin. Osmin persists in

singing to himself – 'You may think you've found a woman'
(Wer ein Liebchen hat gefunden)* – and in taking no notice
of his questioner. He discloses, however, that he hates Pedrillo, who is also in the Pasha's service. And when Belmont
leaves and Pedrillo appears, Osmin shows his hatred.

Osmin leaves. Belmont returns, finds Pedrillo (his own
former servant, now the Pasha's gardener), and learns that
Constanze is still true to him. Belmont decides to pose as an
eminent visiting architect who could be useful to the Pasha.
Before he leaves, he sings of his love: 'How I'm trembling'
(O wie ängstlich).

The Pasha enters, attended by his suite. He attempts to
woo Constanze but she declares she loves another: 'How enchanting, how enraptured' (Ach, ich liebte). Constanze leaves,
the Pasha accepts the proffered services of Belmont, and the
enmity of Osmin towards Belmont and Pedrillo is shown in
a brisk trio.

ACT II

In the garden, Blonde (Constanze's maid) sings of her longing for a tender wooer, and in her duet with the coarse Osmin
shows the cool disdain appropriate to an Englishwoman.

Constanze, after the Pasha has again attempted to woo her,
bewails her sad fate and then voices her defiance: 'Torture
me and flay me' (Martern aller Arten).

A catchy song for Blonde, looking forward to her release,
is followed by one in which Pedrillo sings of his approaching 'battle' – the battle being concerned with overcoming
Osmin by making him drunk, despite the Prophet's injunction against liquor. This is accomplished in a rapid, brief
drinking duet, 'Vivat Bacchus', and Osmin is led off. The
four lovers are united, Belmont greeting Constanze ecstatically, and then all join in a quartet in which the two men are
ready to suspect the women of infidelity but are convincingly
reprimanded (Pedrillo with a box on the ear from Blonde).
The quartet is developed at length, to affirm the sentiments
of love.

* English version by Edward J. Dent (O.U.P.).

ACT III

It is midnight; Belmont and Pedrillo are about to put their plan of escape into action. Pedrillo sings, as a signal to the women, the 'oriental' serenade 'Once on Arabia's golden shore' (In Mohrenland). But Osmin, waking, interrupts the attempted abduction, refuses a bribe from Belmont, arrests the four would-be escapers and rejoices: 'Now for righteous retribution!' (Ha! wie will ich triumphieren).

The Pasha, hearing who Belmont really is, discloses that he himself was wronged by Belmont's father. In revenge, all four captives shall be tortured. A duet of anguish for Belmont and Constanze follows. But the Pasha, reappearing, announces that he despises Belmont's father too much to follow his example and will set the captives free. All four join in giving thanks to the Pasha for his magnanimity; and the frustrated Osmin joins in too, with an empty repetition of the threats in his original song of hatred against Pedrillo (Act I). Osmin apart, their rejoicing is universal as the opera ends.

*   *   *   *   *

At the opening of the 18th century the percussion instruments characteristic of Turkish music began to invade European military music. From this came the employment of bass drum, cymbals and triangle in the modern orchestra – and Mozart employs them in the overture to *The Seraglio* precisely to convey oriental 'local colour'. This 'Janissary music', as music with this special percussion effect is called (from the Turkish military corps of Janissaries), recurs in the opera itself; and the male chorus of attendants on the Pasha are themselves described in the score as 'Janissaries'.

The serenade sung in the third act by Pedrillo was presumably also intended by Mozart to have an oriental atmosphere; it has a curious modal scale (not in our modern major or minor keys) which sounds generally 'foreign' rather than specifically oriental to us. The serenade tells of a fair maiden kept prisoner in a Moorish land.

In Moh-ren-land ge-fan-gen war.___ ein Mä-del hübsch und fein, sah roth und weiss, war schwarz von Haar, seufz' Tag und Nacht und wein-te gar, wollt' gern er-lö-set sein,___ wollt' gern er-lö-set sein.

The two comic servants, Pedrillo and Blonde, seem to have a more approachable humanity in their music than their employers. Blonde is supposed to be an Englishwoman, cool and crafty – which means, in an English performance, that Osmin can directly address his audience when exclaiming: 'What fools are the husbands in England, Such freedom they grant to their wives':

O Eng-län-der, seid ihr nicht Tho-ren; ihr lasst eu-ren Wei-bern den Wil-len!

Belmont and Constanze are personifications of the emotions supposed to be proper to heroes and heroines. Constanze indeed is allowed to take this to extremes in the most famous aria of the work, 'Torture me and flay me' (Martern aller Arten), in which she declares to the Pasha her determination to resist his advances. This aria is on such an enormous scale, with contrasted sections and with sixty bars of instrumental introduction alone, that it seems to hold up the drama. It requires the full agility of a coloratura soprano (high notes, rapid runs, ornamentation) with more dramatic weight than most such singers can give. In fact, many of the songs are over-long.

The finale of the last act, with verses for different characters and a recurring refrain, is a *vaudeville* in the original and technical sense of that word.

LE NOZZE DI FIGARO
(The Marriage of Figaro)

Libretto by Lorenzo da Ponte, after the play by Beaumarchais
First performed: Vienna, 1786

Four Acts

Cast in order of singing:

Figaro, servant to Count Almaviva	*baritone*
Susanna, maid to the Countess Almaviva	*soprano*
Doctor Bartolo	*bass*
Marcellina (former housekeeper of Dr Bartolo)	*soprano*
Cherubino, a young page in Count Almaviva's service	
	mezzo-soprano (or soprano)
Count Almaviva	*baritone*
Don Basilio, a teacher of music	*tenor*
Countess Almaviva	*soprano*
Antonio, a gardener to Count Almaviva, and uncle to Susanna	*bass*
Don Curzio, a lawyer	*tenor*
Barbarina, daughter of Antonio	*soprano*
Chorus of villagers	

The scene is laid in a castle and its grounds near Seville

NOT a few music-lovers would call *The Marriage of Figaro* the greatest comic opera ever written, a spring of bubbling melody set to a sharp, fast-moving, witty plot. It is an opera about masters and servants and the complications in that relationship caused by sex. To the original audience it was an opera on a contemporary subject, with strong political undertones. It was based on a famous French play by an author then still living, Beaumarchais. The play was a sequel to another about the same character, *The Barber of Seville*, which had already been set successfully as an opera – not yet by Rossini but by Giovanni Paisiello (1740–1816).

In *The Barber of Seville* (see page 96), Figaro is the barber and general factotum who outwits Rosina's stupid guardian Bartolo and smoothes the way for the marriage of Count Almaviva and Rosina. Now, in *The Marriage of Figaro*, Rosina has become the Countess and Figaro is the Count's servant. He and the Countess's maid Susanna are betrothed.

The Count and Figaro are both jealous characters, Figaro justifiably so since he knows that the Count himself has designs on Susanna. The words of the libretto make pointed reference to 'the feudal right'. This alludes to the custom by which the lord of the manor, in compensation for the loss of one of his female serfs through marriage, was supposedly allowed to rob the girl of her virginity before the husband took possession. This custom, we learn, has recently been abolished on the Count's estates but, as Figaro puts it, the Count wishes to get back by consent from Susanna the right that he has given up by law.

The situation is complicated not only by the fact that Figaro is virile and self-willed enough to avenge any wrong done to Susanna, but also by the presence in the household of Cherubino, a page – that is, a young man of noble family sent to learn good manners. He is just at an age at which both the Countess and Susanna have to learn not to treat him as a pretty plaything any more. 'He' is sung in the opera by a mezzo-soprano or soprano.

Two arias, one for Marcellina and one for Basilio, are customarily omitted in the final act, and are omitted in the following synopsis.

*   *   *   *   *

ACT I

Susanna is trying on a new hat. Figaro, who is to be married to her, is measuring out a room for a bed. But Susanna insists that this room will never do for their bedroom as it is far too near the Count's, and the Count is by no means to be trusted. Figaro vows, however, that if the Count wants to dance, then he shall dance to Figaro's tune – 'If you are after a little amusement' (Se vuol ballare).* After Figaro's departure Bartolo, who was once outwitted by Figaro, comes in and shows his desire for vengeance. And if Bartolo is angry with Figaro, no less is Marcellina with Susanna, for she wishes to marry Figaro herself. The two women have a duet of mock courtesy: 'I bid you good-day' (Via resti servita). Marcellina leaves.

Now enters Cherubino, the page. He declares his boyish passion for the Countess – but it is really a passion for all womankind, as his song shows: 'Is it pain, is it pleasure' (Non so più). The Count's voice is heard and Cherubino (who should not be there at all) hides behind a chair. The Count suggests an assignation with Susanna, but then he has to hide himself when a voice is heard outside. It is that of Don Basilio – a rascally abbé who is music master and organist in the Count's establishment, and general go-between for all manner of intrigue. So the Count is now hiding *behind* a chair and Cherubino *on* the chair, covered by a dress, while Basilio makes insinuations to Susanna about herself and the Count and about Cherubino's interest in the Countess.

The Count, enraged, reveals himself and declares that he is in any case going to get rid of Cherubino because of what happened the other day: he, the Count, was visiting a young lady called Barbarina, and happened to lift up a cloth from a table just in *this* way (and here the Count draws back the covering of the chair in the room where they are) and there was Cherubino hiding! And there, of course, Cherubino is now discovered hiding in exactly the same position. The Count is furious, particularly because Cherubino must have overheard everything, although Cherubino says he did his best not to listen.

* English version by Edward J. Dent (O.U.P.).

The interchange is interrupted by the entry of Figaro with a group of peasants, who strew flowers before the Count: Figaro has come to ask the Count to join him and Susanna in marriage. The Count promises to do so, but puts him off till later, and now tells Cherubino that he must leave the castle and become an ensign in the Count's regiment. Figaro, also not unrelieved to see Cherubino go, sings gaily of the hazardous military life which now awaits him: 'Say goodbye now to pastime and play, lad' (Non più andrai, farfallone amoroso).

Act II

The Countess, in her boudoir, laments that her husband no longer appears to love her: 'God of love' (Porgi, amor). Susanna enters and tells the Countess that the Count has designs on her (Susanna), and together they plan to outwit him. Cherubino enters and sings a song to the Countess which expresses his boyish love for her: 'Tell me, fair ladies' (Voi che sapete). Susanna and the Countess plan to spite the Count by making an assignation with him in Susanna's name and then sending not Susanna but Cherubino in disguise. For this purpose they start to dress up Cherubino in women's clothes, having prudently locked the door first. But then the Count is heard outside. Cherubino rushes into an inner room and the Countess is in obvious confusion when she lets the Count enter. Meanwhile, Susanna has hidden in an alcove.

His suspicions are aroused, but the Countess insists that in the inner room, which is now locked, is only her maid Susanna. The Count doubts her and says he will go and fetch tools to break the lock of the inner door, and he insists on taking the Countess with him. While Count and Countess are out of the room Susanna dashes out of the alcove in which she has been hiding, unlocks the inner door, and lets out Cherubino, who jumps down out of the window. Susanna then goes into the inner room and locks herself in it.

When the Count and Countess return, therefore, the room looks as if nothing has happened. The Countess, fearing that the Count will find Cherubino in the inner room, confesses to him and asks for pardon. Furious, and with his sword drawn, the Count opens the inner door – and out comes Susanna, to the surprise of the Countess no less than of the Count. Recovering herself, the Countess says that her 'confession' was a ruse to shame the Count and that, of course, it was only Susanna in the inner room all the time. It is the Count's turn now to beg pardon of the Countess.

The intrigue now grows more complex still. Antonio, the gardener, who is also Susanna's uncle, comes in half tipsy and complains that a man jumped down from the window and damaged his plants. Figaro, who has entered, says this was himself and sustains the part with difficulty when Antonio confronts him with the officer's commission which, in reality, Cherubino has dropped. The Count's suspicions are still by no means allayed. Now he welcomes, as allies, Marcellina, Bartolo and Basilio who enter to put forward the case that Figaro is legally obliged to marry Marcellina in compensation for a debt which he is unable to repay. The complication is unresolved as the curtain falls.

ACT III

Susanna, still trying to mislead the Count, promises in a duet to meet him in the garden – though with some confusion between 'yes' and 'no' which arouses his suspicion. When she goes, the Count again becomes suspicious as he overhears some tell-tale words which she says to Figaro. He vents his anger: 'Must I forgo my pleasure?' (Vedrò mentr'io sospiro).

Now Marcellina, accompanied by Bartolo and the Count's lawyer, Don Curzio, confronts Figaro with his promise to marry her. Figaro prevaricates, saying he is of noble birth and cannot marry without the consent of his parents. In token of his noble birth he says that not only can he show them the fine garments in which he was found when an infant, but also a curious mark on his right arm. On seeing this mark Marcellina exclaims with excitement that Figaro is her son and, what is more, Bartolo is Figaro's father.

There follows a sextet of comic reconciliation. Even the

Count is reduced to angry inaction. Figaro naturally enough embraces his new-found mother, Marcellina. But when Susanna enters – having raised from the Countess a sum of money to pay the debt and release Figaro from Marcellina's claim – she misconstrues the embrace, she goes straight up to Figaro and boxes him on the ear. Marcellina then takes the lead in explaining the new situation to Susanna, who repeats the words 'His mother? His father?' (Sua madre? suo padre?) and insists that all should confirm them – which they cheerfully do.

They leave, and the Countess enters. She is still unhappy: 'I remember the days' (Dove sono). Can she truly regain her husband's affection? She still hankers to punish him by a false assignation with Susanna in which he will find himself trapped, and instructs Susanna to write a letter to the Count accordingly: in their 'Letter Duet', Susanna repeats what the Countess dictates.

Now the Count rejoins the Countess, and two happy couples come to claim the Count's blessing – not only Figaro and Susanna, but also Marcellina and Bartolo, who have decided to get married. A crowd assembles to witness the ceremony. While a fandango is being danced Susanna slips a little note to the Count – the note which she has written at the Countess's dictation. Thus, at the very moment of performing the betrothal ceremony, the Count is looking forward to achieving his seduction of Susanna that same evening.

Such is the Countess's plot, however, that when the Count turns up for his rendezvous with Susanna he will find, not Susanna, and not even Cherubino whom it had originally been planned to send in Susanna's place, but the Countess herself. Susanna and the Countess will have exchanged cloaks.

ACT IV

In the garden Figaro encounters Barbarina, Susanna's cousin (and Antonio's daughter): the Count entrusted her with the errand of taking back to Susanna – as confirmation of their rendezvous – the pin that sealed her original note; but Barbarina has let it drop and is searching for it. Thus Figaro gathers that Susanna has a rendezvous with the Count, but does not discover that it is to be a faked rendezvous. Furious with his wife – his unfaithful wife, as he thinks – he invites Bartolo and Basilio to come along and witness her shameful meeting with the Count. Alone, he denounces the unfaithfulness of women: 'Yes, fools ye are and will be' (Aprite un po' quegli occhi).

As he retires, the Countess and Susanna enter, each disguised as the other. Susanna looks forward to the pleasures of love: 'O come, my heart's delight' (Deh vieni, non tardar). She knows that the jealous Figaro is watching her.

Now the complicated rendezvous begins, complicated further still by the fact that Cherubino is there too for a rendezvous with Barbarina. Cherubino sees the Countess, takes her for Susanna and attempts to kiss her. The Count steps in just at that moment and receives the kiss – but the Count's intended box on the ear for Cherubino goes to Figaro, who also intervenes just then. Now the Count starts to make love to Susanna (as he thinks – but really to the Countess, dressed in Susanna's cloak). Figaro thinks he will pay the Count back and starts to dislose the 'plot' to the woman he imagines to be the Countess. It is, of course, Susanna; and when she forgets to disguise her voice Figaro spots who she is, and begins in fun to make love to her – which infuriates her, as she believes that Figaro thinks she is the Countess. Soon she realizes the truth, and they continue for the benefit of the Count, who now sees Figaro apparently making love to the Countess. The Count prepares to denounce them both – but is astonished when the real Countess comes forth and shows that the figure in her cloak is Susanna.

It is the Count's turn once again to be humbled and to apologize to his wife, both for suspecting her and for his own misdemeanours. The Countess forgives him and the company gives itself up to revelry for the rest of the night.

*   *   *   *   *

The Marriage of Figaro, distinguished though it is for famous solo numbers, is also a marvellously conversational opera. The recitative is extensive, quick and complex: in the theatre an inability to grasp it must mean failure to follow the complicated plot. Moreover, at least three of the formal numbers have a conversational element worked with particular musical skill and particular dramatic effectiveness. One is the Letter Duet, in which Susanna takes down a love letter at the Countess's dictation, and then reads it back. It is a letter making an amorous rendezvous in words that hint obliquely at the real message: 'How delightful 'tis to wander in the breath of evening fair' (see p. 56).

Later comes the sextet in the third act in which it emerges that Figaro is the son of old Marcellina and of Bartolo, when the phrase 'his mother?', followed by 'his father?', passes from one character to another. And a little extra fun may occur because one of the participants, Don Curzio, the lawyer, is traditionally a stammerer; so it is 'm-m-mother' and 'f-f-father' when his turn comes.

But perhaps Mozart's greatest skill shows in the long, complicated finales to Acts II and IV, in which the orchestra seems to take its own part in the musical intrigue. In the former, Figaro is confronted by the Count with a paper and is trying with all his wits to identify it: it is (as the Countess whispers to Susanna and Susanna whispers to Figaro) the officer's commission ('la patente del paggio') which Cherubino had dropped. Figaro's racking of his brains is virtually made audible in the repeated phrase of the orchestra (while, amid the talking of the others, Figaro himself is tongue-tied) (see top of p. 57).

In the first part of the finale of Act IV Mozart uses a pointed change of key three times at crucial moments. The first is when the Countess (disguised as Susanna) realizes that the Count may discover her with the importunate Cherubino. The next is the point when Susanna, Figaro and the Count see her with him. Then (most tellingly of all) comes the point marked *: here the Count steps in and receives the kiss that Cherubino wants to give, 'Take this now' (Prendi intanto), to the Countess, whom he takes for Susanna; and Figaro, at 'I want to see' (Vo' veder), steps forward and receives the box on the ear intended by the Count for Cherubino (see pp. 57–58).

There is, we may suspect, one special orchestral joke. In Figaro's song about the faithlessness of women, 'Yes, fools you are and will be' (Aprite un po' quegli occhi), the reference to female deception is accompanied by a prominent figure on the horns – alluding to the well-known dramatic convention by which a pair of horns sprouting from a husband's head was a sign that he had been cuckolded. We quote Figaro's words: 'You all of you know!'.

DON GIOVANNI

Il Dissoluto Punito, ossia Il Don Giovanni
(The Rake Punished, or Don Juan)
Libretto by Lorenzo da Ponte
First performed: Prague, 1787

Two Acts

Cast in order of singing:

Leporello, servant to Don Giovanni	*bass*
Donna Anna, betrothed to Don Ottavio	*soprano*
Don Giovanni, a licentious young nobleman	*baritone*
The Commendatore, father of Donna Anna	*bass*
Don Ottavio, friend of Don Giovanni	*tenor*
Donna Elvira, a lady of Burgos, deserted by Don Giovanni	*soprano*
Zerlina, a peasant girl, betrothed to Masetto	*soprano*
Masetto, a peasant	*bass*

[The role of Donna Elvira's maid is silent]
Chorus of peasants and invisible demons

The scene is laid in Seville

THE French and Germans call this opera *Don Juan*: and so,
rightly, should we, for it provides a ready identification with
the legendary hero, celebrated in many other works for
the stage before Mozart's. (One was the English play of 1676,
The Libertine, by Thomas Shadwell, for a revival of which
Purcell wrote incidental music; another was an opera by Mozart's contemporary Gazzaniga, whose libretto by Bertati was
freely drawn upon by Da Ponte in his libretto for Mozart.)
However, *Don Giovanni* (Giovanni being simply the Italian
form for Juan in Spanish or John in English) has become
established in British usage, and the other characters have
retained their Italian form too.

Mozart called the opera a *dramma giocoso*, meaning comic opera, neither more nor less. Not that profoundly serious elements are excluded: for in its treatment of moral issues *Don Giovanni* steps considerably beyond the traditional comic-opera framework. But certain scenes and characters are wholly comic and the entire action is presented in a comic context. When the 'great seducer' is eventually dragged down to hell by the statue of the man he killed, the remaining characters come on stage and warn the audience to learn from this to behave themselves! This they do in no solemn tones but in merry, scampering music of an absolutely 'comic opera' kind.

Don Giovanni is indeed an opera striking in both its dramatic force and its comic situations, and the characters are so memorably drawn as seemingly to have a life of their own outside the opera: Leporello (one of the great comic creations of musical drama) can be imagined in many other situations from what we know of him here. And the whole action is infused with music showing Mozart's genius at its height.

* * * * *

ACT I

The action opens outside Donna Anna's house. Don Giovanni is inside, masked and trying to seduce her. (He may perhaps have succeeded: interpretations of the opera vary on this point.) The first voice we hear is that of Leporello, Don Giovanni's servant, who is waiting outside and complaining at the drudgery of his life.

Don Giovanni appears from the house, with Donna Anna holding on to him: she wants to identify her masked attacker. Her old father, referred to as the Commendatore (a title of honour with no special relevance to the action) comes out and insists on fighting Don Giovanni. In the ensuing duel, the Commendatore is killed. As he dies he joins in a trio with Don Giovanni and Leporello.

Don Giovanni and Leporello escape. Donna Anna, attended by her betrothed, Don Ottavio, discovers her father's dead body, and before they leave she makes Don Ottavio swear vengeance on the unknown attacker.

A woman appears, singing about a lover who has deserted her. Don Giovanni decides she needs his 'consolation' – but then, addressing her, sees that she is Donna Elvira of Burgos whom he himself has deserted. He slips away and leaves Leporello to play the cruel trick of forcing Elvira to listen to a list of Don Giovanni's international conquests: 'Pray allow me' (Madamina, il catalogo) * – the Catalogue Song.

The scene changes to a nearby country village. Two peasants, Masetto and Zerlina, are about to be married. Don Giovanni approaches, gives Leporello the task of hustling Masetto away and has no difficulty in exerting his aristocratic charm on Zerlina. 'You'll lay your hand in mine dear' (Là ci darem la mano). Don Giovanni is on the point of leading Zerlina away when Donna Elvira steps in, sings an aria warning Zerlina, and guides her off.

Donna Anna and Don Ottavio enter; in a quartet, Donna Elvira tells them that Giovanni is a rogue, while he says that she is unbalanced. From Don Giovanni's own voice Donna Anna recognizes the masked attacker of the previous night. She announces her discovery to Don Ottavio: 'You know now for certain' (Or sai chi l'onore). Alone, Don Ottavio sings 'Mine be her burden' (Dalla sua pace).

Now Don Giovanni, alone, sings of his intention to invite the countryfolk to a party (the so-called Champagne Aria). Then he leaves. Masetto returns, offended with his flirtatious Zerlina. But Zerlina twists him round her little finger: 'Beat me, beat me' (Batti, batti); and they are reconciled. Don Giovanni enters, but Masetto's wish for vengeance on him is sidetracked when all are invited to the party. Don Ottavio, Donna Anna and Donna Elvira, masked, plan to join the party uninvited and trap Don Giovanni there. The three utter a short but intense prayer: 'May Heaven's eternal justice' (Protegga il giusto cielo).

At a party a minuet (for the gentry), a contre-danse (for the villagers), and a German waltz (which Leporello insists Masetto shall dance with him) are heard together. Don Gio-

* English version by Edward J. Dent (O.U.P.).

vanni again makes an attempt on Zerlina's not too elusive
virtue and, when she screams, drags forward Leporello as the
supposed villain. But he is confronted and denounced by Don
Ottavio, Donna Anna and Donna Elvira, who have unmasked.
With drawn sword he escapes as the curtain falls.

ACT II

For the moment, Don Giovanni's quarry has changed again:
now it is a maid of Donna Elvira's. He exchanges cloaks with
Leporello for the purpose. After Don Giovanni has played
another cruel trick on the passionate Elvira (luring her on to
believe he still loves her, and sending her off with the disguised Leporello), he serenades the maid, with a mandolin:
'Look down from out your window' (Deh vieni alla finestra).

Masetto arrives with friends to kill Don Giovanni. But Don
Giovanni in Leporello's cloak pretends in the darkness to be
Leporello; he sends Masetto's friends away and contrives to
give Masetto himself a sound beating. Zerlina arrives and consoles Masetto: 'If you will promise me' (Vedrai carino).

In turn Zerlina, Masetto, Donna Anna, Don Ottavio and
Donna Elvira mistake Leporello for Don Giovanni, whom
they are intent on punishing. They discover their error in a
sextet; then, with an aria, Leporello manages to escape.

Ottavio sings yet again of his love for Anna: 'Speak for me
to my lady' (Il mio tesoro); and Donna Elvira yet again voices
her sense of betrayal: 'All my love on him I lavished' (Mi
tradì quell'alma ingrata).

In a cemetery, Don Giovanni and Leporello see a statue of
the murdered Commendatore (the erection of statues has
never been so quick since). The statue speaks, admonishing
Don Giovanni, to Leporello's (but not Giovanni's) terror.
Don Giovanni audaciously invites the statue to supper and
the invitation is accepted.

To Don Ottavio, Donna Anna excuses her delay in marrying him: 'Say no more that I am cruel' (Non mi dir).

Later, Don Giovanni is dining cheerily at home. His private band is playing and Leporello is waiting on him. (Properly, by the Italian words sung, Don Giovanni has female

company; in most modern productions he dines alone.) Donna
Elvira comes in with another entreaty to him; but again it is
vain. As she leaves she screams at something she has seen outside. So does Leporello when he goes to look. It is the statue
of the Commendatore, approaching to fulfil the invitation
to dine with Don Giovanni. It enters, speaks, and drags the
still defiant Don Giovanni down to hell as flames arise and an
invisible chorus of demons sings.

When the others enter, bent on vengeance, Leporello has to
explain that they have been anticipated! Severally, they settle
their affairs – Donna Elvira will go to a convent, Donna Anna
will observe a year's mourning before marrying Don Ottavio,
Zerlina and Masetto will go home to supper, Leporello will
seek a new master. All, light-heartedly, tell the audience to
learn a serious lesson from Don Giovanni's fate.

*   *   *   *   *

The part of Don Ottavio, the suitor of Donna Anna, is dramatically weak; but through historical accident it included not
one but two of the greatest arias Mozart ever wrote for tenor.
For the first production in Prague Mozart wrote the aria
'Speak for me to my lady' (Il mio tesoro). When the opera
came to be staged in Vienna, in 1788, the leading tenor proved
unable to sing this difficult song and an easier one (but not
very easy!) was given to him: 'Mine be her burden' (Dalla
sua pace). This, however, was placed by Mozart at a different
point in the action. It rather holds up the drama; but, in most
productions today, both arias are nevertheless given.

Also for the Vienna performance, Mozart wrote – at the
insistence of the singer – a big solo aria for Donna Elvira, 'All
my love on him I lavished' (Mi tradì quell'alma ingrata). This
again holds up the action; but, again, it is usually included. A
third insertion demanded of Mozart by his Vienna cast, a
rather foolish duet for Zerlina and Leporello, is *not* performed
today. Of course, it would be quite reasonable for a modern
production to stick entirely to the more concisely dramatic
Prague score, at the acknowledged sacrifice of two superb
musical items.

The orchestral score includes trombones. The trombone was primarily a church instrument in those days; to import it, therefore, was to bring in a special atmosphere of solemnity,* just like the importation of the organ into *Faust* or *The Mastersingers.* The trombones accompany the statue of the murdered man: they are heard only when the statue speaks on the stage – not even when, in the overture, the statue music is anticipated. There is an awesome moment when, in the cemetery, a lively conversation between Don Giovanni and Leporello on the subject of seduction is interrupted by the voice of the statue ('Before tomorrow's dawn your laughter's ended'):

There is an even more unusual instrument than the trombone in the score of *Don Giovanni*: the mandolin. Don Giovanni uses it to accompany himself in the serenade to Donna Elvira's maid (a character who never sings a word in the opera, though in the theatre we should see her face). One precedent for the use of the mandolin was in *A Rare Thing* (Una Cosa Rara) by Vicente Martín y Soler (1754–1806), a Spanish composer of Italian operas. A song from this opera, and also a

* See also page 42.

song from *The Two Litigants* (I Due Litiganti) by Giuseppe
Sarti (1729–1802) are played by Don Giovanni's private band
in the supper scene: they also play 'Say goodbye now to pastime and play, lad' (Non più andrai) from *The Marriage of
Figaro*, which Leporello greets with the observation: 'I know
this tune rather too well!'. The gay, easy-going music here
is cleverly planned to set off the intensity of the scene which
follows.

Mozart's high point of sheer musical skill, however, comes
in the ballroom scene, when three small orchestras on the
stage play three different tunes in different dance-rhythms
which all fit astonishingly together. (In the score there is even
provision for the musicians to tune up.)

A notable feature of the opera is the way in which Mozart
provides distinctive music to portray the characters of the
three women. The simple peasant girl, Zerlina, has essentially
simple, tuneful music, like 'Beat me, beat me' (Batti, batti),
the song in which she wheedles her stupid but honest lover,
Masetto:

Donna Anna's music, especially her Act I aria, 'You know now
for certain' (Or sai chi l'onore), shows her rather stiff nobility.
In her determination to have revenge, she calls on the services of her accepted lover like a general commanding his
troops:

The personality of Donna Elvira is more complex. Her tem-
perament is passionate, her situation is tragic, but – in tune

with the rather hard attitude of 18th-century society to a jilted woman – there is something slightly absurd about her. Mozart conveys this in the old-fashioned pseudo-Handelian idiom of 'Be warned in time' (Ah! fuggi il traditor!), where she warns Zerlina of Don Giovanni, and, most of all, in the almost grotesque leaps in the melody of her opening song 'Where shall I find the traitor' (Ah, chi mi dice mai). In this she threatens to slaughter her seducer and tear out his heart!

COSÌ FAN TUTTE

Così fan tutte, ossia La scuola degli amanti
(All Women do it, or The School for Lovers)

Libretto by Lorenzo da Ponte

First performed: Vienna, 1790

Two Acts

Cast in order of singing:

Ferrando, an officer, in love with Dorabella   *tenor*
Guglielmo, an officer, in love with Fiordiligi   *baritone*
Don Alfonso, an elderly philosopher   *bass*
Fiordiligi ⎫ sisters, young ladies of Ferrara   *soprano*
Dorabella ⎭   *mezzo-soprano*
Despina, their maid   *soprano*
    Chorus of soldiers, townspeople, servants and musicians
The scene is laid in a village near Naples

'ALL women do it': that is, all women show fickleness in love.
Such is the idea of the opera. Literally the title is 'Thus do
all (*feminine*)'. Since the title-words have actually to be sung
in the course of the opera, in five syllables with an emphasis
on the fourth, an English version might be 'Just like a
woman!'. The conception throughout is one of artificial
comedy. The fickle young ladies do not realize that the two
'new' lovers who come to court them are their old lovers in
ridiculous disguise, nor that the 'notary' is similarly their own
maid, disguised.

But whereas such disguising in other operas is meant to be
dramatically credible, even occasioning tragic consequence,
here we are not called on to believe anything. *Così fan tutte*
makes fun of the theatre as well as of life. Its appeal is thus of
sophisticated comedy with moments of broader humour;
Mozart unerringly finds the right musical expression for both.

* * * * *

ACT I

In a café, Ferrando claims that Dorabella will always be faithful to him. Guglielmo makes the same claim for Fiordiligi.
But Don Alfonso is an older man and says he knows better.
The young men are irritated and, challenged by Don Alfonso,
agree to bet on their mistresses' honour against whatever
scheme of temptation he may propose. Gaily all anticipate
their winnings.

In a garden we discover two girls looking adoringly at
miniature pictures of their lovers. Don Alfonso enters (this
is the start of his scheme) with a pathetic song of bad tidings:
Ferrando and Guglielmo, as officers, have been ordered away.
Now they enter. In a quintet, led off by Guglielmo – 'Courage
fails me' (Sento, o Dio)* – the four lovers express undying
passion, the men breaking off with winks at Don Alfonso.
After a little duet for the men, a march is heard. The officers'
troops enter, surrounded by townspeople. There are more

* English version by the Rev. Marmaduke E. Browne (Novello).

farewells (in a quintet, with Don Alfonso's laughter in the background) and the officers march off with their men.

The pert Despina, the girls' maid, enters, complaining of her work. She is somewhat incredulous when her mistresses give vent to extreme misery (aria for Dorabella). To their protestations that they cannot live without their lovers, Despina advises them to take love lightly.

Don Alfonso enters; he determines to take Despina into his confidence and gives her some money. He introduces Ferrando and Guglielmo – now comically and extravagantly disguised as a pair of Albanian noblemen who have come to court the girls. Despina allows them to approach her mistresses. In a sextet, during which the girls react indignantly to the intrusion, Don Alfonso sings his part aside, unseen by the girls; then he finally enters, 'recognizes' the Albanians as old friends and commends them to the girls. But Fiordiligi, in an aria, says she will be 'Firm as rock' (Come scoglio). Ferrando presses his and Guglielmo's claims in an aria, 'O vision so charming' (Non siate ritrosi), commending their fine noses and other masculine attractions. The girls leave in an attitude of disdain and the laughing suitors join in a trio with the still confident Don Alfonso.

Alone (and now seriously) Ferrando sings of his continuing love: 'Her eye so alluring' (Un'aura amorosa). Alfonso and Despina plan the next stage. Ferrando and Guglielmo enter and pretend, in the presence of the girls and Don Alfonso, to take poison and sink lifeless to the ground. Despina and Don Alfonso hurry away for the doctor. Meanwhile such pathetic devotion begins to have its effect on the girls, on which the 'dead' men (when the girls are not looking) comment amusedly.

Don Alfonso returns with the 'doctor' (Despina, disguised and spouting bogus Latin). Despina produces an outsize magnet, topically referred to as an invention of the celebrated Dr Mesmer, and waves it over the bodies. They 'wake' and demand kisses as a restorative. A long sextet ends the act.

ACT II

Despina further urges her mistresses to try a flirtation. Left alone, the girls decide they will do so after all – Dorabella chooses 'the dark one' (that is, Guglielmo) and Fiordiligi the other – each, in fact, choosing the other's lover!

In a garden Ferrando and Guglielmo have summoned musicians to sing and play for the girls, who enter with Don Alfonso but are bashful – so Despina and Don Alfonso, in a quartet with Ferrando and Guglielmo, demonstrate the ritual of courtship for them.

Despina and Don Alfonso leave the four lovers alone. They start talking about the weather at first, then proceeding to other topics. Ferrando leads Fiordiligi away. Guglielmo persuades Dorabella to give him as a keepsake the miniature she wears (it is Ferrando's portrait) and in return gives her a heart-shaped locket: 'This heart that I give you' (Il core vi dono).

They leave, and Ferrando and Fiordiligi enter. He presses his case, but she still does not yield. Left alone she admits fonder feelings for the stranger but resists in the name of her duty to her absent lover. The two men meet: Ferrando reports to Guglielmo this obstinacy of Fiordiligi's – but he has to be told that his Dorabella is weakening, and is shown the portrait with which she parted to Guglielmo. Guglielmo, with Fiordiligi still faithful, can afford to sing lightly of woman's inconstancy: 'Ladies have such variations' (Donne mie, la fate a tanti). But Ferrando, alone again, takes the case more seriously. Then Don Alfonso tells Guglielmo and Ferrando that the next stage is about to begin.

In the girls' apartment, Dorabella is cheerful. Fiordiligi decides that they must save their honour and leave the house dressed up in the soldiers' uniforms that their lovers have left. But Ferrando, still in disguise, comes in, renews his wooing – and eventually Fiordiligi yields. Don Alfonso, Ferrando and Guglielmo meet and sum it up: 'Così fan tutte'.

A room is lit for the party which is now to celebrate the approaching marriage of the girls and their 'Albanians'.

Despina shows the servants and musicians their duties. Don Alfonso enters and leaves with Despina. The four lovers (now, of course, each man paired off with the other's girl) sing an affectionate quartet with chorus – with some furious 'asides' from Guglielmo. Don Alfonso announces the arrival of the notary (Despina in disguise) with the marriage contract. But just as all are about to sign, the soldiers' chorus (as in Act I) is heard. The 'Albanians' go off to hide themselves and the 'real' Ferrando and Guglielmo enter in their own clothes. They smell a rat – and spot the 'lawyer', who reveals himself to the astonished girls as Despina. The girls tremble as they admit that they were preparing a wedding.

The men surprise *them* by confessing the plot, and all ends happily with Don Alfonso the winner and the girls reunited with their lovers – their original lovers, one presumes!

*   *   *   *   *

Da Ponte's words mock the conventions of ever-faithful love. So does Mozart's music. In old-fashioned heroic style, Fiordiligi declares that she will stand 'Firm as rock':

But of course a singer has the same opportunity to display her (or his) voice when a composer means his music ironically as when he means it seriously. This is a particular joy of this particularly sophisticated opera.

Mozart three times makes notable use of recurrent themes. Firstly, the overture (at the end of its slow introduction) presages the tune of the words 'Così fan tutte' itself:

Secondly, when the masquerade is exposed, the two suitors quote music from their and Despina's disguises. The last of these is the nonsense of Dr Mesmer's magnet, previously heard when Despina was dressed as a doctor.

FERRANDO
GUGLIELMO
[Allegretto]
[mf]

Ed al ma - gne - ti - co Si - gnor Dot - to - re ren - do l'o -
- no - - - re Che me - - - ri - to.

Note the exaggerated trill for the waving of the magnet in action. Thirdly, the soldiers' chorus of the first act returns in the last.

The opera is very long, though in only two acts, and certain arias are sometimes cut. The action, be it noted, takes place within a single day – an old dramatic convention which here serves to emphasize the splendid artificiality of the comic tale.

DIE ZAUBERFLÖTE

(The Magic Flute)

Libretto by Emanuel Schikaneder

First performed: Vienna, 1791

Two Acts

Cast in order of singing:

Tamino, a prince   *tenor*
Three Ladies, in attendance on the
  Queen of the Night   *two sopranos, mezzo-soprano*
Papageno, a bird-catcher   *baritone*
The Queen of the Night   *soprano*
Monostatos, a Moor, Sarastro's captain of the guard   *tenor*
Pamina, daughter of the Queen of the Night   *soprano*

Three Genii	*two sopranos, mezzo-soprano (or boys)*
The Speaker of the Temple	*bass*
Sarastro, High Priest of Isis and Osiris	*bass*
Two Priests of the Temple	*tenor, bass*
Papagena	*soprano*
Two men in armour	*tenor, bass*

Chorus of priests, onlookers, etc.

The scene is laid in ancient Egypt

The Magic Flute is like an English pantomime. That is, it is
in the form of a popular entertainment with songs; it allowed
a well-known comedian to gag (in this case Schikaneder, the
actor-manager-librettist); it is highly moral, with personifications of good and evil on the stage; and in the use of trans-
formations and other theatrical devices it suggests the work-
ings of the supernatural in the middle of a tale about ordinary
human beings.

Schikaneder and Mozart were both keen Freemasons at a
time when Freemasonry was officially frowned upon in
Austria as hostile to the Roman Catholic Church and even to
the state itself. In laying the scene in ancient Egypt (where
Freemasonry was believed to have its origins), in the rites of
purification enacted in the opera in Sarastro's temple, and in
some of the actual words of the libretto, Schikaneder and
Mozart were obviously alluding to their creed. Moreover,
some of the actual music has Masonic significance. And if
Sarastro stood for Enlightenment, then the wicked Queen of
the Night would seem to represent the Roman Catholic
Church, or the Empress Maria Theresa, who upheld the
Church and proscribed the Freemasons.

For some reason, the story of The Magic Flute had to be
altered while it was being written, a fact which has left some
oddities in the plot. The flute itself, presented to the hero by
the 'bad' Queen of the Night, aids him in his 'good' quest
later. None the less, the plot is still acceptable in the theatre.
It is part of the richness of The Magic Flute that its music
ranges from the 'pop-song' (Papageno's first utterance) to a con-

trapuntal style suggesting Bach (the duet of the men in armour) and that it can be enjoyed on many levels, from sheer fooling to that which caused Bernard Shaw to say: 'I am highly susceptible to the force of all truly religious music, no matter to what church it belongs; but the music of my own church – for which I may be allowed, like other people, to have a partiality – is to be found in *Die Zauberflöte* and the Ninth Symphony.'

* * * * *

ACT I

Prince Tamino, trying to escape from a huge snake, falls unconscious. The three Ladies-in-Waiting to the Queen of the Night enter, kill the snake, and leave. On recovering consciousness Tamino sees an odd-looking man approaching him: Papageno, the bird-catcher, covered with feathers as his trade demands. He introduces himself by singing a ditty in popular style, and playing his own pan-pipes. Papageno boasts to Tamino that it was he who killed the snake – for which lie he is punished by the Ladies-in-Waiting (who now re-enter) by having his mouth padlocked.

The Ladies show Tamino the miniature portrait of the Queen of the Night's daughter, Pamina, with whom he at once falls in love: 'O loveliness beyond compare!' (Dies Bildnis ist bezaubernd schön).* When the Ladies tell him she is a prisoner of Sarastro, whom they represent to be evil, he resolves to rescue her. The Queen of the Night herself appears and urges him on.

The quintet that follows for the three Ladies, Tamino and Papageno, begins 'Hm, hm, hm, hm' – for Papageno, his mouth still padlocked, can only hum and not sing. But now the Ladies take off the padlock, give Tamino a magic flute to help him in his rescue, and give Papageno (who is to accompany and support Tamino) a magic chime of bells. They set off, and are told that three Genii or Boys will show them the way.

The scene changes to a room in Sarastro's palace, where

---

* English version by Edward J. Dent (O.U.P.).

the imprisoned Pamina is importunately wooed by Monostatos, a Moor, Sarastro's captain of the guard. Papageno, who
has somehow become separated from Tamino, bursts in – and
Papageno and Monostatos have evidently an equally frighten-
ing effect on each other. Monostatos runs away. Papageno
assures Pamina that she will be rescued soon by one who loves
her, and in a duet she assures him that he, too, will find love:
'The kindly voice of Mother Nature' (Bei Männern, welche
Liebe fühlen).

Again the scene changes. The three Boys are seen leading
Tamino to a temple with three doors. From within the first
door a hidden voice bids Tamino 'Stand back' (Zurück!),
similarly within the second door. But from the third door
emerges the Speaker of the temple, whose utterance awakens
in Tamino a desire for wisdom and a suspicion of the Queen
of the Night. A hidden chorus assures him that Pamina still
lives. Tamino plays his flute and hears an answer from Papageno's pan-pipes. He hastens off in search of Papageno, who,
with Pamina, rushes on in search of him – but they are
caught by Monostatos. He and his band of slaves are about
to arrest them when Papageno, at a touch of his magic bell-
chime, stops them in their tracks and makes them dance.

Solemn music heralding Sarastro himself and his attendants
is heard. Papageno asks Pamina what they should say to him
when accused of attempted flight. 'The truth, friend!' (Die
Wahrheit), says Pamina, in a solemn phrase. She confesses to
Sarastro, who emphasizes that she is held captive in order to
escape her mother's influence: woman's true destiny is to
follow a man's guidance. Monostatos, who has now apprehended Tamino, brings him in. After a brief, rapt recognition
between Tamino and Pamina, Monostatos tells Sarastro about
his vigilance in thwarting an attempted abduction of Pamina
and asks for his reward. He gets it – a sentence of beating. All
others unite in Sarastro's praise.

Act II

The priests enter to a solemn march. Sarastro announces that
Tamino, before marrying Pamina, must prove himself worthy

of admission to the Temple. The priests signify their accord on their trumpets. Sarastro prays for Tamino in his coming ordeal: 'O Isis and Osiris'.

Warned by two priests to keep silent and to pay no attention to women, Tamino and Papageno (who is to undergo an ordeal less arduous than Tamino's) find themselves confronted by the three Ladies-in-Waiting but ignore them. The first part of the ordeal is over.

The scene changes to where Pamina is sleeping. Monostatos is excitedly approaching her when Pamina's mother, the Queen of the Night, appears, and gives her daughter a dagger with the instruction to kill Sarastro. Thus, she says, 'I'll have revenge' (Der Hölle Rache).

The Queen of the Night disappears. Monostatos re-enters, still with designs on Pamina, but Sarastro arrives and dismisses him. Pamina asks Sarastro not to take revenge on her mother. He answers that in his temple 'We know no thought of vengeance' (In diesen heil'gen Hallen).

Tamino and Papageno now await the next stage of their ordeal. Papageno is confronted by an old crone who says she is his sweetheart Papagena (which he treats as a joke). The three Boys appear and bring Tamino his magic flute and Papageno his magic bells again. Pamina arrives and, when Tamino (as part of his ordeal) refuses to speak to her, gives way to utter grief: 'Ah, 'tis gone for ever' (Ach, ich fühl's).

Sarastro tells Tamino and Pamina to take their last farewell of each other. Papageno sighs for someone to love: ''Tis love, they say, love only that makes the world go round' (Ein Mädchen oder Weibchen wünscht Papageno sich) – on which the crone reappears, makes him swear to be true to her, and then reveals herself as young, beautiful and feathered like himself! But a priest prevents him from seizing her – for the present.

In a garden, the three Boys sing symbolically of the dawn. Pamina, distressed at Tamino's apparent desertion, contemplates taking her life, but is restrained by the Boys. Two men in armour, singing a solemn chorale, supervise the last stage of Tamino's initiation – ordeals by fire and water, in which he is joined by Pamina herself. The flute, which Tamino plays, leads them safely through.

Papageno, frustrated, comically contemplates suicide, but finally the Boys prompt him to try his magic bells again. He jingles them and finds his beautiful sweetheart at last. Their comic (yet ecstatic) stammering recognition provides a duet which starts: 'Pa-pa-pa-pa . . . (*forty-eight times!*) – geno!'.

One more attempt to defeat Sarastro is made by the Queen of the Night, her ladies and Monostatos, who reappear in darkness with appropriately stormy music. But they are driven away by the light: under Sarastro's benevolent guidance, Beauty and Wisdom shall be crowned for ever.

* * * * *

Papageno, as a bird-catcher, lures the birds by means of a set of pan-pipes, and Mozart writes a suitably light-hearted part for the instrument. Papageno sings in his first song of how the birds respond to his pipes' call and make him happy:

As equipment to see him through his ritual ordeal, Papageno is given a 'magic' set of bells, and these too enter the opera score: a bell-like instrument with a keyboard is needed (because of the way the music is written), not the usual orchestral glockenspiel played with small hammers held in the hand.

These, and other features of the score, are Mozart's counterpart to fooling. At the other extreme is the solemnity of the music associated with the Temple and with Enlightenment – not only with Sarastro but with the Speaker (or Orator, as this Priest is sometimes called) of the Temple.

This musical solemnity is first of all foreshadowed by the weighty chords at the opening bars of the overture. When the solemn chord-sequence returns in altered form in the *middle* of the overture, in many performances all the chords sound the same. They should not. The top note of the chord properly rises with each set of chords – a musical gesture full of meaning as is seen when the chords are repeated (supposedly played on the Priests' trumpets) in the temple at the opening of the second act:

This chord-sequence, by the way, brings in the sound of trombones, instruments whose particular significance has been noted in our consideration of *Don Giovanni,* above.

Another notable musical solemnity arises from the fact that the two Men in Armour, supervising part of the hero's ordeal, sing a Lutheran chorale – 'Ah God, from heaven look within' (Ach Gott, vom Himmel sieh' darein); Mozart perhaps got the idea from his brief study of some of Bach's works on a visit to Leipzig. The opera audience at Vienna (a Roman Catholic city) might not have recognized it, nor do most modern audiences today; but the peculiarly intense atmosphere of the music – the slow, measured melody sung in octaves by tenor and bass soloists, while contrapuntal phrases are uttered by the orchestra – is unmistakable, unique in this opera and all operas:

The part of the Queen of the Night is famous for its high notes and rapid pace: Josefa Hofer (Mozart's sister-in-law), for whom it was written, must have had a high F (above so-called top C) in her voice.

III

LUDWIG VAN BEETHOVEN

(1770–1827)

MOZART'S greatest contemporary, Haydn, also wrote operas – mostly for the noble Esterházy family, to whom he was in service for much of his career. These operas, written in Italian or occasionally German, were formal classical dramas (one on the story of Orpheus and Eurydice) or light comedies such as *The World of the Moon* (Il Mondo della Luna), which has recently been revived. But in general Haydn lacked Mozart's sense of the theatre. His stage works were no models for the earnest young German composer who came to Vienna to study with Haydn and then made Vienna his home: Ludwig van Beethoven.

Nor was Beethoven satisfied with Mozart's ideas on opera. 'I could not compose operas like *Don Giovanni* or *The Marriage of Figaro*', he declared. 'They are repugnant to me. I could not have chosen such subjects. They are too frivolous for me!'. The serious moral aspect of *The Magic Flute*, however, was another matter. Beethoven's one opera, *Fidelio*, was likewise an 'ethical' one. But its action, instead of being that of a fairy-tale, concerns real life. In having a rescue as its point of climax it is indebted to Cherubini's *The Water Carrier* (1800; original French title *Les Deux Journées*, 'The Two Days'). Luigi Cherubini (1760–1842) was an Italian who lived in Paris from 1788: his *Medea* (1797; originally in French, as *Médée*) has enjoyed modern revivals.

FIDELIO

Fidelio, oder die eheliche Liebe
(Fidelio, or Married Love)

*Libretto by Josef Sonnleithner after a libretto by
J. N. Bouilly; revision by G. F. Treitschke*

First performed: Vienna, 1805
Final revised version: Vienna, 1814

Two Acts

Cast in order of singing:

Jacquino, porter at the prison	*tenor*
Marzelline, Rocco's daughter	*soprano*
Leonore, wife of Florestan, disguised as 'Fidelio', a youth	*soprano*
Rocco, jailer of the prison	*bass*
Don Pizarro, governor of the prison	*baritone*
Florestan, a Spanish nobleman	*tenor*
Don Fernando, Minister of State	*bass*

Chorus of soldiers, prisoners and people

The scene is laid in a fortress near Seville

THE urge which later led Beethoven to incorporate a setting of part of Schiller's *Ode to Freedom* (camouflaged as an *Ode to Joy*) in the Ninth Symphony also led him to write an opera which is really about freedom. The contrast in *Fidelio* between the darkness of imprisonment – which is taken as unjust political imprisonment – and the light of justice and liberty is both heard in the music and seen on the stage. It is this ethical force in addition to the purely musical strength and beauty of Beethoven's score that gives *Fidelio* its unique appeal among the great operas.

Against the blackness of the villainous governor of the jail, Pizarro, is set the character of the Minister of State: a brief role, but one which must embody in performance the all-important idea of light triumphant. The ethical tone is sustained by the fact that the hero and heroine of the work are already married – a comparative rarity in opera.

The story (of a woman who dresses in male clothes in order to rescue her husband) is said to be a true one, happening within the knowledge of J. N. Bouilly, a Frenchman who cast it originally as an opera libretto for Pierre Gaveaux (1761–1825). Not only Gaveaux made an opera of it but also the composers Simon Mayr (1763–1845) and Ferdinando Paer (1771–1839).

Beethoven called the heroine by the German form 'Leonore'; the name is often changed in English usage to 'Leonora', especially in the concert hall (see below, page 83).

*   *   *   *   *

Act I

In the lodgings of Rocco, the jailer, his daughter Marzelline is being courted by Jacquino, the young porter of the prison. But she does not care for him; her love is for the young man, known as Fidelio, who has been engaged as her father's assistant.

Rocco, her father, enters, and then Fidelio himself. But the 'young man' who has so taken Marzelline's fancy is really a woman in disguise. 'Fidelio' (the word, of course, suggesting *fidelity*) is the name which has been assumed by Leonore, wife of Florestan. Her aim in entering the prison's service is to find and rescue her husband, whom she suspects is languishing there, unjustly imprisoned. Even at the cost of seeming to accept Marzelline's devotion she cannot reveal her true identity.

Rocco, Marzelline, Leonore and Jacquino (who re-enters) now join in a quartet 'My heart had told me so' (Mir ist so winderbar)*. Jacquino leaves. Rocco points out in an aria that young people about to marry need money. A trio follows: Marzelline is now happy that Fidelio is her approved suitor,

* English version by Edward J. Dent (O.U.P.).

but Leonore thinks only of the rescue.

The scene changes. A military march announces the arrival of Pizarro, governor of the prison: it is he who has unjustly imprisoned Florestan. A message warns him that the Minister of State is coming on an inspection. He decides to have Florestan killed: 'Now is the moment come!' (Ha! welch' ein Augenblick!). Bribing Rocco to dig the grave, he resolves to kill Florestan himself.

Leonore has overheard the plot. Alone, she delivers her feelings of loathing for Pizarro and love for her husband: 'Foul murderer!' (Abscheulicher!).

Now, on Leonore's intercession, the ordinary prisoners (not Florestan, in solitary confinement) are allowed out of their cells for a brief opportunity to breathe the open air. In the Prisoners' Chorus, they utter the word 'freedom' – but guardedly, as they remember that their every word is overheard. Leonore learns that she is to be given an opportunity to help dig the grave intended for a certain special prisoner. Meanwhile Pizarro is enraged that the prisoners have been allowed out, and is only calmed when Rocco remembers that it is the king's name-day and that this therefore is a legitimate celebration.

But now the prisoners are sent back to their cells, their voices joining with the commands of Pizarro to Rocco and the private comments of Marzelline, Leonore and Jacquino.

ACT II

In the deepest dungeon, chained and in darkness, lies one man. It is Florestan. 'God! this awful dark!' (Gott, welch' Dunkel hier!), he sings. His aria takes on the quality of hope when he sees, as in a vision, his 'angel, Leonore'. He sinks back and does not hear when Rocco and Leonore arrive to dig the grave in the cell itself. In dialogue interrupted by music we learn that Leonore cannot at first see the prisoner's face. But, having gained Rocco's permission to give the prisoner some food and drink, she becomes sure that it is Florestan indeed. Florestan, grateful for her human pity, still cannot recognize her.

Now Pizarro, who has warned a trumpeter to sound the alarm should the Minister be seen approaching, enters and reveals himself to Florestan. He is about to kill Florestan when 'Fidelio' throws herself in front of Florestan declaring that Pizarro must first kill Florestan's wife: 'Tödt erst sein Weib!' Her declaration of identity stuns both Pizarro and Florestan. Pizarro would now kill Leonore as well, but she produces a pistol – and suddenly a trumpet-call sounds. The Minister is at the gates. Guards enter with lights. Pizarro and Rocco go to meet him and a duet of joy follows between the reunited Leonore and Florestan.

The scene changes. The Minister recognizes his friend Florestan, sends Pizarro away under arrest, and gives to Leonore the joyous task of unlocking Florestan's chains. Marzelline turns her affections back to Jacquino, and the chorus (now including onlookers as well as prisoners) salute the happy day and the strength of a wife's love.

*   *   *   *   *

The overture begins with a quick, arresting figure, as imperious as an upraised hand. This, the 'Fidelio overture', is not the overture which Beethoven's first audience heard. They heard the overture which is now sometimes heard at concerts under the name of 'Leonora No. 2': 'Leonora' because that is the real name of the heroine of the opera, the title of the original libretto and also the title under which Beethoven himself wanted the opera to be known (the theatre authorities decided otherwise), and 'No. 2' because Beethoven had already composed and rejected an overture now known as 'Leonora No. 1'.

At its first performance the opera was a failure. Originally in three acts, it was cut down to two for a performance in 1806, but this also was unsatisfactory. Beethoven wrote for the occasion another overture, now called 'Leonora No. 3'. (The numbering of these overtures represents the order of their composition. The statement in many books of reference that No. 1 came last is now held to be false.) Leonora No. 3

is one of Beethoven's masterpieces, more an orchestral expression of the entire opera than a mere introduction to it. So Beethoven must himself have felt, for at the final revision of the opera (1814) he introduced a new and simpler overture. This we call the *Fidelio* overture.

Opera conductors, however, can be as vainglorious as any prima donna. Some of them *will* have their *Leonora No. 3*. In Victorian times in England this overture was sometimes inserted between the two acts. Then Mahler, as conductor at the Vienna Court Opera (1879–1907) established the practice of putting it in the middle of the last act, before the last scene – a practice followed by many other conductors, even today. But this is totally without Beethoven's authority or any valid dramatic pretext.

Other liberties have in recent years been taken with *Fidelio* – the reversal of the order of the opening two numbers (this is in fact a return to the first version of the opera); the omission of Rocco's song about money; the curtailment of the choral part of the final scene. Such retouching may be considered presumptuous. It is not as if the opera needed it in order to be rescued from oblivion. On the contrary, *Fidelio* has immensely moving theatrical power just as Beethoven finally left it.

A particularly audacious stroke of Beethoven's, and a masterly one, is the quartet in the first act. This is a canon; here are four people expressing their different innermost feelings to the *same* melody in turn. Yet somehow the unity of mood embraces all. The melody is first sung by Marzelline; then – in the following stanza, from which we quote – it is sung by Leonore to new words ('How great the danger is!') while Marzelline puts her original words to a new melody (p. 85).

Leonore's great aria in Act I harnesses the 'modernity' of Beethoven's language to an old-fashioned operatic 'scena' in three parts – introductory recitative, slow section, fast section. The slow section – to the words 'Come, hope, ...' takes the form of a sublime dialogue with three horns and strings (p. 86).

The opera's great climax occurs when Leonore levels her pistol at Pizarro and suddenly (as she tells him 'One word and you are dead!') the trumpet-call is heard off-stage. The suddenness is emphasized by a dramatic key-change (D major to B flat):

CARL MARIA VON WEBER

(1786–1826)

THE peculiar intensity of Beethoven's musical language left its stamp on the musicians who followed. But German opera, so far following the realistic, ethical (one might say 'political') path of *Fidelio*, turned mainly to the cultivation of the fantastic, the grotesque, the supernatural. This 'romanticism' is a feature of German literature no less than of German music of the period, and both are evident in the art of Carl Maria von Weber. His *Freischütz* remains the only German work between Beethoven and Wagner to have held the international stage.

Weber died prematurely, of tuberculosis, in London, having come for the first performance of his opera *Oberon* (1826). This was commissioned to an English libretto, which now needs thoroughly re-writing if the delightful music is to gain the currency it deserves.

DER FREISCHÜTZ

(The Marksman with Magic Bullets)
Libretto by Johann Friedrich Kind
First performed: Berlin, 1821

Three Acts

Cast in order of singing or speaking:

Max, a young forester, in love with Agathe	*tenor*
Kilian, a peasant	*bass*
Cuno, the Head Ranger	*bass*
Caspar, another young forester	*bass*
Aennchen, Agathe's cousin	*soprano*
Agathe, Cuno's daughter	*soprano*
The demon Zamiel	*speaking part*
Ottokar, prince of the region	*baritone*
A hermit	*bass*

The scene is laid in Bohemia shortly after the end of the Seven Years' War (1756–63)

Der Freischütz is one of the very few opera titles which cannot be more or less straightforwardly translated. Literally it means 'The free-shooter'; it might be paraphrased 'The marksman with magic bullets'. The casting of these magic bullets under the Devil's supervision, and the use thereafter made of them, forms one chief interest in the opera; the other two are romantic love and conventional rustic and hunting jollification. The music unites all three. Spoken dialogue (usually shortened in performance) links the music. The following synopsis makes the omissions which are customary in modern performances.

The score has a richness of melody (both solo and choral) and a warmth of feeling which have kept it alive even in an age which would never endure in a non-musical play such naïve representation of the supernatural.

*   *   *   *   *

ACT I

Max, a forester, is derided because, at a shooting contest, he has been beaten by Kilian, a peasant. Cuno, hereditary Head Ranger, is worried too: his daughter, Agathe, is betrothed to Max. The very next day, Max is due to demonstrate his marksmanship (and thus his right to become Cuno's son-in-law and succeed him eventually) before Prince Ottokar. But on this showing Max is unlikely to acquit himself satisfactorily.

Alone, Max sings of his despair: 'Through the woodlands' (Durch die Wälder).* During this, unseen by Max, the figure of the demon Zamiel makes a brief appearance. Now Max's fellow-forester, Caspar, after a drinking-song, hands Max a gun and bids him fire at an eagle high above – which falls dead at his feet. Caspar explains that the shot was made with a magic bullet which always hit its mark, and if Max will meet him in the Wolf's Glen at midnight they will cast more such bullets, enabling Max to win tomorrow's contest. Despite the stories of evil attached to the Wolf's Glen, Max consents. Caspar, alone, exults. He has in fact sold himself to Zamiel and now hopes to extend his own respite by substituting Max as Zamiel's victim.

ACT II

In Agathe's room, her cousin Aennchen is hammering in a new nail for a picture that has fallen. Aennchen sings coquettishly, but Agathe is sad. Left alone, she sings of her love and her sense of anxiety: 'May my prayer' (Leise, leise); her song becomes more impassioned as she sees her lover approach. Max enters, and Aennchen too returns. But Max soon declares he must leave them and go to the Wolf's Glen, and despite the girls' pleas he sets off.

The scene changes to the Wolf's Glen itself – with an owl,

* English version by Edward J. Dent (O.U.P.).

crows, a terrifying woodland landscape, a chorus of invisible spirits and Caspar, who is waiting for Max. At his bidding, Zamiel appears, but leaves before Max arrives. Despite ghostly warnings (one in the form of Max's mother, another in the form of Agathe) Max persists in his resolve. Together he and Caspar cast, by spells, the seven magic bullets, counting them. At each number some evil thing happens on the stage, and at the seventh, in place of a rotting tree, there stands Zamiel himself, reaching out his hand to grasp Max's own. Six bullets will hit as the marksman wishes; the seventh will do Zamiel's work.

ACT III

It is the day of the shooting trial and of the intended wedding. In her room, Agathe, in white bridal dress, is sad. After a song, alone, she tells Aennchen of an ill-omened dream. Aennchen pooh-poohs omens and then makes fun of Agathe by telling her of 'An aunt of mine whom you'll remember' (Einst träumte meiner sel'gen Base) — a tale involving a 'ghost' that turned out to be a dog. Agathe is not amused.

A chorus of bridesmaids arrives and Aennchen brings in a box which should contain a bridal bouquet. When the box is opened, however, there is a shock which cuts the bridesmaids' chorus short: it is a silver funeral wreath. A mistake in delivery, says Aennchen, but Agathe sees another bad omen. The bridesmaids' chorus, somewhat subdued, is resumed.

The scene changes to an open place. Prince Ottokar has been hunting and a chorus celebrates the sport as the huntsmen carouse. Max (who has evidently made three successful shots) is ordered by the prince to shoot at a white dove visible in a tree. 'Don't shoot, Max! I'm the dove!' (Schiess nicht! ich bin die Taube!) says Agathe's voice; it seems too late, for her body falls and is picked up by a hermit who now appears. But she has only fainted. It is Caspar who has been hit; Zamiel (silent and unseen by anyone else) appears and claims him. Caspar dies.

Max relates the whole story. The prince sentences him to banishment, but the hermit comes forward and bids the prince to be merciful. He relents. Max and Agathe may look forward to being married, and all join in praise to heaven.

* * * * *

We have seen that Mozart, in several of his operas, quoted in the overture from the music of the opera itself. In *Der Freischütz* the overture is entirely built from melodies found in the opera. Noteworthy are the extra two notes on the trombones which give a sinister afterthought (which only just fails to sound unintentionally comic) to the passionate melody with which Agathe later greets her love to the words 'Heav'n, accept the tears I'm weeping' (Himmel, nimm des Dankes Zähren):

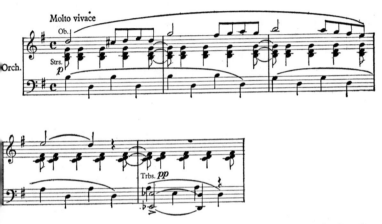

But the real sinister element in *Der Freischütz* is in the music to the Wolf's Glen – an unseen chorus, drum rolls, high woodwind shrieks and *tremolo* on the strings. In the theatre it can still seem astonishingly gripping as an accompaniment to the ever-increasing supernatural storm.

Agathe's music is one of the peaks of German romantic expression and Agathe herself stands musically between Leonore in *Fidelio* and Senta in *The Flying Dutchman*. A theme from her passionate first-act aria has been quoted above; her quieter aria in the final act (expressing her belief in God's loving care) is equally characteristic – of herself and of Weber's style.

Highly characteristic of German romantic opera too is the Huntsman's Chorus. The convivial male choral society was an established German institution for which a considerable repertory was provided by Schubert, Schumann, Brahms and others, and the opera admirably seizes on its special character.

IV

GIOACCHINO ROSSINI

(1792–1868)

S TENDHAL, that witty champion of Rossini, wrote that he
admittedly had his partiality as a critic but could still be
good-natured: 'I have no craving actually to hang anyone,
not even Herr Maria Weber, the composer of *Der Freischütz.*' Gioacchino Rossini and Carl Maria von Weber were,
indeed, contemporaries – and opposites. Stendhal himself
acutely pointed out the difference between the storm-music
in Der *Freischütz*, which musically conveys the evil atmosphere during the casting of the magic bullets, and the storm
music in *The Barber of Seville*, which just represents a
storm.

Although *The Marriage of Figaro, Don Giovanni* and *Così
fan tutte* were written in Italian, the tradition of Italian comic
opera which had grown up in the 18th century is of a
lighter kind than Mozart's. That tradition fully realizes itself
in *The Secret Marriage* (Il Matrimonio Segreto; 1792) by
Domenico Cimarosa (1749–1801). Ten years before *The
Secret Marriage, The Barber of Seville* had already become
operatically famous – not in Rossini's setting but in one by
Giovanni Paisiello (1740–1816). Paisiello's version reigned
internationally until superseded by Rossini's more vigorous
score and has occasionally been revived in our own day.

Rossini worked substantially in three well-defined varieties
of opera. First, comic opera, to which belonged *The Barber of
Seville* and *Cinderella* (both treated below), *The Italian Girl
in Algiers* (L'Italiana in Algeri) and (in French) *Count Ory*
(Le Comte Ory); second, old-fashioned Italian 'serious opera',
Rossini's most famous example being *Semiramis* ('Semira-
mide' is the Italian form); thirdly, historical 'grand opera' of
distinctively French, 19th-century kind, exemplified in

William Tell (Guillaume Tell; 1829). This work concluded Rossini's operatic activity, though he lived nearly forty years longer.

IL BARBIERE DI SIVIGLIA

(The Barber of Seville)

Libretto by Cesare Sterbini, after Beaumarchais's play

First performed: Rome, 1816

Two Acts

Cast in order of singing:

Fiorello, servant to Almaviva	*bass*
Count Almaviva, a young nobleman visiting Seville	*tenor*
Figaro, barber and factotum	*baritone*
Rosina, a rich ward of Dr Bartolo	*mezzo-soprano*
Bartolo, a doctor	*bass*
Berta, an elderly maid to Dr Bartolo	*soprano*
Ambrogio, servant to Dr Bartolo	*bass*
Don Basilio, cleric and music teacher	*bass*
A police officer	*baritone*

[The part of a notary is silent.]

Chorus (men only) of soldiers, police and musicians

The scene is laid in Seville

THE French dramatist Beaumarchais (1733–99) wrote a cycle of three plays about Figaro. No well-known composer has set the third play as an opera. The first, however, *The Barber of Seville*, is the subject of Rossini's best known opera; the second, *The Marriage of Figaro*, is the source of Mozart's. Thus Mozart's comes after Rossini's in time of action. The characters' names mostly correspond.

The Barber of Seville has not the seriously element of pathos notable in *The Marriage of Figaro*. Its music is the music of wit, coquetry, intrigue and excitement. The sparkle of the young Rosina, the comic nastiness of Basilio with his recipe for a successful slander, and the breezy bounce of the barber himself ('Figaro here, Figaro there') – Rossini characterizes all these with skill, verve and human insight. The score is always cut in stage performances, and the story as given below follows the action usually performed. The heroine's part was written for a mezzo-soprano; it has been grabbed by countless sopranos (who usually have to alter the notes considerably) but there is now a disposition to restore it to its proper voice.

In the Lesson Scene, prima donnas have sung songs of their own choice, even 'Home, Sweet Home' (composed long after the opera and ludicrously inappropriate to the situation). But Rossini, as a matter of fact, provided his own song for the Lesson Scene: ''Gainst a heart aflame with love' (Contro un cor che accende d'amore); and it is the new-fangled coloratura of this which Bartolo cries down in favour of good old-fashioned music of which he gives a comic example. This coloratura aria is introduced as coming from a new opera called 'The Useless Precaution'; so, too, is the piece of music which Rosina pretends to drop from the balcony in the opening scene. The subtitle 'or, The Useless Precaution' in fact belongs to *The Barber of Seville* itself.

*　　*　　*　　*　　*

ACT I

In a street by Bartolo's house a band of musicians is assembling under the direction of Fiorello, Count Almaviva's servant. To their accompaniment Almaviva sings a serenade 'Far in the eastern heaven' (Ecco ridente in cielo)* underneath Rosina's window in the house. The musicians make a noisy exit. The Count stands aside as Figaro enters: 'I'm the factotum of the town, make way!' (Largo al factotum della città). He and Almaviva recognize each other and Figaro, having the position of visiting barber-factotum in Bartolo's house, agrees to help further Almaviva's plans.

Rosina, who appears on her balcony with Bartolo, drops a

* English version by Edward J. Dent (O.U.P.).

not into the street and asks Bartolo to go and retrieve it
saying it is the music of a song which she let fall by accident
Almaviva (for whom it was really intended) picks it up: in it
Rosina asks to know his name. In a song (accompanied, properly, by himself on the guitar) he tells her it is Lindoro. (He
does not wish to divulge his true rank.)

Stimulated by money from Almaviva, Figaro has the idea
of introducing him into Bartolo's house as a drunken soldier
demanding a billet. Figaro leaves Almaviva with a pattering
description of how to find his shop 'with five wigs in the
window'.

The scene changes to a room within Bartolo's house. In
'Once a song at break of day' (Una voce poco fa) Rosina shows
her mettle: she can appear docile on the surface but will get
her way. When she leaves, Bartolo tells Don Basilio – a cleric
and scandal-monger as well as a music-master – that he has
heard that Count Almaviva is in town and is pursuing her.
Basilio advises spreading a scandal about him – and in his
aria 'Slander's whisper' (La calunnia) shows how a little
rumour may grow and grow until it explodes like a thunder-
clap.

Figaro tells Rosina that 'Lindoro' is deeply in love with her
and asks her to write a note to him. But she, the cunning crea-
ture, has prepared one already! Bartolo re-enters and warns
Rosina not to try to deceive him. Then arrives the 'drunken
soldier' (Almaviva in disguise), who cannot even pronounce
Bartolo's name rightly. Rosina sees the game at once. Eventually Bartolo produces a document exempting him from billet-
ting, but the 'soldier' brushes it aside and the comic disorder
(now involving Basilio and Figaro too) increases.

Suddenly there is a knock. It is the police: they have come
to investigate the noise. All except Almaviva try to catch the
officer's ear simultaneously. The officer arrests Almaviva but,
when Almaviva secretly identifies himself to him, releases and
salutes him, to everyone's stupefaction. All in turn (Rosina
first) join in an ensemble – 'I don't know what to think'
(Fredda ed immobile) – in which the excitement gradually
mounts.

Act II

An unknown music-master enters the house and greets the surprised Dr Bartolo. Like Basilio, he is a cleric, and endlessly repeats his blessing: 'Peace and gladness on this dwelling' (Pace e gioia sia con voi). He declares that he is deputizing for Don Basilio, who is sick. It is Almaviva, in another disguise. To convince Bartolo he gives him the letter he had from Rosina, as if he had received it from someone else by means of intrigue. Rosina sings a song (this is the Lesson Scene) which enables her to come amorously near the 'teacher'. Bartolo comically demonstrates what *his* idea of good music is. Figaro enters, with an appointment to shave Bartolo.

Basilio enters. All are disconcerted, but the lovers and Figaro tell him he really *is* ill. A purse slipped to him by Almaviva gives a firm hint to him and he goes, with endless repetition of 'So goodnight, then!' (Buona sera!). Bartolo is shaved. The lovers, aided by Figaro, plan to elope at midnight.

Berta, the elderly maidservant, alone, sings pointedly about her employer wanting to marry his ward: ' 'Spite of sixty years to carry' (Il vecchiotto cerca moglie).

Bartolo confronts Rosina with her letter and insinuates that Figaro and the false 'music master' are conspiring to deliver her to another man – namely, Count Almaviva. The angry Rosina (not realizing that Almaviva and Lindoro are the same) discloses the plan for elopement and agrees to marry Bartolo.

The stage empties. There is a storm outside as Figaro and Almaviva enter. They explain matters to Rosina and disclose that Lindoro is in fact Almaviva himself. A notary, procured by Bartolo for his own marriage to Rosina, unites Rosina and Almaviva, with Basilio (at pistol-point) and Figaro as witnesses. Bartolo, entering with an officer and soldiers, orders the arrest of the miscreants – but then, learning what has happened, realizes he is too late and accepts the situation. A gay ensemble (backed by the soldiers as male chorus) ends the opera.

*   *   *   *   *

Rossini makes *The Barber of Seville* a real play-in-music, with a constantly developing plot, and at the same time he provides real display-pieces for the singers. The barber's own self-introducing aria, with its rapid patter of 'Figaro here, Figaro there' is too well-known to need quotation. Equally appropriate to situation and personality is Don Basilio's Slander Song (with its musical illustration of how malicious rumour explodes on the victim's head 'like a cannon-shot').

When Rosina reveals herself to us at the beginning of the second scene, the elaborated repetition of one of her phrases becomes a musical demonstration of the cunning coquetry by which she will twist her guardian round her little finger. She declares she will lay 'a hundred traps' for him:

Rossini was thought in his day to be a very noisy composer. The 'Rossini *crescendo*' – a very long, gradual *crescendo* extending over a whole ensemble with repeated sections – is indeed characteristic of him, though he did not invent it. But it is a real dramatic device, and never better used than in the finale of Act I of *The Barber of Seville*, when it indicates a growing atmosphere of confusion and accusation. Shortly before this, with similar skill, Rossini uses the pace and style of a patter-song not for one soloist but for six people addressing the officer of police simultaneously. It is often com-

plained that in operatic ensembles one cannot hear different
sets of words because they are all uttered together: this is
exactly what happens here, but this time it is on purpose!
The audience's reaction exactly corresponds to that of the
bewildered officer. The repeated 'Si, signor' is tossed comically
from one character to another in a section which begins with
Bartolo's complaint at having been molested by 'this pest of
a soldier':

The overture, by the way, was originally used by Rossini
in an earlier opera altogether: so was the Count's serenade in
Act I. In turn, an aria of the Count's in Act II (now usually
omitted) was re-used as the heroine's final joyous strain (Non
più mesta) in *Cinderella*.

LA CENERENTOLA

(Cinderella)

Libretto by Jacopo Ferretti
First performed: Rome, 1817

Two Acts

Cast in order of singing:

Clorinda ⎱ daughters of Don Magnifico and		*soprano*
Tisbe ⎰ half-sisters to Cinderella		*mezzo-soprano*
Angelina (known as Cenerentola, i.e. Cinderella),		
step-daughter to Don Magnifico		*mezzo-soprano*
Alidoro, tutor to Prince Ramiro		*bass*
Don Magnifico, an impoverished nobleman		*bass*
Ramiro, Prince of Salerno		*tenor*
Dandini, the Prince's valet		*baritone*

Chorus of ladies, gentlemen and servants
of the prince's court

*The scene is laid in Don Magnifico's home
and a nearby palace*

PATHOS and comedy, coloratura fireworks and witty patter are all in this operatic *Cinderella,* which the heroine concludes with one of Rossini's most celebrated vocal show-pieces. It is no wonder that this opera has had a prominent place in the post-war theatrical revival of Rossini's work.

But the opera was heard in London as early as 1820, well before the pantomime version; indeed it seems to have contributed to the shaping of the pantomime. Yet so familiar is the latter that English-speaking audiences have now to be warned of the 'oddity' of the opera – namely, that there is no element of magic in its plot. Instead of a fairy godmother there is a plotting tutor, Alidoro, who pulls the strings and attends matter-of-factly to the details of Cinderella's going to the ball. Incidentally, Alidoro, after casting off his disguise as a beggar, is revealed 'in philosopher's clothing', according to the libretto. Anyone wishing to know the proper clothing for a philosopher has, therefore, only to see the opera.

To the baron, Cinderella's stepfather, Rossini gave two big comic arias. In modern English productions he has been allotted only the first of these, but it has been put in the place occupied by the second (that is, the opening of Act II). In the following synopsis this rearrangement is observed and so are some cuts which are usually made; but Alidoro's aria is included – for, although sometimes cut, it might well not be. The part of the heroine, it will be noted, is for a mezzo-soprano, as in *The Barber of Seville* (and also *The Italian Girl in Algiers*). Her half-sisters are vain and silly; but they are not grotesque and are not called 'the Ugly Sisters'.

*   *   *   *   *

ACT I

While her half-sisters, Clorinda and Tisbe, are preening themselves, Cinderella is doing household tasks and singing her pathetic little song 'Long ago there lived a king' (Una volta c'era un rè).* The entry of Alidoro, disguised as a beggar, shows up Cinderella's kindness and her half-sisters' lack of feeling. A group of courtiers enters with the announcement that Prince Ramiro will soon be here to bid Don Magnifico's daughters to a ball, where he will choose the fairest woman as his bride. Clorinda and Tisbe redouble their efforts to look attractive, each calling on Cinderella to bring her this and that.

The noise brings in Don Magnifico, angry at being wakened out of a dream. He tells it to Clorinda and Tisbe: though the dream involves his being turned into an ass he is sure it means that his daughters are to marry princes. Gleefully he anticipates dandling his royal grandchildren. Naturally, the news of the coming ball only strengthens his feeling.

Alidoro has persuaded Prince Ramiro to change identities

* English version by Arthur Jacobs.

with his valet, Dandini, and has advised him that a daughter of the baron will be the best bride for him. He arrives on a reconnaissance and is beguiled by the charms of the nervous girl who appears, and whom he takes to be a serving-maid: Cinderella. Her tender feelings are aroused too, and there follows a duet, 'O so ardently I gaze' (Un soave non so che). Don Magnifico re-enters fussily. Clorinda and Tisbe are still dressing themselves up when Dandini (masquerading as the prince himself) arrives, escorted by courtiers.

Dandini sings an affected song in stilted language and flowing musical phrases. He puts on a ridiculous 'grand manner' which mightily impresses Clorinda and Tisbe (who now enter) and their father. He extends 'his' invitation to the ball. Cinderella begs Don Magnifico to take her to the ball too – 'for just a half-hour, even for a quarter!' – but he rudely repulses her, and tries to justify himself to Dandini and Ramiro who have overheard.

Alidoro returns, this time as an official with a census-register, demanding to know where Don Magnifico's 'third daughter' is. Confused, Don Magnifico alleges that she died. There is a moment of doubt: in a quintet, each entering in turn, all present voice their suspicions of what is going on: 'It's plain enough to see' (Nel volto estatico).

When all the others leave, Alidoro surprises Cinderella by telling her she *will* go to the ball, and he will take her. She can hardly believe him – is this just a play they are supposed to be acting? 'Yes, my daughter – all the world's a stage'. Alidoro's aria, which follows, is devoted to this theme.

The scene changes to Prince Ramiro's palace, where Dandini (still disguised as the prince) tells Don Magnifico that he will recognize his knowledge of wines by promoting him steward of his household. Then he pretends in his grand manner to make love simultaneously to Clorinda and Tisbe, who have become jealous rivals of each other. But, left alone with Ramiro, Dandini tells him that he has found out both are boobies: 'Tell me quickly in a whisper' (Zitto, zitto, piano, piano).

Again confronted with Clorinda and Tisbe, Dandini says

he will marry one of them and give the other to his squire (pointing to the real prince). Both girls recoil in horror while Dandini and Ramiro enjoy the joke.

Alidoro enters with the announcement that a strange lady, veiled, has arrived. Clorinda and Tisbe feel agitated. The strange lady (Cinderella, of course) sings: 'All is not gold that glitters' (Sprezzo quei don che versa). Dandini is delighted; Ramiro strangely moved. She unveils. Her beauty – and to Clorinda and Tisbe, her resemblance to Cinderella – are an astonishment.

Don Magnifico, who has been in the cellar, re-enters and does not know what to believe. All express doubt, confusion and excitement in a big ensemble.

ACT II

Enjoying the freedom of the princely cellar, the Baron (with chorus of courtiers) dictates a proclamation against the diluting of wine.

Dandini has himself fallen in love with Cinderella but she tells him she loves his squire The 'squire' (that is, the real Prince Ramiro) overhears this and claims her. But she gives him a bracelet and then, telling him he must find its companion and so discover who she is, she leaves. Resuming his true identity, the prince summons his courtiers and declares he will go in search of her.

Dandini, piqued at having to resume his station, is interrupted by the baron, whom he leads further by the nose before revealing at last that he is not the prince but only a valet. The baron is furious.

Back in the baron's house, Cinderella is in her shabby clothes once more when her father and half-sisters return from the ball. A storm rages, and Alidoro contrives that the prince's coach shall break down outside the house and he shall ask for shelter. He does so, and recognizes Cinderella, who learns that her squire is really the prince. A big sextet of confusion follows – 'Here's a plot, there's no denying' (Questo è un nodo avvilupato). Ramiro flings back in the faces of Clorinda and Tisbe their expressions of horror at the idea of marrying him (in Act I, when they thought him a courtier), and after another sextet he leaves with Cinderella. Clorinda and Tisbe face the problem of begging for pardon.

Back in the palace Cinderella, richly dressed, is welcomed as a princess. She forgives her step-father and his daughters and sings of her transformation: 'Born to a life that was lonely' (Nacqui all'affano, al pianto). Then, in exultant style, supported by all present, she brings the story to an end: 'Now no longer by the cinders' (Non più mesta accanto al fuoco).

*   *   *   *   *

The transformation from the household drudge to the princess is expressed in the distance from Cinderella's pathetic little opening air to the brilliant, joyous runs of her final one – that is, from her ditty 'Long ago there lived a king':

to the ecstasy when she dismisses her long suffering as only a vanished nightmare:

– the latter using the entire range of the voice.

The ensembles, steadily building up in volume and tension, and allowing one character at a time to break out into individually passionate expression, are a notable feature of the score. So is the use of the orchestra to add to the gaiety. In the dazzling patter-duet for Ramiro and Dandini, 'Tell me quickly in a whisper', it is the violins that keep the rhythm and melody dancing along in short notes when the voice has an emphatic long one:

GAETANO DONIZETTI

(1797–1848)

Among Rossini's lesser-known operas is one called The *Lady of the Lake* (La Donna del lago), after Sir Walter Scott's poem. Scott's works inspired various other composers of the period (Byron is his only competitor among British authors after Shakespeare) and it is not surprising that Gaetano Donizetti's sixty-two operas include a now forgotten *Kenilworth Castle* (after Scott's *Kenilworth*) and the celebrated *Lucia di Lammermoor* (after *The Bride of Lammermoor*).

Donizetti's audiences went to see the *latest* opera as modern theatre-goers seek the latest play. These audiences loved the sheer thrill of technically difficult singing, but reports of the time show that they were also emotionally moved by the characterization as conveyed in the voices. To a later generation, for whom Verdi's late works were still fresh and Puccini's were newly-arrived, it was difficult to consider Donizetti's (or Bellini's) pretty warblings as adequate to the extremely dramatic scenes (of madness, betrayal, violence and so forth) which they had to represent at points of climax. Now that Verdi's and Puccini's conventions belong, with Donizetti's, to history, modern audiences have been re-attracted to Donizetti's serious works, especially when singers are available who can do justice to them. Donizetti's output also includes comic operas, for which he had a lively aptitude.

He followed the Italian tradition of using recitative (not speech), setting in relief the arias and ensembles. The climax of dramatic complexity is musically represented (again in a traditional way) by a big ensemble for all the characters at the end of the penultimate act. Besides *Lucia di Lammermoor*, his operas include *Don Pasquale* (1843), still an oft-performed comic opera, and *The Daughter of the Regiment* (1840; one of his several operas in French).

L'ELISIR D'AMORE

(The Elixir of Love)

Libretto by Felice Romani
First performed: Milan, 1832

Two Acts

Cast in order of singing:

Giannetta, a country girl	*soprano*
Nemorino, a young farm labourer	*tenor*
Adina, a rich young proprietress of a farm	*soprano*
Belcore, a sergeant	*baritone*
Dulcamara, a quack doctor	*bass*

Chorus of villagers and soldiers

The scene is laid in a Basque village

THE 'elixir of love' is a bottle of wine which a quack doctor sells to a credulous country villager. We might from this expect uproarious comedy throughout. But this villager – who remains credulous, almost a simpleton – is the hero of the opera and moreover has a famous song which is genuinely (not mockingly) pathetic in appeal.

This balance between comedy and pathos is the distinguishing feature of the opera and shows a finely artistic judgement first of all from Felice Romani, the librettist. (He wrote not only this and other texts for Donizetti, but also those of the two Bellini operas treated in this book, and some for Rossini too; no hack-writer, he enjoys an honourable position in Italian literature.) An equally judged balance between comic and serious elements was shown by Donizetti himself. The sophisticated city opera-goers are allowed to laugh at the naiveties of country-life – but not to laugh too hard.

The whole subject of the elixir is raised because the heroine, Adina, has been reading the story of Tristan and Isolde ('Tristano' and 'Isotta' in the Italian). In Adina's book Tristan used a love-potion to win Isolde. Wagner saw the matter differently.

*   *   *   *   *

ACT I

The rich, beautiful Adina mocks at the bashful attempts of Nemorino to woo her and prefers to read aloud from her book about Tristan and Isolde. The villagers wish they had an elixir of love such as Tristan secured. Belcore, a sergeant at the head of a detachment, comes in and courts Adina, to Nemorino's despair.

A trumpet off-stage heralds the entrance of a gilded cart. In it stands Dr Dulcamara, a quack who eloquently proclaims his wares: 'Attention, you country-folk' (Udite, o rustici).* The crowd is impressed. When Nemorino asks for 'the elixir that won Queen Isolde' Dulcamara says he has it. He hands Nemorino a bottle really containing Bordeaux wine, and declares he has never seen such a simpleton. They have a comic duet: 'Thank you kindly' (Obligato).

Nemorino settles down to eat and drink. Happy that he will shortly win Adina by magic (the elixir is supposed to work after twenty-four hours) he sings to himself and does not bother Adina when she re-enters. Of course, this is just what stirs her interest in him.

Belcore receives a message that he and his detachment must leave. He asks Adina to marry him that very day, and she – to stimulate and pique Nemorino – appears to consent. Nemorino now becomes despairing again (after the elixir's twenty-four hours it will be too late!). He entreats Adina to postpone the wedding by a day; she refuses, and while all others look forward in lively manner to the wedding celebrations, Nemorino feels hopeless.

* English version by Arthur Jacobs (O.U.P.).

ACT II

On Adina's farm the wedding feast has been prepared. After a merry chorus Dulcamara produces the latest piece of music, a 'barcarolle' from Venice about a beautiful poor girl who rejects the advances of a rich old senator. Dulcamara and Adina sing it, to the applause of the guests: 'I have riches, you have beauty' (Io son ricco, e tu sei bella).

The crowd departs to watch the signing of the marriage contract, leaving Dulcamara to finish the food. Nemorino, who has been missing, comes in. Dulcamara offers him another bottle of 'elixir', to take instant effect this time. The sly Adina has postponed, after all, the signing of the contract, and Belcore re-enters. To gain money to pay for the new bottle, Nemorino enlists in Belcore's regiment, singing with him a duet, 'Twenty florins' (Venti scudi).

Back in the village square, Giannetta tells the villagers a secret: Nemorino's uncle has died, leaving him (though he does not yet know it) now a rich man. The girls now pay Nemorino considerable attention – which he ascribes to the elixir! Adina is touched when she learns that Nemorino has enlisted for her sake. Nemorino, delighted with his new popularity among the girls, leaves with the others. Adina learns from Dulcamara that he has sold Nemorino an 'elixir' – but she says (and Dulcamara agrees!) that as a beautiful woman she owns a powerful elixir of her own.

Nemorino re-enters; he has observed a change in Adina's attitude towards him, and once again his love for her emerges: 'Did not a tear unwillingly' (Una furtiva lagrima). Adina returns. She has bought Nemorino's discharge from the army, and hands him the papers. She declares her love for him, and she and Nemorino are united at last.

Belcore, returning with his soldiers, finds himself thrown over but consoles himself with the thought that the world is full of girls. Dulcamara does a brisk trade among the villagers with his evidently successful elixir – it brings not only love but money. The happy villagers give their enthusiastic

thanks to Dulcamara as he leaves in his cart and the opera
ends.

*   *   *   *   *

It is richness and range of melody, not of harmonic language
or structural subtlety, that carries *The Elixir of Love*. Sullivan must have learned a trick or two for his operettas from
the duet 'I have riches, you have beauty' of which we may
quote not the beginning but a catchy later fragment. Adina
is here singing in the character of a humble Venetian girl and
modestly rejects the honour of a Senator's love: notice the
way the music exposes the clever internal rhyme (*onore,
Senatore, amore*):

Nemorina's famous pathetic song, 'Did not a tear unwillingly' (Una furtiva lagrima) has an introduction surprisingly,
and most effectively, using a solo bassoon. Later in the song,
after expressing a wish to mingle his sighs with those of his
beloved, Nemorino has a long note which breaks out into the
word 'Heaven!' (cielo). At this very point the music breaks
out from the minor to the major key, with touching effect:

LUCIA DI LAMMERMOOR

(Lucy of Lammermoor)

*Libretto by Salvatore Cammarano, after the
novel by Sir Walter Scott*

First performed: Naples, 1835

Three Acts

Cast in order of singing:

Norman, an officer of Henry Ashton's household	*tenor*
Henry Ashton, lord of the castle of Lammermoor	*baritone*
Bide-the-Bent, chaplain at Lammermoor	*bass*
Lucy Ashton, Henry's sister	*soprano*
Ailsie, her companion	*mezzo-soprano*
Edgar, Master of Ravenswood, in love with Lucy	*tenor*
Arthur Bucklaw	*tenor*

Chorus of friends, relations and retainers
of the house of Lammermoor

*The scene is laid in Scotland towards the
end of the 17th century*

Emilia di Liverpool, the title of one of Donizetti's operas, must have sounded excitingly exotic to his Italian audiences: and *Lucia di Lammermoor*, in like manner, took these audiences to the life of a strange people living in feudal conflict in almost barbaric surroundings. Sir Walter Scott's novel was raided for a libretto by Cammarano (who later wrote *Il Trovatore* and three other librettos for Verdi).

The names of characters are Italianized in Italian performances as Enrico, Lucia, *etc*. Scott's 'Bide-the-Bent' seems to have defeated translation and is made into 'Raimondo'. In our synopsis we return to the literary originals of the names; but the whole libretto of the opera is very free (or careless) with the original. Cammarano made Bucklaw and Henry both

'Lords' but they are not so in the original – nor does the form 'Lord Henry Ashton' make proper sense here. Nor, in the original, is there a 'Castle of Lammermoor': Lammermoor is only the region of Scotland in which the action takes place. Incidentally, in the novel Lucy does not murder her husband – she attempts to, but he recovers.

Musically there are two high points – the sextet (with chorus) in Act II, which is the opera's climax of dramatic complexity, and the Mad Scene in Act III, the point of greatest self-expression for the heroine. The opera very much 'belongs' to the heroine, and it is as a vehicle for the dramatic intensity and vocal suppleness of a Maria Callas or a Joan Sutherland that it continues to be revived.

A scene of confrontation between Henry and Edgar at the beginning of Act II is omitted from most performances and from the ensuing synopsis.

*　　*　　*　　*　　*

ACT I

Henry Ashton, in conversation with his follower Norman, is agitated because his sister, Lucy, refuses the marriage with Arthur Bucklaw which has been arranged for her and which would strengthen Henry's house. Henry has found that Lucy has secretly been meeting her lover, Edgar, whose inheritance Henry as usurped. A hunting-party returns with the news that Edgar is in the neighbourhood. Henry expresses his hatred for Edgar: 'Cruel, fatal rage' (Cruda, funesta smania).

In a park by a fountain, Lucy is awaiting her love – with Ailsie, her companion, to keep watch. Lucy tells how she saw a spectre rising from the fountain: 'When all was silent' (Regnava nel silenzio); then she passes to rapturous anticipation of Edgar's coming: 'When in his joy and rapture' (Quando, rapito in estasi). Edgar arrives – but with the news that he must go at once to France, and they bid one another a loving farewell.

ACT II

Norman, conspiring with Henry, has intercepted the letters written by Edgar to Lucy and has written a forged one to the effect that Edgar is marrying someone else. In a duet, Henry gives the forged letters to Lucy. Festive music announces the arrival of Arthur Bucklaw, whom Henry intends Lucy to marry. Even in her grief over Edgar's 'unfaithfulness' she is still unwilling. The chaplain, Bide-the-Bent, to whom she turns for advice, tells her to resign herself to the marriage.

In a decked-out hall the company welcomes Arthur Bucklaw: 'We all rejoice to see you here' (Per te d'immenso giubilo). Lucy, trembling and in misery, is induced to sign the marriage contract. Suddenly there is a commotion; Edgar has returned and confronts them all, and a sextet follows: 'What restrains me?' (Chi mi frena?). Bide-the-Bent stops Henry's men from attacking Edgar and himself shows Edgar the marriage contract which Lucy has signed. Edgar curses Lucy for her lack of trust and a further ensemble expresses the passionate feelings of all.

ACT III

The company is celebrating the marriage when Bide-the-Bent interrupts the revelry with awful news: Lucy has gone mad and killed her husband. Lucy herself, her wedding garment stained with blood, enters. In this, her Mad Scene, she imagines that she and Edgar are beside the fountain but that a spectre rises up between them; she imagines the marriage that was to have taken place between them: 'Now, now I am yours' (Alfin son tua). Finally she prays Edgar to shed a tear on her grave. She falls senseless.

By night, Edgar has come to the graveyard outside the castle. He prepares to die in a duel with Henry, thinking that Lucy has willingly married Arthur Bucklaw and is happy. The chorus enters to tell him she is dying; the castle bell tolls; Bide-the-Bent enters to announce that she is dead. Edgar is now overcome with grief and kills himself, thinking of her as he dies: 'Thou who heavenward art flying' (Tu che a Dio spiegasti l'ali).

* * * * *

The sextet in Act II is remarkable for **its** building-up of tension. It is begun by Edgar and Henry (as the chief opponents) alone, afterwards joined by Lucy and then by Arthur Bucklaw, Bide-the-Bent and Ailsie, with the bystanders in chorus. Edgar, Henry and Lucy each have their moments of dominating the sextet. Here is one of Lucy's, as she sings 'Ah, I should like to weep and cannot; tears still desert me':

The chorus, as is usual in such numbers, provides little more than an *oom-pah* marking of the rhythm. But in the welcome which they sing on Arthur's arrival they become musically and dramatically prominent. Here, as elsewhere, we may see Donizetti's technique as foreshadowing Verdi's.

Already in the first act, when she was waiting for Edgar, Lucy's florid, graceful music had displayed her character as romantic heroine. But it is the Mad Scene which gives the pathos and the coloratura another turn of the screw, so to speak. There is a poignant moment here when the orchestra, playing a melody from her love-duet with Edgar (Act I), suggests that she is recollecting that meeting; but now, terrified, she sees 'the fearful phantom' of her murdered husband rise to separate her lover from herself:

The companionship – or even rivalry – of voice and flute is a feature of the scene. Here, for instance, voice and flute ripple away together as Lucy sings of bliss for herself and her lover in heaven:

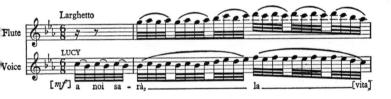

It may sometimes seem that this music speaks more of prima donnas' showmanship than of madness; yet in the theatre a great artist can even make us forget that we no longer think madness a romantic state of mind.

VINCENZO BELLINI

(1801–35)

O_F the same type as Donizetti's operas were those of a composer four years younger, Vincenzo Bellini. In his last opera, *The Puritans* (I Puritani, 1835), he not only showed a new adventurousness in harmony, but also set the recitative to be accompanied by the orchestra (not the piano, which had succeeded the harpsichord). This, a procedure occasionally followed by Gluck and certain of Bellini's more immediate predecessors, was designed to lessen the rigid differentiation in the audience's ear between recitative and aria.

What, we may wonder, would Bellini's later works have been like if he had not died at thirty-three?

LA SONNAMBULA

(The Sleep-Walker)

Libretto by Felice Romani

First performed: Milan, 1831

Two Acts

Cast in order of singing:

Lisa, keeper of the village inn	*soprano*
Alessio, a young peasant, in love with Lisa	*bass*
Amina, a village girl	*soprano*
Teresa, Amina's foster-mother	*mezzo-soprano*
A notary	*baritone*
Elvino, a young farmer, engaged to Amina	*tenor*
Count Rodolfo	*baritone*

Chorus of villagers

The scene is laid in Switzerland

THE title gives away the element which imparts an unusual twist to the plot. Amina is caught in Count Rodolfo's bed-room at night, but is cleared of suspicion when it is shown that it was only somnambulism that led her there. (The age of Freud would have a different comment on this 'excuse', especially since certain undeveloped hints suggest the possibility that the Count is Amina's father.) Her actual sleep-walking is, by theatrical tradition, demonstrated by her perilous crossing of a rickety footbridge.

In the opera's kindly depiction of the simplicity of country-folk (they have not even heard of somnambulism until the Count explains) it is a kind of 'serious' complement to Donizetti's comic *Elixir of Love* – another tale of country simplicity from the pen of the same librettist. But *La Sonnambula* lives most of all through the appeal of its melodies to coloratura sopranos and their fans.

*   *   *   *   *

ACT I

All the villagers rejoice at the forthcoming wedding of Amina and Elvino – all except Lisa, who keeps the inn. She, repulsing the advances of Alessio, who loves her, is jealous of Amina's good fortune. Amina sings of her joy: 'See how the day serenely' (Come per me sereno). The notary arrives, preceding Elvino, and a betrothal duet follows: 'Take now the ring' (Prendi, l'anel ti dono).

The sound of horses heralds the arrival of Count Rodolfo on an expedition. He decides to stay the night in the village, which evidently has associations for him: 'Ah, how pleasant once more to see it' (Vi ravviso, o luoghi ameni). He pays rather too much attention to Amina for Elvino's liking. Led by Teresa, the villagers warn him of a local phantom. When they have gone, Elvino reproaches Amina for apparently flirting with the Count, but they are reconciled and sing a duet.

Rodolfo is conducted to his room by Lisa, who is not reluctant to flirt with him. Shortly afterwards Amina, in her nightdress, walks into the Count's room. He realizes that she is sleep-walking, hearing her speak of her coming marriage.

The villagers and afterwards Elvino are brought in by the jealous Lisa; they put another construction on Amina's behaviour and her protests. There is a prolonged ensemble (for all the characters except the Count) begun by Amina's 'I am guiltless' (D'un pensiero). The combined expression of tension and doubt, during which Elvino breaks off the engagement, ends the act.

Act II

The villagers are on their way to Count Rodolfo's castle, where they intend to beg him to establish Amina's innocence. They leave. Amina in her distress is comforted by her foster-mother Teresa, but Elvino spurns her. The villagers return to say the Count will be coming to testify for her. Unconvinced, Elvino takes back the ring he gave Amina. But, aside, he admits his feelings: 'Ah, why then can I not hate you?' (Ah, perchè non posso odiarti?).

Nevertheless, he agrees to marry Lisa instead. Lisa rejects, once again, the pleas of Alessio, and rejoices at her new good fortune. While Elvino is about to arrange this new marriage, the Count attempts to dissuade him. He is adamant and disbelieves the Count's explanation about somnambulism, voiced in a quartet (for Lisa, Teresa, Elvino and the Count) and chorus: 'No, your Lordship!' (Signor Conte).

Suddenly Amina herself is seen, again sleep-walking, on a dangerous ledge or bridge. The villagers watch, not daring to cry out and wake her – and hear her complaining in her sleep that, though innocent, she has lost Elvino. As Amina comes down, still sleep-walking, she sings of her unhappiness: 'Ah! could I think to see you' (Ah! non credea mirarti). Elvino, agonized at his own lack of faith in her, interrupts and places the ring on her finger again. Amina wakes to a joyful chorus, and sings of the happiness now restored to her and Elvino: 'Never was there' (Ah! non giunge); the others (except Lisa, who has withdrawn) join in to end the opera.

*　　*　　*　　*　　*

Bellini's lyrical writing does not confine itself only to the
heroine and her lover. An extract from the Count's aria in the
first act gives an idea of the warm expression of Bellini's solo
music and of how, like Rossini and Donizetti, he often used
the chorus merely to mark the beat. The Count is greeting
those 'dear places' he is now revisiting after many years:

The big ensemble which ends the first act, consequent on
the discovery of Amina in the Count's room, was the direct
model (even as to key) for Sullivan's parody in *Trial by Jury*,
'A nice dilemma'. Amina leads it; then, when Elvino enters
expressing his anguish at the situation, Amina follows him in
canon and with words addressing him directly – 'Do not believe that I am guilty'. The effect is as if she were trying to
enter his thoughts:

The heroine's vocal fireworks come chiefly at the end. The singer must emphasize the musical contrast between the tender, introspective strain sung while sleep-walking and the brilliant expression of joy. Here the excitement rises as the voice does when Amina sings of the earth transformed by her happiness into 'a heaven of love'.

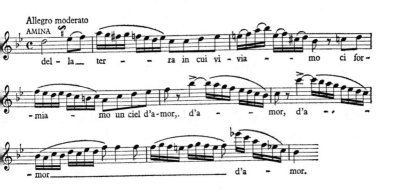

NORMA

Libretto by Felice Romani
First performed: Milan, 1831

TWO ACTS

Cast in order of singing:

Oroveso, arch-Druid	*bass*
Pollio, a Roman pro-consul	*tenor*
Flavius, his friend	*tenor*

Norma, a Druid priestess, daughter of Orovesco   *soprano*
Adalgisa, a younger priestess   *soprano*
Clotilda, attendant to Norma   *soprano*
    Chorus of Druids, soldiers and people

The scene is laid in Gaul in Roman times

THE conflict in a hero or heroine between love and duty is
the mainspring of many operas. In this one, Norma's holy
obligations as a Druid priestess are opposed to her love for
the Roman pro-consul, Pollio, and involve her finally in suicide. An exotic background to the human struggle is provided by the setting in ancient Gaul. The point is emphasized
when, before her great invocation to the moon – the 'Chaste
Goddess' (Casta diva) of the famous aria – Norma cuts off a
spray of mistletoe with a sickle from the sacred oak. She is,
by the way, no girlish heroine; her maturity and strength are
contrasted with the inexperience of the younger priestess,
Adalgisa. A performance which reverses the two is a perversion. Norma is a positive rather than a passive heroine, her
acts of will influencing the plot: there is a power of characterization here, as well as a brilliance of vocal writing in the
role, which contributes to the opera's strength.

    The Roman names are here given in the authentic Latin
forms: 'Pollione' and 'Flavio' are used in the Italian original.

      *   *   *   *   *

ACT I

To the sacred oak come the people of Gaul in procession, followed by the Druids, who are addressed by Oroveso, their
head. They pray for victory over the Romans and retire. The
Roman officers, Pollio and Flavius, enter. Pollio, formerly in
illicit love with Norma, chief Druid priestess, by whom he
has two children, mentions that he now loves a younger
priestess, Adalgisa. In an aria 'We at the shrine of Venus'
(Meco all'altar di Venere) he voices his foreboding of
Norma's vengeance. In the distance the Druids' rites are
heard.

Now the Romans retire as the Druids return to welcome Norma, who advances and speaks prophetically of Rome's coming fall. Then, cutting off the sacred mistletoe, Norma addresses the rising moon – 'Chaste Goddess' (Casta diva) – supported by Oroveso and the chorus of people. Aside, she discloses her love for Pollio. All then leave.

Adalgisa enters and prays for the protection of her gods. Pollio reveals himself and woos her: Adalgisa is at first hesitant, but then admits that she returns his love.

Norma is at home with her children and reveals her sorely disturbed feelings. She bids Clotilda, her attendant, hide the children as the young Adalgisa approaches. There follows a duet for Adalgisa and Norma: 'I was the same' (Io fui così). Adalgisa's confession to Norma of her illicit love awakens Norma's sympathy: for she too broke her priestly vow of chastity. But then Norma asks Adalgisa who her lover is. 'Here he comes', Adalgisa replies, for Pollio approaches. Passions rise as the two women realize his deception. Finally the striking of the sacred shield is heard, in the distance, summoning Norma to inspire the people. The distant chorus of Druids add their voices to those of the three soloists.

ACT II

It is night. Norma holds a dagger and contemplates her sleeping children, whom, in her agony, she is tempted to kill. But she refrains, and sends Clotilda to bring Adalgisa. Norma presents the children to Adalgisa and bids her take them when she goes with Pollio to Rome, while Norma will die. Adalgisa begs Norma, instead, to live for the children's sake and says she will turn Pollio's affections back to Norma. The duet for the two women – 'Take thou then' (Deh! con te) – ends in passionate avowal together.

Within the Druids' forest, Oroveso and chorus show their hatred of the Romans but feel powerless until Norma advises them. At the temple, Norma hears from Clotilda that Adalgisa wishes to renew her vows as priestess but that Pollio has sworn to tear Adalgisa from the altar. Norma strikes the sacred shield three times and the Druids, entering to hear her, sing a chorus of war. Clotilda runs in with the announcement that a Roman attempting to enter has been caught. It is Pollio. Norma takes a dagger to kill the interloper but cannot strike the blow.

Norma takes Pollio aside. When he rejects her demand that he shall leave Adalgisa, she vows that Adalgisa shall be burnt as a priestess who has betrayed her vows. The people are told to prepare for a burning. But when Norma is asked to name the guilty priestess she replies 'I'. The people are incredulous, but Norma persists. When her children are brought in Norma asks Pollio to take care of them, but he stands aside.

Anguished, Norma's people prepare to sacrifice her. Much moved, Pollio goes with her to be sacrificed.

*   *   *   *   *

Among Bellini's melodies, with their smooth flow and long spans, Norma's invocation to the moon, 'Chaste Goddess', is perhaps the most famous of all:

The duet of Norma and Adalgisa in Act II, after presenting the two women as opposed, finally shows them united in mutual feelings. Adalgisa begs Norma to have regard to her 'darling children', now kneeling before her and Norma feels her resolution weakening. This new unity between the women is naturally paralleled in the music:

But Norma herself is no mere mouthpiece for euphonious music. This is a genuinely dramatic part. The trio just before the end of Act II has been well said to foreshadow the end of Verdi's *Aida*. In her final duet with Pollio, Norma has to 'punch' out a simple melody to make it carry a menacing text ('Already I am relishing your glances, your grief, and her death'):

The Druids are characterized as 'noble savages'. The exotic sound of a gong among the orchestral instruments, the solemnity of the off-stage choruses, and the striking of the sacred shield are musical evocations of this.

V

GIUSEPPE VERDI

(1813–1901)

'Viva Verdi' was the popular slogan when the composer went to Naples in 1858. It was a slogan with a hidden political meaning: 'Viva Vittorio Emanuele Rè D'Italia!' – a cheer (which could not be voiced openly in Naples under the Bourbons) for King Victor Emanuel of Piedmont, whom liberal opinion hoped to make king of a united Italy (as actually happened in 1861).

The identification of Verdi with liberal ideals was not just an acrostic. He was sympathetic to the liberal cause (which, in the 19th-century Italian context, meant the anti-clerical as well as anti-despotic cause) and eventually accepted nomination as a deputy in the parliament of the new Italy, though he was not active in politics. Moreover many of his operas made biting social or political comment and ran into trouble with censorship (see *Rigoletto* and *A Masked Ball*, below); and even in a work like *Aida*, the casting of the priests as an intolerant and vindictive force behind the throne would not have been considered accidental in Verdi's Italy. In the early *Nabucco* (short for Nabucodnosor, *i.e.* Nebuchadnezzar, 1842) the celebrated chorus of exiled Hebrews was heard as a patriotic lament of contemporary Italians in political exile. So was the chorus of Scottish exiles in *Macbeth* (1847).

Verdi was not, in fact, writing a kind of refined diversion for an international audience of canary-fanciers. He was writing a kind of romantic drama intended to appeal – in its melodies, its plots and its stagecraft – to the Italy of Cavour (one of Verdi's great heroes), Garibaldi and Manzoni (the patriotic novelist in whose memory Verdi wrote his Requiem). It is the achievement of Verdi's genius to have lifted this type of drama beyond the circumstances of its creation.

Love-duets, bold and catchy choruses, brilliant arias for

soprano and heroic ones for tenor – these are the traditional ingredients for Italian opera, and Verdi started off with them. But as he progressed, he came to place less stress on such individual numbers, each complete and rounded off and ready to be followed by applause. Instead he developed a greater continuity of drama-through-music, prominently using the device of musical recall (re-introducing a theme when the drama recalls some person or situation previously encountered. Verdi's last two operas, *Otello* and *Falstaff*, depend much more on their total sweep, less on their individual songs and choruses, than do the earlier works.

Apart from works mentioned above and those discussed in the following pages, some of Verdi's other operas such as *I Lombardi* (1843) and *Ernani* (1844) are occasionally revived.

RIGOLETTO

Libretto by Francesco Maria Piave, after Victor Hugo
First performed: Venice, 1851

Three Acts

Cast in order of singing:

The Duke of Mantua	*tenor*
Borsa, a courtier	*tenor*
Countess Ceprano	*mezzo-soprano*
Marullo, a courtier	*baritone*
Rigoletto, the Duke's jester, a hunchback	*baritone*
Count Ceprano, a nobleman of Mantua	*bass*
Count Monterone, a nobleman of Mantua	*baritone*
Sparafucile, a professional assassin	*bass*
Gilda, Rigoletto's daughter	*soprano*
Giovanna, her attendant	*mezzo-soprano*
A page	*mezzo-soprano*
An usher	*baritone*
Maddalena, Sparafucile's sister	*mezzo-soprano*

Chorus of courtiers, servants, etc.

The scene is laid in Mantua in the 16th century

Rigoletto is an opera to stir the moral passions. It is this quality that helps to make the opera a persistent favourite – apart from the sheer musical gifts of Verdi that have made 'La donna è mobile' and the major-key theme of the quartet among the best known tunes of the world. The hero of the opera is a hunchback jester who is made the cruel sport of an idle court. But the hunchback's vengeance is terribly turned back on himself. A dramatic force is made of the curse laid on the jester – *The Curse* was the opera's originally intended title. (It may seem curious that, in this and later operas too, the 'progressive' Verdi attached such dramatic validity to the superstition of cursing.)

The opera's implied attack on court life, doubtless appealing to Verdi himself and his original audiences, brought composer and librettist into conflict with the censor at Venice (at that time under Austrian imperial rule) who banned the original libretto as enshrining 'revolting immorality and obscene triviality'; however, after some changes of names, the plot was eventually accepted.

*   *   *   *   *

ACT I

To music from a band back-stage (light music suitable for a gay gathering), the curtain rises to show the Duke's palace. In conversation with Borsa the Duke mentions the latest girl he has his eye on, whose name he does not know. He shows his devil-may-care attitude towards women: 'Shall I bind me?' (Questa o quella).* The band strikes up a minuet in which the Duke dances with Countess Ceprano, whom he has also been pursuing.

Marullo brings the courtiers a surprising discovery: their ugly hunchback jester, Rigoletto, keeps a mistress. Now Rigoletto himself enters and mocks Ceprano, whom his master is openly attempting to cuckold. There is a big ensemble, mainly of revelry, but Ceprano is planning vengeance. Suddenly Monterone, a nobleman whose daughter the Duke has se-

* English version by Edward J. Dent (O.U.P.).

duced, pushes his way in; the Duke allows Rigoletto to mock Monterone, then orders his arrest. Monterone curses Rigoletto – and continues to do so as he is led out. For the others, the revelry continues.

A change of scene shows Rigoletto returning home as the evening darkens, Monterone's curse still preying on his mind. He is accosted by an assassin, Sparafucile, who offers his services and explains his methods. Rigoletto says he has no use for him – at present. As Sparafucile leaves, Rigoletto thinks of his own pitiful state. He, too, is a hireling – like an assassin, except that he uses his mocking tongue instead of a dagger: 'We are equals!' (Pari siamo).

Entering his home, he is greeted by Gilda. She is his daughter, not (as Marullo had told the courtiers) his mistress. They have been here three months, but he has kept her locked up, and he now emphasizes that she must never go out except to church. He tells her of her dead mother, showing a grief which Gilda tries to comfort. He sternly warns her attendant, Giovanna, to guard her well.

Unseen, outside, the Duke has arrived. Gilda is the new girl he was pursuing, and only now does he realize that she is Rigoletto's daughter. When Rigoletto, hearing some noise outside, opens the gate, the Duke slips into the garden, throws a bribe to Giovanna and conceals himself. Before leaving the house again Rigoletto sings in an impassioned duet with Gilda and again warns Giovanna to guard her. Gilda now confides to Giovanni that she has been attracted by a youth she saw in church. It is the Duke, who now shows himself and professes his love; together they sing 'Love to the heart is the fair light of morning' (E il sol dell'anima). He declares that he is a student, by name Gualtier Maldè. Outside, unknown to both, the courtiers are gathering; Ceprano's and Borsa's voices are heard. They are planning to abduct Rigoletto's 'mistress'. After a passionate farewell to Gilda, the Duke leaves.

Gilda, alone, echoes the words 'Gualtier Maldè', and declares 'Ah, how dear to me that name!' (Caro nome). The words Gualtier Maldè die away on her lips as she enters the house by an outside stairway; the conspirators can see her over the wall, and marvel at her beauty. It is now dark. Rigoletto is accosted by the conspiring noblemen who pretend to him that they are going to abduct Ceprano's wife. Rigoletto joins them. Under pretence of masking him they blindfold him. There is a softly excited chorus of conspiracy as they make the blindfold dupe hold a ladder against the wall of his own house and abduct Gilda before Rigoletto discovers – as he now does, too late – that his eyes are bandaged. He rushes into the house and finds her gone. In anguish he recalls Monterone's curse (Ah! la maledizione!).

ACT II

Back in the palace the Duke is disconsolate because, on returning to Rigoletto's house, he could not find Gilda. (The abduction had been made without his knowledge.) He sings with genuine passion of Gilda: 'Ah me, could I but wipe away' (Parmi veder le lagrime). Then the courtiers enter and tell him that they have abducted and brought to the palace Rigoletto's 'mistress'. The Duke realizes it is Gilda and goes off to 'console' her.

Enter Rigoletto, arrayed as jester but in anguish. The appearance of a page discloses that the Duke is 'busy'. Rigoletto's anguish bursts out: 'I'll have my daughter!'. The word 'daughter' stuns the courtiers, whom Rigoletto now denounces: 'Oh ye courtiers, vile rabble' (Cortigiani, vil razza) – his fury then softening into a plea to have Gilda restored to him. She rushes in. Rigoletto orders the courtiers out. Gilda tells her story: 'Every Sunday morning' (Tutte le feste al tempio); Rigoletto consoles her. Just then Monterone is led, under guard, across the scene. Seeing Rigoletto, Monterone declares that his curse was evidently in vain. But Rigoletto now plans revenge on the Duke both for his own sake and for Monterone's. In the duet 'I pronounce thy fatal sentence' (Sì, vendetta) Gilda pleads with her father for mercy on the Duke but he refuses.

ACT III

Sparafucile keeps an inn where his sister Maddalena acts as a decoy for robbery or murder. The Duke, inside, is observed from outside by Rigoletto and Gilda (who has been brought by her father to see the kind of man the Duke really is). The Duke sings his opinion of women: 'Wayward as thistledown' (La donna è mobile). Sparafucile comes out of the house and asks Rigoletto – on whose instructions he has evidently lured the Duke there – for further orders. A quartet follows: inside the house the Duke is light-heartedly making love to Maddalena (who affects to resist him, but is charmed), while Gilda and Rigoletto look on from outside.

Rigoletto, thinking that the town will be unsafe for them when he has accomplished the deed he has in mind, instructs Gilda to go home, put on boy's clothing and leave for Verona. She departs unwillingly. Rigoletto arranges payment with Sparafucile for killing the Duke – whose body is to be sewn up in a sack – and says he will return at midnight. A storm rises as Maddalena shows the Duke the way to the upper room for the night. She descends to the lower room and pleads with her brother not to kill the young man ('he's an Apollo') and to murder Rigoletto instead – a suggestion Sparafucile indignantly repudiates as unworthy of an honest assassin under contract to his client. But he agrees to substitute for the Duke any other male victim who may present himself before midnight. Gilda, now in boy's clothes, has returned and stands outside: she knocks, deciding to sacrifice herself for the Duke, and enters. What happens in the house amid the storm and darkness is left to the imagination.

The storm ceases. Rigoletto enters as midnight strikes; he receives from Sparafucile a sack with a body in it and goes exultantly to throw it in the river. Suddenly from the house a voice is heard – the Duke's voice, with his unmistakable song, 'Wayward as thistledown' (La donna è mobile). The horrified Rigoletto opens the sack and in it discovers Gilda, not quite dead. She asks forgiveness for disobeying him, and dies. With

a cry from Rigoletto – who recalls Monterone's curse – the
opera ends.

*   *   *   *   *

The musical drama in *Rigoletto* is much more closely inte-
grated than in the older (Donizetti-Bellini) kind of Italian
opera. Instead of a formal overture there is the orchestral
pronouncement of the 'curse' theme which appears throughout the opera.

And just as the orchestra thus becomes a voice, so the chorus
become instruments: in the storm scene they sing wordlessly
for purely atmospheric effect. The element of display in the
vocal parts, while sufficient for the characters to be musically
conveyed, is subordinated to drama. Gilda disappears into her
room at her father's house with her lover's supposed name of
'Gualtier Maldè' on her lips, and the name fades out on a
dreamy trill:

That is what Verdi wrote. (We omit the subdued chorus of
those who are about to abduct her.) The prima donna who
puts it up to top E (an octave above what Verdi wrote) is
impertinently thinking of herself, not of Gilda. The tune in
which the Duke sings of woman's fickleness ('La donna è mobile') is marvellously catchy – and its catchiness is itself part
of the drama: a few bars must serve to identify both the tune
and its singer at the moment of climax when Rigoletto is

bearing on his shoulders the sack supposedly containing the Duke's body.

Verdi does not need a solo to establish every character: Maddalena has none, but her concerted music defines her as clearly as anyone else on the stage. The high point of the opera is no solo at all but the quartet where even Maddalena's laughing – she says, but only half-truly, that she does not believe the Duke's pretensions of love – is woven into the texture at the same time as the Duke light-heartedly woos her. Meanwhile Gilda pours out her anguish in a long phrase which is paralleled in her father's vocal line (note Verdi's way of conveying sympathy between characters):

IL TROVATORE

(The Troubadour)

Libretto by Salvatore Cammarano

First performed: Rome, 1853

Four Acts

Cast in order of singing:

Ferrando, captain of the guard to the Count of Luna	*bass*
Inez, confidential maid to Leonora	*soprano*
Leonora, a lady-in-waiting at the Court of Aragon	*soprano*
The Count of Luna, a young nobleman, in love with Leonora	*baritone*
Manrico, a troubadour, reputed son of Azucena	*tenor*
Azucena, a gipsy	*mezzo-soprano*
A gipsy	*baritone*
A messenger	*baritone*
Ruiz, a soldier in Manrico's service	*tenor*

Chorus of followers of the Count and of Manrico, soldiers, nuns and gipsies

The scene is laid in Spain in the 15th century

IL TROVATORE lives by its stream of memorable melodies. The Miserere, the Anvil Chorus, the Soldiers' Chorus, Manrico's 'Di quella pira', Luna's 'Il balen', Azecuna's 'Stride la vampa', the duet 'Ai nostri monti' – all these would inevitably be in a short-list of the most popular of all operatic tunes, tunes heard repeatedly with delight in thousands of drawing-rooms and band-stands. But the opera was also intended to be exciting dramatically, with its scenes of gipsy life and of abduction from a convent. This is romantic opera, in which the characters display their romantic aspects as a means of moving the drama forward: the soldiers, even in private, still sing about the splendours and glory of fighting.

The plot is complicated, and far-fetched in an old-fashioned way: we are to believe that, before the opera opened, the gipsy Azucena, raving, 'hurled into the flames her own child, instead of the young Count (thus preserving, with an almost supernatural instinct for opera, the baby that was destined to grow up into a tenor with a voice high enough to sing "Di quella pira").' We quote this from one of the classics of operatic literature* – though we must spoil the fun a little by adding that the high C's with which the tenors insist on preening themselves in this aria are not Verdi's at all, but an interpolation.

It is further demanded that the Troubadour, instead of flying off to the rescue of his mother for whom the stake is already burning, shall stay and sing of his intentions for two verses of that very song (an extreme example of a 'contradiction' implicit in opera and mocked by Gilbert and Sullivan). The second verse is therefore often cut in performance.

Much of the story happens *between* the acts and before the opera begins, as indeed is explained in Ferrando's opening narration. Performances in Italian before English-speaking audiences, who fail to follow this narration and subsequent explanatory passages, have given the opera the reputation of being much more absurd than it really is.

*   *   *   *   *

ACT I

The curtain rises on a guard-room. Ferrando, captain of the guard, reminds his men that their master, the Count, loves Leonora and wishes to track down a mysterious troubadour in whose serenading of her he detects a rival. Ferrando also tells about the gipsy Azucena's misdeed of many years ago: when her mother was being burned at the stake, Azucena threw a baby (the present Count's abducted young brother, as all believe) into the flames.

The scene changes to the garden. Leonora confesses to her

* Kobbé's *Complete Opera Book* (1919, with later revisions).

attendant· Inez that she loves the unknown knight who comes to serenade her. She expresses her love: 'Within my heart a flame is raging' (Di tale amor che dirsi mai può).* The Count, who loves (but is not loved by) Leonora, enters the garden, when the sound of a harp discloses the presence of the serenader. It is the troubadour, Manrico, who now woos Leonora in song. A trio follows for Leonora, Manrico and (unseen at first, then fiercely denouncing the lovers) the Count. The two men face each other in anger as the curtain falls.

Act II

We see Manrico again – in the gipsies' camp. The mysterious troubadour is thus presented as a gipsy, the son (as he supposes) of Azucena. After the gipsies' opening 'Anvil Chorus', as they begin their day's work, Azucena sings of the harrowing sight she witnessed when they burnt her mother: 'Harsh roars the greedy flame' (Stride la vampa). After the others have left, she explains in a further song that she was ready to avenge her mother by throwing the present Count's abducted infant brother into the flames but instead, distracted, threw in her own son.

Then who is Manrico, if not her son? He himself tells her of meeting the Count in battle and being prevented by some mysterious feeling from killing him. Now a message arrives telling him that Leonora believing him dead is to enter a convent that evening. After a duet with Azucena reflecting his agitation, he leaves.

Outside the convent the Count, attended by Ferrando, sings of his love for Leonora: 'No faint star' (Il balen del suo sorriso). He plans to abduct her before she takes the vow. He and his followers retire and comment, unseen by the nuns who now approach in procession. Leonora, attended by Inez, is ready to enter the convent building, but the Count and his men step forward to abduct her. Suddenly Manrico appears, attended by Ruiz and other followers. Leonora can hardly believe her senses. Her voice rides above the big ensemble

* English version by Edward J. Dent (O.U.P.).

which expresses the agitation of all. Manrico's forces prevail and he leads Leonora away.

ACT III

The soldiers of the Count, who is now laying siege to the castle to which Manrico has taken Leonora, are in camp. Led by Ferrando they sing of the coming assault in the Soldiers' Chorus. Ferrando brings the Count news that an old gipsy has been apprehended. It is Azucena, whom the Count and Ferrando interrogate and recognize; not only is she held responsible for the baby-killing of long ago but she declares herself the mother of their enemy, Manrico. She is condemned to the stake.

In the besieged castle Manrico sings to Leonora of his love: 'When I to thee in bonds of love' (Ah sì, ben mio). They are about to be married and an organ from the chapel of the castle is heard. Ruiz enters with the message that Azucena has been captured by the enemy. Manrico sings of his determination to leave the castle (and his bride) to save his mother: 'That foul flame yonder' (Di quella pira); Leonora, Ruiz and a chorus of Manrico's soldiers join in. He leaves hastily.

ACT IV

Manrico's effort has failed. He and Azucena lie in a prison-tower of the Count's. But unknown to him, at night, Leonora is outside with Ruiz. She sings of her love: 'Borne on the wings of love so bright' (D'amor sull'ali rosee). In the distance, a choir is heard chanting the Miserere for an approaching death, over which are heard the lamenting of Manrico and the forebodings of Leonora. The Count enters. Leonora accosts him and eventually offers to marry him if he will free Manrico (she plans to take poison herself): 'O see, the bitter tears I shed' (Mira, d'acerbe lagrime). He accepts the offer jubilantly.

Inside the tower Azucena is delirious and Manrico tries to soothe her: 'Home to our mountains' (Ai nostri monti). Leonora enters to tell Manrico he is free but he, saying that he guesses the terms, repels her. She then explains that she has taken poison, and dies in Manrico's arms. The Count comes in and finds himself tricked. Manrico is taken outside for execution. Azucena informs the Count he has executed his own brother, and exultantly declares that her mother has been, after all, avenged.

Italian opera in Verdi's day was meant to provide 'hit tunes', and Verdi did not fail. Not to be missed is the essentially popular, downright, strongly rhythmic nature of the gipsies' Anvil Chorus:

Even in the numbers expressing the soloists' private thoughts of anguish or desire, Verdi manages to keep the melodies in immediately memorable form, with here and there an ornament that adds an emphasis – like a sigh or an indrawn breath – to emotion:

The latter is Manrico's despairing utterance ('Ah, death, thou comest slowly') when he and his mother are imprisoned and when the mood has been set by the chanted Miserere. The continuation sums up Verdi's power of ensemble. In the first bar Manrico dominates, with his high A flat as he cries 'Do not forget me!' to Leonora (far away, as he thinks). But she is hidden outside his prison and hears him: 'I forget thee?' she cries in the third bar, her voice now rising to dominate the music. At the same bar the orchestra begins a 'drumming' rhythm characteristic of Verdi's expression of

moments of fatality; and meanwhile the death-warning of the
Miserere continues:

LA TRAVIATA

(The Woman Gone Astray)

Libretto by Francesco Maria Piave, after the play
'La Dame aux Camélias' by Alexandre Dumas the younger

First performed: Venice, 1853

Three Acts

Cast in order of singing:

Violetta Valéry, a courtesan	*soprano*
Flora Bervoix, her friend	*mezzo-soprano*
Baron Douphol, suitor to Violetta	*baritone*
Grenvil, a doctor	*bass*
Marquis d'Obigny	*bass*
Viscount Gastone de Letorières	*tenor*
Alfredo Germont, in love with Violetta	*tenor*
Annina, maid to Violetta	*soprano*
Joseph, servant at the country house	*tenor*
Giorgio Germont, Alfredo's father	*baritone*
A messenger	*baritone*

Chorus of party guests, street revellers, etc.

The scene is laid in and near Paris

'THE death of Violetta is of a grand realistic effect, and has drawn many a tear from many fair eyes.' So says the introduction to an edition of the score published for English readers during Verdi's lifetime. This is, indeed, an opera meant to affect the audience by its true-to-life nature: the way the street-noises from the carnival burst into the dying heroine's bedroom is an example. With this dramatic method Verdi drew as strong a set of principal characters as any opera knows. Soprano, tenor and baritone have constantly changing personal relationships – and from the light-hearted drinking-song (Brindisi) of the first act to the heroine's final farewell

Verdi gives each change its own memorable music.

La Traviata was originally set (like the play on which it is based) in the audience's own time. It was, however, a failure at its first performance and later was put back into the period of Louis XIV. Today there is every reason for restoring it to Verdi's own period. There would indeed be a case for presenting it now as a modern-dress drama (that is, set in our own time), were it not that the situation of the central character – a woman not accepted in 'society' but ready to sacrifice herself so that her lover's sister may make a 'good' marriage – could hardly seem even remotely plausible today.

Dumas' names for the two leading characters were Marguerite and Armand; Verdi's librettist Italianized them as Violetta and Alfredo.

*   *   *   *   *

ACT I

The rise of the curtain discloses the well-to-do house of Violetta, a courtesan. (Not a prostitute, selling her favours casually and privately; a courtesan of Violetta's type was a woman who lived a regular social life, attaching herself to one man at a time in an 'underworld' which was frequented by men of fashion but which was not officially recognized by respectable married society.)

A party is in progress to which Violetta welcomes Flora and her other friends. Among them is Baron Douphol, an old admirer of hers. Gastone, another friend, enters and brings with him Alfredo, introducing him to Violetta as one who has long admired her. Beneath her gay manner she is touched. When Alfredo, called on by the other guests, leads a drinking song or Brindisi, 'Let's drink, let us drink from the wine-cup o'er-flowing' (Libiamo, libiamo ne' lieti calici),* Violetta rises and sings the second stanza; the chorus of guests joins in festively.

Dance-music is heard from an adjoining room. As the guests are about to go to dance, Violetta is seized with coughing. She asks her guests to proceed to the dance, but, as she

* English version by Edward J. Dent (O.U.P.).

looks in a mirror and sees how pale she is, she finds that one guest has stayed with her. It is Alfredo, who declares that he has loved her from afar for a year. Gaston calls from the other room, and Violetta dismisses Alfredo tenderly.

The other guests return and take their leave. Alone, Violetta reflects on Alfredo: 'How curious' (E strano), and then, 'Ah, is it he' (Ah! fors' è lui). She seems to see a new, purer life in what Alfredo offers to her. But finally (for she is no more than half persuaded that such a new life would be possible) she declares – 'Free as ever' (Sempre libera) – that she can only pursue the gay round of social pleasures.

ACT II

But Alfredo has evidently won her over. He and Violetta have now settled in a country villa not far from Paris. Alfredo, alone, sings of his new happy existence: 'After a wild unruly life' (De' miei bollenti spiriti). But when Annina, Violetta's servant, comes in, he learns that she has been in Paris on Violetta's instructions, selling off her mistress's possessions, in order to pay for the idyllic life they have been living. Alfredo is ashamed and embarrassed and immediately leaves for Paris to attend to their finances.

Violetta enters and receives a letter from Flora inviting her to a dance that evening. She is expecting a caller on business, but there enters Giorgio Germont. As Alfredo's father, he comes to denounce Violetta, first of all for squandering his son's money – but discovers that, after all, it is Violetta who has had to sell her possessions. Then he asks her for a sacrifice on behalf of his daughter, 'Pure as an angel from above' (Pura siccome un angelo). His daughter, he explains, faces the breaking of her engagement because of Alfredo's 'disgrace'. He asks Violetta to leave Alfredo but not to tell him why. At first she refuses, but eventually she sadly consents, asking Germont only that he should tell his daughter that someone made such a sacrifice: 'Tell her, your daughter dear' (Dite alla giovine). Violetta writes a note telling Alfredo that she has left him – without explanation, so that he will think her false to him. Germont has been more and more moved by

Violetta's nobility of spirit and he embraces her as a father. He leaves.

Violetta rings the bell and is about to give Annina the note for Alfredo when Alfredo himself enters. Passionately she asks Alfredo to love her as she loves him: 'Love me for ever' (Amami, Alfredo). She leaves. He does not understand what is happening until a messenger gives him a letter. It is Violetta's, saying she has left him. In anguish, he sees his father enter. Germont attempts to console his son and proposes to take him home: 'To our home in fair Provence' (Di Provenza, il mar, il suol'). But Alfredo already suspects that Violetta has gone to Douphol, her old admirer. Seeing the letter which Violetta received from Flora he resolves to go to the party, meet Violetta there, and take his revenge.

The scene now changes to Flora's party. Some of the guests enter dressed up as Spanish fortune-telling gipsies, others as matadors, with appropriate music. Suddenly Alfredo enters and joins a group of card-players. Violetta enters, on Baron Douphol's arm. Alfredo, who is winning at cards, makes insulting remarks which can only be taken to refer to Violetta. Tension rises between him and the baron and a duel seems imminent.

Left alone with Alfredo, Violetta asks him to leave for his safety's sake. Alfredo's fury only rises, reaching a climax when she says (to avoid telling him the truth) that she loves the baron. He calls in the other guests, insults Violetta, and tells them to witness (flinging a purse at Violetta) that he has now paid his debts in full. While the other guests show their indignation at Alfredo's behaviour, Giorgio Germont enters and denounces his son's conduct. In the final ensemble the miserable Violetta is heard affirming that she loves Alfredo still.

Act III

Violetta, separated from Alfredo is living alone with the devoted Annina; she is ill with consumption and they have hardly any money left. She is in bed when, early in the morning, the doctor comes to see her. He reassures her, but tells

Annina that Violetta has really only a few hours to live. Annina leaves and Violetta re-reads a letter she has received from Giorgio Germont, revealing that he has told Alfredo of Violetta's sacrifice and that Alfredo is coming to beg her forgiveness. As she reads she hears (in the orchestra) a strain from the melody Alfredo sang when he first declared himself to her – the strain she had taken up in her song at the end of the first act.

She feels her illness, and laments: 'For ever has faded that dream' (Addio, del passato bei sogni ridenti).*

From outside her window the carnival revellers are heard in the street. Annina returns and admits a visitor: Alfredo. All bitterness is forgotten as the lovers embrace. He speaks of taking her away: 'Come, O my dearest, far from this city' (Parigi, o cara, noi lasceremo). But after the exhilaration Violetta feels weak and has to send Annina for the doctor. She realizes that she is going to die. Giorgio Germont enters. Violetta gives Alfredo a medallion, asking him to give it to the girl he eventually marries. Annina has returned with the doctor and all join in as Violetta utters her plea to Alfredo.

Suddenly her agitation leaves her. Reliving the joyful first moments of their love, Violetta dies.

*   *   *   *   *

All Verdi's dramatic insight and human sympathy are poured into the delineation of Violetta and her relationship with the other characters. The contrast between the 'brilliant' but hard life of Parisian parties and the idyll of the country retreat is paralleled by the contrast within Violetta's music – between her song at the end of Act I (very remarkably, Verdi does not end the act with Violetta as transformed by Alfredo but with Violetta still the courtesan) and the tenderness of her final 'farewell' song. Particularly subtle is the musical expression of her response to Alfredo. As soon as he has struck up the

---

* Literally, 'Farewell, smiling dreams of the past'. The common shortening to 'Addio del passato' as if that could mean 'Farewell to the past' is misleading. It is in this aria that Violetta refers to herself as *traviata*, a woman gone astray.

drinking-song in the first act, Violetta feels drawn to sing the second stanza to the company herself. Then, when he has made his suit to her and left, it is his musical phrase and his very words she takes over in her own aria:

This also recurs twice (as though returning in Violetta's memory) as she lies dying in the final scene. Similarly, in this scene Violetta is drawn to repeat the words and melody used by Alfredo when he spoke of taking her away from Paris.

This particular section of music corresponds in fact to the slow section of the old-fashioned operatic aria divided into a slow, pathetic opening and a more brilliant concluding part. Verdi, like other composers before him, modified the convention for the sake of dramatic realism. After the slow section there is an agitated interruption, when Annina is sent again for the doctor. Only after that is the quick concluding part allowed to follow: 'Oh, God, I am too young to die' (Ah! gran Dio! morir si giovine):

Here, in fact, Verdi unites the psychological strength of slow-followed-by-fast music with the dramatic strength of 'realistic' interruption.

As remarkable as the portrayal of the lovers is that of Giorgio Germont who – unlike almost all such 'baritone father' parts – undergoes a real development of character. Violetta softens even him. His music is noble in the conventional operatic sense, but never heavy or blustering. Even his self-righteousness is transformed into tenderness:

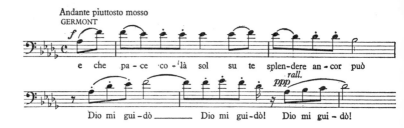

SIMON BOCCANEGRA

Libretto by Francesco Maria Piave, after a play by Antonio García Gutierrez; revised version with alterations by Arrigo Boito

First performed: Venice, 1857

(Revised version: Milan, 1881)

Prologue and Three Acts

Cast in order of singing:

Paolo Albiani, leader of the plebeian party, later a
    favourite associate of Boccanegra as Doge   *baritone*
Pietro, a Genoese goldsmith, later an associate of
    Boccanegra as Doge   *baritone*
Simon Boccanegra, Corsair in the service of the
    Genoese Republic, later the Doge   *baritone*

Jacopo Fiesco, a Genoese nobleman, later going
    under the name of Andrea   *bass*
Amelia, going under the surname Grimaldi, not
    knowing herself to be Boccanegra's daughter   *soprano*
Gabriele Adorno, a Genoese of noble family   *tenor*
Amelia's maid   *soprano*
Captain of the Archers   *tenor*
    Chorus of sailors, people, soldiers, servants to Fiesco,
    the Doge's courtiers, senators, *etc.*

The scene is laid in and near Genoa, in the 14th century

SIMON BOCCANEGRA was a historical Doge (ruler) of Genoa
in the 14th century. He was a plebeian (that is, he was not
of noble birth) and was poisoned – facts which were incorporated into Gutierrez's Spanish drama and into the opera
which Verdi based on it. There is, as often with Verdi, a
strong intermingling of political and personal passions in such
a way as to provide strong emotional situations – a villain
forced to pronounce a curse on himself, a father recognizing
his long-lost daughter, a death-bed forgiveness and so on. It
adds up to a forceful drama: and if the score has not the
memorable melodies of Verdi's earlier operas it has power and
psychological truth.

But the opera was originally (1857) a failure and Verdi not
only got Arrigo Boito to revise the over-complicated libretto
(the great Council Scene is entirely Boito's addition) but himself made many additions and alterations, both small and
great. (Boito as an original librettist we shall consider under
Otello, p. 191 and *Falstaff*, p. 198.) The result is still dramatically rather complex and 'difficult' (especially the twenty-five-
year gap between the Prologue and Act I); but Norman
Tucker in his successful English version (Sadler's Wells, 1948)
simplified the action a little further, and it is his version that
is followed in the ensuing synopsis. We have, however, desig-
nated the final scene Act III (on its own, as in the original) and
not as Act II, Scene 2 as in Tucker's version. Incidentally,
Tucker preferred the more familiar Italian form of 'Simone'

in the title; but 'Simon' is Verdi's original (though in the opera itself 'Simone' is also sung).

* * * * *

PROLOGUE

In Genoa, in a square showing the church of San Lorenzo and the Fiesco Palace, Paolo, leader of the plebeian party, is discussing with Pietro the forthcoming choice of a Doge. It is night. Paolo suggests Simon Boccanegra, who has lately restored Genoa's maritime glory by driving the African pirates from the seas. On promise of a suitable reward, Pietro guarantees popular support.

Pietro leaves and Boccanegra enters. At first he is unwilling to accept nomination; but Paolo tempts him with the observation that as Doge he could no longer be refused the hand of the girl he loves – Maria Fiesco, who has already borne him a child and is now held prisoner by her father (the present Doge) in the Fiesco Palace. He agrees to accept nomination. As Boccanegra leaves, a crowd of workmen and sailors enters, led by Pietro. He and Paolo counsel them to support Boccanegra. Paolo angrily points to the palace where Maria is incarcerated: 'See yonder gloomy dwelling' (L'atra magion vedete).*

As they move off, Fiesco emerges from the palace. His daughter Maria has just died and he expresses his own sorrow: 'Weary and worn with suffering' (Il lacerato spirito). Sounds of mourning for Maria's death are heard from the palace as he sings.

Boccanegra enters, hoping that he may soon be united with Maria. Fiesco angrily reproaches him, refusing to forgive him even when he offers to pay for his seduction with his life. But Fiesco is prepared to forgive Boccanegra if he will yield up the child Maria bore him. Boccanegra explains that this is impossible, as the child has vanished. Coldly, Fiesco turns away, refusing to hear Boccanegra's plea for reconciliation. Boccanegra knocks at the door of the palace, demanding to see

* English version by Norman Tucker (Ricordi).

Maria; he finds within only silence and gloom, and discovers that she is dead. As he comes out, horror-struck, voices in the distance are proclaiming him as the new Doge. Paolo and Pietro come to tell him of his election, the news of which dismays Fiesco. Crowds acclaim Boccanegra and bells ring out in his honour.

ACT I

Twenty-five years have elapsed. Simon Boccanegra is still Doge; Fiesco, now using the name 'Andrea', is conspiring against him.

In the garden of the Grimaldi Palace outside Genoa, by the sea, Amelia is admiring the beautiful scene: 'See how sky and ocean' (Come in quest'ora bruna). (She calls herself by the surname Grimaldi and regards Andrea as her guardian.) Her lover, Gabriele, approaches. She warns him that his and Andrea's political intrigues against the present Doge may lead to trouble. Amelia's maid enters, announcing a messenger from the Doge. It is Pietro, who asks Amelia to receive Boccanegra himself. When Pietro has left, Amelia explains to Gabriele that Boccanegra wishes her to wed Paolo; she, of course, wants to marry Gabriele, and asks him to hurry and find Andrea and obtain his consent to their speedy marriage.

Amelia goes into the palace. As Gabriele is about to depart he meets Fiesco, who tells him that Amelia is not a Grimaldi but of unknown humble stock, having been substituted for a child of Count Grimaldi who had died, in order to save the family fortunes from confiscation by the Doge (Count Grimaldi himself is in political exile). Fiesco blesses Gabriele and consents to their marriage.

The sound of trumpets introduces Boccanegra, and Fiesco and Gabriele (as the Doge's enemies) leave hastily. Paolo and others are with Boccanegra, but he sends them away; then, alone with Amelia, Boccanegra hands her a pardon for her 'father', Count Grimaldi. She tells him that she has a lover and does not wish to marry the rapacious Paolo (who seeks the Grimaldi fortunes), and goes on to explain that she is not a Grimaldi by birth but an orphan. It becomes clear to Boccanegra from what she says that she is in fact his long-lost daughter,* and this is confirmed when they compare pictures of her mother. They rejoice in the discovery: 'Daughter! when I recall this name' (Figlia, a tal nome io palpito).

As Amelia leaves, Paolo enters. Boccanegra, before he goes, tells Paolo to abandon any hopes of marrying her, but Paolo refuses to accept the decision and arranges with Pietro for her abduction.

The scene changes to the council chamber, where Boccanegra, as Doge, presides over an assembly comprising twelve patricians, twelve plebeians (including Paolo) and various officers. He tries unsuccessfully to persuade the council to agree to peace with Venice. In the distance the shouts of an angry mob are heard; Boccanegra sees from a window that Gabriele and another man are being attacked. Paolo is about to flee, but Boccanegra orders the doors to be guarded. The people are calling 'Death to the nobles!' (Morte ai patrizi!), to the alarm of the twelve patrician councillors, and even 'Death to the Doge'. Boccanegra sends out a herald to say that he awaits the people. They are quickly pacified, but they enter the chamber demanding the blood of Gabriele. It emerges that Gabriele has killed Pietro, who abducted Amelia; and now Gabriele, believing that Pietro acted on Boccanegra's instructions, attempts to attack Boccanegra himself.

Suddenly Amelia enters and throws herself between the two men. She tells the true story of her abduction. She thinks she knows the man responsible, staring pointedly at Paolo. A fight nearly breaks out between the two sides of the assembly and Boccanegra steps angrily between them: 'Nobles! Plebeians!' (Plebe! Patrizi!). An elaborate ensemble follows.

Gabriele yields his sword to Boccanegra, who says he must be a prisoner for one night, till the plot is unravelled. Then Boccanegra calls forcefully on Paolo. He demands that he, as

---

* In the original her real name is stated by Boccanegra to be Maria. Tucker's English version omits this rather unnecessary further complication.

an officer of state, should join in cursing the man who perpetrated these evil doings. Paolo forces himself to pronounce the curse ('Sia maledetto') then shrinks in terror ('Orrore, orror!') of what he has done. All assembled join in the curse and Paolo attempts to flee.

ACT II

Paolo is under guard in a room in the Doge's palace. He sends for one of the guards to bring Andrea, who is also there under surveillance. When Andrea comes, Paolo discloses that he knows he is really Fiesco, but says that he (Paolo) will support Fiesco against the Doge if he may himself marry Amelia. Fiesco rejects such dishonourable terms and leaves. Alone, Paolo pours a slow poison into a glass of wine, planning to kill Boccanegra. But first Gabriele enters. Paolo tells him (falsely) that Amelia, whom Gabriele loves, is Boccanegra's mistress.* Paolo leaves and Gabriele expresses his furious jealousy: 'Fiercely within my bosom' (Sento avvampar nell'anima).

Amelia enters. She is now living privately as Boccanegra's daughter – not, of course, as his mistress – but when Gabriele accuses her she can only assure him that she is faithful to him, and says she cannot yet tell him of her relationship with Boccanegra. As Boccanegra approaches, Gabriele, determining to murder him, hides on the balcony. Seeing Amelia weeping, Boccanegra asks what is wrong; she discloses that she loves Gabriele – to Boccanegra's great distress, for Gabriele and his family, the Adornos, have been plotting against him. As she departs he considers whether he can pardon Gabriele. He drinks of the poisoned wine and falls asleep, dreaming of Amelia.

Gabriele enters to find his enemy asleep. He is on the point of stabbing Boccanegra (partly to avenge his own father's death at Boccanegra's hands) when Amelia enters and stops

* This is Tucker's sequence of events. Verdi's own (revised) score has the order: Paolo soliloquizes and prepares the poison – Fiesco and Gabriele are brought in *together* – Paolo tempts Fiesco, who refuses and leaves – Paolo tells Gabriele that Amelia is the Doge's mistress.

him. Boccanegra wakes and bids him strike, and eventually tells him that by robbing him of his daughter Gabriele has more than avenged his father's death. Gabriele, seeing the situation, is full of remorse, begging Amelia for forgiveness ('Perdon, perdon, Amelia'); Boccanegra prays for the city's peace, and Amelia begs that the spirit of her dead mother may soften her father's heart.

From outside a warlike crowd is heard approaching: a patrician revolt has started, aimed at overthrowing Boccanegra. Boccanegra tells Gabriele to go and join his friends, but he now refuses to fight against Boccanegra and agrees to bear a message of peace to the clamouring rebels. In return, Boccanegra awards him Amelia's hand.

ACT III

The scene is a great hall in the palace. The revolt has been quickly put down, and from outside the people's joyous shouts can be heard. The Captain of the Archers returns his sword to Fiesco, who is now freed. On his way out Fiesco meets Paolo, being brought in under guard: he had escaped to join the rebel cause but now, recaptured, is under sentence of death. Paolo tells Fiesco that he has poisoned Boccanegra. Distant voices are heard intoning a wedding-hymn for Gabriele and Amelia – whom Paolo once again, to Fiesco's fury, calls 'Boccanegra's mistress'.

Paolo is led off to execution and Fiesco conceals himself. From a balcony, a trumpeter calls the people to silence and the Captain announces that the Doge wishes the jubilation to cease as it is offensive to the dead. Alone, Boccanegra enters, unsteadily, feeling ill as the poison begins to take effect. He looks seaward, apostrophizing the element that brought him his glory. Fiesco steps forward and foretells Boccanegra's doom. Boccanegra recognizes the voice as that of Fiesco, long since assumed dead: he tells his old enemy who Amelia is, and the two men are at last reconciled. Sadly Fiesco tells Boccanegra that he has been poisoned.

Amelia and Gabriele enter, with their wedding procession. Boccanegra tells them who 'Andrea' is – Fiesco, father of

Maria (who died before Boccanegra could marry her), and
thus Amelia's grandfather. Their joy at the marriage and reunion is tempered by the realization that Boccanegra is approaching death. Boccanegra blesses them. In an ensemble
he begs her to come close to him and she prays that he may
be spared, while Gabriele and Fiesco, in different ways, be-
wail the ephemeral nature of human happiness and the courtiers express their grief.

As he dies, Boccanegra gathers the senators around him and
in a failing voice decrees that Gabriele shall be his successor.
Fiesco, from the balcony, tells the people that Gabriele Adorno
is their Doge. They call for Boccanegra: he is dead, Fiesco
tells them. They pray for him as the curtain falls.

*   *   *   *   *

The father-daughter relationship dominates *Simon Bocca-*
negra. In the prologue Fiesco laments for his daughter Maria
who has been seduced by Boccanegra and has died: 'Weary
and worn with suffering'. He begins in the minor key; when
he changes to the major (with more consoling thoughts of
God's pardon) the off-stage chorus of mourners insists on the
minor-key sadness (see top of p. 160).

In Act I there is the dramatic scene of recognition between
Boccanegra and Amelia, when the words 'padre' and 'figlia'
('father' and 'daughter') are many times repeated. Finally,
after Amelia has gone off-stage and her father's gaze is lovingly following her, the orchestra plays the tune they have
just been singing, and we hear the tender words once again
(see pp. 160–61).

In contrast with these two 'private' scenes is the great 'public'
drama of the council chamber in which Boccanegra forces
Paolo to pronounce a curse on an unnamed traitor (in reality,
Paolo himself). Preceding it is a long utterance by Boccanegra showing his suspicion of Paolo: musically the expression is shared by the orchestra, with explosive figures displaying the force behind the singer's monotone. His words mean:
'You have authority in all that touches the people: on your

good faith rests the honour of this city; today I need your help':

bra - mo l'au-si - lio tuo

UN BALLO IN MASCHERA

(A Masked Ball)

Libretto by Antonio Somma, after Eugène Scribe
First performed: Rome, 1859

Three Acts

Cast in order of singing:

Oscar, a page   *soprano*
Gustavus III, King of Sweden
  [Riccardo, Governor of Boston] *   *tenor*
Captain Anckarstroem, Gustavus' secretary
  [Renato]   *baritone*
Armfelt, Minister of Justice [A Judge]   *tenor*
Mam'zelle Arvidson, a fortune-teller
  [Ulrica, a negro fortune-teller]   *contralto*
Cristian, a sailor [Silvano]   *bass*
A servant   *tenor*
Amelia, wife of Anckarstroem   *soprano*
Count Ribbing and Count Horn [Samuele, Tomaso],
  enemies of Gustavus   *basses*

  Chorus of deputies, officials, sailors, guards, people,
      conspirators, servants, masked dancers

  *The scene is laid in and near Stockholm at the end of
              the 18th century*

          * For an explanation, see below.

HERE are *two* famous soprano roles (tragic heroine and skittish
page-boy); strong male solo roles; fine choruses; and sharp
dramatic situations. And yet *A Masked Ball* is not quite as
popular as some other Verdi operas preceding and following
it. Part, at least, of the trouble arises from non-musical circumstances surrounding its creation. We must start with an
event 21 years before the composer's birth, when on 16 March
1792 King Gustavus III of Sweden was killed by a shot during a masked ball in the court opera house at Stockholm. The
French dramatist Scribe wrote a libretto on this subject for
an opera by Auber (1782–1871), which was produced in 1833.
On this libretto, Somma's libretto for Verdi – originally to
have been entitled simply *Gustavo III* – was based. But in an
Italy where revolutionary movements were being repressed
with difficulty, an opera depicting the assassination of a king
was frowned on by censorship; and the first performance, in
Rome, was permitted only on condition of transferring the
action to Boston, Mass., in 17th-century America under British rule. Only an English governor, not a king, would then
have to be shown as the assassin's victim!

The ridiculousness of the action in its American setting has
long been felt and, especially in the last few years, the action
has been restored in many opera-houses to Sweden. The names
of the characters are therefore given here in their authentic
Swedish forms, but with Verdi's 'American' (Italianized)
names shown in the cast-list in square brackets, since performances on gramophone records still trundle along in the
old groove.

*   *   *   *   *

ACT I

In the hall of his palace, King Gustavus is about to give an
audience: courtiers are singing his praises, and the mutterings of conspirators (among them Count Ribbing and Count
Horn) can also be heard. Oscar, the page-boy, announces the
approach of the king, who receives various petitions. He
glances over a list of visitors invited to a masked ball, and
sees with delight that Amelia (the wife of his secretary,

Anckarstroem) will be there: secretly, Gustavus loves her. Aside, he shows his feelings: 'I shall behold in ecstasy' (La rivedrò in estasi).* The courtiers depart and Oscar brings in Anckarstroem.

Anckarstroem tells the king of a plot against him. Gustavus does not take it seriously, but in his song 'Life to you looks ever smiling' (Alla vita che t'arride) Anckarstroem bids him do so. Oscar announces the Minister of Justice, who brings for his signature an order to banish Mlle. Arvidson, a fortune-teller. Gustavus asks the opinion of Oscar, whose plea on the fortune-teller's behalf – 'She of the stars above' (Volta la terrea fronte) – arouses Gustavus' interest. When the courtiers (and conspirators) return, the king tells them that he will go in disguise to test the woman's powers: all sing with pleasure of the prospect.

The scene changes to Mlle. Arvidson's hut, where a few women and boys listen to her solemn invocation of the powers of darkness, during which Gustavus enters, dressed as a fisherman. A sailor, Cristian, comes to have his fortune told: Mlle. Arvidson predicts promotion, and Gustavus ensures the truth of her prediction by writing out a commission and slipping it unseen into Cristian's pocket, which the sailor soon discovers, to his pleasure. A servant of Amelia's comes, asking for a private audience for his mistress. Mlle. Arvidson dismisses the crowd but Gustavus manages to hide.

Amelia comes in and tells Mlle. Arvidson that she loves Gustavus (he overhears this with delight) but wishes to exorcise this guilty love. The fortune-teller informs her of a special herb, which will serve the purpose if gathered at the gallows-foot by night. In a trio, Amelia prays for strength, Mlle. Arvidson tells her not to fear, and the concealed Gustavus sings of his love.

As Amelia departs, the courtiers and Oscar arrive. The king steps forward and, pretending to be a gay, devil-may-care fisherman, asks Mlle. Arvidson to tell his fortune: 'To fight for my country' (Di' tu se fedele). His hand is that of a nobleman, she says; she asks him not to press her to tell his fate.

* English version by Edward J. Dent (O.U.P.).

He and the assembled courtiers insist that she should complete the prophecy. She does: he will soon die, and by a friend's hand. All are horrified except Gustavus himself, who does not take it seriously. His murderer, she goes on to predict, will be the next man to shake his hand. The courtiers all decline to do so. Then Anckarstroem enters; the king immediately grasps him by the hand. Gustavus then tells Mlle. Arvidson who he is, and Cristian summons the people to join with the courtiers in singing to him, with only the voices of the conspirators dissenting, and those of Mlle. Arvidson and Anckarstroem singing with foreboding of the future.

ACT II

At midnight, near the gallows outside the city, Amelia is seeking the magic herb: 'When the leaf from the stem' (Ma dall'arido stelo divulsa). Suddenly Gustavus enters. She tries to send him away, but their love proves too strong. They are interrupted by Anckarstroem, who comes to warn the king that the conspirators are around, intending to kill him. The men exchange cloaks, and Gustavus makes Anckarstroem swear to escort Amelia (heavily veiled and unrecognized by her husband) back to the city without inquiring who she is.

Gustavus goes off and the conspirators, led by Ribbing and Horn approach. They are frustrated to discover that it is Anckarstroem, not the king, whom they had seen with the lady. Despite Anckarstroem's protests, they strip off her veil –and he is horrified to find that it is his own wife; Ribbing and the conspirators, however, are amused. To take revenge on the king, Anckarstroem resolves to join the conspiracy, and summons Ribbing and Horn to visit him next day.

ACT III

The next day, Anckarstroem and his wife are at home. He is determined to kill her for her faithlessness. She pleads her innocence and begs for a final favour – 'I die, but ere my hour be come' (Morrò, ma prima in grazia) – to be allowed to see their small son. He agrees, and she goes out. He addresses an accusation to the portrait of Gustavus that hangs on the wall: 'Yes, 'twas you' (Eri, tu), and decides to spare her.

Ribbing and Horn arrive. Anckarstroem says he will join their plot and the three swear to avenge themselves on Gustavus. They draw lots to decide who shall strike the fatal blow. The names are placed in an urn and just as one is to be picked Amelia enters to say that Oscar has come. Before they admit him, Anckarstroem compels his uncomprehending wife to pick a piece of paper from the urn. The one she selects bears her husband's name, to his great satisfaction. Again the three men swear vengeance and Amelia begins to understand that they plan to murder Gustavus.

Oscar enters with the invitations to Gustavus' masked ball. Anckarstroem accepts, realizing that this will provide his ideal opportunity. All join in a quintet, Oscar anticipating the evening's delights – 'The court will all be there' (Di che fulgor) – while Amelia expresses her fears and the others their intention of taking advantage of the chance to kill Gustavus.

The scene changes to Gustavus' palace. The king is alone, writing out an order appointing Anckarstroem Governor of Finland, where he will take Amelia. (The king has thus honourably decided to renounce his illicit love.) Dance music is heard in the distance. Oscar brings in a letter: it is a warning that an attempt will be made on Gustavus' life. But he will not be so cowardly as to stay away, and proceeds with preparations.

The court opera house has been turned into a ballroom, and the masked ball is now in progress. The three conspirators confer, wondering whether the king has arrived. Anckarstroem meets Oscar and tries to find out Gustavus' disguise for the ball, but Oscar declines to say: 'If you'd be asking' (Saper vorreste). Again Anckarstroem presses Oscar, saying that he has imporant matters to discuss with the king; this time the page gives way.

As a waltz strikes up, Gustavus and Amelia meet, and she tells him to fly from the murderers. He fails at first to recognize her in her disguise: when he does, they sing together as the dance proceeds. She again begs him to go. He tells her

hat she will be leaving for Finland with her husband. As they
oid one another farewell, Anckarstroem comes and stabs the
king.

Amelia and Oscar call for help; Anckarstroem is seized and
the crowd call for vengeance. Before he dies, Gustavus assures
Anckarstroem of his wife's purity, and orders that he should
be spared. Anckarstroem repents his action and, mourned by
all, Gustavus dies.

*   *   *   *   *

This is a powerful opera into which – especially when the work
is given in its historically correct setting – the chorus enters
with considerable dramatic point, both as the common people
who support the king and (men only) as the conspirators
who (in Act II) come to assassinate the king and are amused
to have surprised their 'enemy' Anckarstroem taking his own
wife, veiled, for a midnight walk. The private confrontation
of husband and wife next day produces two of the opera's outstanding arias: first for Amelia (when she believes her husband will kill her, but prays to see her young son first):

and then for Anckarstroem who addresses the king's portrait
and delivers an accusation of the king himself: 'Yes, 'twas you
laid the stain of dishonour and shame'. Note the characteristic
'hammering' accompaniment:

Later Anckarstroem's utterance softens as he laments his lost days of love.

The opera also has Verdi's most celebrated page-boy part, that of Oscar, with two arias for a brilliant light soprano voice – in Act I, describing the fascination of the fortune-teller, and in the final scene, when the page's skittish refusal to divulge the king's disguise is dramatically ironic because we know (as the page does not) of the deadly reason why the conspirators are so anxious for him to divulge it. The page replies, 'Oscar knows well, but will not tell!':

LA FORZA DEL DESTINO

(The Force of Destiny)

*Libretto by Francesco Maria Piave, after a Spanish play by
the Duke of Rivas*

First performed: St. Petersburg, 1862

Four Acts

Cast in order of singing:

The Marquis of Calatrava	*bass*
Leonora, his daughter	*soprano*
Curra, her maid	*mezzo-soprano*
Don Alvaro, Leonora's suitor	*tenor*
An official	*bass*
Don Carlo de Vargas, Leonora's brother	*baritone*
Trabuco, a muleteer and pedlar	*tenor*
Preziosilla, a gipsy girl	*mezzo-soprano*
Brother Melitone, a Franciscan monk	*baritone*
The Father Guardian of a Franciscan monastery	*bass*
Two sentries	*tenor, baritone*
A military surgeon	*baritone*

Chorus of muleteers, Spanish and Italian peasants, Spanish
and Italian soldiers, camp-followers, beggars

*The scene is laid in Spain and Italy about the
mid-18th century*

ELOPEMENT, duels, a woman dressed as a man, gay military
music, the chanting of monks ... Such a list of trusted operatic
ingredients made a rich store for Verdi, but (in the event) a
rather confused one. Indeed, the title *The Force of Destiny*
could be more aptly replaced by *The Force of Coincidence*,
for a series of mere chances runs through this opera and
diminishes its dramatic credibility, making it little more than
a chain of unprompted tableaux. Moreover, *The Force of*

Destiny rests on a series of social conventions a good deal more remote from us even than those underlying *La Traviata*. Carlo (Verdi Italianized the Spanish 'Carlos') is justified in killing his sister because she dishonoured the family name in eloping with a lover who killed their father (although accidentally); and Carlo is not, operatically, a 'bad' character.

But the character of Leonora, at least, comes over as a fully sympathetic one; and as an equally sympathetic background we have the consoling figures of the Father Guardian and the serenely chanting Franciscan friars. Among these friars is the heavily humorous Brother Melitone: in his music he is often held to anticipate Falstaff, but because his big scene (the mock-sermon) is based on purposefully bad Italian puns and the crowd's reaction to him, he can hardly make quite the effect that Verdi intended unless the audience follows his every word.

*   *   *   *   *

ACT I

The marquis is bidding goodnight to his daughter in her room at his castle in Seville. He notices her troubled mood, which he attributes to the fact that he has separated her from her suitor (Don Alvaro, whom he regards as unworthy). When he goes she and her maid, Curra, talk of the plans for her elopement, that very night, with Alvaro; she is sorrowful at deceiving her father and leaving her home, singing sadly at the prospect: 'As wanderer and orphan' (Me pellegrina ed orfana).

Alvaro arrives. Overcoming her hesitation, Leonora is on the point of leaving with him when footsteps are heard and her father appears with servants. He angrily orders Alvaro's arrest. Yielding himself, Alvaro throws his pistol at the marquis's feet, but it explodes and the marquis is mortally wounded. As he dies he curses his daughter, who leaves with Alvaro.

ACT II

In an inn at the Spanish mountain village of Hornachuelos, the people are singing and dancing. The clients led by an official sit down to the meal ('A cena!') and a 'student' (in reality the marquis's son Don Carlo, disguised and seeking his sister and her lover) says grace. Leonora arrives – alone, disguised and in male clothes – and realizes who the student is. The student starts to question a muleteer, Trabuco, about his travelling companion (he arrived with Leonora), but before he replies the gipsy Preziosilla enters. She sings a gay patriotic song, echoed by the whole company: 'At the sound of the drum' (Al son del tamburo). It is momentarily interrupted by Carlo, who asks her to tell his fortune: she predicts tragedy, and adds that she can see he is not really a student.

A group of pilgrims is heard approaching: the assembled company joins them in prayer, Leonora praying that she may escape from her vengeful brother. She goes into an inner room. The student then starts questioning Trabuco and the official about the young stranger; Trabuco evades the questions and retires to bed. Next Carlo tries to go upstairs to find the stranger, but the official refuses to let him and asks him who he is himself. Carlo answers: 'I am Pereda, a student' (Son Pereda), saying that he is on the trail of a friend called Vargas. The singing and dancing are resumed until all go to bed. Leonora has evidently escaped safely .

The scene changes to the gateway of Hornachuelos monastery. It is bright moonlight and will soon be dawn. Here we rediscover Leonora, still dressed as a man, still a fugitive, and now exhausted. She prays for forgiveness: 'Help me, O Mother of God' (Madre, Madre, pietosa Vergine). From within she hears the friars chanting. The doorkeeper, Brother Melitone, at first hesitates to call the Father Guardian, but eventually does so. The Father Guardian sends Melitone away and hears her story. During their long scene together, she tells him who she is (he had heard about her from another priest) and he exhorts her to prayer and repentance; he suggests that she should enter a convent, but she protests imploringly ('Un chiostro? un chiostro? no') and asks to be allowed the use of a hermit's cave near the monastery. He agrees, then calls Melitone and tells him to gather the friars together, and she thanks God for his mercy.

In the monastery chapel, the Father Guardian tells the friars that the cave is to be occupied. Anyone disturbing the hermit (whose sex, of course, is undisclosed), or trying to find who it is, is accursed ('Maledizion!'). All pray to 'the Virgin of the angels' (la Vergine degli angeli) to extend her protection to the hermit.

ACT III

At night, in a wood near Velletri in Italy, some soldiers are playing cards. Their officer is Alvaro (under a false name), who has joined the Spanish Army in Italy fighting against the Austrians. He ruminates on his unhappiness and on Leonora, whom he believes dead: 'O sainted soul' (O, tu che in seno). A cry for help is heard; Alvaro rushes off and comes back with Carlo (also now an officer in the Spanish army) whom he has saved from attempted assassination. The two men, who have not met before, exchange names (both false) and swear eternal friendship.

An alarm is sounded and they go off to fight. There is a rapid change of scene. A surgeon and some orderlies watch the battle, in which Alvaro leads his men to victory but is wounded. He is carried in: Carlo, complimenting Alvaro on his bravery, says he will be given the Order of Calatrava (that name, his family name, makes Alvaro tremble). Then Alvaro asks Carlo to carry out his last wish, to destroy unopened a packet of papers: 'In this solemn hour' (Solenne in quest'ora).

Left alone, Carlo wonders whether his new friend, who was disturbed when the name Calatrava was mentioned, is his father's murderer. He struggles with his conscience as to whether he should open the papers: 'Fateful urn of my destiny' (Urna fatale del mio destino). In Carlo's valise he finds a small box without a seal—and in it is a portrait of Leonora, confirming his suspicions. He is glad to learn from the surgeon that Alvaro will recover ('Ah! egli è salvo!'), so that he himself can kill his enemy.

The scene changes to an encampment. A patrol passes. Alvaro is alone, in pensive mood, when Carlo enters. He tells Alvaro who he is and demands a duel. Alvaro is unwilling, pleading that it was fate, not he, that killed the marquis, and he affirms real friendship for Carlo. But Carlo (incidentally revealing that Leonora is not dead, as Alvaro thought) deliberately provokes Alvaro and the two men fight. The patrol, re-entering, separates them. Alvaro, saddened, resolves to retire to a monastery.

The scene changes to the main army camp. First, soldiers and female camp-followers (*vivandières*) sing gaily, with Preziosilla offering to tell fortunes; then, after various toasts, the pedlar Trabuco enters, buying booty and selling trinkets; next, a few poor peasants enter, with children, begging for bread ('Pan, pan per carità'); then a group of homesick boy-recruits arrives, soon to be cheered by the camp-followers and Preziosilla. She leads the company in singing and dancing a tarantella. They are interrupted by Melitone, who delivers a mock-solemn sermon, full of puns ('You prefer bottles to battles!'): eventually he is hustled off by the two groups of soldiers, Italian and Spanish. Another song from Preziosilla ('Rataplan', imitating drums), with chorus, cheers the company.

ACT IV

The scene moves back to Spain, some time later. Outside the monastery at Hornachuelos, beggars are demanding charity and Melitone is distributing food to them. The Father Guardian is also present. It becomes clear that they much prefer a certain Father Raffaello to Melitone, to his irritation. The Father Guardian reproaches Melitone for his impatience and mentions the virtue and self-denial of Father Raffaello – who is in fact Alvaro.

The bell at the gate rings and the Father Guardian sends Melitone to open it. Don Carlo is there: he has at last traced Alvaro, and he asks Melitone to call him. While he waits he reaffirms his resolve to kill Alvaro, and he challenges him when he comes. Feeling no animosity and wanting only to be left in peace as a monk, Alvaro is unwilling to fight: 'Let your threats fly away' (Le minaccie, i fieri accenti). Carlo, however, repeatedly taunts him – finally striking his face. Alvaro, who so far has restrained himself, can do so no longer: they run off to fight.

The scene changes to Leonora's lonely hermitage. She is praying – 'Peace, grant me peace, O Lord' (Pace, pace, mio Dio) – that God may send a speedy end to her suffering. Sounds are heard nearby and she retires into her cavern: then Carlo and Alvaro approach, fighting. Carlo, mortally wounded, calls for a priest, and Alvaro, approaching the cell, calls on the 'hermit' to come. Leonora rings her bell to summon aid and then, coming out, recognizes Alvaro as her lover. In despair, he tells her what has happened, and that her brother lies dying. She rushes off to Carlo. A scream is heard: Carlo has summoned up sufficient strength to strike his 'guilty' sister a mortal blow. Supported by the Father Guardian, she returns to Alvaro, who furiously curses the forces that govern their destiny. In a trio, Leonora and the Father Guardian admonish him. As she dies, Leonora looks forward to a heavenly reunion with Alvaro.

*   *   *   *   *

The Force of Destiny starts with a full-scale overture, more often heard at concerts than any others of Verdi's. The opening three hammer-like blows, repeated, constitute a 'fate' motive, which is followed by an agitated theme (in a minor key) from Leonora's scene in Act II outside the monastery gate; later comes Leonora's great major-key prayer from the scene in Act II in which the heroine has arrived at the monastery gate. But the three-note 'destiny' theme, though it recurs in the course of the overture, does not do so in the actual opera: it is not, therefore, a leading-motive in Wagner's sense.

We may quote from the 'prayer' theme as it occurs in the scene itself, to the words 'Do not abandon me, O God!': it is one of Verdi's most memorable (and most characteristic) tunes, with a vocal line whose rise and fall seem to portray in turn the strength and weakness of the human spirit:

Allegro assai moderato
LEONORA

[f] Deh! non m'ab-ban - do - nar, _____ pie-tà di me, pie-tà Si - gnor.

Equally famous is the duet ('Solenne in quest'ora') in which Alvaro, who thinks he is dying, asks Carlo to do him a service. Carlo consents: 'I swear it, I swear it'.

The part of Preziosilla, a gipsy camp-follower, calls for a brilliant mezzo-soprano. She has nothing to do with the basic plot; her music is very effectively designed to throw a lively element into the sombre story. Her 'Rataplan' with chorus is accompanied only by two side-drums on the stage:

The use of the word 'Rataplan' for this purpose was no new; it became popular in Donizetti's *The Daughter of th Regiment*. The operetta *Cox and Box* (music by Sullivan words by F. C. Burnand) made fun of this usage in 1867, few months before *The Force of Destiny* was first staged i London.

DON CARLOS

Libretto by François-Joseph Méry and Camille du Locle, after Schiller's play

First performed: Paris, 1867

Five Acts

Cast in order of singing:

Don Carlos, Infanta of Spain	*tenor*
Thibaut, page to Elisabeth	*soprano*
Elisabeth de Valois, daughter of the King of France	*soprano*
A monk	*bass*
Rodrigo, Marquis of Posa	*baritone*
Princess Eboli	*mezzo-soprano*
Philip II, King of Spain	*bass*
A herald	*tenor*
A voice from heaven	*soprano*
The Count of Lerma	*tenor*
The Grand Inquisitor, a blind nonagenarian	*bass*

Chorus of huntsmen, courtiers, monks, soldiers, deputies, people, etc.

The scene is laid in France and Spain, about 1560

Two famous soliloquies – of a king recognizing that his young wife does not love him, and of a woman cursing her own beauty – are among the features of *Don Carlos* which show Verdi's dramatic power at its height. Public and private passions run strong in this opera, which requires bold spectacle as well as highly individual characterization.

Don Carlos is a political drama on the familiar theme of

iberty versus tyranny'. Schiller's play presented Don Carlos, on of Philip II of Spain, as a heroic and virtuous young beral (apparently without historical justification); and his ivalry with his father, both in politics and in love, forms the ubject of the play and of Verdi's opera. In Schiller's play the nquisitor's power compels the king, at the very end, to hand iis son over to him; in the opera as written, Carlos is saved rom this fate by being spirited away in the nick of time by he ghost of his royal grandfather. At Sadler's Wells (1951) ichiller's more strongly dramatic, non-supernatural ending vas used for the opera.

Don Carlos was written in French for the Paris Opéra: t was in the long, five-act form, with ballet, which had be-:ome established at that house. In 1884 it was given in Milan is *Don Carlo*, with Italian words by Antonio Ghislanzoni, in i version which jettisoned not only the ballet but the whole irst act. This means the loss of a love-duet not only fine in tself but providing a musical phrase purposefully used in ater scenes. Modern practice is to restore the first act what-:ver other incidental cuts may be made. The synopsis below ollows this scheme whilst omitting the ballet-episode and >ne or two other minor episodes in the drama; but it does in-:lude the final scene of Act IV, which is sometimes omitted. Since performances not in English will generally be encoun-tered in Italian rather than in French, lines quoted are given in their Italian form. In the four-act version Carlos's aria from the first act is inserted – with different words, 'Ah, I have lost her!' (Io l'ho perduto) – in Act II at a point which is indi-cated in the synopsis.

Verdi's original French or Spanish names are kept for the personages mentioned, except for Philip II and Charles V, Spanish emperors always so referred to in English history-books.

*　　*　　*　　*　　*

ACT I

In France, in the forest of Fontainebleau, a hunt is in progress. Princess Elisabeth and her page Thibaut, separated from the

other riders, disappear to look for them. Don Carlos, son of
King Philip of Spain, is to marry Elisabeth and, alone, sings
of his joy. She, however, has never met him; and now, when
she reappears, he introduces himself merely as one of the
Spanish envoy's staff. But he shows her what he declares to
be a portrait of Don Carlos, which she recognizes as himself.
They confess their mutual love.

But then Thibaut, who has left them alone, returns with
the message that the king, Carlos's father, intends to marry
her himself. Her grief contrasts with the jubilant chorus of
courtiers who are heard approaching to greet her on the prospect of becoming a queen.

[By the point of time at which the next act begins – or at
which the four-act version of the opera begins – this has taken
place: Elisabeth is married to King Philip.]

Act II

In the cloister of the Yuste monastery in Madrid, near the
tomb of Charles V, the chanting of monks, led by one of their
number, is heard; they are mourning their late monarch. As
the sun rises, the monks depart and Don Carlos enters. (In
the four-act version of the opera he sings here of his loss of
Elisabeth.) His conversation with a monk discloses that the
ghost of Carlos's grandfather, the Emperor Charles V – or
perhaps the Emperor himself, not in fact dead – is sometimes
seen in the monastery.

Rodrigo, Don Carlos's life-long friend, enters, newly
arrived from the Spanish province of Flanders. He is troubled
by Carlos's anguish and asks what is its cause, Carlos explains that he loves his father's wife; Rodrigo advises him to
leave Madrid, to obtain his father's permission to go to
Flanders and show his worth by helping the oppressed popu-
lace there. They swear eternal friendship and ask God for
strength to fight for freedom: 'Thou who in every man' (Dio,
che nell'alma infondere).* Philip and his wife enter; he kneels
for a moment at the tomb, and they pass on without speaking.
The monks resume their chanting, and Don Carlos, though

* English version by Arthur Jacobs (E.M.I. Records).

momentarily disturbed on seeing Elisabeth, resumes singing with Rodrigo of their friendship.

The scene changes to a garden, where ladies of the court are passing the time. First the page-boy Thibaut joins them, then Princess Eboli, who sings a Moorish song – the Song of the Veil (Canzone del velo) – assisted by Thibaut and the assembled ladies. The queen enters and a moment later Thibaut announces Rodrigo, newly returned from Paris. He presents to the queen a letter from her mother, and also slips another note into her hand.

While Rodrigo and Eboli talk of the news from fashionable Paris, she reads the note: it is from Carlos, asking if he may see her, and Rodrigo adds his own voice to the request. She consents. When Carlos enters the others all withdraw. At first he asks her to persuade the king to make him Governor of Flanders, but when she admits that her love for him is still strong he loses his self-control and addresses her passionately. She draws away, asking if he means to kill his father and marry her, and he rushes off distracted.

Thibaut announces the king, who, angry at finding his wife alone, peremptorily dismisses the lady who should have been waiting on her. She bursts into tears and Elisabeth consoles her: 'Do not weep, my sweet companion' (Non pianger, mia compagna). Rodrigo and the attendant ladies and gentlemen commiserate, and even Philip, who suspects his wife's fidelity, is almost moved into believing in her sincerity.

Rodrigo is left alone with Philip, who asks if he has any favour to request. He asks his harsh king to alleviate the wretched state of affairs in Flanders, but Philip is unmoved, and only warns Rodrigo to beware of the Grand Inquisitor. In a flood of confidence, he tells Rodrigo of his suspicions of the queen and his son, asking him to watch her carefully. But it is with a final warning of the Inquisition that Philip at last dismisses Rodrigo.

ACT III

Don Carlos has received an anonymous note (which he presumes is from the queen) making an assignation. To fulfil it, he now waits in the queen's garden at midnight. A veiled woman enters and Carlos sings of his love. Suddenly he realizes that it is not Elisabeth, but Princess Eboli, to whom he has poured out his heart. She in fact loves him, and quickly guesses that his words were intended for another – the queen. Rodrigo arrives and tries to smooth over the situation, but Eboli is furiously jealous and warns them that she is determined to exact revenge. As she goes, Carlos and Rodrigo pledge their mutual faith, and Carlos entrusts to Rodrigo some vital secret papers – correspondence with the revolutionary leaders in Flanders.

The next scene takes place in a square in front of a cathedral, a funeral pyre prepared for an auto-da-fé is visible. Crowds sing in honour of the king. Monks singing a funeral chant bring forward the prisoners condemned by the Inquisition; then the crowds resume jubilantly as a procession of courtiers, deputies and pages, and including Elisabeth and Rodrigo, draws up before the cathedral. A herald announces the opening of the cathedral doors, disclosing the king; the people prostrate themselves.

Don Carlos leads in six Flemish deputies, who fall in supplication before the king. They make a moving plea for mercy for their people, but it is rejected out of hand by Philip and the monks, although the crowd are sympathetic. Eventually, Carlos steps forward and asks to be appointed ruler of Flanders, so that he may prove his worthiness to become king. Philip rejects his request: he will not give his son power which may be used against himself. Swearing to help the suffering people of Flanders, Carlos draws his sword – an outrage before the king. Despite Philip's call to disarm Carlos, no one steps forward to do it. Then Rodrigo does so; Carlos, astonished, yields his weapon to him, and the king creates Rodrigo a duke in recognition of his service.

The people resume their praises of the king and the monks resume their chant of death. A voice from heaven proclaims future joy for those so cruelly dealt with on earth. The funeral pyre is lit, and all but the condemned deputies sing to the glory of God.

ACT IV

Philip, alone in his apartments, meditates sadly: 'I never had her love' (Ella giammai m'amò). The Count of Lerma brings in the aged Grand Inquisitor. Philip asks what punishment should be administered to Carlos, and the Grand Inquisitor advises death, countering Philip's scruples by pointing out that God sacrificed *his* own son. Then the Inquisitor demands that Philip turn Rodrigo over to the Inquisition on the grounds that he is plotting against king and Church. Philip resists, but, before he departs, the Inquisitor warns that the king himself is not above the Inquisition.

Elisabeth enters. Her casket of jewels has been stolen, and she demands justice. Philip produces the casket, ordering her to open it. She refuses: he opens it himself and confronts her with Carlos's portrait which is inside. She faints when he angrily rejects her explanation that she had been betrothed to Carlos. Rodrigo and Princess Eboli come when he calls for help. Now he regrets his hasty conduct, and Eboli, who had given him the casket, regrets her betrayal of the Queen. In a quartet, each expresses his reaction to the situation; then, after the men have departed, Eboli begs Elisabeth's forgiveness for her betrayal. She discloses that she herself loves Carlos and has been seduced by the king. Elisabeth orders her to leave the court, either in exile or to enter a convent; left alone, Eboli curses her 'fatal gift' of beauty ('O don fatale'), but vows to help rescue Carlos from his threatened punishment.

In Carlos's underground prison, Rodrigo comes to visit him. Rodrigo explains that Carlos's papers have been found in his possession and that he is being hunted by the Inquisition. At that very moment an assassin, under the orders of the Inquisition, enters and shoots him. As he dies he tells Carlos that the queen will meet him the next day, and he charges him to bring freedom to Spain and Flanders: 'O Carlos, now listen' (O Carlo, ascolta).

The king, with grandees in attendance, comes to restore his sword to Carlos, but the son denounces his father for com-

plicity in Rodrigo's murder. Outside, an angry crowd is
clamouring in support of Carlos. The Count of Lerma and
the grandees are afraid, but Philip demands that the doors be
opened. Eboli, in disguise, bids Carlos escape. The Inquisitor
appears and orders the tumultuous crowd to kneel in homage
before God's chosen king. Overawed, they do so, and beg
Philip for mercy.

ACT V

Elisabeth, in profoundly sorrowful mood, is alone in the
cloisters of Yuste, kneeling before the tomb of the Emperor
Charles V, whom she invokes: 'You who know that in vain'
(Tu che le vanità). She bids her joys a sad farewell, and recalls
the happy days of her youth in France. Carlos arrives and
they sing a duet, in which they acknowledge that their love
can be fulfilled only in heaven.

King Philip enters with the Grand Inquisitor and guards.
As the guards move to seize the lovers, the tomb of Charles
V opens and a figure in a monk's robes emerges and, to the
terrified astonishment of all, takes Carlos away.

*   *   *   *   *

Musically the opera is remarkable for its mezzo-soprano and
bass solo parts, rather than the (usually more prominent)
tenor and soprano. Princess Eboli – sharing with Amneris in
Aida the claim to be considered the most compelling of
Verdi's mezzo-soprano roles – has the famous aria in which,
remorseful, she curses her 'fatal gift' of beauty ('O don fatale').
Here Verdi starts in 4/4 time with a rhythm of ordinary
quavers and semi-quavers:

which later gives way to the urgency of triplets and, at the end, after climbing to a testing high note, hammers out strict quavers again:

King Philip may be accounted Verdi's greatest bass part, and his duologue with the blind Grand Inquisitor (two basses, but the king weak in character and the Inquisitor strong) is unique. The measured, pacing orchestral accompaniment is that which served to introduce the Inquisitor just previously. Philip asks whether he should condemn his son to exile or death – and would the Church absolve him if he did? The Inquisitor's firm reply is: 'The peace of your dominions is worth a rebel's dying':

[*mf*] La pa — ce dell' im — pe — ro   i dì val d'un ri — bel — le

This is the 'conversational' musical style of the mature Verdi, dramatically fulfilling the purpose of recitative in older opera.

AIDA

Libretto by Antonio Ghislanzoni, from a French prose text by Camille du Locle and A. E. Mariette

First performed: Cairo, 1871

Four Acts

Cast in order of singing:

Ramfis, high priest of Egypt	*bass*
Radames, captain of the Egyptian guard	*tenor*
Amneris, daughter of the King of Egypt	*mezzo-soprano*
Aida, slave of Amneris and daughter of Amonasro	*soprano*
The King of Egypt	*bass*
A messenger	*tenor*
High priestess	*soprano*
Amonasro, King of Ethiopia	*baritone*

Chorus of priests and priestesses, soldiers, Ethiopian prisoners and slaves, Egyptians

The action is laid in Memphis and Thebes at the time of the Pharaohs

ITALIAN opera began its conquest of the whole world of music in the 18th century and consolidated it in the 19th. In November 1869 an Italian theatre was opened in Cairo, and *Aida* was commissioned for it by the Khedive (ruler) of Egypt and produced there two years later. (The original plan had been for an opera to celebrate the opening of the Suez Canal in 1869.) The plot had been provided by the French Egyptologist Mariette (known as Mariette Bey, for he had received that title from the Egyptian government); the libretto was written in French prose by Camille du Locle and put into Italian verse by Ghislanzoni, with a good deal of direct intervention by the composer himself.

Verdi's *Aida* turned out to be one of the most universally popular of all operas. It has tremendous spectacle, intermingles personal and political plots, and has its major conflict between soprano and mezzo-soprano – features which relate it to *Don Carlos*. In both works, too, the priests are the villains. But musically and dramatically *Aida* is the more compelling, and only in the dances does it show traces of being constrained by superficial theatrical needs. Solos and ensembles of deep personal passion are set off by massive choral effects and great orchestral splendour.

* * * * *

ACT I

The curtain rises on a hall in the royal palace at Memphis, with temples and pyramids visible in the background. The high priest, Ramfis, tells Radames that the Ethiopians have invaded Egypt, and that the goddess Isis will declare who is to lead the Egyptian armies. Hoping to be chosen leader, Radames dreams of returning, after a victorious campaign, to Memphis and to Aida, whom he loves. He sings of her: 'Beauteous Aida' (Celeste Aida).* Aida, a captive Ethiopian, is a domestic slave to Amneris, the daughter of the Egyptian king. Amneris enters and, seeing his elation, suspects that his ardour is not merely for military glory. Her fears – for

---

* English version by Arthur Jacobs.

she is in love with him herself – are reinforced on Aida'
entry. In the ensuing trio she detects the strong feelin
between Aida and Radames.

The king then enters, in procession, with Ramfis an
various officers. A messenger tells of the devastation of th
Egyptian countryside and the threat to the capital, Thebes
from the Ethiopian armies under their king, Amonasro. A
mention of this name, Aida exclaims 'My father!' (Mi
padre!) – but her exclamation is unheard by the Egyptians
who do not know of her royal birth. The king proclaims tha
Isis has chosen Radames to command the Egyptian armies
Led by the king, the assembled Egyptians sing a battl
chorus, and Amneris exhorts Radames to return victorious
'So conquer and return!' (Ritorna vincitor!). Left alone, Aid;
echoes the words with tragic irony; she is torn betweei
loyalty to her father, her country and her people on the on
hand, and her love of Radames on the other.

The scene changes to the Temple of Phtha (a god equatec
in the Italian text with Vulcan, Roman god of fire and th
working of metals), where the high priestess, Ramfis and th
assembled priests and priestesses present Radames with con
secrated arms.

Act II

Radames has been victorious; and Amneris in her apart
ment is being attired for the triumphal feast in celebratior
of the victory. Her Moorish slaves dance for her. Soon Aid;
enters, and Amneris resolves to find out whether her jealou;
suspicions are justified. At first she treats Aida with feignec
kindness. Then she tells her that Radames has been killed ir
battle, leading Aida to reveal her love for him. Then Amneri;
scornfully tells her that he is in fact alive – and how dare ;
mere slave presume to rival the Egyptian princess herself ir
love! The women's duet is joined by the battle song hearc
previously (sung in the distance by the returning warriors).
Then Aida, left alone, implores the gods' pity ('Numi, pietà!').

The scene changes to the outside of a temple near Thebes.
The king arrives in state. After a chorus of praise and thanks-

giving to Isis and the king, a Grand March opens a resplendent procession including soldiers, dancing girls, chariots, banners and idols. At the height of the ceremony Radames enters. The king greets him, orders Amneris to place the victor's crown on his head, and tells Radames that he may ask any boon.

Next the Ethiopian captives arrive, including Amonasro, whom Aida at once recognizes and embraces, with a cry of 'My father' (Mio padre!'). The Egyptians hear this, but he tells Aida not to disclose to them his real identity. Amonasro tells the Egyptians that the Ethiopian king is dead, and pleads for the lives of the prisoners and slaves; his plea is supported by the Egyptian people and by Radames (who claims this as the boon earlier offered him by the king). The priests and Amneris oppose the plea, but the king consents, retaining as hostages (at Ramfis's insistence) Aida and her father. The king awards Amneris's hand to Radames, to her great delight but to the distress of Aida and Radames himself. The final ensemble expresses the jubilation of the people and the diverse reactions of the individual characters.

Act III

From a temple of Isis, by the Nile, priests and priestesses are heard chanting. Ramfis enters with Amneris, leading her to the temple to pray for the goddess's blessing on her marriage, which is to take place the next day. Aida arrives for an assignation with Radames, and sings of her sadness at the prospect of never seeing her beloved homeland again: 'O native skies' (O cieli azzurri). Suddenly Amonasro appears: he tells her that she could return to her home safely if only she could find out from Radames what route the attacking Egyptian armies were planning to take. At first she recoils from the idea, but in face of her father's bitter contempt and his threatened curses she ultimately agrees.

Amonasro hides as Radames enters. With woman's wile, Aida overcomes his scruples and persuades him to fly with her to Ethiopia. As they depart she pauses to ask him by which route they can avoid the army; he tells her that the

army will go through the Gorge of Napata. At this momen
Amonasro, having overheard the vital information, steps fo
ward and reveals himself as the Ethiopian king. Radames ca
hardly comprehend that he has been led into betraying hi
country. As Aida and Amonasro try to lead him away, Am
neris, Ramfis and their guards emerge from the temple; the
have witnessed Radames's disclosure and come to arrest hin
Amonasro attempts to kill Amneris, but Radames steps be
tween them, and he bids Aida and her father flee while h
yields himself to Ramfis.

ACT IV

Amneris is alone in a room in the palace, close to Radames'
prison and above the hall of justice where his fate is bein;
decided. She sends for Radames and offers to intercede o
his behalf and save his life, on condition that he swears neve
to see Aida again. He steadfastly refuses and Amneris, prou
and despairing, lets him go to face judgment. In increasin;
distress she overhears his trial, taking place offstage. He offer
no answer to the charges of Ramfis and the priests; he is con
demned three times as a traitor ('traditor!') and is sentence
to be buried alive. The priests emerge and in an impassione
outburst Amneris curses them for their bloodthirsty cruelty

The final scene is a double one – the Temple of Phth
above, a crypt below. As the scene opens, the crypt is bein;
sealed as a living tomb for Radames, who is within. He dis
covers that Aida had previously concealed herself in th
crypt. While, from the distance, the priests and priestesse
chant the praises of their god, and Amneris in bitter isolatio
prays for Radames's eternal peace, Aida sinks into his arm
and dies.

*　　*　　*　　*　　*

Aida, Radames, Amneris: it is perhaps the most powerfu
'triangle' of love in opera, with each character superbly de
lineated in music. Radames establishes himself at the star
with his aria 'Beauteous Aida', with its long sweeping line
which test a tenor's abilities:

t ends with an ascent from F to high B flat which Verdi
marked 'pianissimo, dying away' – an effect beyond most
tenors, who sing it very loudly instead (and contrive to be ap-
plauded for doing so). The scene when Amneris uncovers
Aida's love for Radames enshrines a double dramatic contrast
– not only between the two women's attitudes, but between
their 'private' scene and the festive air of victory outside.
The chorus off-stage shouts its cry of death to the invader,
while before us Amneris threatens vengeance on Aida and
Aida humbly asks pity from the gods:

Amneris, the 'villain' in her actions towards Aida, is her self trapped when she tries (repenting at last) to make the priests show mercy to Radames. It is a strong dramatic moment, of an almost classical dramatic irony, and Verdi put into it his most intense writing for mezzo-soprano against the relentless unison of the chorus of priests. The role of Amonasro is also one of great power.

The Grand March is famous, with its sudden key-change

but is at its most effective when producers observe (as the generally do not) the remark in the score that it represent one group of trumpeters moving away in procession and new group coming in.

For an oriental subject a composer is faced with the ques tion of whether to include 'oriental' musical effects. Verdi in the scene in Phtha's temple, created an admirable styliza tion using the regular rhythms of 'western' solemnity in the harp accompaniment and the unusual 'oriental' melodic in tervals in the high priestess's solo as she invokes the deity:

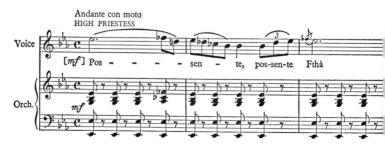

OTELLO

(Othello)

Libretto by Arrigo Boito, after the play by Shakespeare
First performed: Milan, 1887

Four Acts

Cast in order of singing:

Montano, Othello's predecessor as Governor of Cyprus	*bass*
Cassio, Othello's lieutenant	*tenor*
Roderigo, a Venetian gentleman	*tenor*
Iago, Othello's ensign	*baritone*
Othello, a Moor, general in the Venetian army and Governor of Cyprus	*tenor*
Desdemona, Othello's wife	*soprano*
Emilia, Iago's wife and companion to Desdemona	*mezzo-soprano*
A herald	*bass*
Lodovico, Venetian ambassador	*bass*
Chorus of soldiers and sailors, ladies, gentlemen and children	

The action is laid at a seaport in Cyprus,
at the end of the 15th century

THE librettos of Verdi's last two operas were written by Arrigo Boito (1842–1918), who was himself a composer of standing. His opera *Mephistopheles* (in Italian, Mefistofele) which was a failure on its first performance in 1868, has since achieved a modest place in the world's opera-houses. As a librettist his standing is even higher: *Otello* and *Falstaff* are sometimes reckoned the best texts ever written for Italian opera. Certainly they are marvellous abridgements of the original plays. Perhaps the most striking solo in *Otello*, curiously enough, is not from Shakespeare's pen at all: Iago's Creed, 'I believe in a cruel God' (Credo in un Dio crudel), which is a creation of Boito's own.

In *Otello* and *Falstaff* the 'static' element of formally separate numbers is almost banished; the onward development of the drama takes precedence. There is no grandeur of spectacle (or parallel grandeur of choruses) comparable with that of, say, *Aida*. But the role of Othello, immensely heavy and difficult for the tenor, and the hardly less difficult role of Iago give the opera an exciting virtuoso element on top of its dramatic tension.

In the following synopsis we have restored Shakespeare's spelling of his hero; in Italian he drops his 'h'. 'Desdemona' is accented in Italian on the second, not third, syllable; and Iago (in Italian also spelt Jago) is pronounced strictly in two syllables, Yah-go.

*   *   *   *   *

ACT I

A crowd at the quayside, near the castle which is the Governor's residence, is waiting to greet Othello on his return from the wars. There is a violent storm at sea and the crowd are fearful for the safety of his ship, which Montano and Cassio identify. Iago and Roderigo watch too as the storm abates and the ship makes harbour. Othello steps on to the quay, briefly tells the crowd to rejoice ('Esultate!') since the Turks have been defeated, and goes into the castle. After a short chorus of jubilation, it emerges that Roderigo loves Othello's wife, Desdemona, and that Iago hates Othello and is jealous of Cassio, whom Othello has promoted above him.

The people light a fire, singing and dancing around it. Then, while the officers are taking their ease, Iago starts a drinking song – 'Then let me the canakin clink' (Inaffia l'ugola)* – makes Cassio gradually drunk, and engineers a quarrel. Provoked by Roderigo, Cassio draws his sword and in the ensuing brawl Montano is hurt. Meanwhile Iago has sent Roderigo for Othello, who soon exercises his authority, making the men lower their swords ('Abbasso le spade!') and dismissing Cassio from his service. Thus the first part of Iago's plot – to discredit Cassio – has succeeded.

* English version by Francis Hueffer (Ricordi).

Desdemona followed Othello out when he came to stop the brawl but she does not speak till the others are gone and she and Othello are left alone. They sing of their love and of their happy memories of the past: 'Dark is the night and silent' (Già nella notte densa). As their love-duet ends they return to Othello's castle.

ACT II

In a hall of the castle, Iago pretends that he wishes to help Cassio regain Othello's favour: he advises him to ask Desdemona, who has great sway over her husband, to intercede on his behalf. As Cassio walks off into the garden, Iago (alone) reveals that it is part of his plot to sow suspicions in Othello's mind about Desdemona and Cassio. He sings his creed: 'Cruel is he, the God who in his image has fashioned me' (Credo in un Dio crudel che m'ha creato simile a se).

Iago watches Cassio and Desdemona in conversation, and, when Othello approaches, mutters, as if to himself, 'This I like not' (Ciò m'accora), for Othello to overhear. Then he subtly arouses Othello's jealousy, while pretending to warn him against 'the green-eyed monster'.

A chorus of sailors, women and children serenades Desdemona, who is now in the garden. Witnessing the scene, Othello's doubts of her innocence are shaken; but his suspicions well up again when she asks him to forgive Cassio. His gruff manner leads her to think him unwell, and she moves to place her handkerchief on his forehead. He throws it down roughly. It is picked up by Emilia, who has been attending Desdemona; she yields it to Iago at his request, with some foreboding.

The two women leave. Othello gives way to jealous doubts, and says an anguished farewell to his former peace of mind: 'And now for ever farewell' (Ora e per sempre addio). He demands of Iago positive proof of Desdemona's faithlessness. Accordingly Iago relates how, one night recently ('Era la notte'), Cassio talked in his sleep as if making love to Desdemona. He goes on to ask Othello whether Desdemona has a certain spotted handkerchief ('fazzoletto'); Othello says she

has one of this description, his own first gift to her; and Iago
states that such a one is in Cassio's possession (in fact it is
now in Iago's own pocket). For Othello this is the final con
firmation of her guilt, and the two men, kneeling, swear
vengeance: 'Witness, yonder marble heaven' (Si, pel ciel
marmoreo giuro!).

ACT III

In the great hall of the castle, a herald announces to Othello
that messengers from Venice will shortly arrive. As Desde
mona approaches, Iago warns Othello to be watchful, and then
leaves him. His conversation with her is calm, with a touch of
irony; but when she again asks him to forgive Cassio he does
not answer, only asking to see the handkerchief. She says it
is at home, and renews her pleas. He answers by accusing her
of infidelity, which she strenuously denies. Othello thrusts her
away, calling her a strumpet ('cortigiana'). Alone he shows his
anguish: 'Heav'n, had it pleased thee' (Dio, mi potevi
scagliar).

Iago returns, with Cassio following; Othello conceals him
self before Cassio enters. As the two talk, Iago drawing Cassio
on the subject of his amorous conquests, Othello tries to over
hear, but Iago takes care that he only catches remarks that
could apply to Desdemona. Othello expresses his feelings to
himself as he sees Cassio produce Desdemona's handkerchief
which Iago had previously had placed in his room.

Trumpet calls announce the arrival of the messengers
headed by Lodovico. Before they arrive, Othello asks Iago to
obtain poison to kill Desdemona. Iago advises strangling, and
offers his own services for the killing of Cassio. In return for
this advice Othello appoints him his lieutenant. The crowd
welcomes Othello, and Lodovico enters to hand the message to
him.

Still seething with jealousy, and almost striking Desdemona
(to the scandal of Lodovico and the others), Othello reads the
message aloud. He himself is to be recalled to Venice, and
Cassio is to be his successor as governor of Cyprus. In fury,
he throws Desdemona to the ground. She pleads with him

athetically, and in a prolonged ensemble all express their
:actions to the situation, with Iago secretly jubilant. At the
limax, Othello furiously curses his wife. Left alone with Iago,
is imagination runs wild and he faints. As the crowd, outside,
1out their praises of Othello, the 'Lion of Venice', Iago looks
own contemptuously on his inert form – 'See here the lion!'
Ecco il leone!).

.CT IV

1 her bedroom, Desdemona talks sadly with Emilia. Remem-
ering a poor serving-maid of her mother's called Barbara,
orsaken by her lover, she sits before the glass and sings
arbara's song – the Willow Song, with its refrain, 'Willow,
illow' (Salce, salce). As Emilia leaves, Desdemona, full of
oreboding, bids her a passionate farewell. Alone, she kneels
1 prayer (Ave Maria), and when she finishes she lies down
n the bed.

Othello enters, places his scimitar on the table, looks at her
.eeping form, blows out the candle, advances to the bed,
raws aside the curtains and gazes at her, then kisses her three
imes. She stirs. He asks if she has prayed for forgiveness for
er sins, and once more accuses her of loving Cassio. She
gain repeatedly denies it; he tells her that nothing can save
er, refuses her a moment for prayer, and stifles her with a
illow.

Emilia enters to tell Othello that Cassio has been attacked
y Roderigo but has killed him. With horror, she finds Des-
emona dying. She calls for help, and Iago, Cassio, Lodovico
nd others arrive. Iago's cunning plot is exposed by Emilia
nd he runs out, pursued by soldiers: then Othello, realizing
nd repenting his monstrous injustice to Desdemona, stabs
imself, kisses her again, and falls dead.

*   *   *   *   *

~owards the end of the love-duet concluding the first act
omes a memorable recurring phrase as Othello kisses Desde-
nona with the words 'One kiss!'

This is poignantly recalled when Othello kisses his sleeping
wife just before he kills her, and again when he kisses her dead
body, after having realized the truth and stabbed himself, at
the very end of the opera. But this remains a special effect;
the opera is not built on such 'recollections'.

The characterization of the three leading personages is
strong. Othello is a 'heroic' tenor (it is a role whose arduous-
ness *within* the Italian style makes it particularly difficult to
cast). Iago's sinister power is conveyed by the striking *fortis-
simo* octaves in the orchestra before he delivers his Creed
and, equally sinister, the orchestral trills as he begins:

Note the treatment of the 'octaves' theme as it becomes softer towards the end of the creed, sinking to 'And death's a nothing' (La morte è il nulla).

Desdemona's two great set pieces follow one another in the final act: the Willow Song and the Ave Maria (not the traditional Ave Maria in Latin, by the way). It is preceded by a mysterious orchestral chord-sequence and itself opens on a monotone while the chord-sequence continues. The Italian declamation is exact and English words cannot be precisely fitted to the music. A literal translation is: 'Hail to the Mary, full of grace, be elect among married and virgin women; let the fruit be blessed (O thou blessed one!) of thy maternal loins, Jesus.'

Here is the musical language of Verdi's final period at its richest.

FALSTAFF

Libretto by Arrigo Boito, after Shakespeare
First performed: Milan, 1893

Three Acts

Cast in order of singing:

Dr Caius	*tenor*
Sir John Falstaff	*baritone*
Bardolph, follower of Falstaff	*tenor*
Pistol, follower of Falstaff	*bass*
Mistress Ford (Alice)	*soprano*
Mistress Page (Meg)	*mezzo-soprano*
Mistress Quickly	*mezzo-soprano*
Nannetta, daughter of Ford, in love with Fenton	*soprano*
Fenton	*tenor*
Ford	*baritone*

Chorus of townspeople, servants, etc.

The scene is laid in Windsor in the time of Henry IV

AFTER an unparalleled succession of tragic operas, Verdi finished his operatic career with a comedy. It has a thread of intriguing musical cross-references and a great richness of musical resource, as well as subtle delineation of character. It has enchanting love-music, too; but it is the delineation of Falstaff himself and the web of conspiracy round him that gives the opera its chief celebrity.

Boito, having provided one masterly Shakespearian libretto for Verdi in *Otello*, showed equal mastery in this adaptation of *The Merry Wives of Windsor* (he also drew on *King Henry IV, Part I*, for Falstaff's 'Honour Monologue'). Shakespeare's plot, too complex as it stands for operatic treatment, is cleverly shortened by the 'telescoping' of certain incidents and by making the young girl in love with Fenton the daughter of Ford, not – as in *The Merry Wives of Windsor*, and Nicolai's opera of the same title (1849) – the daughter of Page. Page himself does not appear. The Italian name, Nannetta, is retained in the following synopsis, but Bardolph has been reconstituted from the Italianized Bardolfo, and so forth. Dr Caius, in Shakespeare a French physician whose foreign speech is made fun of, is in the opera a silly (but not foreign) pedant, past his youth; and Mistress Quickly is introduced 'on her own', as it were, not as Dr Caius's servant – she is a confidant of Mistress Ford and Mistress Page but not quite their equal.

*   *   *   *   *

Act I

Falstaff is drinking in the Garter Inn; Bardolph (recognizable by his big red rose) and Pistol are in attendance. Dr Caius enters and brushes past the protesting Bardolph, complaining that Falstaff has broken into his house and beaten his servants, and that Bardolph and Pistol made him drunk and robbed him. Falstaff does not deny it, but tells him to keep more sober company – to which Pistol and Bardolph, hustling Caius out, reply 'Amen'.

Falstaff has no money left to pay the innkeeper's bill. He determines to carry on an amorous intrigue with two merry wives of Windsor, Alice Ford and Meg Page, whom he thinks have looked on him favourably, and asks Bardolph and Pistol to take them letters arranging assignations. They decline to act the pandar and he entrusts the letters to his page, haranguing Bardolph and Pistol for their new-found scruples: 'What is honour? A word' (Che è dunque l'onore? una parola).

In the garden of Ford's house, Meg Page, Alice Ford, Mistress Quickly and Nannetta are together. Comparing notes, Mistress Page and Mistress Ford find that they have received identical love-letters from Falstaff, differing only in the names Alice and Meg. They are amused and slightly indignant about their elderly, corpulent admirer (Alice reads out Falstaff's

extravagant phrases in a caricatured voice) and resolve to
make a fool of him.

The women, keeping together, retire into the background as
Ford enters, followed by four men agitatedly talking to him –
Caius, telling him what a rogue Falstaff is; Bardolph and
Pistol (chased out by Falstaff) trying to warn him of Falstaff's
designs on his wife; and Fenton, Nannetta's suitor. Eventually
the women leave and Bardolph tells Ford that Falstaff has
already sent a letter of assignation. The men leave too.

Fenton and Nannetta steal some hurried kisses and sing a
love duet, which is momentarily interrupted when the three
women return, planning to send Mistress Quickly as a messenger to Falstaff. Finally Fenton joins the men when they
return, still discussing plans to deal with the errant knight. A
little later the two groups, men and women, again congregate
on opposite sides of the stage; only Fenton, singing in large
rapturous phrases, is out of the conspiratorial chatter. The
men go off first; then the women complete the hatching of
their plot, repeat the caricature of Falstaff's extravagant
literary phrases, and go off laughing.

ACT II

Back in the Garter Inn, Bardolph and Pistol (now in Ford's
pay) present themselves to Falstaff and feign penitence at
having angered him earlier. When Bardolph and Pistol have
gone, Mistress Quickly enters, with an exaggerated 'Oh, your
worship!' (Reverenza!); she delivers affectionate messages
from both ladies and tells Falstaff that Alice Ford would welcome a visit between two and three o'clock, when her husband
will be out. (Unfortunately, she adds, Meg Page's husband is
rarely away!)

No sooner has Falstaff paid her for her trouble and con-
gratulated himself on his good fortune than Bardolph announces another caller, by name 'Fontana' (in Shakespeare,
Brook). This is Ford himself, who, in order to find out how
things stand between his wife and Falstaff, has come under
the pretence of asking for help in pressing his own suit with

Mistress Ford. So far, he says, he has failed: offering Falstaff a purse of gold, he asks if the knight could first assail her virtue so as to ease his path. With pleasure, says Falstaff: he himself has an assignation with her between two and three that afternoon, when her jealous fool of a husband will be out. Left alone for a moment, Ford bursts out with rage against his apparently faithless wife and Falstaff: 'A dream? or real life?' (E sogno? o realtà?). Sir John returns, dressed up to the nines for his intended seduction, and the two go off together ceremoniously.

In a room in Ford's house, Alice, Meg and (aside) Nannetta are waiting. Mistress Quickly gives a lively account of her interview with Falstaff, with imitations of his words and manner. She tells them that he will be coming in a few minutes' time, between two and three. Nannetta does not join in the others' laughter; she tearfully tells them that she is sad as her father intends her to marry not her beloved Fenton but old Dr Caius. The other ladies tell her not to worry – they will arrange something. Meanwhile, they set about preparing the scene (with such 'props' as a laundry basket and a screen) for Falstaff's arrival. First Alice, then Meg and Nannetta, sing of the 'merry wives of Windsor' (gaie comari di Windsor).

With the others in hiding, Alice plays the lute to herself as she awaits her visitor. He arrives, sings a refrain to her lute, and then converses with her. Falstaff boasts that love is a vocation for him and sings of his gay youth: 'When I was page-boy to the Duke of Norfolk' (Quando ero paggio). Suddenly Mistress Quickly comes in, to say that Meg urgently needs to speak to Alice; so Falstaff is hurried behind a screen and Meg warns Alice that her husband is approaching.

Ford strides up angrily, with Caius and Fenton, Bardolph and Pistol; he accuses his wife and sets about searching the house – emptying the dirty linen from the laundry basket to see if anyone is hidden there before he goes. The agitated Falstaff emerges from behind the screen to find only Meg, tells her he loves her alone and begs her to save him. She and Mistress Quickly stuff him into the basket and fill it with the dirty clothes again. Fenton and Nannetta enter together and, seeing the screen, retire behind it. The other men return, Ford and Caius still ranting angrily and looking in cupboards and up chimneys.

In a moment of silence, a kiss is heard from behind the screen. While Meg and Mistress Quickly hush the suffocating Falstaff in his basket, Ford gives instructions to his assembled servants for the unmasking of his wife and Falstaff – behind the screen, as he supposes. After a step-by-step advance in comic style, Ford throws down the screen, and is scarcely less enraged to find his daughter and her lover than he would have been to find his wife and hers. He strides off to renew the search. Alice summons servants to throw the basket of dirty laundry out of the window and laughingly shows Ford and the other men, who have returned, the magnificent spectacle of Falstaff in the Thames outside. A great outburst of laughter from all ends the act.

ACT III

Outside the Garter Inn, Falstaff is not unnaturally in dampened spirits as he grumbles to the landlord. But he perks up: 'Go on, good old John' (Va, vecchio John). Mistress Quickly enters – with her 'Oh, your worship!' (Reverenza!) again – bearing apologies from Alice; at first Falstaff will not listen, but he eventually calms down and, watched from a distance by the concealed Ford, Alice, Meg, Nannetta, Caius and Fenton, he reads out a note from Alice suggesting an assignation at Herne's Oak in Windsor Forest, to which he should come disguised as the fabled 'black huntsman' (cacciator nero).

Mistress Quickly and Falstaff depart, while Ford and the others discuss plans for the night's revels at Herne's Oak. Alice announces that Nannetta shall be Queen of the Fairies (Regina della Fate), clad in white. As they go off, Ford tells Caius he will make him his son-in-law at the revels: Caius is to come dressed as a monk. Mistress Quickly overhears this, and the women determine to circumvent it. As they go off their voices are heard in the distance. Night begins to fall.

The scene changes to Herne's Oak, by moonlight. Fenton s the first there and is soon joined by Nannetta, Alice, Meg nd Mistress Quickly in their various disguises. They bring nonk's robes for Fenton, to his mystification, and all hide. As he clock strikes midnight Falstaff arrives, costumed as re- quested, in nervous mood. Alice emerges and Falstaff starts to nake love to her. She mentions that Meg is nearby. Suddenly here is a terrified scream from Meg, shouting that witches are :oming; Alice, as if frightened, runs off.

Falstaff is utterly petrified by the fairies, elves and other pirits (in fact Alice's friends, later with Bardolph and Pistol, ʳord and Caius) who suddenly appear. They are led by Nannetta, who sings the fairies' song, 'From secret caverns ınd bowers' (Sul fil d'un soffio etesio). They set about Falstaff, olling him round, pinching him ('Pizzica, pizzica!'), and he is cared out of his wits. Eventually he recognizes Bardolph (by ıis big red nose), fulminates against him, and asks for respite.

While Mistress Quickly sends Bardolph away to don a new lisguise (a white veil), Ford goes up to Falstaff, asking him 'Which of us wears the horns?' (Il cornuto chi è?). Falstaff)egins to address him as Fontana, but Alice interrupts to ntroduce him as – her husband. Then Mistress Quickly iden- :ifies herself to him too, singing the same phrase as on their previous encounters. Falstaff takes it all in good part.

Ford then suggests the formal betrothal of a loving couple, Dr Caius (a man in monk's disguise steps forward) and the 'airy queen; Alice proposes the addition of another pair of overs, both masked. As the couples unmask it is seen that Caius has pledged his troth with Bardolph! – and Fenton with Nannetta, to the astonishment of Ford (not to mention that of Caius himself). 'Which of us is the dupe?' (Lo scornato chi è?), Falstaff asks Ford merrily. All three – Falstaff, Ford and Caius – answer Alice, and she begs Ford to forgive the young lovers. He quickly does so, and, led by Falstaff, the proceedings are brought to a hilarious close: 'Jesting is man's vocation' (Tutto nel mondo è burla).

*   *   *   *   *

The music of the young lovers is ardently romantic, fitting for language that speaks of kisses and of love which renews itself like the moon:

(note that the orchestral tune at bar 6 is the one sung just a moment previously by the lovers).

Memorable too is the exaggerated greeting of Mistress Quickly to Falstaff:

Both these are among the phrases which later recur prominently. Falstaff's own role is marvellously varied – phlegmatic to Caius, angry to Bardolph and Pistol, amorous to Alice. To her he boasts of how nimble a page-boy he used to be:

And it is Falstaff who leads the final ensemble of jollity – a fugue, incidentally:

The whole orchestra seems to join in the laughter. With this ebullient ensemble, Verdi wrote the last pages of his last opera.

VI

RICHARD WAGNER

(1813–83)

WE turn now to a composer who was born in the same year as Verdi and who, with him, dominates opera in the 19th century: Richard Wagner. From *The Flying Dutchman* (produced in 1843) to *Parsifal* (1882), he produced a succession of works for the stage unmatched in their influence on the international development of opera in particular and music in general. We need not be concerned here with Wagner's earlier operas, *Die Feen* (The Fairies, composed in 1833 but not staged till after the composer's death), *Das Liebesverbot* (The Ban on Love, based on Shakespeare's *Measure for Measure*), produced in 1836, and *Rienzi* (based on Bulwer-Lytton's once celebrated novel), produced in 1842.

As a conductor himself, Wagner knew the operas of his own time well, including those of Weber, with their evocation of the romantically supernatural, and those of Meyerbeer, in which the drama served to display vocal set pieces. But his own aim was to portray the human soul with a new force, a force he detected in Beethoven's Ninth Symphony. By fitting a symphonic finale with words Beethoven had attached concreteness to a 'pure' musical form. Wagner wished his operas similarly to be 'music fertilized by poetry', not merely poetry set to music.

Already, as we have seen, composers were increasingly tending to intersperse their operas with recurring musical themes, the recurrence serving a dramatic point. But these recurrences hitherto took place only at special, selected moments of the score. Wagner, from *Tristan und Isolde* on, aimed to make such themes the actual stuff from which his musical fabric was woven. The themes do not each simply represent a mere personage (as Prokofiev in *Peter and the Wolf* has a tune for

the cat, a tune for the duck and so on): they may represent
an emotion, a destiny, an aspect of character, or something
equally abstract. What they represent is to be *deduced* from
their dramatic use in the opera: Wagner wrote the music, not
the labels for the themes.

Through the use of these themes Wagner writes music
which is, in intention, symphonic – and the symphonic argument almost (but not quite) eliminates the division of an act
into separate numbers.

In the three works preceding *Tristan und Isolde* Wagner
still laid out his score in separate numbers, and still made only
a limited, non-symphonic (though considerable) use of recurring themes. Moreover, the orchestra part may still be described as an accompaniment.

Wagner's recurring themes, each bearing a dramatic meaning, are usually called by the name 'leading-motive'—an
anglicization of the German *Leitmotiv* (plural *Leitmotive*).

DER FLIEGENDE HOLLÄNDER

(The Flying Dutchman)

Libretto by the composer, after a story by Heinrich Heine

First performed: Dresden, 1843

Three Acts

Cast in order of singing:

Daland, captain of a Norwegian ship	*bass*
Steersman on Daland's ship	*tenor*
The 'Flying Dutchman', a Dutch sea-captain	*baritone*
Mary, Senta's old nurse	*contralto*
Senta, Daland's daughter	*soprano*
Erik, a huntsman, betrothed to Senta	*tenor*

Chorus of Norwegian sailors, Dutch sailors and
Norwegian girls

*The scene is laid in a Norwegian fishing village
in the 18th century*

WAGNER was his own librettist – and, unlike many composers, a good one. He wrote *The Flying Dutchman* originally as a one-act libretto, and offered it to the director of the Paris Opera hoping for a commission to complete the music. Instead, the director offered the libretto to other composers and paid Wagner five hundred francs for it – a sum much needed by the almost penniless young German musician, who had been obliged to leave Russia (where he had held a conductor's post in Riga) secretly to escape his creditors. The five hundred francs gave Wagner the leisure to convert *The Flying Dutchman* into a full-length work of his own.

Its story is a strong one – of a man supernaturally doomed to sail the seas until he can earn redemption. The supernatural element links it with the operatic world of Weber; the element of man's redemption through womanly love points to Wagner's later works. The music here is striking in its evocation of sea, storm and superstition (first of all in the overture) – and no less striking for its sheer tunefulness, as in Senta's Ballad, the Spinning Chorus and other numbers.

* * * * *

ACT I

The stormy overture sets the atmosphere for the opening scene, in which we see a Norwegian ship just anchored, after a violent tempest, in rough seas off the Norwegian coast. Daland, the captain, finds that they are not far from the port where they were intending to put in. Leaving a steersman on watch, he and the sailors go below for some much-needed rest. The steersman tries to keep awake, singing a ballad 'Through the thunder and storm' (Mit Gewitter und Sturm'),* but eventually succumbs to sleep.

A ghostly ship, with blood-red sails and black masts, approaches. She puts in alongside the other ship, momentarily disturbing the steersman, and in silence the spectral crew make fast. Its captain, the legendary 'Flying Dutchman', comes ashore and sings of the terrible curse upon him. Once,

* English version by Ernest Newman (Breitkopf & Härtel).

rounding the Cape of Good Hope in a storm, he invoked the Devil's aid, and consequently his fate is to sail unceasingly until the Day of Judgment unless he can find a woman 'faithful unto death'. He is allowed to search for her every seven years, and that time has now come. The crew echo his bitter complaint.

Daland comes on the deck of his own ship and rouses his steersman, who signals the other ship. In reply there is only an eerie silence. Then Daland sees the Dutchman himself. The two captains talk: the Dutchman tells Daland of his wanderings, asking for his friendship and for shelter at Daland's home (which is nearby), and offering a magnificent casket of jewels in return. The Dutchman ascertains that Daland has a daughter and begs to be allowed to make her his wife ('Sie sei mein Weib'); to which Daland, though mystified, willingly consents. In a duet, Daland rejoices at the prospect of great riches and the Dutchman at the prospect of finding peace at last. Meanwhile the storm has passed and the steersman reports a favourable south wind ('Süd-wind!'); Daland and his sailors weigh anchor and set sail for their home port, the Dutchman promising to follow as soon as his crew have rested. The Norwegian sailors sing joyfully as their ship moves off.

ACT II

In a room in Daland's house, Senta's friends and Mary, Senta's old nurse, are singing as they sit at their spinning-wheels (Spinning Chorus). Only Senta, Daland's daughter, does not spin: she is preoccupied with a picture hanging on the wall, depicting the Flying Dutchman. Mary reprimands her for her idleness and the others tease her for her interest in the Dutchman when she has a suitor (Erik, the huntsman). Senta asks Mary to tell the tale of the Dutchman, but the old woman refuses, so Senta herself sings of the curse and the hoped-for redemption (Senta's Ballad).

The other girls join in. Finally Senta is seized with the sudden idea that she could be the one to save the doomed Dutchman, to the horror of all – including Erik, who arrives and has overheard her. He mentions that Daland's ship is arriving, to the delight of all the girls, who are excited at the prospect of seeing their menfolk. Mary reminds them of the domestic preparations now to be made.

The girls and Mary go off, leaving Erik and Senta alone. In a duet he begs her to promise to remain faithful to him, but she only wishes to go, to meet her father. She tells Erik of her compassion for the Dutchman: he is deeply troubled and relates to her a dream he has had in which he saw her father lead the Dutchman to her, and saw them embrace and go off together. (She adds an occasional detail, 'identifying' the dream from the picture.) She is now convinced that it is her fate to save the Dutchman, and Erik rushes off in despair.

Alone, Senta gently sings the refrain of her ballad: then the door opens and she sees her father, with the Dutchman himself, standing there. Her eyes remain riveted on the Dutchman as her father greets her. Daland is disconcerted when she does not run to embrace him as usual; then he praises the guest, asking her to receive him kindly and to consider accepting him as her husband. The Dutchman and Senta remain contemplating one another, in silence: Daland, puzzled and none too pleased by their apparent coldness, goes out, leaving them alone.

Senta and the Dutchman, both as if entranced, can hardly believe the fulfilment of their dreams. Their mutual love becomes clear to them both: 'Up from forgotten depths of years' (Wie aus der Ferne). When Daland returns he is delighted to find that she has accepted the visitor as her husband-to-be and that he can announce her betrothal at the forthcoming feast.

ACT III

In a bay, overlooked by Daland's house, the two ships are seen – the Dutchman's shrouded by a ghostly stillness, the Norwegian one full of light as the sailors sing and dance lustily: 'Steersman, leave the watch!' (Steuermann, lass' die Wacht!). The Norwegian women arrive with food and drink. They go to take some to the silent Dutch ship (the Norwegian steersman attributes their silence to their thirst) but there is no response to the women's calls, which they repeat, louder and louder. Eventually they become afraid, especially when the Norwegian sailors jokingly suggest that the ship resembles that of the legendary Flying Dutchman.

When the Norwegian sailors have eaten and drunk they move towards the Dutch ship. Suddenly a sinister dark blue flame is seen on board: the spectral crew come to life, singing a wild chorus, as the wind whistles and the sea rises round their ship. The Norwegian sailors, mystified and frightened, resume their song. Eventually, suspecting evil, they make the sign of the cross and go below, to the eerie laughter of the Dutchman's crew.

Calm returns just as Senta emerges from the house, followed by the agitated Erik, who reproaches her for her behaviour towards him. He begs her to remember her pledge to him of eternal love – which she recollects with terror. He reminds her of her solemn promises: 'Is that sweet day so soon by thee forgotten?' (Willst jenes Tags). The Dutchman steps forward (Erik recognizes him as the man in his dream): he has overheard their conversation and believes Senta untrue to him. He immediately determines to put to sea once more. As the Dutchman rebukes her for her supposed infidelity, she begs him to stay, while Erik pleads with her to leave the Dutchman to go.

Before he leaves, he starts telling her who he is: she answers that she already knows and intends to save him from the terrible curse. In front of Daland, the Norwegian sailors and the girls (who have hurried out), he proclaims his identity as the dreaded Flying Dutchman. Meanwhile, his crew make preparations to put to sea; he steps on board and they depart. Senta rushes to the edge of a cliff and calls to him, then throws herself into the sea. As she does so, the ship is sucked down into a whirlpool: in the sunset, the forms of Senta and the Flying Dutchman are seen rising heavenward from the sinking wreck.

*　　*　　*　　*　　*

The storm-tossed Dutchman is portrayed in the opening bars (beneath a string tremolo which is omitted in the following example):

and a little later the redeeming Senta is portrayed:

These two principal motives persist throughout the opera; they both appear (the Dutchman's motive transformed to a peaceful guise) in the very last moments. Senta's theme is first heard vocally in her Ballad (Act I). The overture thus represents (in miniature and in anticipation) what is going to happen; and like the opera itself it ends quietly. The fact that the Dutchman's theme is used both for the appearance of the actual man (Act I) and for the telling of his legend (by Senta in Act II) musically establishes that this *is* the man of the legend: a point which may seem obvious but which in fact illustrates a basic operatic method of communication.

It is notable that the Dutchman's theme is made up of quite 'ordinary' components of rhythm and of melody (two notes only, D and A!); but Wagner stamps his own originality on it. In *The Flying Dutchman* we also sense the more daring harmonic touch which Wagner fully developed in his later works. The Norwegian sailors hail the Dutch ship (in Act III) in a carefree C major; in place of a human answer there comes, after an ominous pause, an 'other-worldly', musi-

cally unexpected chord (on the horns and bassoon) in the
unrelated key of C sharp minor:

The sequence is shortly repeated twice more, at a different
pitch and with slightly different music for the Norwegians,
but always with the bleak unrelated minor chord (higher
each time) to express the supernatural mystery of the Dutch
vessel.

TANNHÄUSER

Libretto by the composer
First produced: Dresden, 1845

Three Acts

Cast in order of singing:

Venus, goddess of love		soprano
Tannhäuser, minstrel and knight		tenor
A shepherd boy		soprano
Hermann, Landgrave of Thuringia		bass
Walther von der Vogelweide		tenor
Biterolf		bass
Wolfram von Eschinbach	minstrel knights	baritone
Heinrich der Schreiber		tenor
Reinmar von Zweter		bass

Elisabeth, niece of the Landgrave   *soprano*
Pages   *two trebles, two altos*
  Chorus of sirens, pilgrims, Thuringian nobles, knights
                      and their ladies

  The scene is laid in Thuringia at the beginning of the
                      13th century

LIKE *The Flying Dutchman, Tannhäuser* has memorable
tunes, several of them foreshadowed in the overture which is
so well known. Like *The Flying Dutchman* again, it is concerned with redemption – but this time with the conflict of
good and bad represented by the roles of the two principal
sopranos, who never confront each other on the stage.

  Tannhäuser himself was an actual 13th-century minstrel
('minnesinger'), some of whose verse survives. Perhaps because of a 'Song of Repentance' attributed to him, in the 16th
century his name became linked with the legend of the
Venusberg – the hill within which Venus was supposed still
to hold her court and to destroy the souls of men who fall
into her hands. In his opera, Wagner linked this legend with
a contest of song which actually took place in 1210 at the
Wartburg, a castle in Thuringia (central Germany).

  Dramatically, this yields the theme of sacred versus profane love (to which Wagner returned in *Parsifal*), as well as a
contest of song with its obvious operatic opportunities (to
which the composer returned in *The Mastersingers*) – all
against a background of medieval courtly life which exercised
a strong attraction for 'romantic' writers and composers of
Wagner's day. In the opera, Christian love triumphs over
pagan sensuality, but in the older traditional legend Tannhäuser is *not* redeemed and returns to the Venusberg.

  Wagner completed *Tannhäuser* in 1845, and later that year
it had its first performance – in Dresden, where he held a
resident conductor's post. But when the opportunity came to
present the work in Paris, in 1861, Wagner was no longer
the Wagner of 1845: he had by now written *Tristan und
Isolde*, and accordingly he felt he needed to modify the score

of Act I of *Tannhäuser*. In the new version, now known a
'the Paris version' of the score, there are three major changes
The overture does not bring back the opening Pilgrims
Chorus and does not come to a formal close, but merges int
the opening music of the Venusberg. The music to the dance
in the Venusberg, depicting pagan ecstasy, is expanded
with detailed scenic indications to match (for example, 'Num
erous sleeping Cupids are huddled together in a confuse(
tangle like children who, tired after play, have fallen asleep')
Venus's plea to Tannhäuser to stay with her is re-written wit
greater subtlety of expression – Venus is less shrewish, mor
meditative.

These modifications do not affect the actual outline of th
opera; and the Paris version has not universally banished th
earlier (and musically more homogeneous) one from theatrica
performances.

*   *   *   *   *

ACT I

The opening scene is set within the Venusberg, where th
profane rites of love are celebrated to appropriate music
Tannhäuser is resting his head on Venus's lap. He is feelin
discontent with the indolent, abandoned life he has led fo
the past year, and tells Venus so; but she soothes him an(
asks him to sing to her, which he does: 'All praise be thine
(Dir töne Lob)†. But he is determined to leave her, despite he
repeated seductive pleadings. Eventually she dismisses him
with proud anger, telling him that he can have no hopes o
salvation. His hope rests in the Virgin, he replies; Venus an(
the Venusberg disappear at the mention of her name.

The scene changes suddenly to a valley near the Wartburg
where Tannhäuser finds himself. A shepherd boy is playin;
on his pipe and singing, and a group of chanting pilgrim:
moves past. The shepherd wishes them God speed; the

---

* In concerts this is known as the Bacchanal or the Venusberε
Music.

† English version by Natalia Macfarren (Novello).

Tannhäuser, deeply moved, falls to his knees and raises his voice in fervent prayer. As the pilgrims finally disappear, the sounds of approaching huntsmen are heard. It is the Landgrave (ruler) of Thuringia with his minstrel knights.

The Landgrave and the knights Walther and Biterolf do not at first recognize Tannhäuser; then another knight, Wolfram, realizes who the stranger is. Wolfram, Walther and Biterolf in turn welcome him. Reinmar and Schreiber join in the greeting, which the Landgrave takes up: they all beg him to return to their company, but Tannhäuser feels that he cannot go back to the past after his transgressions. Only when Wolfram mentions the Landgrave's niece Elisabeth, and tells Tannhäuser that she loves him (a self-sacrificing disclosure, for Wolfram loves her himself), does he agree to return. They all sing joyfully at the prospect of reunion.

ACT II

Elisabeth, alone in the Minstrels' Hall, sings happily of Tannhäuser's return: 'Oh, hall of song' (Dich, teure Halle) – Elisabeth's Greeting. Tannhäuser, led in by Wolfram, throws himself at her feet; she is confused. When she asks about his long absence, he answers vaguely: then the two sing a long love duet, while Wolfram, in the background, comments briefly on the hopelessness of his own passion for Elisabeth.

Tannhäuser and Wolfram go and the Landgrave enters, greeting his niece. Flourishes of trumpets announce the arrival of the guests for a contest of the minstrel knights. As the nobles and their ladies enter, to the strains of a choral march – 'Hail, bright abode' (Freudig begrüssen wir) – they are greeted by the Landgrave and Elisabeth: then they raise their voices in praise of song and in praise of the Landgrave. Next the minstrels enter. The Landgrave rises and addresses them, telling them that Love is to be the theme of the song-contest about to take place.

The nobles seat themselves while pages collect slips of paper bearing the minstrels' names, one of which Elisabeth draws from a cup. The first contestant, the pages announce, is Wolfram. He duly rises and, with harp accompaniment, sings a simple, restrained song about the purity of love, hinting at Elisabeth as the source of his inspiration. The assembled company express their approbation. Tannhäuser comments briefly on the more passionate nature of love; then the second contestant, Walther, sings like Wolfram of love's purity.

Now Tannhäuser rises impatiently and startles his audience by singing of the sensual delights of love and its fulfilment. Angrily, Biterolf challenges him to fight, to the approval of the nobles and the other minstrels, who are only more angered by Tannhäuser's answer. The Landgrave and Wolfram restore peace, but no sooner has Wolfram finished than Tannhäuser, carried away, sings his song of impassioned praise to Venus (which was heard in Act I).

All now are scandalized: the ladies rush out in alarm and the minstrels and nobles close on Tannhäuser with their swords drawn, calling curses upon him. But Elisabeth stands in front of Tannhäuser to protect him, and passionately pleads with them to spare him and grant him an opportunity of salvation. In a long ensemble, the outraged company agree to spare him in view of Elisabeth's intercession, though they still consider him accursed, while she continues pleading and Tannhäuser prays to God for forgiveness.

The Landgrave steps forward and pronounces his verdict. Tannhäuser's only prospect of salvation lies in his joining a second party of pilgrims, on the point of departure for Rome, and seeking absolution from the Pope. All echo his words, threatening Tannhäuser with death if he does not go. The chanting of the pilgrims is heard in the distance, and with a cry of 'To Rome' (Nach Rom!) Tannhäuser rushes off to join them.

ACT III

Elisabeth is seen kneeling before a shrine in the valley by the Wartburg, praying for the absent Tannhäuser's redemption and return. Wolfram watches her, reflecting on her love. The song of the pilgrims, returning at last, is heard. Elisabeth and Wolfram, watching as the pilgrims pass by, see that Tannhäuser is not among them.

Elisabeth kneels again in prayer: 'Oh blessed Virgin' (Allmächt'ge Jungfrau). When she finishes, she moves off, declining Wolfram's offer to accompany her. As night falls, he sings to the accompaniment of his harp, comparing Elisabeth with the bright evening star: 'Oh star of eve' (O du mein holder Abendstern).

As he finishes, a weary, ragged pilgrim enters. It is Tannhäuser: he is seeking the path to Venusberg. At first he mistrusts Wolfram, whom he takes as his enemy, but Wolfram's kindness moves him. He tells Wolfram of the ordeals he subjected himself to on his pilgrimage, and how he approached the Pope, who had forgiven thousands that day. He was met with a stern refusal: it was as impossible that he should be absolved as that the Pope's barren staff should flower. So now, he explains, he is turning to Venus once more.

As he calls on Venus, visions of her appear and her voice is heard. Wolfram tries to hold Tannhäuser back as she calls to him: as he struggles, Wolfram mentions Elisabeth's name. Tannhäuser, rapt, repeats it – and at this moment voices are heard: Elisabeth has died and her funeral cortege is approaching, attended by the Landgrave, nobles and minstrels. The pagan visions disappear as Venus calls 'I have lost him!' (Mir verloren). Wolfram, telling Tannhäuser that he is absolved as a result of Elisabeth's intercession, signs them to halt and guides Tannhäuser to her bier; he falls beside it and dies. As the new day breaks, the second group of pilgrims arrives, exalted by the news they bear: the Pope's staff has miraculously burst into flower. Tannhäuser is indeed saved. All raise their voices in praise of God.

*　　*　　*　　*　　*

Wagner 'tells the story' of the opera in advance in the overture, which is built from motives of the opera – but the 'story-telling' is more obvious in the earlier (Dresden, not Paris) version when the Pilgrims' Chorus, which opened the overture softly, returns to close it loudly: Christianity has triumphed.

Tannhäuser, as a minstrel, apostrophizes Venus in Act I

to the accompaniment of his harp and with words beginning (literally) 'Thanks be to thy grace!':

This is the air which in English is often called 'O gracious fair', and which recurs – to Tannhäuser's disgrace – in the contest in Act II. Venus herself is musically characterized by all the allurements of the Venusberg music as well as by her own sensuous appeal to Tannhäuser (note its free, 'airy' declamation of the words 'Beloved, come!' with no insistent beat below):

Elisabeth is characterized with equal clarity. Her great moment of self-revelation (Elisabeth's Greeting to the hall of song in Act II) has such distinctive phrases as this, as she speaks of the pride in her bosom in recalling Tannhäuser's former triumphs:

The climax of Tannhäuser's part comes in what is often
called (in clumsy, mock-German English) the Rome Narration – that is, his account in Act III of his pilgrimage to
Rome and his bitter disappointment. As an orchestral counter-
point to Tannhäuser's words about the day breaking in Rome
to the sound of bells, we hear a theme which has already been
stated in the prelude to the act, anticipating the narration:

The theme signifies Christian salvation, and Wagner carries
it over into *Lohengrin* and *Parsifal* where it is usually called
the Grail Motive – on which, see p. 227.

Thirty-seven distinct motives have been identified and
labelled (according to the emotions or situations they represent) in *Tannhäuser*. Wagner had already advanced considerably towards the total penetration of the drama by recurring motives which is found in his later works.

LOHENGRIN

Libretto by the composer
First performed: Weimar, 1850

Three Acts

Cast in order of singing:

A herald	*bass*
King Henry I of Germany	*bass*
Friedrich von Telramund, a noble of Brabant	*bass*
Elsa, daughter of the late Duke of Brabant	*soprano*

Lohengrin, knight of the Grail   *tenο*
Ortrud, a sorceress, wife of Telramund   *mezzo-sopran*
Four nobles   *two tenors, two bassε*
Four pages   *two sopranos, two altο*
[The role of Gottfried, Elsa's brother, is silent.]
Chorus of Saxon and Brabantian nobles and retainers, ladieϛ
pages, etc.

The scene is laid in Antwerp in the first half of
the 10th century

THE romantic, picturesque and dramatic appeal of medievaΙ
Christianity furnished Wagner, after *Tannhäuser*, with *Lohen*
grin. The opera's famous Bridal Chorus is the one piece ο
Wagner known to those who do not know Wagner. The firϛ
conductor of the opera was Liszt who, as conductor at thϵ
court of Weimar (central Germany) was a keen champion ο
the most vital new music of his day. For the production ο
Lohengrin at his theatre, he spared no expense and sent ouϮ
to buy a bass clarinet – a recently invented instrument whic├
Wagner's score calls for.

According to medieval legend, the Holy Grail is 'the plattϵ
used by our Saviour at the Last Supper, in which Joseph ο
Arimathea received the Saviour's blood at the cross ... Some
times, the Grail or Sangreal has been erroneously supposed Ϯ
be the cup or chalice used at the Last Supper' (*Oxford Eng*
lish Dictionary). Wagner appears to have held this 'erroneouϛ
view. The legendary Knights of the Holy Grail had the Graϊ
in their possession.

With this legendary element Wagner links the historicϊ
German king, Henry I ('the Fowler'; ?876–936), who madϵ
war on the Hungarians and who, in the opera, is supposed Ϯ
be visiting Antwerp to raise an army to fight the Hungariaϊ
invader. It was only in the 12th century that Brabant bϵ
came a Duchy, carrying with it the marquisate of Antwerϸ
Wagner mistakenly (or deliberately ?) antedates the dukedoϜ

*　　　*　　　*　　　*　　　*

ACT I

By the banks of the Scheldt, near Antwerp, a herald calls the people of Brabant to arms. They respond gladly. King Henry explains that before going to war in defence of his kingdom against the Hungarian barbarians, he wishes to resolve the disunion evident in Brabant itself. He calls on Telramund, who is present with his wife Ortrud, to give an account of the dispute.

Telramund tells the king that he was left in charge of the late duke's children when the duke died. One day the son, Gottfried, disappeared when alone with his sister, Elsa; Telramund now accuses Elsa of having killed her brother so as to have the dukedom for herself. Consequently he resigned his previous claim to her hand, marrying Ortrud instead, through whose noble descent he now claims to be ruler of Brabant. The assembled nobles and the king are horrified by his accusation. The king sends for Elsa, determined to find out the truth and pass judgement.

Elsa comes. She can give no clear answer to the king's questions, but she relates a dream, to everyone's mystification, in which a knight in shining armour appeared as her champion: 'Oft when the hours were lonely' (Einsam in trüben Tagen).* Telramund presses his case further, and the king and Brabantines are inclined to believe him. The king rules that the matter shall be decided by combat between Telramund and any man who will act as Elsa's champion.

At the king's command the herald, with a flourish of trumpets, calls upon such a man to step forth. Twice the proclamation is read out, but no one comes. Then, as Elsa and the attendant ladies kneel in prayer, the crowd is astonished to see a swan ('Ein Schwan!') appear on the river, drawing a boat in which there is a knight in silver armour. All greet him (except Telramund and Ortrud): he bids farewell to the swan and steps on to the shore. He asks Elsa if he may act as her champion, but imposes the condition that she must never

* English version by Natalia Macfarren (Novello).

ask him his name or his origin. With absolute trust, she agrees and they pledge mutual love.

Lohengrin (for it is he) steps forward and challenges Telramund, whose friends advise him to withdraw. The herald announces the combat and all call on God to see that justice prevails. The two men fight: Lohengrin defeats Telramund but spares his life. All applaud his success and Elsa expresses her joy; the only dissident voices are those of Ortrud and Telramund.

Act II

On the cathedral steps at night, Telramund and Ortrud are musing on their defeat. Sounds of revelry are heard from the palace. Telramund blames his disgrace on the evil machinations of his wife, who is a sorceress. She tells him that the power of the victorious knight can only be overcome if Elsa can be induced to ask about his name and origins, or if he should be wounded. They determine to seek vengeance.

Elsa appears on the balcony of the Kemenate (the women's dwelling), singing of her happiness. Ortrud sends Telramund away and calls to Elsa, bemoaning her own fate – but while Elsa is on her way down (and thus out of earshot), Ortrud exults in the prospect of revenge. Elsa enters and tells Ortrud she forgives her and promises to try to restore her and Telramund to favour; in their duet, Ortrud cunningly sows in Elsa's mind the seeds of doubt about her champion.

They go off and Telramund enters, concealing himself when, as dawn breaks, trumpeters sound the reveille and a summons to the people. The nobles and retainers arrive. A herald announces that Telramund is banished and that the mysterious knight (Lohengrin) shall marry Elsa, become Guardian of Brabant and lead the Brabantians in war. The royal decrees are acclaimed. Four disaffected nobles, Telramund's friends, are displeased at the prospect of following Lohengrin, and Telramund, defying the decree, reveals himself to them. They conceal him.

Four pages announce the arrival of Elsa and a train of ladies. As she is about to enter the cathedral Ortrud interenes, saying angrily that Elsa occupies her (Ortrud's) right-ul place. She taunts Elsa for not knowing her lover's name. Elsa, astonished, replies that she has entire trust in him, but Ortrud continues to assert that he is a traitor. Lohengrin arrives with the king and comforts Elsa, but now Telramund boldly presents himself. At first all refuse to listen, but Telramund demands of Lohengrin that he disclose his identity, for otherwise he may be suspected of having his origins in evil magic.

Lohengrin contemptuously refuses to answer. Only Elsa can compel him to speak, he says – and he sees that she is deeply troubled. In an ensemble, Ortrud and Telramund rejoice in her doubts, Elsa expresses her wish to know Lohengrin's secret, he prays to heaven to shield her and the king and people reaffirm their confidence. Telramund speaks for a moment to Elsa against Lohengrin, but Lohengrin draws her away and all enter the cathedral.

ACT III

The scene shows the bridal chamber. To the strains of the wedding march, Elsa is led in by the ladies and Lohengrin by the king and nobles, and the couple are soon left alone together. They sing tenderly of their love: but when Lohengrin calls Elsa by her name she is sad at not being able to answer with his, and asks if she may know it. He begs her not to ask, but she presses him more and more impetuously – saying she foresees the day when the swan will come again and Lohengrin will leave her.

At the climax of her demand, the door is flung open and Telramund enters with his four friends. With a single blow, Lohengrin kills him, and the four nobles kneel before Lohengrin. He tells Elsa that their happiness is over, and summons ladies to lead her into the king's presence, where he will disclose his identity to all.

The scene changes to the banks of the Scheldt, where the king and nobles assemble. It is early morning and they are preparing to march off to war. The four nobles enter bearing Telramund's body, followed by Elsa, in mournful mood, and a train of ladies. Finally Lohengrin enters. He tells the king, to everyone's consternation, that he cannot lead the campaign and that Elsa has broken the vow she made and has demanded to know his name and origins.

He now discloses his secret: he is a knight of the Holy Grail, by name Lohengrin, son of Parsifal; and now that his secret is known his power has departed and he must return. He reproaches Elsa, who is crushed by the realization of what she has brought upon them. In despair, she begs him not to leave her, and the king and people add their voices to her plea. But Lohengrin cannot stay. He predicts a glorious victory for the German armies: then the swan appears, drawing an empty boat. He greets it: 'My trusty swan' (Mein lieber Schwan); then he embraces Elsa in a final farewell, handing her his sword, horn and ring to give to her brother Gottfried if he should return.

Suddenly Ortrud steps forward in apparent triumph. She tells Elsa that she had transformed Gottfried into a swan, the swan who now serves Lohengrin; if Lohengrin had been able to stay he would have been able to restore him to human form, but now the opportunity is gone. Lohengrin sinks to his knees in prayer. In response, a white dove appears over his boat, the swan sinks and re-emerges as Gottfried, to Ortrud's rage. The Brabantians bow before Gottfried, who will now rule them. The dove draws the boat away, Lohengrin in it. As Elsa sees him go she falls lifeless into her brother's arms.

* * * * *

Lohengrin is an opera of patriotism and spectacle (the two often go together in the theatre). Wagner asks for twelve trumpets on the stage in the opening and final scenes, as well as those in the orchestra, and in the final scene the noblemen are also supposed to arrive on horseback. Musically, however, it is distinguished not by 'big' effects but for its evocation of intimate, lyrical feeling. The overture opens with a suggestion of high, ethereal mystery (the 'divine' mission of Lohengrin):

and towards the end of the overture a theme rings out from
trumpets and trombones to signify the triumph not of Lohengrin's earthly love, but of that divine mission, the mission of
the knights of the Holy Grail to which Lohengrin belongs:

The kinship of this to the example on p. 221 and the first on
p. 272 will be noted.

When Elsa in the first scene tells of her dream of a knight
coming to her rescue it is the 'ethereal' theme which is given
to the orchestra, and Lohengrin on his arrival sings his thanks
to his swan to a phrase which evokes this theme. Naturally,
the return of the swan in the final act brings a return of the
same music.

When Lohengrin first approaches Elsa and declares his
love for her he adds a warning not to ask what his name is:

This is usually called the 'Motive of Warning' (or we might
retitle it 'Ban on Inquiry' – Wagner's actual musical motives
are more precise than any names for them can be). It recurs
prominently – with that bass clarinet which Liszt's orchestra
had to buy! – when Ortrud tempts Elsa to put the forbidden
question to Lohengrin.

TRISTAN UND ISOLDE

Libretto by the composer
First performed: Munich, 1865

Three Acts

Cast in order of singing:

A sailor	*teno*
Isolde, an Irish princess	*sopran*
Brangäne, her attendant	*sopran*
Kurwenal, Tristan's squire	*bariton*
Tristan, a Cornish knight, nephew of King Marke	*teno*
Melot, a courtier	*teno*
King Marke of Cornwall	*bas*
A shepherd	*teno*
A steersman	*bariton*

Chorus of sailors, knights, attendants, etc.

The scene is laid on a ship near Cornwall,
in Cornwall and in Brittany, in legendary times

THIS is a long opera about love and about almost nothing else: sexual passion is expressed with the full force of Wagner's newly enlarged musical language and the full splendour of his newly enlarged orchestra.

Tristan und Isolde is, moreover, the first of Wagner's new-style operas (he preferred the word 'music-dramas') in which a symphonic texture, an interplay of leading-motives and a use of 'endless melody' (Wagner's term) replace the old operatic style, and in which there are no formal ensemble numbers. Dramatically, Wagner clung to the domain of legend, but characteristically altered the old story. In the original, Tristan and Isolde's love is purely the result of sorcery – that is, of the magic potion. In Wagner, their mutual

ove is present from the beginning, and the potion only 'fixes'
t and makes it dominant.

*   *   *   *   *

ACT I

A young sailor is heard singing on board the ship on which
Isolde, with her attendant Brangäne, is being carried from
Ireland, lately conquered, to be the bride of the ageing King
Marke of Cornwall. His voice arouses Isolde, who in conversation with Brangäne vents her angry grief at her fate. When
Isolde asks for air ('Luft!'), Brangäne draws aside the cur-
ains, and a further part of the ship is seen: Tristan, the
king's nephew (who has been charged to bring Isolde back),
and his squire Kurwenal are there with the sailors.

The voice of the young sailor is again heard. Isolde gazes
contemptuously at Tristan; then she orders Brangäne to
summon him. Kurwenal warns Tristan of Brangäne's approach. Tristan is unwilling to go to Isolde and Kurwenal,
rather insolently, makes his excuses – that Tristan owes no
allegiance to an Irishwoman. Tristan is embarrassed, especially when Kurwenal sings loudly (echoed by the crew) as
Brangäne goes.

Isolde, alone with Brangäne, is enraged by Tristan's refusal
to come. She tells Brangäne how Tristan, wounded in a fight
in which he had killed her betrothed, came to her, under the
false name of Tantris, and how she overcame her desire for
revenge and nursed him back to strength. And now she, Ireland's princess, has to submit to the indignity of being conveyed by the man whose life she saved to be the bride of his
elderly monarch. She curses him angrily.

Brangäne tries to comfort her by pointing out that Tristan
is bringing her to be a queen. She does not perceive the true
cause for Isolde's grief and humiliation – her love for Tristan:
when Isolde mentions love, Brangäne thinks she refers to her
future husband, and says that the magic potions of Isolde's
mother can be used to keep his love alive and strong. Thoughts
of such potions lead Isolde to the idea of poisoning herself
and Tristan.

Shouts are heard from the sailors: the ship is nearing land
Kurwenal comes to call the women, but Isolde tells him tha
she will not consent to be led ashore by Tristan unless h
first comes to seek her forgiveness. When Kurwenal goe
Isolde tells Brangäne to prepare poisoned drinks for hersel
and Tristan. Brangäne, horrified, protests vehemently. Kur
wenal announces Tristan and retires. Isolde reminds Trista
of the past and how she saved his life when he had killed he
betrothed. He offers her his sword so that she can take re
venge, but instead she suggests that they drink to the end o
their strife. She signs to Brangäne to prepare the draught. I
the distance, the sailors' voices are heard.

Isolde hands him the drink, still taunting him bitterly. A
he takes it he realizes she means to poison them both, and h
– in love with her as he is, but having hitherto concealed ;
love which he knows cannot be fulfilled – drinks willingly
But Brangäne has substituted a love-potion for the poison
They are both instantly overwhelmed by their longing and
fall into each other's arms. As the sailors greet King Marke
Brangäne realizes the consequences of what she has done
Tristan and Isolde sing passionately, unaware of what is happening. Brangäne calls to them as the ship reaches land, to
shouts from the crew, and Kurwenal tells Tristan that Marke
is coming to greet his bride. Brangäne confesses to Isolde that
she gave them a love-potion. As the ship berths and people
clamber on board, Isolde faints on Tristan's breast.

ACT II

From a garden outside King Marke's castle, overlooked by
Isolde's room, sounds of a hunt are heard. It is night, and
Isolde, with Brangäne, impatiently awaits Tristan. As the
sound of horns fades, Isolde prepares to give Tristan the
signal. But Brangäne suspects treachery from a courtier,
Melot (who organized the hunting party), and begs her not
to be reckless. Isolde sends Brangäne to where she can keep
watch, while she signals to Tristan by extinguishing the torch
burning on the castle wall.

Tristan comes. In their prolonged duet, they explore their

ove; they denounce the day (which keeps them apart) and welcome the night. Passionate strains lead to the quieter ecstasy of 'O sink upon us, night of love' (O sink hernieder, Nacht der Liebe). As they embrace, the voice of the watchful Brangäne is heard for a moment in warning. Later, as the night is succeeded by day, Brangäne warns them again.

Suddenly Kurwenal enters, calling to Tristan to save himself. At the same time the courtiers, led by Melot and King Marke, arrive, and Brangäne comes from her watching-place. The lovers are discovered. Melot asks Marke if he now thinks his warnings justified. Marke, in a long soliloquy, shows his bitter grief at the faithlessness of his long-truted friend and nephew.

Tristan asks Isolde if she would follow him to the gloomy land to which he must go. She says that she would. In fury, Melot draws his sword to challenge Tristan; Tristan charges him with duplicity and is about to fight, but then lowers his guard, allowing Melot to wound him. He sinks into Kurwenal's arms and Isolde flings herself on to his breast.

ACT III

Tristan, gravely wounded, has withdrawn to his father's castle in Brittany. A shepherd plays a melancholy strain on his pipe and inquires from the faithful Kurwenal about the health of Tristan, who is sleeping on a couch which has been placed under a lime tree. Tristan stirs and, bewildered, asks Kurwenal where he is: he can remember little except of Isolde, for whom he expresses his great longing. To his delight, Kurwenal promises to have Isolde brought to him.

Tristan expresses his warmth of feeling towards Kurwenal, and excitedly anticipates Isolde's coming. But – as the shepherd's pipe is heard, still on its former strain – no ship is within sight, and he lapses again into melancholy. He goes over the past, then becomes agitated again as he remembers the love-potion. Eventually he falls back, unconscious, but soon revives, still thinking of Isolde's coming and growing agitated once more.

At long last the shepherd's pipe gives out a livelier melody

and Kurwenal tells Tristan that it is indeed Isolde's ship.
With mounting excitement Tristan, with Kurwenal, watches
the ship approach. He sends Kurwenal to bring Isolde. As he
waits, Tristan, almost frenzied, tears the bandage from his
wound. Isolde enters and he falls into her arms; in a few
moments he is dead. After trying to revive him she falls upon
his body.

The shepherd comes to tell Kurwenal that a second ship
has arrived. Kurwenal, seeing King Marke and Melot, orders
his men to prepare to defend the castle, despite the entry of
the steersman saying that defence is useless. Brangäne's voice
is heard from below, asking for admittance, then Melot's.
Kurwenal attacks Melot and kills him, shouts defiance to
Marke and fights with Marke's men; he is wounded and dies,
falling at Tristan's feet. Meanwhile Brangäne has entered,
climbing over a wall, and is relieved to find Isolde still living.
Marke had come with only peaceful intentions (Brangäne had
told him about the potions), and is sad and dismayed to find
Tristan dead. Isolde, hardly aware of what is happening,
raptly sings her lament over Tristan's body: 'Mild and softly'
(Mild und leise). At the end she sinks lifeless into Brangäne's
arms, over Tristan's body, and Marke silently invokes a bene-
diction over the dead lovers.

*   *   *   *   *

There are no more famous bars in the history of music
than those which open the prelude of *Tristan und Isolde*:

While the historic novelty of the harmony, and the novelty
of beginning an opera in this way, may not now concern us, the theme is still arresting in itself and for what

Wagner does with it. This is the chief love-motive of the opera and can be melodically separated into two phrases, as quoted in the example on page 232, which have been respectively called 'Avowal' and 'Desire' (this at any rate seems more plausible than an alternative allocation of the first to Tristan and the second to Isolde). Very shortly follows a motive related to this, and usually called the 'Motive of the Love Glance':

The love-duet in Act II prominently quotes and 'develops' the first of these. Then, at the height of ecstasy, Tristan suggests that this is how they should die, never parting, and his melody announces a new theme, that of Love-as-Death (Liebestod):

In the last act when Tristan is dead and Isolde, over his body, is herself looking forward to death, it is this that she sings to the words beginning 'Mild and softly' (Mild und leise). Hence the word 'Liebestod' has been applied – by Liszt first of all, not by Wagner – to the final pages of the work, accompanying Isolde's death. (It is frequently joined to the end of the prelude in concert performances, often with the voice-part taken over by the orchestra.)

Tristan and Isolde's love-music is by intention concretely erotic: its chromatic sensuousness is tellingly contrasted with the diatonic 'upright', extraverted music of Kurwenal and the sailors in Act I.

The music which the shepherd in Act III plays on his pipe

is of a kind never heard before, with its strange intervals and
repetitions:

The pipe is simulated in the orchestra by an English horn —
until a quicker tune is reached (Isolde's ship is sighted at
last!), when, in the modern theatre, the melody is sometimes
taken over by a powerful Hungarian single-reed instrument,
the tárogató, or, regrettably, a trumpet.

DIE MEISTERSINGER
VON NURNBERG

(The Mastersingers of Nuremberg)
Libretto by the composer
First performed: Munich, 1868

Three Acts

Cast in order of singing

Walther von Stolzing, a young Franconian knight		*tenor*
Eva, daughter to Pogner		*soprano*
Magdalene, Eva's maid		*mezzo-soprano*
David, apprentice to Hans Sachs		*tenor*
Veit Pogner, a goldsmith		*bass*
Sixtus Beckmesser, town clerk		*bass*
Hans Sachs, a cobbler		*bass*
Kunz Vogelgesang, a furrier		*tenor*
Konrad Nachtigall, a tinsmith		*bass*
Fritz Kothner, a baker	Mastersingers	*bass*
Hermann Ortel, a soap-boiler		*bass*
Balthasar Zorn, a pewterer		*tenor*
Augustin Moser, a tailor		*tenor*
Ulrich Eisslinger, a grocer		*tenor*

Hans Foltz, a coppersmith   }   { *bass*
Hans Schwarz, a stocking-weaver } Mastersingers { *bass*
A nightwatchman   *bass*
          Chorus of apprentices, burghers, girls, etc.

The scene is laid in Nuremberg in the mid-16th century

The Mastersingers (as the title is usually abbreviated) is Wagner's only comic opera – and a most successful one, with real comedy backed by the lyric inspiration of the Prize Song and the springing vigour of the various choruses. It is an opera about the triumph of real, living art over false academic art, and Wagner saw the victory of the young knight Walther as representing his own victory over crabbed criticism. Such criticism is represented in the opera by the character of Beckmesser whom, in the original form of the libretto, Wagner named Hans Lick. No wonder that Eduard Hanslick, the bitterly anti-Wagnerian Viennese music critic, walked out of a private reading of the libretto!

Hans Sachs, the central character among the Mastersingers, was a historical personage (1494–1576), a shoemaker and poet. The chorus of acclamation to Sachs in Act III of the opera ('Wach' auf') is in fact a setting of words by the real Sachs. The Mastersingers were, historically, a middle-class type of minstrel as distinct from the aristocratic minstrels (Minnesingers) whom Wagner had already celebrated in *Tannhäuser*. The opera is not without its patriotic appeal: at the end, the triumphant Walther is ready to turn his back on the Mastersingers who originally spurned him, but is persuaded to join them when Sachs puts forward the claim of 'holy German art'.

*   *   *   *   *

ACT I

At a service in the church of St Catherine, at Nuremberg, the final hymn is being sung. The young knight Walther von Stolzing, a visitor to the town, is watching Eva, the daughter

of Pogner the goldsmith. As the service ends he approaches
her; she contrives to send her maid, Magdalene, away
momentarily and he asks if she is betrothed. Magdalene, over-
hearing as she returns, explains that Eva's hand is to be the
prize in a song contest to be held by the Mastersingers the
next day. Walther does not fully understand. But presently
David (an apprentice, betrothed to Magdalene) comes, with
other apprentices, to prepare the scene for a preliminary
song trial; and, after Eva and Magdalene have gone, he
explains to Walther some of the complexities of the rules of
song.

The apprentices, their preparations complete, retire to the
back as Pogner enters, with Beckmesser, who is not only
town clerk but also himself an aspirant to Eva's hand. Walther
greets Pogner, saying he wishes to become a Mastersinger;
Pogner welcomes him and introduces him to the other Masters
as they enter. Finally Sachs arrives and Kothner calls the
roll. When this is done Pogner addresses the Masters – 'Now
hear!' (Nun hört)* – announcing that the victor in the next
day's contest may claim the hand of Eva, as long as she is
willing to accept him. The Masters and apprentices are excited by this and a discussion ensues, Beckmesser demanding
strict adherence to the rules of song while Sachs would permit
a freer style.

Pogner inroduces Walther as a candidate for membership of
the guild. In answer to their questions he says, in his song
'By silent hearth' (Am stillen Herd), that his teacher was
Walther von der Vogelweide, an ancient Minnesinger, and
that he studied 'in nature'. The Masters are unimpressed, but
he is allowed to proceed with a song. Beckmesser is appointed
Marker (to count the faults in his song) and retires into the
Marker's box with a slate and chalk. Kothner tells Walther
some of the rules and Beckmesser calls to him to begin. He
sings a song of love: 'So cried the spring' (So rief der Lenz).
As he sings, noisy scratchings are heard from the marker's
box, and before he has finished Beckmesser emerges, his slate
completely covered with chalk marks (he has realized that

* English version by Ernest Newman (Breitkopf & Härtel).

Walther is a rival for Eva's hand and is at pains to discredit him).

The other Masters agree that the song was not in accord with the rules and that Walther should be rejected, but Sachs speaks up for Walther, saying that although his song does not conform to the Masters' rules it is different in kind and demands new rules of its own. He also mentions that Beckmesser is not as disinterested as a marker must be. Beckmesser replies that the cobbler should stick to his last. Sachs tells Walther to continue singing. As he does so, Beckmesser angrily shows his catalogue of faults to the other Masters, who agree that Walther is not qualified to be a Mastersinger (and so cannot enter the contest). The apprentices and David join in the general hubbub. As he finishes, Walther proudly goes off and the meeting breaks up in disorder, Sachs remaining deep in thought as the others disperse.

ACT II

That evening, the apprentices sing of the morrow, St John's Day ('Johannistag') as, in the street, they close their masters' shutters. Magdalene comes and learns from David that Walther has failed. The other apprentices are teasing David about Magdalene when Sachs arrives and takes him into the workshop. Pogner and Eva enter, and sit talking on a bench. Before Eva follows her father indoors she learns from Magdalene of Walther's failure.

Sachs emerges from his shop, sends David off and settles down to work out of doors under an elder tree: 'The elder's scent subdues me' (Was duftet doch der Flieder) – the 'Fliedermonolog'. Eva comes to seek his advice. Sachs, a widower, is deeply fond of her himself, though he realizes not only that he is far too old but also, by her reaction to his apparently slighting reference to Walther, that she really loves the young knight. As Sachs goes indoors, Eva joins Magdalene, who tells her that Beckmesser is coming to serenade her and tries to lead her indoors. Eva asks Magdalene to take her place at the window, and as Walther arrives she goes to his side. He declares his love for her and tells her of his contempt for the Masters and their rules. They arrange to elope and she goes indoors.

The nightwatchman, sounding his horn, comes past. Sachs has overheard their plan to elope and considers it unwise, so he arranges his light to shine on the street so that they would be seen. Eva comes out in Magdalene's clothes and at that moment Beckmesser arrives, with his lute. Walther and Eva conceal themselves as he prepares to sing his serenade. But before Beckmesser begins Sachs starts a noisy cobbling song. Angrily Beckmesser tries to silence him, especially when he sees a woman (Magdalene, whom he takes for Eva) at the window. Sachs continues tormenting him and Beckmesser gets more and more irritated.

Eventually they agree that Sachs shall act as marker during Beckmesser's serenade, being allowed to sound one hammer-stroke on the shoes for each fault in the singing. Beckmesser's grotesque, misaccentuated serenade brings forth blow after blow from Sachs's hammer, to Beckmesser's fury. He sings louder and louder, bringing all the neighbours to their windows. David sees him serenading Magdalene, whom he recognizes, and comes down with a cudgel and gives him a good beating. Neighbours and others are aroused and a general brawl breaks out. In the confusion Walther and Eva try to escape, but Sachs seizes Walther, hands the false Magdalene (really Eva) over to Pogner, who is standing anxiously in his doorway, and pulls Walther into his shop. The nightwatchman's horn is heard and the crowd quickly disperses. When the nightwatchman appears all is peaceful again.

ACT III

Sachs is in his workshop, reading. David enters, in some trepidation after the previous night's doings, but finds his master in benevolent mood. It is St John's Day (Midsummer Day) which, David realizes with a start, must be his master's name-day [Hans = Johannes = John]. When he goes, Sachs ruminates on human folly: 'Mad! Mad!' (Wahn! Wahn!) –

the 'Wahnmonolog'. Walther, who has been staying overnight at Sachs's house, comes in. He tells Sachs of a song revealed to him in a dream and eventually sings it to him: 'Bright in the sunlight' (Morgenlich leuchtend). Sachs, impressed, writes down the words of the two stanzas Walther sings. They go off to prepare themselves for the contest of song.

A moment later Beckmesser enters the shop, looking somewhat the worse for his drubbing the previous night. He notices the manuscript in Sachs's handwriting on the table and, seeing Sachs coming, quickly pockets it. In their ensuing conversation Beckmesser accuses Sachs of trying to discredit him because he is intending to compete himself, producing the song as evidence. Sachs assures him that he is not, saying that he may keep the song and sing it if he wishes to, promising, in answer to Beckmesser's request, that he will not claim its authorship for himself.

Beckmesser departs and Eva enters, on the pretext of an uncomfortable shoe. Walther comes in and the lovers stare raptly at one another. While Sachs repairs Eva's shoe, Walther bursts into song (producing spontaneously the third, final verse required to give his song complete musical form). In profound gratitude and emotion, Eva falls weeping on Sachs's breast. He passes her to Walther and talks of the sad life of a cobbler. Eva says that she would happily have chosen Sachs as her husband if she were not so much in love with Walther. Magdalene and David come in and Sachs promotes David (with the customary box on the ear) from apprentice to journeyman ('Geselle'). Then all, led by Eva, join in a quintet of happiness: 'Blessed as the dawning' (Selig, wie die Sonne).

As horns and trumpets ring out festively, the scene changes to a meadow outside Nuremberg. Large crowds are gathering, the various guilds of the city marching ceremoniously in with banners flying. The apprentices, festively attired, guide people to their places. The tailors sing a story of Nuremberg which involves comic choral imitation of a goat. There is lively dancing from the journeymen, the apprentices (with them David) and girls. The gathering is completed by the majestic entry of the Mastersingers themselves, heralded by trumpets. Pogner leads in Eva, who is attended by Magdalene and other maidens.

The apprentices call for silence and Sachs steps forward to be acclaimed by the people: 'Arise, the day is dawning (Wach' auf!). With some emotion, he announces the terms of the contest. Pogner thanks him. Meanwhile Beckmesser has vainly been trying to memorize the words of the pirated song. (The music was not written down; he must compose his own.) He is the first contestant and Kothner calls on him to sing. He clambers up on to the rostrum, almost falling as he does so, and looking so ludicrous that the crowd begins to titter. Rather uneasily, he plays some chords on his lute and starts. His melody is ridiculously ugly and he confuses Walther's words so hopelessly that they emerge as completely absurd. The Masters and people are astonished. Eventually Beckmesser, having provoked everyone's ridicule, rounds on Sachs, saying that he was the writer of the song. The Masters and people are shocked and demand an explanation. Sachs says that he could not write so fine a song himself and he calls on its true composer.

Walther bows to the Masters and steps forward. As he sings his song – the Prize Song – all are struck with its beauty. Though Walther was debarred from the Mastersingers' guild, his is plainly the victory. When he finishes, Eva crowns him with the victor's wreath and they kneel before Pogner, who blesses them. He is about to invest Walther as a Master, but Walther proudly declines. Sachs, however, in an address on the glory of German art, persuades him to accept. Walther accepts the honour from Sachs himself, while Eva takes the wreath from Walther's brow and places it on Sachs's. The people echo Sachs's words and pay him homage.

*   *   *   *   *

The recurring musical motives in *The Mastersingers* are used with great subtlety – great dramatic subtlety, that is, apart from the musical skill with which so many are combined successively and contrapuntally in the overture.

Hardly has the curtain gone up when, after the first line of the congregational hymn, we hear in the orchestra:

Walther is in church to snatch an opportunity of speaking to Eva, and this melody anticipates the Prize Song which Eva's beauty later inspires in Walther and which, in its turn, wins him Eva as his bride.

There is even a reference by means of motive to Wagner's own *Tristan und Isolde* – in Act III (after Beckmesser has left Sachs's room). Sachs as a widower might well have been a suitor for Eva's hand; but he tells Eva that he well knows the story of Tristan and Isolde and does not wish to have the role of King Marke!

Beckmesser's role has rare comedy in music, especially in the scene of his serenade to the disguised Magdalene, whom he takes for Eva. In this serenade, with its absurdly 'decorative' lute accompaniment (usually played in the theatre on a harp with newspaper between the strings!), each false accent committed by Beckmesser is marked by a blow of Sachs's hammer. For instance, the accent should fall on the first syllable of 'schönes' and 'Fräulein' but does not:

We may wonder indeed how Beckmesser ever came to be made a Mastersinger in the first place!

The lute serves also to emphasize the period atmosphere of the opera, as does the Nightwatchman's song and the hymn which opens the first act. In a further deliberate ges-

ture, Wagner also founded two of his principal leading-
motives on two old tunes reproduced in a 17th-century book.
One of these old tunes became the march of the Mastersingers:

We encounter this in full in the overture and again in the
final scene – both times in C major, the key which significantly also begins and ends the opera. In this key too we
encounter Walther's Prize Song, both when it is 'composed'
(Act II) and when it is delivered (Act III); and nothing is
more magical in it than the orchestral chord of C major which
precedes it. The special lay-out and tone-colour of this chord
gives it the distinctiveness of a leading-motive in itself!

DER RING DES NIBELUNGEN

(The Nibelung's Ring)

IN 1848 Wagner completed a libretto for an opera to be called *The Death of Siegfried*. He later decided that three other operas should precede it in performance, dealing with earlier events in the same story. He completed and published the librettos of all four in 1853 and in the same year began working on the music. He finished the last opera in 1874, and the first performance of the complete cycle of four was given in 1876 in the opening season of the new Festival Theatre at Bayreuth (Bavaria) – a theatre built to Wagner's own specification. The two first operas of the cycle had already been given separately at Munich.

The cycle itself Wagner named *Der Ring des Nibelungen*, or *The Nibelung's Ring*. (Only *one* Nibelung in the title, be it noted: it is Alberich.) He described it as 'a theatre festival play for three days and a preliminary evening'. The individual operas are named *Das Rheingold* (The Rhinegold), *Die Walküre* (The Valkyrie), *Siegfried* and *Götterdämmerung** (Twilight of the Gods) – the last of these corresponding to the original conception of *The Death of Siegfried*.

The basic material of the story was taken by Wagner from the old legend – which appears in German form as an epic poem, the Nibelunglied, and in Scandinavian form in prose, the Volsunga Saga (not identical with the other in detail). Apart from the now standardized English forms Valkyrie and Valhalla (both from the Scandinavian source) Wagner's own German forms of proper names are used, as is customary, in the following pages. The Nibelungs are a race of dwarfs; the story also deals with gods, men and giants.

Theatrically *The Ring* is opera's colossus. The sheer musical planning involved would compel admiration; but we must add to this an amazing psychological skill in the shaping of

---

* Not '*Die* Götterdämmerung'.

the actual themes. The use of myth, though far from new in opera, was intended to give a special and symbolic universality to the drama – a universality which has been seized upon in the style of production associated particularly with post-war Bayreuth.

Wagner made opera not only bigger but more solemn. It was Bayreuth which established the modern convention that the auditorium is darkened during the performance and that late-comers to opera are prevented from taking their seats in mid-act. Opera as an after-dinner diversion is not consistent with a performance of *Das Rheingold*, in one unbroken act lasting more than two-and-a-half hours.

A continuous development of leading-motives goes right through all the four operas of *The Ring*. In the following pages, therefore, we first of all tell the story itself as it runs through all four, and then discuss some of the musical aspects of the complete work.

DAS RHEINGOLD

(The Rhinegold)

Part I of 'The Ring'

Libretto by the composer
First performed: Munich, 1869

One Act

Cast in order of singing:

Woglinde ⎫		*soprano*
Wellgunde ⎬ Rhinemaidens		*soprano*
Flosshilde ⎭		*mezzo-soprano*
Alberich, a Nibelung		bass-baritone
Fricka, wife of Wotan and goddess of marriage		*mezzo-soprano*
Wotan, ruler of the gods		bass-baritone
Freia, sister of Fricka and goddess of love and spring		*soprano*

| Fasolt | } giants | { | bass-baritone |
| Fafner | | | bass |

Froh, god of joy and youth .... *tenor*
Donner, god of thunder .... *bass-baritone*
Loge, god of fire and cunning .... *tenor*
Mime, a Nibelung, Alberich's brother .... *tenor*
Erda, goddess of earth and wisdom .... *mezzo-soprano*

*The scene is laid in the Rhine, on a mountain above
the Rhine and in the underground caverns of
Nibelheim, in legendary times*

IN the waters of the Rhine, the three Rhinemaidens, Wog-inde, Wellgunde and Flosshilde, are playing. Their task is to guard the river's treasure, the Rhinegold. The grotesque dwarf Alberich comes and watches; entranced by their beauty, he longs to possess one of them. All three in turn tease him cruelly. As he angrily pursues them, his eye is caught by the gleam of the Rhinegold. They tell him of its magic – of how the man who fashions a ring from it, if he renounces love, will become supremely powerful. As the maidens idly play, Alberich, angry and frustrated, moves towards the gold and suddenly snatches it away, to the Rhinemaidens' consternation – uttering the required reunuciation, 'Love I curse now for ever!' (So verfluch ich die Liebe).

The waves and rocks disappear into darkness: in their place there appears a splendid castle on a mountain height, with the Rhine visible far below. It is the newly built home of the gods. Outside it Wotan, ruler of the gods, and his wife Fricka are sleeping. As they awake, Wotan contemplates the great castle. Fricka chides Wotan for the promise he made to its builders, the giants Fafner and Fasolt, to give them her sister Freia as their reward. Freia herself enters, asking to be protected from the giants. Wotan is relying on help from Loge, god of fire and cunning, to extricate him from his promise.

The giants come and Fasolt demands their reward. Wotan temporizes. In response to Freia's call for help, two more

gods, Froh and Donner, enter. Donner threatens the giant
with his hammer while Froh embraces Freia. Then Loge
arrives. He admits, to Wotan's anger, that he has found no
alternative payment to suggest; but he goes on (deliberately
tempting the giants) to tell of the theft by Alberich of the
Rhinegold, mentioning that the Rhinemaidens have asked
Wotan to help them recover it.

The giants, listening, begin to covet the gold as an alternative to Freia. But Wotan, wishing to have the gold himself
refuses. The giants seize Freia and bear her off as a pledge
giving Wotan until the evening to decide.

Loge watches them depart and turns back to the gods. He
is surprised to see them looking aged and weary. Freia, goddess of youth, has left them. Aroused from his lethargy
Wotan decides to go to Nibelheim (the land of the Nibelungs)
with Loge. The scene changes as they descend deep into the
earth, and the banging of anvils is heard as they reach Nibelheim.

In an underground cavern in Nibelheim Alberich, who
now possesses a Ring formed from the gold, is berating his
brother Mime. Mime has just forged from the gold a magic
helmet, the Tarnhelm, which allows its wearer to take on any
form or become invisible. Alberich puts it on, becomes invisible, beats his brother and goes off, triumphant in his possession of the gold and its power. Wotan and Loge arrive and try
unsuccessfully to console Mime. Alberich returns, driving
before him more Nibelungs, carrying gold and silver trinkets
which they pile up. He brutally sends them back to work,
Mime among them.

In the course of a long scene between the two gods and
Alberich, Loge cleverly leads on the dwarf, who boasts of
his power and predicts the gods' downfall. Wotan overcomes
his anger as he sees Loge's plan working. Alberich tells how
he can transform himself into different forms. Loge pretends
to doubt him, so he changes himself first into a dragon, then
into a toad – when Wotan promptly puts his foot on him
Loge seizes the Tarnhelm. As Alberich returns to human
shape they bind him and take him off as their prisoner.

The reverse of the previous scene-change takes place, and we are transported back to the mountain heights where the gods' new castle stands, shrouded in mist. As ransom for Alberich's freedom, Wotan and Loge demand the Rhinegold. Angrily and grudgingly, he agrees. They untie him, as the Nibelungs bring the treasures and pile them up at his command. He asks to be released, but first Loge demands the Tarnhelm, then Wotan the Ring. Defiantly, Alberich refuses to part with the Ring and finally Wotan has to tear it from his finger. Contorted with rage, he curses the Ring and all who shall possess it ('Verflucht sei dieser Ring!') before he departs.

The mist clears as Donner, Froh and Fricka enter, and a few moments later Fasolt and Fafner bring in Freia. They refuse to hand her over until the ransom is paid, and Fasolt is so sorry to part with her that he insists that the amount of gold be sufficient to hide her. Wotan agrees, and Loge and Froh pile up the hoard. Fricka and Donner are much grieved at Freia's humiliation. To conceal her hair, visible at the top, the Tarnhelm is added, and, finally, when a crevice in the great pile discloses her eyes, the giants demand the Ring. When Wotan refuses, Fasolt angrily seizes Freia and makes as if to go. All press Wotan to give way. Then Erda, goddess of the earth, wisdom and destiny, appears, and solemnly warns him to part with the cursed Ring.

Wotan eventually decides to do so: Freia is freed, and embraces the other gods joyfully. The giants start sharing out the gold. Fafner demands that he should have the larger share, as it was Fasolt who was particularly willing to resign all the gold for Freia. When it comes to the Ring itself, the two fight and Fasolt is killed. The curse laid on the Ring is already working.

Fafner goes off: Loge ironically congratulates Wotan on having parted with the Ring. As Wotan, deeply troubled, determines to consult Erda, Fricka bids him enter their castle with her. Swinging his hammer, Donner now calls forth a mighty thunderstorm ('Heda, hedo!'); then the clouds disperse, and Donner and Froh are seen at the foot of a dazz-

ling, radiant rainbow bridge stretching across the valley t
the castle. After being seized with a new, grand idea, Wota
greets the castle, names it Valhalla (Walhall) and leads Frick
across the rainbow bridge, followed by Froh, Freia an
Donner, while Loge stands by and watches them with wr
detachment. From below, the mournful singing of the robbec
Rhinemaidens is heard, to Wotan's irritation: the security o
mighty Valhalla is threatened by the curse on one smal
golden ring.

DIE WALKÜRE

(The Valkyrie)

Part II of 'The Ring'

Libretto by the composer

First performed: Munich, 1870

Three Acts

Cast in order of singing:

Siegmund ⎱ the Wälsungs, twin brother and sister, ⎰		*teno*
Sieglinde ⎰ children of Wotan by a mortal woman ⎱		*sopran*
Hunding, husband of Sieglinde		*bas*
Wotan, ruler of the gods		*bass-bariton*
Brünnhilde, a Valkyrie, daughter of Wotan and the goddess Erda		*sopran*
Fricka, wife of Wotan and goddess of marriage		*mezzo-sopran*

Gerhilde
Helmwige
Waltraute
Schwertleite } Valkyries, daughters of Wotan and Erda, sisters of Brünnhilde   *sopranos an*
Ortlinde   *mezzo-soprano*
Siegrune
Grimgerde
Rossweisse

*The scene is laid in Hunding's hut, a rocky place, and
at the summit of a mountain, in legendary times*

SINCE the events of *Das Rheingold*, Wotan, in union with Erda, has fathered nine warrior-maidens, the Valkyries, whose task is to bring fallen heroes to Valhalla where they can form an army for the gods' defence. Wotan's favourite among these is Brünnhilde. Disguised as a mortal, 'Wälse', he has also fathered twin brother and sister, Siegmund and Sieglinde (known as the Wälsungs), by a mortal mother, in the hope that, as half-gods, his children would help the gods in their struggles against the Nibelungs for the repossession of the Ring.

ACT I

The scene is a forest hut, enclosing the stem of a huge ash tree, belonging to Hunding and his wife Sieglinde. During a storm, Siegmund enters the hut, exhausted and in flight from his enemies, the Neidings. Finding it empty, he lies down to rest. Sieglinde enters. She sees the stranger and brings him water, pressing him to accept shelter until Hunding returns. The two are strongly attracted to one another.

Hunding enters. Suspicious at finding a stranger in his hut, and noting his resemblance to Sieglinde, he asks his name and story. Siegmund says his name is Wehwalt ('Woeful'), son of Wolfe: he tells his story – of the loss of his mother and twin sister, the pursuit of his father and himself by their enemies, and of his fight to save a woman from a marriage she abhorred, a fight in which he lost his weapons. Hunding realizes that this man is an enemy of his race. He tells Siegmund he may stay overnight but the next morning they must meet in combat. He sends Sieglinde off to the other room, but before she goes she looks meaningfully at a particular spot in the ash tree's trunk. Then Hunding follows her.

Alone in the subdued firelight, Siegmund muses on his position, defenceless in his enemy's home, and in love with his enemy's wife. He recalls his father's promise to provide a sword when he needs it. A shaft of light illuminates the point on the ash stem which Sieglinde had indicated.

As it becomes completely dark, Sieglinde, in night clothes, enters. She has drugged Hunding and comes to warn Siegmund to escape. She relates the story of her wedding-feast, where she sat in sadness as Hunding's kinsmen celebrated, and an old man clad in grey came in and plunged a sword deep into the ash tree; many strong men have tried, without success, to withdraw it. Both Siegmund and she realize that he is the man for whom it was intended. The two feel themselves irresistibly drawn together: they embrace passionately. The door flies open, disclosing the beauty of the night, and Siegmund sings of love and spring: 'Winter storms have waned' (Winterstürme wichen). She responds passionately. He tells her that his father's name was really Wälse, and he is a Wälsung: they know now that they are brother and sister, and she gives him his true name, Siegmund ('Victory'). He pulls forth the sword, to Sieglinde's delight, calling it Nothung ('Needful'). With renewed ecstasy the lovers again embrace.

Act II

Siegmund has taken Sieglinde away with him and Hunding is in pursuit. Wotan, wishing to protect Siegmund as his son, has summoned Brünnhilde to the wild, rocky place where he stands. He tells her to support Siegmund against Hunding. She sounds her war-cry ('Ho-jo-to-ho!'), warns Wotan of Fricka's approach, and goes off.

Fricka arrives, in a chariot drawn by two rams. As goddess of marriage, she demands of Wotan that Siegmund be punished by being duly killed by Hunding. Wotan is unwilling but finally consents: 'Take my oath!' (Nimm' den Eid!).

Brünnhilde's war-cry as she returns has already been heard. Now, as Fricka leaves, she enters. She is distressed to see her father so unhappy. He tells her the story of Alberich and the Ring, of Erda's prediction of the gods' downfall, and the gods' struggle to avert it – through the Valkyries (who will bring an army of heroes to Valhalla) and through Wotan's own half-godly children. But now Siegmund has to die, to satisfy Fricka. In bitter despair, he realizes the inevitability of the gods' downfall. Brünnhilde, appalled, remonstrates with him and begs that Siegmund be allowed to win, as Wotan had at

irst ordered. But now, with anger, he orders Brünnhilde to
ensure Hunding's victory.

Both go off. Shortly Siegmund and Sieglinde enter, in
light; Siegmund is trying to calm the agitated Sieglinde, now
ull of remorse. In her fevered imagination, she hears the
distant sound of horns – she believes that Hunding and his
kinsmen, with hounds, are in hot pursuit, and she visualizes
he scene of Siegmund's death at their hands. She faints, and
Brünnhilde enters.

[Now begins the part of the opera known as the 'Announcement of Death' (Todesverkündigung).] Brünnhilde tells
Siegmund that he is to go to Valhalla with her. But when, in
reply to his questioning, she says that Sieglinde cannot go
with him, he refuses even the honour of Valhalla. She offers
to protect Sieglinde and their unborn child after his death,
but Siegmund draws his sword: he will kill the sleeping Sieglinde rather than leave her defenceless. Brünnhilde, much
moved, stops him, saying that she will, after all, ensure his
victory.

Brünnhilde departs. Siegmund bids farewell to the sleeping Sieglinde and goes off to meet Hunding in battle. As she
stirs in her sleep, a thunderstorm breaks. In the lightning
flashes, Hunding and Siegmund can be seen as they seek one
another, shouting their defiance. Soon they meet and fight.
Brünnhilde is seen protecting Siegmund with her shield. As
Siegmund is about to strike Hunding down, Wotan himself
appears, in a red glow: Siegmund's sword shatters on Wotan's
spear, and Hunding kills Siegmund. Brünnhilde lifts Sieglinde on to her horse and bears her off, gathering up the
broken pieces of the sword. Wotan sadly contemplates Siegmund's body, and, at a wave of his hand, Hunding falls dead.
Then, vowing to punish Brünnhilde's disobedience, Wotan
disappears.

ACT III

The 'Ride of the Valkyries' is heard. The Valkyries have been
carrying the bodies of heroes to Valhalla on their horses, and

now they gradually assemble on a mountain peak. They comment that Brünnhilde is missing. Eventually she comes – supporting Sieglinde. They are all horrified to learn of her defiance of Wotan's command and are unwilling to help her conceal Sieglinde from their father.

Sieglinde revives and tells them that she does not wish to live, but rallies when she is told that she is to bear Siegmund's child. Brünnhilde sends her eastward, to the forests – Wotan is unlikely to go there, since in that region are the Ring and the rest of the Rhine's treasure, protected by Fafner in his shape as a dragon. Before Sieglinde goes, Brünnhilde gives her the fragments of Siegmund's sword, telling her that her unborn son is to be a great hero, to be called Siegfried; he must re-forge the sword, and will be universally victorious.

Wotan arrives, in a fierce storm. The eight Valkyries at first shield Brünnhilde, but she steps forward when he calls on her. In furious rage, he pronounces his sentence. She was his favourite, he says, but she has turned against him. He rejects her completely: she is no longer to be a Valkyrie but an ordinary mortal, to lie in sleep until a man shall awaken her and take her as his wife. The Valkyries, appalled at his severity, beg for leniency, but he refuses to give way and dismisses them, warning them not to help her.

The Valkyries ride off and Brünnhilde is left alone with her father. She begs him to be merciful, pleading that she carried out his true wishes in defending the Wälsung, despite his later command. She tells him of her meeting with Siegmund and mentions the child that Sieglinde is to bear. Wotan remains unmoved and repeats his sentence.

Brünnhilde falls on her knees before him and asks that some great difficulty be placed before anyone wishing to awaken her, so that only a hero dares to venture there. Deeply affected, he agrees to encircle her with fire. They embrace and bid each other a solemn farewell. He closes the visor of her helmet and covers her with her shield. Then he describes a circle round her with his spear, calling on Loge, the god of fire. The ring of fire appears. Wotan proclaims that no one who fears his (Wotan's) spear shall penetrate the fire. With a

orrowful look back at Brünnhilde, Wotan disappears through
he flames.

SIEGFRIED

Part III of 'The Ring'

Libretto by the composer
First performed: Bayreuth, 1876

Three Acts

Cast in order of singing:

Mime, a Nibelung, brother of Alberich	*tenor*
Siegfried, son of Siegmund and Sieglinde	*tenor*
The Wanderer (Wotan, ruler of the gods, disguised)	*bass-baritone*
Alberich, a Nibelung	*bass-baritone*
Fafner, a giant, now in the form of a dragon	*bass*
The voice of a wood-bird	*soprano*
Erda, goddess of earth and wisdom	*mezzo-soprano*
Brünnhilde, formerly a Valkyrie	*soprano*

*The scene is laid in a forest and on a mountain,
in legendary times*

IN the time that has elapsed since the action of *Die Walküure*,
Sieglinde has died in giving birth to Siegfried. The dwarf,
Mime, brought up Siegfried in the knowledge that Siegfried
would be able to kill Fafner, who obtained possession of the
Ring and, to guard it, has assumed the form of a dragon.
Mime plans that he will thereupon kill Siegfried and obtain
the Ring and the treasure which Fafner now holds.

ACT I

The opening scene takes place in Mime's cavern, where the
dwarf is at work forging a sword. No ordinary sword, he re-

flects, will do for Siegfried, who simply breaks them like toys
only his father's sword, Nothung, will suffice, and Mime i
unable to repair the fragments of it which Siegfried's dyin
mother left behind.

Siegfried enters, driving a bear (to Mime's terror), whic
he soon despatches back into the forest. Mime hands Sieg
fried his newest sword, which Siegfried tries and promptl
breaks, expressing his contempt for Mime's work. Mim
chides him for his ingratitude, and reminds Siegfried of ho
he has cared for him. Siegfried only expresses his arrogan
loathing of the dwarf.

Siegfried now demands to know who his mother an
father were. Mime at first says he is both father and mothe
to Siegfried; then, when Siegfried threatens to strangle hin
if he does not reveal the truth, he tells him of Sieglinde an
shows Siegfried the fragments of 'Nothung'. Siegfried order
Mime to make a new sword from it, so that he can go awa
properly armed, and never return to see Mime again. H
goes out, leaving Mime to prepare the sword.

Mime tries unsuccessfully to forge the sword. A Wandere
enters (Wotan, in disguise). He asks for hospitality, whic
Mime is unwilling to grant. The Wanderer asks Mime to tes
his wits with three questions, with his head as forfeit if h
fails. He answers all three correctly – about the Nibelungs
the giants and the gods – then asks Mime to answer three i
return, on the same conditions. In fear and trembling, Mim
agrees and correctly gives the answer to the first (the race o
Wälsungs) and to the second (Nothung). For the third ques
tion, the Wanderer asks who will repair the sword. The terri
fied Mime cannot answer, and the Wanderer tells him tha
the sword can only be mended by one who has never know
fear.

The Wanderer goes off – forbearing to claim Mime's life
saying that the 'fearless' one will take it – and a few moment
later Siegfried returns, to find Mime hiding. Mime tells hin
what the Wanderer said and tries to explain, but Siegfrie
cannot understand: he does not know what 'fear' means. H
impatiently decides to re-make the sword himself; as he doe

ɔ, Mime resolves presently to guide Siegfried to Fafner (the
ɾragon), then poison Siegfried when he has killed Fafner and
ɪken the Ring. Siegfried sings his forging song – 'Nothung!
Ɍothung!' – and eventually finishes his hammering. Finally,
ɔ Mime's terror, with one mighty blow of the refashioned
ꞁword he splits the anvil in two.

ꞁcᴛ II

ꞁn the wood, outside the cavern which is Fafner's lair, Albe-
ꞁich is keeping watch at night. The Wanderer arrives: Albe-
ꞁich quickly recognizes him as Wotan and treats him with
ꞁngry contempt, boasting of how, when Fafner dies, he him-
ꞁelf (Alberich) will regain the Ring and conquer Valhalla.
Ꞇhe Wanderer tells him that a young hero, ignorant of the
Ꞧing and the treasure, will soon come and kill Fafner. He
ꞷakens Fafner and both tell him of the boy's coming. Wotan
ꞡoes off and Alberich, aside, continues his watch.

As morning dawns, Siegfried and Mime arrive – Mime has
ꞕromised to teach Siegfried what fear is by showing him the
ꞁragon. Siegfried is dissatisfied with the lesson and sends
Ɇime off. He sits there musing for a while on Mime and on
ꞕis mother, then, during an interlude (the 'Forest Murmurs'),
ꞁistens with growing enchantment to the sounds of the forest
ꞁnd the songs of the birds. He tries to imitate the bird song
ꞁn a reed, then lifts his silver horn and sounds a long call. It
ꞧouses Fafner, the dragon. Siegfried defies him. They fight
ꞁnd Siegfried kills Fafner, who before dying warns him
ꞁgainst Mime.

As Siegfried removes his sword, he is burnt by the dragon's
ꞕlood and automatically puts his hand to his mouth. This
ꞡives him the power to understand bird-song, and he hears
ꞇhe voice of a wood-bird tell of the hoard of treasure, includ-
ꞟng the Tarnhelm and Ring, within the cave. Mime and Al-
ꞕerich arrive as he goes into the cave, quarrelling over the
ꞇreasure. They hide as Siegfried comes out, with the Tarn-
ꞕelm and Ring. Again he hears the bird's voice, this time
ꞷarning him of Mime's treachery. Just then Mime approaches,
ꞇhinking to entrap Siegfried. But the dragon's blood enables

Siegfried to hear what Mime *thinks*, not what he intends t
say. Thus Mime reveals that the drink he now offers Siegfrie
is poison. Siegfried kills him.

Siegfried now sinks down to rest and thought. He cal
again on the bird. This time he is told that a bride, Brünn
hilde, awaits him and at present is sleeping on a rock withi
a circle of fire. In answer to his excited questioning, the bir
says that she can be awakened by a man who knows no fear
Siegfried realizes that he is the man, and the bird leads hin
away towards Brünnhilde. He bears the Tarnhelm and th
Ring.

Act III

At night, in a wild, rocky place, the Wanderer (Wotan) sum
mons the earth-goddess Erda (here also called the Wala), wh
appears from a deep chasm. She suggests that he consult
the Norns (Fates), but he presses her to answer his query -
how can the wheel of destiny be halted, and the fall of th
gods be averted? Erda mentions Brünnhilde, her child and
Wotan's; Wotan recalls her disobedience and punishment
Erda wants only to return to sleep, but Wotan will not let he
go. He tells her that he is now resigned to the gods' downfall
and has bequeathed the world to Siegfried who, feeling no
greed and happy in love, is immune from the Ring's curse
Siegfried will awaken Brünnhilde and they will redeem the
world. He dismisses Erda, who returns underground.

As day dawns, the Wanderer sees Siegfried approaching
led by the bird's voice. He asks Siegfried various questions
about Mime, Fafner, the sword, and how he came to seek
the woman encircled by fire. The answers please him. But
Siegfried grows impatient with the 'old man' and speaks
insolently to him, which annoys Wotan. Eventually, in irritation, Wotan bars the way with his spear. In the gathering
darkness, he points up the mountain towards the glow of the
fire, telling Siegfried he will be unable to pass through the
flames. Both become angrier, and when Wotan says that his
spear broke the sword previously, when Siegfried's father
wielded it, Siegfried is all the more determined. At a single

low, Siegfried shatters Wotan's spear; defeated, Wotan gathers the fragments and goes off.

Siegfried continues on his way up the mountain, as the fire
grows increasingly brighter. Fearless, he sounds his horn and
plunges into the flames. Soon the flames disappear, for Siegfried has passed through them. Brünnhilde is seen sleeping,
in her armour, covered by her shield, wearing her helmet,
with her weapons by her. Her horse too is sleeping there.
Siegfried is astonished and at first thinks that the 'warrior'
is a man. He loosens the helmet and armour, cutting the iron
with his sword. When he realizes it is a woman he is still more
amazed and bewildered – he does not know whom to summon
for help, and calls on his mother. He thinks the strange emotions and desires he feels are the mysterious 'fear', about
which he has heard so much.

He calls on the woman to wake, bends over her and kisses
her. Slowly Brünnhilde awakens from her long sleep. She
hails the sun and light, and is enraptured when she realizes
that it is Siegfried who has awakened her. Now Brünnhilde
feels many conflicting emotions – joy at awakening, love of
Siegfried, nostalgic regret at the loss of her identity as a
warrior, shame and even anger at the coming loss of her
maidenhood. She even asks him to leave her, untouched: but
finally his intense ardour arouses her, and they embrace
passionately.

GÖTTERDÄMMERUNG

(Twilight of the Gods)

Part IV of 'The Ring'

Libretto by the composer

First performed: Bayreuth, 1876

Prologue and Three Acts

Cast in order of singing:

The Three Norns (Fates)	*contralto, mezzo-soprano, soprano*
Brünnhilde	*soprano*
Siegfried	*tenor*
Gunther, lord of the Gibichungs	*baritone*
Hagen, son of Alberich and half-brother to Gunther	*bass*
Gutrune, Gunther's sister	*soprano*
Waltraute, a Valkyrie	*mezzo-soprano*
Alberich, a Nibelung	*bass-baritone*
Woglinde ⎫	*soprano*
Wellgunde ⎬ Rhinemaidens	*soprano*
Flosshilde ⎭	*mezzo-soprano*

Chorus of Gibich vassals and female attendants

The scene is laid on a rocky mountain, in the Gibichung castle by the Rhine and in a wood by the Rhine, in legendary times

PROLOGUE

AT night, by the rock on which Brünnhilde slept, the three Norns are weaving the rope of Fate. They sing of the crumbling of Wotan's power. The rope breaks. The Norns descend into the earth for ever.

The sun begins to rise and Brünnhilde and Siegfried enter from a cave. They sing of their love. But Siegfried must go in quest of further heroic adventure. As a token of love he gives her the Ring and in return she gives him her horse

Grane. She watches him depart, listening to the sound of his horn fading away in the distance. She is still encircled by the flames – now her defence against any man but Siegfried.

[An orchestral interlude (known as 'Siegfried's Journey down the Rhine') links the Prologue to the next scene.]

Act I

In the castle of the Gibichungs, on the Rhine, live the half-brothers Hagen (Alberich's son) and Gunther, with Gunther's sister Gutrune. They talk of their plans to enhance the Gibichung's fame. Hagen wishes that Gunther should marry Brünnhilde and that Gutrune should become Siegfried's wife. Much cunning will be necessary to arrange this, he says, as only Siegfried can penetrate the flames surrounding Brünnhilde; he suggests that a love-potion be administered to Siegfried by Gutrune so that he should forget Brünnhilde.

In the distance Siegfried's horn is heard. Soon he arrives and is welcomed into the castle hall. The three men talk of the Nibelung's hoard, Siegfried mentioning that he has the Tarnhelm and has given the Ring to a woman. Gutrune, who had gone out, returns with a drinking horn which she gives to Siegfried. He drinks to Brünnhilde; but in doing so (the drink contains a love-potion) he conceives a violent passion for Gutrune. She retires again, and Siegfried asks Gunther if he has a wife. He says he has not, for he wishes only to marry Brünnhilde, who is unattainable as he cannot pass the wall of fire: Siegfried has now altogether forgotten Brünnhilde and in exchange for a promise of Gutrune's hand offers to help him. With a solemn ceremony of blood sacrament, they swear eternal brotherhood. Then they go off, in a boat on the Rhine, to bring back Brünnhilde. Gutrune watches them go, delighted that she is to be Siegfried's wife. Hagen too watches, contemplating the prospect of obtaining the Ring, which he, as Alberich's son, thinks of as his heritage.

The scene changes to the rocky mountain (as in the Prologue) where Brünnhilde is fondly contemplating Siegfried's Ring. She is excited to hear the voice of her sister, Waltraute, and greets her affectionately, telling her of her great joy in

Siegfried's love. Waltraute, desperate with anxiety over the terrible decline in Wotan's power, has come to ask Brünnhilde to give her the Ring, so that it can be returned to the Rhine, thereby allaying the curse on the gods and the world. But to Brünnhilde the Ring is the symbol of Siegfried's love. She sends her sister away empty-handed.

Darkness falls and the flames round the mountain glow more vividly. Brünnhilde hears Siegfried's horn call and prepares to greet him, but is horrified to see a different man approaching. (It is in fact Siegfried, wearing the Tarnhelm and in Gunther's form; his memories of Brünnhilde are entirely erased.) He is a Gibichung, he says, by name Gunther, and he commands her to follow him. She refuses, invoking the Ring's protection. But in a struggle he wrenches it from her finger. Her spirit is now broken. He drives her into the cave, calling on his sword to stand between them during the night, in token of his faith to his blood-brother.

ACT II

At night, outside the Gibichungs' Hall, Alberich comes to the sleeping Hagen. He urges his son to act with cunning so as to defeat their enemies, telling him to help complete the overthrow of the declining gods and to obtain the Ring from Siegfried.

As day dawns, Alberich goes; soon Siegfried arrives and tells Hagen of his success. Hagen calls Gutrune, who questions Siegfried about events on the mountain and greets him as her betrothed. They enter the hall together to prepare for the wedding.

Hagen places a cowhorn to his lips, summoning the Gibich vassals to come at once and bring their weapons. They arrive in force, anticipating danger. But Hagen tells them that the occasion is a wedding party for Gunther and his bride; sacrifices must be made to Froh, Donner and Fricka, and then all can drink and make merry. The vassals are surprised. A boat bearing Gunther and Brünnhilde draws up and the vassals sing in welcome.

Gunther presents his bride to his people and greets Sieg-

ried, who comes from the hall with Gutrune. Brünnhilde
sees Siegfried and almost faints. She is bewildered at his
failure to recognize her; then bursts out angrily on seeing the
Ring (taken from her by Gunther, as she imagines) on Siegfried's hand. Gunther is puzzled and cannot answer; Brünnhilde then accuses Siegfried, who says he obtained it when
he killed the dragon. Now Hagen intervenes, saying that Siegfried must have won it by guile, and Brünnhilde, in terrible
anguish, charges Siegfried with betraying her. But he, his
memory of his love for Brünnhilde completely blotted out by
the potion, denies it – his sword, he says, separated them
during their night on the mountain. Gunther, Gutrune and
the people are much disturbed.

Siegfried, placing his hand on the point of Hagen's spear,
and invoking the 'bright weapon' (helle Wehr), takes a
solemn oath on the truth of his story; and Brünnhilde, with
a like invocation, dedicates the spear to his destruction. The
bystanders call the gods as witness. Siegfried nonchalantly
advises Gunther to send Brünnhilde to where she can rest,
then, taking Gutrune by the arm, he calls on the men to follow him in to the wedding feast.

Brünnhilde, Hagen and Gunther remain. Brünnhilde bewails her terrible dilemma, with its conflict of love and hate.
Hagen approaches and offers to help her. Eventually she discloses that Siegfried's one vulnerable spot is his back. Hagen
turns to the downcast Gunther, telling him that only Siegfried's death can purge his shame. Brünnhilde willingly agrees,
and all three determine that he shall die. Hagen suggests that
the deed be done during a hunting party the next day. The
bridal procession emerges from the hall and Gunther and
Brünnhilde join it.

ACT III

Near where Siegfried and others are out hunting, the three
Rhinemaidens are seen swimming in the river where it passes
through a woody and rocky valley. They are lamenting the
loss of their gold. Siegfried, separated from the rest of the
huntsmen, enters. The Rhinemaidens talk to him teasingly

and ask if he will give them his Ring. He refuses, then late
offers it to them. They tell him to keep it, saying that its curs
will soon be fulfilled on him. Their threats leave him all th
more determined to keep the Ring, and they swim off.

Hagen, Gunther and other huntsmen arrive, and a meal i
prepared. Hagen asks Siegfried what game he has won: none
he tells them, but he met some 'water birds' who predicte
his death. The three men drink, then Hagen asks Siegfrie
about his understanding of bird-song. In reply, Siegfried tell
the story of the sword, his killing of Fafner and his contac
with the dragon's blood, his understanding of the birds, hi
taking of the Tarnhelm and Ring, his killing of Mime. Afte
drinking further from a horn in which Hagen has squeeze
the juice of a herb, to revive his memory, he resumes, an
begins to recall how he passed through the fire and arouse
Brünnhilde. Gunther, astonished, begins to comprehend Sieg
fried's relationship to Brünnhilde before he arrived at th
Gibichungs' castle.

Some ravens, portents of death, fly over. Hagen draws Sieg
fried's attention to them and as he turns to watch them Hager
plunges his spear into Siegfried's back. Hagen walks slowl
off as Gunther and the vassals, horrified, kneel at Siegfried'
side. As he lies dying, he recollects his awakening of Brünn
hilde and their love. Night falls: Gunther commands the
vassals to lift up Siegfried's body, and convey it to its funeral
The procession moves off slowly and solemnly in the moon
light.

Mists rise from the Rhine, obscuring the scene: when they
clear we find ourselves once more in the Gibichungs' Hall
Here Gutrune is alone, waiting anxiously for Siegfried to re
turn. Hagen soon comes, and tells her that he has been killed
by a boar, to her intense grief. His body is borne in and she
falls upon it. Gutrune blames her brother, but Gunther tells
her that Hagen was responsible. He defiantly admits it, claim
ing that he was justified: then he goes on to demand the
Ring. Gunther denies his claim and the two fight; despite the
intervention of his vassals, Gunther is killed. Hagen advances
to take the Ring off Siegfried's hand; but suddenly the hand

raises itself menacingly.

Now Brünnhilde enters, having understood all. As Siegfried's rightful wife, she demands vengeance. Gutrune angrily blames her for what has occurred, but Brünnhilde soon silences her. Brünnhilde orders a great funeral pyre to be prepared for Siegfried. As the men build it and the women decorate it with flowers, she recalls his nobility and purity. Ordering Siegfried's body to be taken to the pyre, she draws the Ring from his finger and places it on her own. With a firebrand in her hand, she sends two ravens (Wotan's messengers) to tell Wotan what has happened and to bid Loge to the burning of Valhalla. She lights the pyre and, mounting Grane, she rides into the flames to join Siegfried.

The flames burn more fiercely. As they threaten to burn the hall itself, the Rhine overflows and quenches them. The three Rhinemaidens are in its waves. Hagen, still coveting the Ring, leaps forward into the flood: he is seized by two of the Rhinemaidens and drawn away beneath the waters while the third joyously holds aloft the Ring. As the three swim merrily, playing with the Ring, the Rhine waters subside, and in the distance a glow of fire appears in the sky. The hall of Valhalla, with the gods all assembled, is seen consumed by flames.

*   *   *   *   *

In the admirable exposition of *The Ring* by Aylmer Buesst* no fewer than 112 motives are given. We confine ourselves here to showing *how* a few of them are used.

Certain motives identify *things*. This, in the opening scene of *Das Rheingold*, is one of those which represent the gold itself:

* *The Nibelung's Ring: a handbook to Wagner's opera cycle*, 1952.

In other cases, musical meaning is extended from a thing to
what that thing stands for. When the giants are bickering
with the gods over the payment for Valhalla, Wotan quells
the quarrel by uttering the command 'Halt, wild one! Nothing through force!' and by brandishing his spear:

Wotan's spear stands for the sanctity of contract and oath; so
this motive is also heard, during *Götterdämmerung*, when
Siegfried takes an oath of blood-brotherhood with Hagen.
Siegfried does this only after having been deceived by
Gutrune's love-potion: but an oath remains an oath, so the
'spear motive' recurs.

The meaning of the first example was doubly identified –
on the stage (we *see* the Rhinegold glinting at this point) and
by the word 'Rheingold!'. But the 'spear motive' on its first
full appearance is not identified by words, nor is it sung: it
is enunciated by trombones. It is none the less identified because we see the spear as Wotan brandishes it, and we learn
from Wotan's own conduct to associate his spear with 'contract'. Thus the motive has meaning also in the swearing of
blood-brotherhood in *Götterdämmerung*.

Motives may be musically related because their meanings
are related. Loge the god of fire enters thus (orchestra only):

The flickering semiquavers representing 'fire' reappear in the
'Magic Fire' music to which, in *Die Walküre*, Wotan lays
Brünnhilde to sleep. First they retain their agitated character:
then they are lulled into more restful harmony as the 'sleep
motive' (*y*) and another motive representing 'destiny' or 'inevitability' (*x*) are combined with them:

Sometimes the significance of a motive is deliberately not
made clear at first. At the end of *Das Rheingold*, when Wotan
– just before leading Fricka to Valhalla – is seized with a grand
idea, we hear a trumpet:

Only in *Die Walküre* do we identify this with 'the sword' –
the sword which Wotan places in the hands of the Wälsung
race he has begotten, and which (in *Siegfried*) shatters even
Wotan's own spear.

Similarly at the end of *Die Walküre*, after encircling
Brünnhilde with magic fire, Wotan sings that only one who
knows no fear shall break through it; and his stirring melody,
in Wagner's typical fashion, only half-coincides with the
actual motive which the trombone is busy announcing:

This theme is discovered (in *Siegfried*) to represent Siegfried himself, who *is* fearless.

The 'heroine' of *The Ring* is Brünnhilde, even though she does not appear in Wagner's 'preliminary evening' (*Das Rheingold*) at all. We first meet her as a Valkyrie, when she shares the characteristic music of the other Valkyries and utters her war-cry in this famous (and, to the singer, extremely difficult) melody against a tumultuous orchestral accompaniment:

When in *Siegfried* she awakens from her magic sleep, now all woman and no longer a Valkyrie, her music is changed. Her themes are new (but a subdued snatch of the Valkyrie motive, above, comes through in a reminiscence). At first Brünnhilde is ashamed and upset before Siegfried; then a new motive arises which we might call 'Love's Content', to the words 'Eternal was I, eternal am I':

It is a theme familiar from Wagner's separate concert piece, the *Siegfried Idyll*. Its mood is never struck again in the relationship of Siegfried and Brünnhilde. The theme does not recur in *Götterdämmerung*: the non-recurrence of a motive is as significant as its recurrence.

PARSIFAL

Libretto by the composer
First performed: Bayreuth, 1882

Three Acts

Cast in order of singing:

Gurnemanz, a veteran knight of the Grail	*bass*
A knight of the Grail	*bass*
Two esquires attendant on the knights of the Grail	*soprano, alto*
A knight of the Grail	*tenor*
Kundry, a sorceress	*soprano*
Amfortas, ruler of the knights of the Grail	*baritone*
Third and fourth esquires	*two tenors*
Parsifal, a youth of unknown origin	*tenor*
Titurel, father of Amfortas and former ruler of the knights of the Grail	*bass*
A celestial voice	*alto*
Klingsor, a magician	*bass*
Six flower-maidens	*sopranos*

Chorus of knights, esquires, youths, flower-maidens

The scene is laid in Spain in the 10th century

WE have noted how Lohengrin finally reveals his identity by referring to 'my father Parsifal'. The legend of Parsifal (also spelt Parzival) was set down in the 13th century by Wolfram von Eschinbach (a minstrel whom Wagner brought into *Tannhäuser*). There is a connection with yet a third of Wagner's operas: Wagner originally planned to have Parsifal, in his quest for the Holy Grail, come as a pilgrim to where the dying Tristan lies in the third act of *Tristan und Isolde*. (As Robert L. Jacobs says in his book on Wagner: 'Tristan renounces life for the sake of passion – Parsifal renounces passion for the sake of eternal life'.) Parsifal is the 'Percival' of Malory's *Morte d'Arthur* and Tennyson's *Idylls of the King*.

Thus, after the heathen legend of *The Ring*, Wagner turned to the Christian legend of the Grail for his last opera. He called *Parsifal* '*ein Bühnenweihfestspiel*', perhaps best translated 'a sacred festival drama'; and something like a Holy Communion is enacted on the stage. Consequently the request is often made of audiences to abstain from applause. This may be logically indefensible (the make-believe rite is not the real rite) but it is the culmination of Wagner's own tendency to make the theatre into a temple. The atmosphere of mystic exaltation is remarkably conveyed in this music.

'Monsalvat' (Mont Salvagge) in Spain is here named as the site of the stronghold of the knights of the Holy Grail, to whose company the 'guileless fool' Parsifal is admitted. Part of Spain at this period was under Arab rule; in that part Wagner places the castle of the knights' antagonist, Klingsor. As to the grail, see p. 227: Wagner uses the word in its erroneous sense of a chalice from the Last Supper, supposing that in the same chalice Christ's blood was collected from the Cross.

*　　　*　　　*　　　*　　　*

ACT I

Reveille sounds in a forest in the domain of the knights of the Holy Grail. Gurnemanz, an aged knight of the Grail, calls his two esquires to prayer, then sets them to work preparing for the arrival of the king of the knights, Amfortas, who is coming to bathe in the nearby lake. Two knights come, one telling him that Amfortas's wound is more painful than ever. The mysterious heathen sorceress Kundry, in a wild, dishevelled state, enters with a phial of balsam for Amfortas, which she gives to Gurnemanz; then she flings herself wearily to the ground.

Amfortas is borne in on a litter, with a train of knights and esquires. He talks with a knight, mentioning the prediction that a 'guileless fool, made wise by pity' (Durch Mitleid wissend ... der reine Thor) will bring him relief. Gurnemanz hands him the phial from Kundry, whom Amfortas thanks before he goes off. Four esquires talk with Gurnemanz, who tells how the holy Spear and the Grail (the spear which wounded Christ and the cup used at the Last Supper) were delivered to Titurel, who founded a band of knights to guard them and eventually handed them on to his son, Amfortas.

We learn that Klingsor, a knight who on account of his transgressions had been refused admittance to the brotherhood, magically created a garden of seductive women to tempt the Knights of the Grail. Amfortas succumbed to the charms of one of them, and while he was with her Klingsor stole the Spear and wounded Amfortas's side with it. His wound can never heal, nor the Spear be recovered, except through the agency of 'the guileless fool, made wise through pity'. The esquires repeat Gurnemanz's words.

At that moment a wounded swan flies across the lake – to the horror of the knights and esquires, for animal life is sacred in the domain of the Grail. The swan was shot by a young man, who is brought forward; he is deeply contrite. It is Parsifal: but, to Gurnemanz's question he cannot even declare his name and origins. After the esquires have taken the body of the swan away, Kundry, who is still present, discloses that Parsifal's father was slain in battle and he was brought up in innocence by his mother, who is now dead (Parsifal is filled with wild rage at this).

Gurnemanz leads Parsifal away and, as the scene changes, they reappear in the great hall of the knights. Bells are heard and knights, esquires and youths are assembling for a sacred feast. Voices are heard from a dome aloft. The aged Titurel bids his son, Amfortas, uncover the Grail. Amfortas, with his burden of guilt and pain, can receive no comfort from the Grail and does not wish to: 'No! leave it unrevealed!' (Nein! lasst ihn unenthüllt!). But eventually at Titurel's command the crystal cup is uncovered; it glows in the darkness; and Amfortas consecrates with it the bread and wine which are then distributed to the knights who sing in praise of its holy powers of regeneration. The knights and others move off, with Amfortas, whose agony is renewed. Parsifal, who has watched in silence, clutches his own heart and slightly shakes his head. Gurnemanz, irritated at what seems Parsifal's dumb stupidity, sends him off. But from above the words ring out: 'Made wise by pity, the guileless fool . . .'.

Act II

In his magic castle, Klingsor anticipates the coming of Parsifal to his domain and resolves to trap him by magical means. He summons Kundry from a deep slumber (she is half in his power, half drawn to the knights) and orders her to seduce Parsifal. She is unwilling, but has to agree. Klingsor sounds a horn to alert his own company of defenders against the attack being led by Parsifal.

The tower with Klingsor and Kundry disappears and a magic garden, full of beautiful maidens, appears in its place. Parsifal, who has routed Klingsor's warriors, enters. The maidens angrily reproach Parsifal for killing their friends, but their anger changes to gaiety as he approaches and talks with them. They deck themselves in flowers and dance around him, all competing for his attention and love. He is about to leave when Kundry, transformed into a beautiful woman, calls to him, and the flower-maidens go off.

Kundry tells Parsifal the story of his mother, who died of grief when he went away; then she tries to console his sorrow with a passionate kiss. As she kisses him, he remembers Amfortas and the wound he received from the spear. Momentarily he feels Amfortas's pain himself. Kundry is disconcerted as Parsifal, almost in a trance, recalls the sight of the Grail.

As she approaches him again, he realizes what is happening and repulses her. She tries to persuade him to save her, telling him of the terrible curse that has lain upon her since she once reviled Christ himself. Parsifal tells her he can save her, but not in the way she wishes. Becoming more and more frenzied, she begs him to spend one hour in her arms, but he continues to repulse her. Enraged, she curses him and calls Klingsor, who appears on the castle walls overlooking the garden and hurls the sacred Spear at Parsifal. Miraculously, it remains suspended over his head: he grasps it and makes the sign of the cross, whereupon the castle falls in ruin and the magic garden withers and becomes an arid desert. As Parsifal goes off with the Spear he calls to Kundry that she knows where to find him.

ACT III

It is some years later. The aged Gurnemanz is outside his hermit's hut, where he finds Kundry, dressed as a penitent, half-dead in a thicket. He revives her. Her former wildness is gone and she starts to act like a servant to him. She goes into the hut as a man approaches. It is Parsifal, clad in black armour. Gurnemanz does not recognize him, but says that no man must come armed into the domain of the Grail, especially on Good Friday. Parsifal removes his armour and Gurnemanz sees that he was the foolish boy who killed the swan.

Parsifal tells Gurnemanz that owing to a curse (Kundry's) he has hitherto been unable to find his way back, but now he brings the holy Spear. Gurnemanz is thankful, for the knights are in a piteous state: Amfortas refuses to show the Grail, and as a result of that deprivation Titurel has just died. Parsifal is deeply grieved. Kundry and Gurnemanz bathe Parsifal's feet and sprinkle water on his head; he says he is to be their king, as Titurel's true successor, and Gurnemanz anoints him. Then Parsifal baptizes Kundry. He and Gurnemanz gaze with wonderment on the beautiful scene of the Good Friday morning. Bells are heard in the distance: it is midday and Gurnemanz must lead Parsifal, as king, to the knights. They go off, Parsifal bearing the Spear and wearing the mantle of a knight of the Grail.

The scene changes to the great hall of the Grail. Two processions are seen, one with Amfortas and the Grail, the other with Titurel's coffin. The knights express their woe as the coffin is set down before the altar and Titurel's body is uncovered; the weary Amfortas adds his voice, praying to be released by death. They press him to reveal the Grail, but he refuses animatedly: he is dying, he says, and does not want to be revived. Instead he begs them to kill him.

At that moment Parsifal enters. He holds the Spear to Amfortas's wound, which heals instantly. Amfortas is absolved, he tells the knights, but he, Parsifal, is now their king. All stare, enraptured, at the Spear; then Parsifal commands that the Grail be shown. As before, it glows. Voices are heard from above. As Parsifal silently blesses the assembled company with the Grail, a white dove hovers above his head. All kneel before him, and Kundry, her curse removed, sinks lifeless to the ground.

*   *   *   *   *

The prelude introduces three of the work's prominent motives. First is heard the 'motive of sacrament', which we shall meet when Amfortas (in the second scene of Act I) answers Titurel's request to have the Grail shown.

Then, after a pause, the Prelude goes on to announce two motives in succession:

In this (a) is the motive of the Grail, which we shall meet when Gurnemanz first mentions the Grail to Parsifal and Parsifal ignorantly asks 'Who is the Grail?'. Following it, (b) is the motive of Faith, which will first be sung by the boys' voices issuing from above in the second scene of Act I.

But the motive which prophesies the coming of Parsifal himself is not heard in the Prelude. It is sung by Gurnemanz ('With knowledge gained through pity, the guileless fool') in the opening scene, and repeated by the esquires:

In the last act, after Parsifal has baptized Kundry, a motive which has already been hinted at comes to the fore. It is the Good Friday Spell motive:

(The Good Friday Music as played in orchestral concerts includes the passage *preceding* this, as well as the music of the Spell itself: all, of course, minus the voices.)

VII

HECTOR BERLIOZ

(1803–69)

ROSSINI (to revert for a moment to p. 107) conquered not merely Italy but the whole world of European music. In 1823, after visiting London, he took up a musical director's position in Paris – the capital which was then attracting young, enterprising musical geniuses from everywhere, among them Chopin, Liszt and a German known as Giacomo Meyerbeer (1791–1864), whose career reached its climax with the opera *Les Huguenots* (Paris, 1836). It is a pre-eminent example of French 'grand opera' – in five acts, historical in setting, spectacular in action, making full use of chorus and ballet.

Of native French operas of this period, however, none has lasted securely into today's repertory. We may just mention the work of two composers. Great success was won by Daniel Auber (1782–1871) with *La Muette de Portici* (The Dumb Girl of Portici), otherwise *Masaniello* (1828), and with *Fra Diavolo* (1830). Fromental Halévy (1799–1862) created in *La Juive* (The Jewess; 1835) a French 'grand opera' of Meyerbeer's type, which enjoyed many revivals, principally because of its tenor role.

Unlike these composers, Hector Berlioz was never in his life a successful composer for the theatre, but today his repute in the general world of music has compelled a reconsideration of his operatic work. He was led to opera both by his musical bent and by his literary enthusiasm. For him, opera at its highest was a means of experiencing psychological dramatic truth: Gluck and Beethoven were his gods. His opera *Benvenuto Cellini* (Paris, 1838) enshrines his idea of the artist as a kind of romantic hero, and in this respect has been called an anticipation of Wagner's *The Mastersingers*. Berlioz's enthusiasm for Shakespeare led him to write an operatic version of *Much Ado About Nothing* which he called *Béatrice et Bénédict* (which, in English, ought to be *Beatrice and Benedick*, reproducing Shakespeare's spelling of the hero's name. It was produced in 1862 – not in France, but in Germany, where Liszt (as court musical director at Weimar) had already conducted *Benvenuto Cellini*. Between these two operas Berlioz composed *Les Troyens* (The Trojans), completing it in 1858. Paris mounted only the second part, *The Trojans at Carthage* in 1863, but the first part was not given until 1890 when the whole work was produced at Karlsruhe (in Germany again!)

None of Berlioz's operas, in fact, has become standard in the world's opera houses at any period from that day to this. But all, today, are thought worthy of the occasional revival. If *Benvenuto Cellini* is dramatically stiff, and if *Beatrice and Benedick* dauntingly asks opera-singers to speak Shakespeare as well as to sing Berlioz, in *Les Troyens* music and drama are splendidly unified.

LES TROYENS

(The Trojans)

Libretto by the composer, after Virgil

First performed complete: Karlsruhe, 1890

Five Acts (see below)

Cast in order of singing:

A Trojan soldier	*baritone*
Cassandra, daughter of Priam	*soprano*
Choroebus, betrothed to Cassandra	*baritone*
Aeneas, a Trojan warrior	*tenor*
Helenus, son of Priam	*tenor*
Ascanius, son of Aeneas	*soprano*
Hecuba, wife of Priam	*mezzo-soprano*
Pantheus, a Trojan priest	*bass*
Priam, King of Troy	*bass*

The ghost of Hector — *bass*
Polyxena, daughter of Priam — *soprano*
A Greek chieftain — *bass*
Dido, Queen of Carthage — *soprano*
Anna, sister of Dido — *mezzo-soprano*
Iopas, a Carthaginian poet — *tenor*
Narbal, minister of Dido — *bass*
Mercury — *bass*
Hylas, a young Trojan soldier — *tenor*
The parts of Andromache and Astyanax (Hector's widow
and infant son) are silent.]
Chorus of Trojans, Greeks, Carthaginians, spirits, nymphs, etc.

*The scene is laid in Troy at the end of its siege by
the Greeks, and then in Carthage*

BERLIOZ'S gift for tender expression as well as for musical
excitement is shown in *The Trojans*. Its huge, fresco-like
score still permits fine shading of personal detail. The opera
was dedicated by Berlioz 'divo Vergilio' (to the divine Virgil).
The Roman poet had been a passion of Berlioz's since his
boyhood, and he tells of having been moved to tears on hearing of Aeneas's desertion of Dido. He based his own libretto
for *Les Troyens* on the original Latin (*Aeneid*, Books II, IV).
Note the title of the work. The innumerable 18th-century
operas on classical subjects nearly all took their titles from the
name of a particular hero or heroine: Berlioz instead depicts
the story of a nation, the Trojans. The first part is dominated
by Cassandra, who dies at the end of it, the second by Dido
and Aeneas.

The two parts (*The Capture of Troy* and *The Trojans at
Carthage*) were issued at the original publisher's insistence as
separate entities, divided into three and four acts respectively.
But Berlioz had intended the whole work to be given in a
single evening, in five acts, to take about 4½ hours including
intervals. This five-act division has been followed here.

The Royal Hunt and Storm, which (usually with the small
vocal cries omitted) is so well known in the concert-hall, was
placed by Berlioz at the end of Act III; here, as in modern

productions generally, it is placed at the end of Act IV. Th
Trojan March, also familiar in concerts, reproduces the musi
to which the Greeks' wooden horse is dragged inside the cit
by the unsuspecting Trojans.

*   *   *   *   *

Part I: *The Capture of Troy*

ACT I

On the plain of Troy, a Trojan soldier shows some peopl
the grave of the Greek captain, Achilles. It appears that th
Greeks have abandoned the siege of Troy – but left a gian
wooden horse behind: the people go to view it, outside th
city walls. Cassandra enters and, with her gift of prophecy
foretells the city's doom: her lover Choroebus tries to ban
ish her fears, but in vain.

In front of the Citadel (outside the city proper), the Troja
people give thanks for their deliverance from the Greeks. An
dromache, Hector's widow, and her infant son Astyana
enter in the mourning colour of white but speak no word
Cassandra foretells yet more sorrow. Aeneas suddenly enter
with dread news: the priest Laocoon, suspecting an ambus
in the wooden horse, had thrown a javelin at it, whereupo
two sea-serpents had arisen and devoured him. The peopl
are appalled at the portent. King Priam orders the horse t
be brought within the city walls.

Cassandra is left alone. In agitation she sings of the im
pending destruction of the city. The sound of the people joy
ously dragging in the wooden horse comes nearer. Suddenl
the joyous music stops – an ominous clash of arms has bee
heard within the horse – but then is resumed. The processio
with the horse passes. Cassandra is left alone.

ACT II

Aeneas is asleep in his bedroom; his young son Ascanius, hav
ing heard a noise of fighting, runs in terrified, then leaves
The ghost of Hector appears; Aeneas wakes and recognize
him. The ghost bids Aeneas flee from Troy and found a ne
empire. The priest Pantheus, wounded, enters with the new

that the horse contained a Greek ambush and that Priam is dead. Ascanius and Choroebus, entering, add to the tidings. Aeneas and the others rush off to fight.

In the temple of Cybele (the goddess Vesta), the Trojan priestesses and other women, including King Priam's daughter Polyxena, are praying in terror. Cassandra, as chief priestess, rushes in. She tells the others that Aeneas and his men will escape and will found a new Troy; that Choroebus is dead; and that only death can save the women from violation by the triumphant Greeks.

The majority of the women, taking up their lyres, sing heroically and prepare to kill themselves; a smaller group are afraid and are driven out by the others. A Greek chieftain and his soldiers are astonished at the sight of the defiant women. Cassandra stabs herself and hands the dagger to Polyxena; the other women follow their example.

Part 2: *The Trojans at Carthage*

ACT III

Dido and her people, who came to this region seven years ago as refugees from Tyre (and so are sometimes referred to in the text as 'Tyrian'), are holding a festival to celebrate their progress in building the new city of Carthage. The people sing and then greet their queen on her entry: 'Hail, all hail to the queen' (Gloire, gloire à Didon!).* With her sister Anna and her minister Narbal at her side, Dido addresses the people and tells them that Iarbas, the Numidian king, threatens invasion in order to force her to marriage. The people swear to defend her against him. After a ceremony in honour of the construction of the city, they leave.

Dido is left alone with Anna, who wishes that Dido would re-marry and Carthage acquire a king. Dido swears she must be faithful to the ring she wears, a gift from her dead husband, but (aside) confesses that Anna's plan is attractive to her. Iopas, a poet, enters to tell her that a fleet of foreign sailors has been driven on to their shores; Dido sends him to bring them and, while waiting, expresses a strange apprehension.

* English version by Edward J. Dent (O.U.P.).

The foreigners are brought in: they are the Trojans. Aeneas, their leader, is disguised. His young son Ascanius presents Dido with ceremonial gifts, supported by Pantheus.

Narbal rushes in with news that the Numidians have invaded; Aeneas throws off his disguise and promises to lead the defence of Dido's realm, leaving Ascanius to her care. The Carthaginians rally to him and prepare to fight.

ACT IV

Aeneas has been victorious. Anna is in conversation with Narbal, who expresses anxiety because Dido is neglecting all else for Aeneas's company – the very thing which delights Anna.

Dido and Aeneas enter with Ascanius, Iopas and attendants. A ballet (with chorus of made-up 'Nubian' words) is performed for them. At Dido's command, Iopas sings. Then Aeneas relates to Dido the fate of Andromache, mentioning that Andromache has now wed the son of the man who slew her first husband, Hector. In that case, Dido thinks, may she herself not think of remarriage? Absently she allows Ascanius to remove her former husband's ring from her finger. Dido and Aeneas hail the beautiful evening, with Anna, Iopas, Ascanius, Narbal, and Pantheus: 'Night throws a veil of enchantment all around' (Tout n'est que paix et charme). Then, left alone, they declare their love: 'On such a night' (Par une telle nuit, the text is modelled on the famous lines in Shakespeare's *The Merchant of Venice*). As they depart together they receive a fateful warning: Mercury appears and reminds Aeneas of appointed destiny: 'To Italia!' (Italie!).

[Symphonic entr'acte: Royal Hunt and Storm.] In a forest, naiads swim and a storm is heard; Dido dressed as Diana enters with Aeneas dressed as a warrior, and they take shelter in a cave. Their ecstasy together is portrayed in the music and visually symbolized by lightning. Fauns and other creatures dance and cry out the fateful message, 'To Italia!'.

ACT V

The harbour at Carthage is seen, with the Trojan encampment nearby. A young sailor on board one of the Trojan hips sings with nostalgia of his homeland; the two sentries comment on his song. Pantheus and other Trojan chiefs enter, having been told by Aeneas to prepare to sail. (A ghostly cry of 'To Italia!' is again heard.) The two sentries are annoyed at having to sail: life has been easy at Carthage. They retire as Aeneas comes. He soliloquizes: 'There is no turning back' (Inutiles regrets); he is torn between Dido's love and the gods' command. The ghosts of Priam, Choroebus, Hector and Cassandra appear and reinforce the command. Aeneas stirs up the Trojans asleep in their tents.

Dido enters precipitately and begs Aeneas to stay. The sound of the Trojan March (first heard when the wooden horse was being dragged into Troy, now a rallying-tune for the Trojan force) recalls him to duty. Dido, heart-broken, leaves; Aeneas, escorted by his men, embarks.

In a room in her palace, Dido is in agony at Aeneas's desertion. To Anna, Narbal and Iopas (who enters to announce that the Trojan fleet has sailed) she proclaims her fury. But when they have left, her bitterness turns inward in an intense, tragic soliloquy: 'Now must I die' (Je vais mourir).

On a terrace overlooking the sea a funeral pyre has been lit. The priests of Pluto pray for infernal aid; Anna and Narbal solemnly curse Aeneas. Dido throws into the fire her own veil and a toga which belonged to Aeneas; prophetically, she is inspired to utter the name of the man who will one day avenge Carthage – Hannibal. Then she stabs herself. The people lament. In another prophetic inspiration Dido sees a vision of her people's coming enemy, Rome. She dies. The people vow the vengeance of Carthage on the Rome that is to be.

*   *   *   *   *

Les Troyens contains some of Berlioz's greatest music: it also contains it in a truly dramatic framework. The brassy pride of the Trojan march, first heard in procession as the Trojans pull the wooden horse within their walls –

— comes again at the very end of the work to indicate that
for all Dido's hope and her people's curses, it is Rome (the
successor to Troy) which will triumph over Carthage.

This is in Berlioz's heroic manner, and so is the strain to
which Dido is hailed by her courtiers (Act III, scene 1) and
which — as Edward J. Dent pointed out—may have been
based by Berlioz, who had visited England, on *God save the
Queen:*

Likewise couched in this heroic manner is the tremendous
chorus to which Cassandra and the other Trojan women im-
molate themselves before the eyes of the astonished Greeks.

No less remarkable is the more intimate music – the two
great soliloquies in Act V (for Aeneas in scene 1, for Dido
in scene 2) and the nocturne-duet for them both ('O sweet
night, night of ecstasy unending'):

– a number which may be compared with the equally ravish-
ing one for Hero and Ursula (two women this time) in *Beatrice
and Benedick*.

One of the peculiar and fascinating features of Berlioz's
music is the irregularity of its rhythmic patterns. Note the
strange, haunting refrain of the young sailor's song in Act V,
scene I ('Rock me gently, on thy bosom lying, mighty mother
sea!'):

CHARLES FRANÇOIS GOUNOD

(1818–93)

BERLIOZ wrote a *Damnation of Faust* for the concert-hall which has occasionally been staged as an opera; but *Faust* in opera belongs to Gounod. It was the greatest single success of a composer who was enormously successful and enormously prolific. Since the Second World War the position of *Faust* in the international public repertory has significantly declined, much as the position of Rossini, Donizetti and Bellini has risen; it would be rash to prophesy that the decline will be permanent. Gounod's *Roméo et Juliette* (1867; after Shakespeare), formerly often given, has slumped too; *Mireille* (1864), a romance set in Provence, is still given in French theatres.

FAUST

*Libretto by Jules Barbier and Michel Carré,
after the play by Goethe*

First performed: Paris, 1850

Five Acts

Cast in order of singing:

Faust, a learned doctor	*tenor*
Mephistopheles	*baritone*
Wagner, a student	*bass*
Valentin, a soldier, Marguerite's brother	*baritone*
Siebel, a village youth, in love with	
Marguerite	*mezzo-soprano*
Marguerite	*soprano*
Marthe, Marguerite's neighbour	*mezzo-soprano*

Chorus of students, soldiers, villagers, angels, demons,
legendary figures, *etc.*

The scene is laid in Germany in the 16th century

THE first part of Goethe's drama *Faust* was finished in 1808, the second not till 1831. It had great influence on the romantic composers of the 19th century (among them Schumann, Wagner, Liszt and Boito – see page 191) and Gounod's *Faust* is founded on it, or rather on that part concerned with Gretchen, known in the opera as Marguerite.

Originally the opera was an 'opéra-comique' in the French sense – that is, using spoken dialogue (the term does not necessarily imply 'comic' opera). But later Gounod arranged it for the Paris Opéra where recitative had to replace speech: and this has become standard form. It was also for the Opéra that Gounod added the long ballet in Act V (often cut, in part or altogether, today). For the first London production in 1863 Gounod wrote Valentin's air, known in the lament ble standard English version as 'Even bravest heart may well', to a tune which he had used in the prelude to the pera.

A word about Mephistopheles – a classic role for baritone s Faust is for tenor and Marguerite for soprano. Mephisto-pheles is not a pantomime demon with green eye-shadow and o forth. He expressly describes his own first appearance to Faust (we translate literally):

> Here I am! Why are you surprised?
> Am I not as you imagined me? –
> Sword at my side, feather in my hat,
> A full purse and a rich cloak over my shoulder –
> In a word, a proper gentleman!

$$* \quad * \quad * \quad * \quad *$$

ACT I

Old Dr Faust is alone in his study, disillusioned and weary of life. He is contemplating suicide when he hears in the distance the happy voices of young people. Faust takes up their injunction to prayer, as the voices fade away, but then bursts out bitterly, cursing his learning, his prayers and his patience, and calling on the powers of darkness.

To his astonishment, Mephistopheles appears. He identi-fies himself, then asks Faust what he wants – is it gold, honour, power? 'My youth restore me' (Je veux la jeunesse!),* Faust replies. When Faust hesitates before signing away his soul, Mephistopheles summons up a vision of a young and beautiful girl, Marguerite, promising her to Faust, who hesi-tates no longer. Faust is suddenly transformed into an eager youth, and the two sing of pleasures in store.

ACT II

A gay crowd is gathered at a 'Kermesse' (festival fairground). The chorus 'Red or white liquor' (Vin ou bière) introduces, in turn, the voices of students (led by Wagner, one of their number), soldiers, older citizens, girls and matrons, and men. Valentin Marguerite's brother, sings of his regrets at going

* English version by Henry F. Chorley (Novello).

to war and leaving his sister unprotected – 'Even braves heart may swell' (Avant de quitter ces lieux) – though he young admirer Siebel has promised to look after her.

Wagner has just embarked on a song when Mephistophele enters and interrupts, asking if he may sing instead. He sing a profane song: 'Clear the way for the Calf of Gold' (Le veau d'or). Valentin and Wagner invite him to drink, bu before doing so he tells Valentin's and Siebel's fortunes – gloomy, foreboding ones; Siebel will find that flowers fade at his touch. Mephistopheles then draws wine by sorcery from the barrel forming the inn-sign, and proposes Mar guerite's health, to Valentin's annoyance: Valentin draws hi sword, but finds himself powerless to use it. The men, recog nizing the powers of evil, form the sign of the cross with their swords, and Mephistopheles, angry and impotent recoils.

The crowd leaves and Faust enters. Seeing Mephistopheles he asks him if he may meet Marguerite. Mephistopheles tell him that the waltz which now begins will bring her. Young people re-enter, dancing in high spirits, and the older people follow them. Siebel, longing only for Marguerite, refuses to dance. When Marguerite enters, Siebel's approach to her is foiled by Mephistopheles, and Faust proffers his arm. She politely declines, but has evidently been impressed. She leaves. Mephistopheles and Faust depart to plan the next steps, and the dance goes on in rousing fashion.

ACT III

Siebel is alone in Marguerite's garden, singing of his love for her. He picks a flower, which withers in his hand (as Mephis topheles had predicted); but the next flower, picked after he has dipped his fingers in holy water, stays alive. He leaves.

Faust and Mephistopheles enter and Siebel returns with a nosegay for Marguerite, to outshine it, Mephistophele goes to fetch a casket of jewels. Meanwhile, Faust sings the romance 'All hail, thou dwelling pure and lowly' (Salut! demeure chaste et pure). Mephistopheles returns with the jewels. Faust overcomes his scruples; Mephistopheles place he jewels where she will see them, and they leave.

Marguerite enters. She is thinking about the charming man (Faust) who spoke to her. Sitting at her spinning wheel, she sings an old ballad about the King of Thule, interrupting it from time to time with thoughts of the stranger. As she enters the house she sees Siebel's flowers, then the casket of jewels. She opens it and is astonished to see its contents: she cannot resist bedecking herself in them, and sings with delight: 'Oh, the joy' (Oh, je ris de me voir) – the Jewel Song.

Marthe, an older neighbour of Marguerite, enters and admires Marguerite in her finery. Mephistopheles comes to tell Marthe that her husband has been killed, to her distress (which is short-lived). In a quartet Faust converses with Marguerite while Mephistopheles makes himself pleasant to Marthe. Soon Mephistopheles draws her away so as to leave Faust and Marguerite alone. By now they are both in love, and as evening falls they sing tenderly together. Faust bids her goodnight, arranging to meet her in the morning, and leaves; but Mephistopheles stops him and draws his attention to Marguerite's window, where she is singing rapturously of her love. Mephistopheles's mocking laughter is heard as Faust climbs through the window to embrace her passionately.

ACT IV

Marguerite has borne Faust's child but has been deserted by him. She is in her room, spinning; her wretchedness contrasts with the gay snatch of song heard from the street. Siebel offers his love but she still hopes for Faust's return.

A scene in a church follows. Marguerite is praying for forgiveness, but Mephistopheles and the distant voices of demons intervene: he tells her that it is too late for repentance and that her soul is his. The voices of a choir in the church, with organ, proclaim the coming Day of Judgement. She prays all the more fervently but the voice of Mephistopheles pursues her.

The scene changes to the street, with the church on one side and Marguerite's house on the other. A march is heard. The soldiers, Valentin among them, are returning from war

and sing a rousing chorus: 'Glory and love to the men <
yore' (Gloire immortelle). It is momentarily interrupted :
Valentin greets Siebel. When it is finished Siebel begs Vale
tin to forgive his sister. Valentin – puzzled, for he has n<
heard of what has happened – rushes into the house. Mephi
topheles, arriving with Faust (who, against Mephistopheles
advice, still wants to see Marguerite), sings a cynical ser<
nade to his own guitar accompaniment.

Valentin angrily emerges from the house, having lear
about Marguerite, and challenges one of them to a due
After a trio (during which Valentin throws away his meda
lion of the Madonna, given to him by Marguerite, who
he now rejects), Valentin and Faust fight. With Mephist<
pheles's supernatural aid, Faust triumphs. As Valentin li<
dying, Marthe and other people come to help him, and Mai
guerite throws herself over his body. But despite pleas fror
onlookers and from Siebel to forgive her, Valentin curses he
angrily.

[The three scenes in this act are sometimes played in th
order Street–Room–Church.]

ACT V

A chorus of will-o'-the-wisps leads off the infernal Walpurgi
Night celebrations in the Harz Mountains. Faust is conducte<
there by Mephistopheles, who presides over the revels, i
which many legendary and historical characters appear (in
ballet). A drinking-duet for Faust and Mephistopheles is in
terrupted when Faust sees a vision of Marguerite with bloo<
round her neck as though from the blow of an axe. Faus
orders Mephistopheles to take him to see Marguerite again

She is by now in prison, having been condemned to deatl
for the murder of her child during a fit of madness. Mephisto
pheles leads Faust to her cell, to effect her escape, and leave
them alone together. They sing of their happiness at bein<
reunited. But her deranged mind wanders – recalling thei
meeting at the Kermesse and their evening in the garden <
and Faust cannot persuade her to leave with him, for she i
now content to die. Mephistopheles returns to hurry then

efore they are all discovered.

She prays to heaven for salvation while Faust presses her
fly with him and Mephistopheles tries to persuade Faust
leave, even without her. At its climax she makes the mean-
gful gesture of pushing Faust away. 'She is damned!'
ugée!) says Mephistopheles, exultantly; but a chorus of
gels contradicts him with 'Saved!' (Sauvée!). Her soul is
orne away. Faust sinks to his knees and (to quote the stage
irection) 'Mephistopheles is half bent back under the lumi-
ous sword of the Archangel'. A choral outburst – the Easter
ymn of Christ's resurrection – ends the opera.

* * * * *

Jo opera has produced more 'hit tunes' – we use the words
vithout a hint of being patronizing – than *Faust*. The Fair
;cene; the Soldiers' Chorus; 'Even bravest heart' (Valentin's
arewell); the Choral Waltz in Act II; Siebel's song when
ringing his bouquet for Marguerite; Faust's 'All hail, thou
lwelling'; Marguerite's Jewel Song; Marguerite and Faust's
ove-duet; the tune of the final trio; several of the tunes from
he ballet music – all these came down from the opera stage
o conquer the 19th-century public in song-albums, piano
elections, arrangements for bands and orchestras of all kinds.
Today *Faust* sounds (to borrow the old joke about *Hamlet*)
full of quotations', and the very familiarity of the music may
nake us overlook its inventiveness. Take for example the
nusical delineation of the different groups of participants in
he Choral Waltz ('Like the breeze at early morning'):

The orchestral tune (which is the main one, the choru
accompanying) starts off in such a way that it could b
notated in 2/4 time.

Another melody from this waltz recurs later in the opera
when Marguerite, in prison and half delirious, begins to re
call in Faust's presence the scene where they first met. Not
the dramatic aptness: Marguerite, her thoughts turning in
wards in concentration, can manage only a single note (i
fact she keeps that single note for thirty-two bars of music
and it is on the orchestra that the reminiscence steals in
moreover, it does so with a modulation (from F to D) whicl
is simple but which exactly hits off the change of 'plane' be
tween the present and the memory of the past:

Marguerite's words as the vision appears to her are 'But wait! ... Here is the street ...'. The introspective aspect of Marguerite's character makes an admirable foil to the brilliance of the Jewel Song – and there, again subtly, the brilliance is never over-done: Marguerite still manages to be her innocent, unspoilt self, suddenly swept off her feet.

The final trio has one of the most powerful strokes in opera, the repetition of a melody at a higher pitch to screw up the excitement. (Verdi did it later in the trumpet tune of the Triumphal March in *Aida*.) Marguerite, asking the angels to transport her to heaven, leads off in G:

Note the harp accompaniment; its 'celestial' connotations are obvious, just as are the connotations of the organ in the church scene.

Faust asks her to fly with him; her prayer gets more intense by being pushed into A; Mephistopheles adds his plea but Marguerite now pushes the tune up to B. And even this is not the end; the angelic interruption of 'Saved!' (harps again!) leads to the key of C major, the actual chord being struck when the Easter hymn of the resurrection (organ again!) begins. This is musical language absolutely wedded to the dramatic action.

JACQUES OFFENBACH

(1819–80)

AMONG the many musicians attracted to Paris from other countries (see p. 275) was Jacques Offenbach (born Jakob Eberst, in Cologne; his family came from Offenbach), who in 1833 came to study the cello at the Paris Conservatory and became, from the 1850s, the leading composer of French operettas. He turned out nearly a hundred of these (including *Orpheus in the Underworld*, first version 1858; *La Belle Hélène*, 1864; and *La Vie Parisienne*, 1866), but wrote only one serious opera and did not quite finish it nor live to see it performed. It is a masterpiece and – with its peculiar dramatic intermingling of reality and fantasy – a work like no other in the opera repertory: *The Tales of Hoffmann*.

LES CONTES D'HOFFMANN

(The Tales of Hoffmann)

Libretto by Jules Barbier and Michel Carré, after a play of their own based on stories of E. T. A. Hoffmann

First performed: Paris, 1881

Prologue, Three Acts and Epilogue

Cast in order of singing or speaking:

Prologue and Epilogue

Councillor Lindorf	*baritone*
Andreas, servant of Stella	*tenor*
Luther, keeper of a beer-cellar	*bass*
Herman ⎱ students	*baritone*
Nathaniel ⎰	*tenor*
Hoffmann, a poet	*tenor*
Nicklaus, his friend	*mezzo-soprano*
Stella, an opera singer	*speaking part*
The Muse of Poetry	*speaking part*

Chorus of students

*   *   *   *   *

Acts I, II and III

Spalanzani, a physicist and inventor	*tenor*
Hoffmann	*tenor*
Cochenille, Spalanzani's servant	*tenor*
Nicklaus	*mezzo-soprano*
Dr Coppelius, a spectacle-maker	*baritone*
Olympia, Spalanzani's 'daughter', loved by Hoffmann	*soprano*
Antonia, a girl, loved by Hoffmann	*soprano*
Crespel, her father, a councillor	*baritone*
Franz, Crespel's servant	*tenor*
Dr Miracle, an evil physician	*baritone*

A voice (Antonio's mother)		mezzo-soprano
Giulietta, a Venetian courtesan, loved by Hoffmann		soprano
Schlemil ⎱ two other admirers	⎧	bass
Pittichinaccio ⎰ of Giulietta	⎨	tenor
Dapertutto, an evil magician	⎩	baritone

Chorus of guests at Spalanzani's house and of Venetian
ladies and gentleman, etc.

*In the Prologue and Epilogue the scene is laid in
Nuremberg, and in the three Acts respectively in Paris,
Munich and Venice in the early 19th century*

E. T. A. HOFFMANN (1776–1882) was a German novelist and
amateur composer; his writings occupy an important place
in the German literary romantic movement and he wrote a
famous 'romantic' interpretation of Mozart's *Don Giovanni*.
So it is appropriate that a strain from *Don Giovanni* is quoted
in Offenbach's opera, in which Hoffmann is the hero. Hoffmann himself appears as story-teller in the prologue and epilogue: between come the three acts (each founded on one
of the real Hoffmann's stories) which tell of his different
loves.

Because Offenbach died before finishing the work, Ernest
Guiraud (1837–92) undertook its orchestration; he also wrote
recitatives for the work. (He did similarly for *Carmen*: see
p. 307.) But in recent years there has been a tendency for
opera houses to eliminate the recitatives and to give the work
with spoken dialogue, as Offenbach intended. Moreover,
though the published vocal score gives the three acts (with
three different heroines) in the order Olympia – Giulietta –
Antonia, it was Offenbach's intention to have the 'Giulietta'
act last, as a reference in the prologue and another in the epilogue make clear. Various modern productions have adopted
this authentic order, and we do so in the following synopsis.

Ideally, all three heroines – being dramatically treated as
different incarnations of Hoffmann's beloved – should be sung
by the same soprano. This has occasionally, but not often,
been done. But it is normal, on the same dramatic grounds,

for the four 'villain' roles (Lindorf, Coppelius, Dr Miracl and Dapertutto) to be sung by the same baritone, as an in carnation of the evil genius who foils Hoffmann at every turn Certain other roles may also be doubled.

The voice of Stella must be the only example of a role it opera which is that of an opera-singer and which calls for n singing! The role of Nicklaus is given to a mezzo-soprand representing a youth; it has been observed that Nicklaus i apparently never addressed by anyone in the opera excep Hoffmann – as if he were, so to speak, a projection of Hoff mann, his 'better self', pressing the claims of conscience and duty on a being who is ruled by passion.

*   *   *   *   *

PROLOGUE

In Luther's beer-cellar at Nuremberg (sited next to an opera house, where the celebrated singer Stella is appearing in Don Giovanni), voices are heard singing in praise of beer and wine. Lindorf – a married man, but pursuing Stella – enters and bribes Stella's servant Andreas into handing over a lette addressed by Stella to Hoffmann. The letter encloses the key of her room and Lindorf eagerly looks forward to keeping th assignation in Hoffmann's place.

Luther comes in with waiters to prepare the room for i crowd of students, who soon arrive, singing lustily, led by Hermann and Nathaniel. Nathaniel proposes a toast to Stella then Hermann and he ask Luther where Hoffmann is: jus then Hoffmann arrives, with his friend Nicklaus, who ironic ally quotes from the music of Leporello's opening song it Don Giovanni and applies the words to the way Hoffmann's escapades tire him out night and day – 'Notte e giornd faticar'.

Hoffmann is at first in reflective mood. In response to eager requests he sings a comic song about a dwarf, Kleinzach – but his romantic musings lead him astray in the middle and he sings of his pursuit of love. Soon after, Hoffmann sees Lindorf, who mocks him; Hoffmann recognizes in Lindorf the force of evil which has always dogged him, and the two

xchange insults. The conversation turns to the students'
:irls: Hoffmann talks of his three loves (all now embodied in
tella). Disregarding Luther's warning that the curtain is
bout to rise on the next act of the opera, the students pre-
are to listen as Hoffmann relates the stories of his three en-
ounters ... 'The first was called Olympia ...'.

ACT I

n Paris, the physicist and inventor Spalanzani boasts a
daughter', Olympia. Hoffmann, who has become Spalan-
:ani's pupil and fancies himself in love with Olympia, comes
n. Spalanzani, after giving orders to his servant Cochenille,
eaves Hoffmann alone. Hoffmann peeps behind a curtain and
ees Olympia, apparently sleeping. Enraptured, he sings: 'To
ive with thee' (Ah! vivre deux).* Nicklaus enters and tells
Hoffmann that Spalanzani's sole interest is science and that
le makes lifelike dolls: 'He has a doll with eyes of grey' (Une
poupée aux yeux d'émail).

But Hoffmann fails, or refuses, to take the obvious hint.
Coppelius, an inventor and Spalanzani's rival, arrives. He
,ings of his scientific wares and sells Hoffmann a pair of
magic 'eyes' through which Olympia seems still more won-
derful. Spalanzani returns, and, out of earshot of Hoffmann,
Coppelius claims his share of the income which Spalanzani
will earn from Olympia, for Coppelius made her eyes. Spalanzani pays Coppelius with a cheque drawn on a banker whom
he knows is really bankrupt.

The guests now begin to arrive for Olympia's splendid
coming-out dance. Nicklaus and Hoffmann look forward to
seeing the beautiful girl. Soon Spalanzani leads her out, to the
admiration of all assembled, especially Hoffmann. Spalanzani
offers to have her sing to her own harp accompaniment. She
sings a coloratura aria – 'Ev'ry grove with song-birds laden'
(Les oiseaux dans la charmille) – but there is a strange
running-down in the middle which Spalanzani has to remedy
by winding up a mechanism. Hoffmann, utterly enchanted,
and still not realizing what Olympia is, wishes to take her to

* English version by Edward Agate (Cramer).

supper, but Spalanzani cunningly asks him to stay behind
with her. The guests go down. Hoffmann, alone with Olympia, sings lovingly to her: as he touches her shoulder she
makes a mechanical response. Finally, he takes her hand
she rises, moves around in various directions and goes off, to
Hoffmann's dismay. Nicklaus comes in and tries to tell him
the truth about her, but he will not listen.

Coppelius enters, having found that Spalanzani's cheque is
worthless and eager for revenge. He disappears, to conceal
himself in Olympia's room and wait for her. The guests re-
assemble and the dance begins. Hoffmann takes Olympia as
his partner; they dance for a while, whirling more and more
rapidly, until Spalanzani taps her and stops them (after Nicklaus has tried and failed). Hoffmann has fallen and is dazed;
his spectacles (the 'eyes' Coppelius gave him) are broken. As
he begins to recover, there is a sound of breaking machinery:
Coppelius, in an inner room, has destroyed Olympia. Hoffmann, aghast, at last begins to realize that she was only a
puppet. As Coppelius and Spalanzani shout abuse at one
another, the guests deride the deluded Hoffmann.

ACT II

The second story takes place in Munich. Antonia, whom
Hoffmann loves, is seated at the harpsichord in her room
singing unhappily: 'Thou art flown' (Elle a fui). Her father,
Crespel, enters and reminds her of her promise never to sing
– she inherits her mother's voice and also her mother's fatal
tendency to tuberculosis, which her singing aggravates. She
goes off, renewing her promise. Crespel, worried that Hoffmann is disturbing her peace of mind, orders his deaf servant
Franz to admit no one. After a comic song for Franz, Hoffmann arrives with Nicklaus, and Franz, having misheard his
instructions, admits them.

Hoffmann sings a snatch of the love-duet he and Antonia
used to sing. Antonia comes and the lovers embrace passionately; Nicklaus leaves them to express their love. She mentions that she is forbidden to sing, but he presses her; she
goes to the harpsichord and they sing a duet (incorporating

the strain which Hoffmann had previously sung). At the end she becomes faint, then, hearing her father coming, she goes off to her room. Hoffmann hides.

Franz comes in and announces Dr Miracle. Crespel orders him to be sent off – he does not want his daughter killed by Miracle's treatment, just as his wife was. But he enters and insists on treating her, to the fear of both Crespel and the concealed Hoffmann. By magical means he diagnoses her illness in her absence and, despite Crespel's angry protests, prescribes for her. As if she hears Miracle's command, 'Now sing!' (Chantez!), her voice is heard. Miracle remains unruffled during Crespel's furious attempts to eject him, returning through the wall when pushed out by the door. Eventually he leaves, followed by Crespel.

Antonia returns to find Hoffmann alone. Before he goes he warns her to forget her dreams of becoming a singer. She agrees never to sing again ('Je ne chanterai plus'). Then Miracle returns, as if by magic: he takes up her words, reproaching her for wasting so great a talent and telling her of the dazzling future in store for her as a singer. She is disturbed and looks to her mother's portrait for comfort. It comes to life and speaks to her, bidding her to sing, and Miracle plays wildly on a violin to rouse her excitement. At the end, Miracle disappears into the earth, the portrait resumes its old form and Antonia falls, dying.

Crespel comes in, exchanging only a few words with his daughter before she dies. As Hoffmann enters, Crespel turns on him and accuses him of being responsible. Hoffmann merely tells Nicklaus to fetch a doctor, in response to which Miracle appears. He pronounces her dead.

ACT III

Hoffmann's third tale is enacted in Venice. The setting is a palace overlooking the Grand Canal; a Barcarolle is sung by Nicklaus and the courtesan Giulietta with the assembled company. Hoffmann then sings a gay drinking song: 'When love is but tender' (Amis, l'amour tendre). He loves Giulietta but her accepted companion is at present Schlemil. Now

Giulietta introduces Hoffmann to Schlemil and also to another admirer of hers, Pittichinaccio, and suggests a game of cards.

They go off, leaving Nicklaus and Hoffmann alone: Nicklaus warns his friend not to be foolish, but Hoffmann is in love with Giulietta and will not easily be restrained. As they depart Dapertutto enters – a sorcerer who uses Giulietta to enslave his victims. He has already enslaved Schlemil and is determined to capture Hoffmann. He exhibits the diamond with which he will again bribe Giulietta to do his will: 'As jewels divine' (Scintille, diamant).

Giulietta enters and Dapertutto asks her to captivate Hoffmann so that he can capture his soul by stealing his reflection in her mirror. Hoffmann, coming in as Dapertutto departs, sings passionately of his love for her. She warns him of Schlemil's jealousy but says she loves him; then she begs him to look in her mirror, so that when he goes she can retain his likeness for ever. He is mystified but consents.

Schlemil enters with Pittichinaccio, Nicklaus, Dapertutto and others. Dapertutto hands Hoffmann a mirror: he is horrified to find that his reflection has vanished. Nicklaus tries vainly to lead the distracted Hoffmann away. Hoffmann proclaims that he both hates and adores Giulietta, and the others comment on the situation. Now (in spoken dialogue, as the Barcarolle is heard again in the background) Hoffmann demands of Schlemil the key to Giulietta's room: they fight, Hoffmann using Dapertutto's sword, and Schlemil is killed. Hoffmann grabs the key and rushes off to Giulietta's room – but returns as Giulietta approaches, below, in a gondola. She is alone. But instead of accepting Hoffmann as a lover, she abandons him as a victim to Dapertutto and takes Pittichinaccio into her arms. Nicklaus drags the disillusioned Hoffmann away.

EPILOGUE

Back in Luther's inn, Hoffmann tells his friends that his tales are finished. In the distance, cheers are heard, which Luther says are for Stella. Lindorf slips out. In answer to a remark of Nathaniel's, Nicklaus explains that Stella is the embodiment of Olympia, Antonia and Giulietta, and all drink to her. At first this infuriates Hoffmann, but then he decides that drowning his sorrows in punch is the only solution. The students go off, leaving Hoffmann slumped over the table, dead drunk. In a vision, the Muse of Poetry appears and asks him to devote his life to her, to which he joyfully consents.

Stella enters and sees Hoffmann. Nicklaus explains that he is drunk; Lindorf comes in and draws her towards him. The students' voices, lifted in a drinking-song, are heard again.

*   *   *   *   *

The puppet Olympia is characterized by an aria that is at once expressive yet capable of being delivered (by a skilled soprano) in a slightly mechanical, left-hand-then-right-hand sort of way. It is also extremely difficult to sing accurately in tune!

In complete contrast, Antonia introduces herself with a rather slow, intense song about a turtle-dove, with the most delicately-hinted accompaniment:

Giulietta has, rather remarkably, no comparable solo – but the Barcarolle, which Nicklaus begins and in which Giulietta presently joins, is the strongest indication of her (and Venice's)

seductive charms. The most notable solo in this act is the famous baritone song 'As jewels divine' (showing the power of the evil genius who confronts Hoffmann). Hoffmann's own romantic, expansive nature is shown in the opening of his duet with Giulietta. He is intoxicated with love:

Although Hoffmann and Giulietta sing ecstatically together later in the duet, Giulietta's feeling for Hoffmann is merely a courtesan's fancy; so Offenbach never gives her the phrase of genuine passion we have quoted from Hoffmann's part.

The celebrated Barcarolle, perhaps unexpectedly given to two women's voices (at the opening of Act III), was transferred from Offenbach's unsuccessful opera *Sprites of the Rhine* (Rheinnixen), produced at Vienna in 1864.

GEORGES BIZET

(1838–75)

ORIENTAL subjects, with opportunities for exotic-sounding music, were much favoured in 19th-century Paris. It is ironical that *Samson and Delilah* by Camille Saint-Saëns (1835–1921), though written for the Paris Opéra, was declined by its management and first staged in 1877 at Weimar in Germany. (Owing to objections to its biblical plot, it was not staged in London till 1909.) In 1883 Paris saw the first performance of an opera about the daughter of a Brahmin priest in love with a British officer in India – *Lakmé* by Léo Delibes (1836–91). It is still performed today, though it has hardly the 'classic' status of Delibes's two celebrated ballets, *Coppélia* (on the story by E. T. A. Hoffmann which also furnished the 'Olympia' episode in Offenbach's *Tales of Hoffmann*) and *Sylvia*.

Oriental subjects were also used by Georges Bizet in two operas: *The Pearl Fishers* (1865) and *Djamileh* (1872; one act, unsuccessful). And Bizet found another 'orient' (that is, a setting giving dramatic opportunity for an exceptional, exotic touch in the music) at the very door of France: in Spain. *Carmen* was produced in 1875; displeased most of the critics; was reckoned a failure. Tchaikovsky, visiting Paris at the time, prophesied that within ten years it would be the most popular opera in the world. He overestimated, but not by much. Incidentally, Tchaikovsky's own use of a boy's chorus imitating soldiers at the opening of *The Queen of Spades* is the frankest of tributes to Bizet's masterpiece.

Among Bizet's other works is the opera *The Fair Maid of Perth* (1867), based on Scott's novel.

CARMEN

Libretto by Henri Meilhac and Ludovic Halévy,
after Prosper Merimée

First performed: Paris, 1875

Four Acts

Cast in order of singing:

Morales, a corporal	*baritone*
Micaela, a peasant girl from Navarre	*soprano*
Don José, a corporal from Navarre	*tenor*
Zuniga, a lieutenant	*bass*
Carmen, a gipsy	*mezzo-soprano*
Frasquita, a gipsy	*soprano*
Mercedes, a gipsy	*soprano*
Escamillo, a toreador	*baritone*
El Dancairo, a smuggler	*baritone*
El Remendado, a smuggler	*tenor*
Two gipsies	*mezzo-soprano, baritone*

Chorus of soldiers, street-boys, townspeople,
cigarette girls, gipsies, smugglers

The scene is laid in Seville in the 1820s

SAY 'seductive Spanish gipsy' and we think of Carmen; say 'Toreador' and we think of Escamillo's swaggering tune. Bizet's opera has come to have an almost proverbial status. Its ever-fresh score, admired by such dissimilar musicians as Brahms and Debussy, has combined with its dramatic story to preserve its popularity the world over.

Indeed, its tunes are now so well loved, its plot so well understood, and its heroine so widely recognized as representing a whole type of female behaviour, that we scarcely think of what a shocker the opera originally seemed. Girls smoking on the stage (in 1875); such a disgusting death for the heroine – and on the stage of the Opéra-Comique, dedicated by tradition to much less sordid fare!

Not that 'opéra-comique' in France means precisely 'comic-opera'. As we have noted in considering Gounod's *Faust* (see page 286), its distinguishing feature was the use of spoken dialogue – in place of recitative, which was used in works presented at the larger theatre, the Paris Opéra. Later (after Bizet's death) *Carmen* was performed and published in an all-sung version, with recitatives added by Bizet's friend Ernest Guiraud (1837–92). The modern tendency is to restore the spoken dialogue, which makes the action much clearer, and also to restore certain parts of Bizet's original score which were omitted from the published version.

*   *   *   *   *

ACT I

The curtain rises on a square in Seville, with a tobacco factory on one side and a guard-house on the other. Soldiers, led by Morales, sing as they lounge and watch the bustle of people in the street. Micaela, a simple country girl, comes to ask Morales if he knows a corporal called Don José, who is her sweetheart; he tries to flirt a little with her and tells her that José will soon come, when the guard changes. She goes, and the soldiers briefly resume their song.

Trumpets off-stage signal the approach of the new guard, a crowd of urchins following and imitating them admiringly. The children sing as the guard is changed, José commanding the relief. Morales tells José that a girl has enquired after him.

Zuniga, an officer only recently posted to Seville, asks José about the girls in the cigarette factory. They are 'fast' by reputation, but they do not interest José, who loves only Micaela. A bell sounds and the girls come out of the factory smoking, watched by a crowd of men, with whom they exchange pleasantries. The last girl to appear from the factory is Carmen, a seductive gipsy beauty. Only José ignores her. She sings a habanera: 'Love is like an elusive bird' (L'amour est un oiseau rebelle).* All the young men sue for her favours,

* English version by Hermann Klein (Cramer).

but her eye has fallen on José, and she tosses a flower to him before going back into the factory.

José, left alone, is disturbed by the incident. Then Micaela arrives: she has come to give José a letter – and a kiss – from his mother. In their duet, 'Tell me then of my mother' (Parlemoi de ma mère), the two sing nostalgically of the village which was his home. When she goes he reads the letter, which urges him to marry Micaela.

Suddenly there is a commotion in the factory and girls come running out, chattering about a quarrel involving Carmen. Zuniga sends José with two soldiers to investigate. He soon comes out with Carmen, who sings an impudent 'Trala-la!' in reply to Zuniga's questions. It seems that she attacked another girl with a knife, so Zuniga sends her off to prison, in José's charge.

Carmen and José are left alone in the square. She speaks seductively to him; he forbids her to speak to him, so she sings – to herself, she pretends – a seguidilla, 'Close by the ramparts of Seville' (Pres des remparts de Séville). Soon José is entirely captivated. In response to her promise that she will give him her love at Lillas Pastia's inn, he loosens the cord round her wrists. Zuniga returns with the warrant for her arrest. While a crowd watches, José begins to march Carmen away. But suddenly she turns, gives him a push (as she had arranged with him) and rushes away, to the amusement of the crowd. [In stage performances, José is usually put under arrest immediately by Zuniga for permitting Carmen's escape.]

ACT II

It is two months later. In Lillas Pastia's tavern, where Carmen had told José she would wait for him, gipsies are dancing. Carmen sings the Gipsy Song, 'Ah, when of gay guitars the sound' (Les tringles des sistres tintaient), in which Frasquita and Mercedes join. Zuniga is present and tries to lead Carmen off, but she refuses to go; he mentions that José, who had been imprisoned for permitting Carmen's escape, has just been released. Soon Escamillo, a famous

toreador, arrives. He is cheered by all present and sings the
Toreador's Song, 'Sirs, your toast' (Votre toast), with their
support, and before he leaves he makes a bid for Carmen.
Zuniga and the rest of the crowd soon follow, hurried off by
the innkeeper, leaving Carmen, Frasquita and Mercedes.

Two smugglers, Dancairo and Remendado, enter and ask
the three women for immediate help in a venture. Carmen
refuses, knowing that José will come – but she agrees to
try to persuade him to desert and join them. The others leave
Carmen as José is heard approaching: 'Dragoon of Alcala'
(Dragon d'Alcala). He comes and declares his love. She is
dancing for him when, hearing bugles calling him to duty, he
prepares to leave. She is angry and sarcastic – this is love that
can be quelled by a bugle-call! He tries to assure her of his
love, telling her that he has kept, throughout the imprisonment, the flower she threw to him: 'See here your flower' (La
fleur que tu m'avais jetée) – the Flower Song. She tempts
him with visions of a free and happy life together among the
smugglers and gipsies in the mountains.

He resists and is about to leave when there is a knock at
the door and Zuniga enters. He asks Carmen if she prefers a
common soldier to an officer, and orders José back to camp.
José refuses and draws his sword against his officer. The smugglers, who have been in hiding, disarm Zuniga and send him
off in the custody of some gipsies. By defying his officer José
has turned his back on the army. To leave with Carmen is
now the only way for him, and he joins in a chorus in praise
of the free life.

Act III

In the smugglers' mountain lair, preparations are being made
for an exploit, led by Dancairo. By now Carmen is tiring of
José, who is unhappy at the kind of life he is leading; she suggests that he should leave them, but he is bitterly jealous and
threatens her angrily. As the men rest, Frasquita, Mercedes
and Carmen read their fortunes in the cards. Carmen sees
only death for herself – 'and later for him'.

Dancairo leads the smugglers off, singing of their plans;

the women go with them, to beguile the customs officers. The stage is empty when a figure appears in the darkness: it is Micaela, who has paid a guide to take her to the smugglers' lair and prays that God will help her to lead José back to his mother: 'I said nought should frighten me here' (Je dis que rien m'épouvante). She sees him approaching; then, as a shot rings out, she hides. José had seen a man coming and only just missed him. The man identifies himself as Escamillo, who has been in the region rounding up bulls for his next fight. In a duet Escamillo says he has come to see Carmen, who is tiring of her latest lover, a soldier ('her affairs only last six months'). José's jealousy is aroused; he challenges Escamillo, who then realizes that José is the man, and they fight.

José is about to kill his rival when Carmen arrives and seizes his arm. Dancairo tells Escamillo to go, which he does, but not before he has taunted José, who has to be held back by the smugglers. They are leaving again when Remendado finds Micaela in hiding. She pleads with José to come away with her. Carmen and the smugglers too tell him to go, but he swears that only death can part him from Carmen. But when Micaela says that his mother is dying he consents to leave, and even then he threateningly tells Carmen that they will meet again. Escamillo's voice is heard from a distance and Carmen moves towards him, but José menacingly bars her way.

ACT IV

Tradesmen, gipsies, children and townspeople are seen filling the square in Seville, outside the amphitheatre where a bull-fight is to be held. Zuniga is there, making small purchases from the gipsies. Soon the colourful procession of those taking part in the bull-fight starts, hailed by the bystanders (including children); Escamillo brings up the rear in triumph, to shouts of his name. After a brief love duet with Carmen, who is with him, he goes off to prepare for the fight. Frasquita and Mercedes have seen José in the crowd and warn Carmen to take care, but she is unafraid.

José intercepts Carmen as she moves towards the arena. He

begs her to return to him, to go away with him, forgetting the past; but she says her love is dead and he demands the impossible. Despite his repeated pleas she remains adamant. From the arena, cheers for Escamillo are heard. Carmen tries to enter but he bars her way, determined that she shall not go to her new lover. Again the cheers are heard. José becomes more violent. She demands that he kills her or lets her pass. Then she throws his ring at him and tries to slip past him, but he catches her and plunges his knife into her back. As she falls dead the crowd, singing the Toreador Song, comes out of the amphitheatre and sees her. Kneeling by her lifeless body, José gives himself up.

*   *   *   *   *

The cigarette-girls come out of the factory with a studiedly languid air as they puff at their cigarettes, and the music which they sing in languid too. Then, suddenly loud and with an abrupt change of tempo, Carmen enters:

Even opera-goers familiar with *Carmen* would not necessarily recognize this tune, played here on the violins, but it is metamorphosed later in the scene into a theme which is unforgettable:

This has already been heard in the prelude, and is first heard in the opera when Carmen throws the flower at Don José, thus establishing her power over him; it recurs at various points, up to the very end of the opera when José gives himself up for her murder. But this recurrence is not part of a general web of leading-motives used symphonically; it is a unique 'fate' motive.

The Toreador's Song is also re-quoted. It is the best-known piece in the opera, and has to be delivered with swagger by Escamillo: Bizet marked it to be sung 'with fatuity' – which shows just how he viewed Escamillo's character.

The habanera sung by Carmen – 'Love is like an elusive bird' –

is an adaptation of a Spanish-American song by Sebastian Yradier (1809–65); and the entr'acte before Act IV and the snatch of melody with which Carmen defies Zuniga in Act I are also borrowings from Spanish sources.

But the atmosphere which is so striking in this opera is not mainly a matter of borrowing but of a daringly original mind working on his material. When Carmen dances for José in Lillas Pastia's tavern she has her own tune (sung to 'la'); with this she (or a performer in the orchestra) plays the castanets in a typically Spanish rhythm; and at the same time two bugles (Bizet specified that instrument, not trumpets) sound the retreat, summoning José back to barracks. The three strains intertwine in a whole which represents exactly what is in José's mind.

As remarkable as anything in the work is the characteriza

tion of Micaela. As the opposite of Carmen she might have been simpering and pale. But her music is strong:

Notice the force of the unorthodox harmony at *.

Dramatically, Micaela is strong partly because she represents not only herself but also José's mother from whom she comes. This is one of the incidental virtues of a libretto which, in itself, is one of the best ever written.

JULES MASSENET

(1842–1912)

MUCH of Massenet's music may seem today too obvious in its sensuous charm, and we need not look for a revival of most of his operas: he wrote no fewer than twenty-seven, excluding those unfinished and unperformed! The mixing of the religious and the erotic (which had already provided two major operatic successes in Wagner's *Tannhäuser* and Gounod's *Faust*, and was to come to its musical climax in Richard Strauss's *Salome*) was congenial to Massenet. His *Hérodiade* (Herodias; 1881) and *Thaïs* had considerable success and are still occasionally given, especially in France. So, on a quite different kind of 'domestic' subject, is *Werther* (1892). But *Manon* (in which, it will be noted, the interplay of religious and erotic impulses again has a place) is reckoned its composer's masterpiece. He also wrote a little-known sequel to it, *Le Portrait de Manon* (1894).

MANON

*Libretto by Henri Meilhac and Philippe Gille, after
the novel by the Abbé Prévost*
First performed: Paris, 1884

Five Acts

Cast in order of singing:

Guillot de Morfontaine, Minister of Finance, an old roué		*tenor*
De Brétigny, a nobleman		*baritone*
Poussette	⎱ described as actresses ⎰	*soprano*
Javotte		*soprano*
Rosette		*mezzo-soprano*
Innkeeper		*baritone*
Lescaut, of the Royal Guard, Manon's cousin		*baritone*
Two Guardsmen		*tenors*
Manon Lescaut		*soprano*
The Chevalier des Grieux		*tenor*
The Count des Grieux, his father		*bass*

Chorus of citizens, travellers, postillions, porters,
street-vendors, worshippers, gamblers, soldiers

*The scene is laid in France (Amiens, Paris
and near Le Havre) in 1721*

THE Abbé Prévost (1697–1763) was a soldier (in his youth), a novelist, and a translator into French of Richardson's English novels, as well as a member of the Benedictine order. His most famous work is the novel *Manon Lescaut* (1731), a classic treatment of the bad girl as literary heroine (dying in the end, of course). It has the peculiar distinction of having inspired four operas over ninety-six years, from *Manon Lescaut* by Auber (1856) to Hans Werner Henze's *Boulevard*

Solitude (a modern-dress adaptation, 1952) – with the two best known examples in between, Massenet's *Manon* (1884) and Puccini's *Manon Lescaut* (1893).

Dramatically, a notable difference between these two is that Puccini follows the novel in showing Manon as dying in the wilds of America, after her sentence of transportation; in Massenet's opera she dies before the planned embarkation at Le Havre. Massenet gives his heroine much sentimental charm, and the same kind of appeal goes into the musical portrayal of the hero, in the romantic dilemma of having to choose between passion and priesthood.

* * * * *

ACT I

In the courtyard of an inn at Amiens, two well-to-do clients, Guillot and de Brétigny, have arrived with their gay companions, Poussette, Javotte and Rosette – described as actresses, really Guillot's mistresses. They clamour impatiently for a meal. Soon the innkeeper announces that it is ready and they go to a pavilion to eat.

People gather to watch the arrival of the stage-coach, and the innkeeper comments on it. Lescaut, a young guardsman, enters with two travelling-companions whom he sends off into the inn while he awaits the coach. (He is to meet his young cousin Manon, who is travelling in the coach on her way to entering a convent.) The coach arrives and there is a general bustle of passengers, porters and others. Lescaut finds Manon among the crowd and they introduce themselves to one another; he comments on her beauty. Rather confused after the journey, Manon tells Lescaut of her feelings: 'I can't express all my emotion' (Je suis encore tout étourdie).* Once more there is a flurry of activity as preparations are made for the coach's departure. Lescaut goes off to fetch Manon's baggage; Guillot offers to elope with her; she laughs at him and his companions call him back. But he tells Manon that his coach will call in a few minutes and is at her service.

Lescaut comes back and Guillot rejoins his friends. Intend-

* English version by Norman Feasey.

ing to go and play cards with the guardsmen, Lescaut solemnly warns Manon not to listen to any frivolous propositions.
Left alone, she sings with sad resignation of her dreams as
she sees the prettily dressed 'actresses' at the inn: 'So I will
stay' (Restons ici).

The Chevalier des Grieux enters, musing on his coming
reunion with his father. Suddenly he sees Manon, and is at
once enchanted by her. Within a few moments both are
deeply in love. She tells him that she is destined for a convent, but he begs her to come to Paris with him and they sing
together rapturously. The coach ordered by Guillot arrives
and they decide to go to Paris together in it.

From inside the inn, the girls' laughter is heard, and Lescaut's voice. Lescaut and Guillot come out. In fury, Lescaut
charges Guillot with the abduction of Manon. The innkeeper
tells Lescaut that Manon went off with a young man in Guillot's coach. The bystanders mock Guillot as he vows revenge
on the eloping pair.

Act II

Des Grieux and Manon are living in a small Paris apartment.
He is writing to his father, asking his consent to his marriage
with Manon, and he and Manon read the letter over together.
(From it we learn that she is only just sixteen.) Two men in
soldier's uniform are brought in by the maid. One is Lescaut;
the other, pretending to be Lescaut's fellow-guardsman, is de
Brétigny, who hopes to become Manon's lover. (Manon recognizes him; des Grieux does not.) Des Grieux and Lescaut at
first quarrel angrily; Manon is afraid, and de Brétigny tries
to restrain his friend. But des Grieux assures Lescaut of his
honourable intentions. While he shows him the letter he was
writing, de Brétigny draws Manon aside and tells her that des
Grieux's father plans to take him away from Paris by force
that very evening. De Brétigny dissuades her from warning
her lover; would she not prefer a life of luxury with de
Brétigny to poverty with des Grieux?

The visitors depart and des Grieux goes to send off his
letter. Alone, Manon reflects on her weakness in failing to

reject de Brétigny's offer and on the coming end of her idyll
with des Grieux: 'Farewell, our table that we love so' (Adieu,
notre petite table). Des Grieux returns and finds her in a sad
mood. As they have their supper he tells her of a dream he
has had, a dream of happiness with her: 'Oh, moment sweet'
(Instant charmant). He is interrupted by a knock on the door.
Manon is distressed and asks him not to answer it. But he
goes. Sounds of a scuffle are heard and he does not return.

Act III

At the Cours-la-Reine, a place of promenading for fashionable
Paris, street vendors are crying their wares amid a general
bustle. Poussette, Javotte and Rosette come out of a pavilion
where they have been dancing. Lescaut arrives, makes some
purchases and leaves. Guillot arrives and then de Brétigny,
who speaks of Manon, with whom he is now living. Presently
Manon herself enters. She is much admired by all the men
present and sings a coquettish song to them – expressing her
mood in the gavotte 'Let us enjoy the days of beauty' (Pro-
fitons bien de la jeunesse).

Eventually Manon moves off to make some purchases.
Meanwhile de Brétigny meets an old acquaintance, the Count
des Grieux (father of Manon's previous lover), who tells him
that his son has gone to a seminary to train for the priesthood,
after an unhappy love affair. Manon overhears part of their
conversation and, with some embarrassment, questions the
Count, pretending that his son's lover was a friend of hers.
The Count tells her that his son has now begun to overcome
his unhappiness.

Guillot arrives, with some friends (including Lescaut) and
the ballet dancers from the Opéra – brought by him to
amuse and impress Manon, whom he in turn hopes to win
from de Brétigny. Greeted by the crowds, the dancers perform a ballet. But Manon is uninterested, thinking only of des
Grieux; she asks Lescaut to call her carriage and, to Guillot's
stupefaction, goes off to St. Sulpice.

The scene changes to the St. Sulpice seminary. Worshippers are gathered there, praising the oratory of 'the Abbé des

Grieux'. He enters and his father talks to him, trying to dissuade him from entering the priesthood. But he will not be dissuaded. Left alone, he sings of his new desire – to forget Manon and find heavenly peace: 'Ah! Begone, vision fair' (Ah! fuyez, douce image). He goes. Manon arrives at the seminary and, while the sound of prayer is heard from the chapel, she gives money to a porter who fetches des Grieux. In their long duet which follows, he at first rejects her and tries to send her away. But she begs him to have pity and eventually he gives way: he can no longer overcome his love for her, and they go off together.

ACT IV

At a gambling hall in Paris, Lescaut, Poussette, Javotte and Rosette are among the crowds. Guillot enters, soon followed by Manon, who has brought des Grieux, against his better judgment. Manon and Lescaut try to persuade the unwilling des Grieux to retrieve his fortunes at the tables. Singing of her love for him, she eventually succeeds, and when Guillot challenges him to a game he agrees. They play, watched excitedly by Manon and the three girls, for extravagant stakes.

Des Grieux consistently wins, and at length Guillot rises from the table and suggests he has been cheated. Des Grieux challenges him, but order is restored and Guillot goes off, threatening the lovers. The agitated crowd points suspiciously at des Grieux. Soon there is a knock at the door: Guillot has returned with the police, to arrest des Grieux for cheating and Manon as his accomplice. Des Grieux's indignation changes to remorse when his father enters. In an ensemble, Guillot rejoices in the prospect of revenge while the others plead for mercy. The Count promises his son that he will soon be freed, but he has no pity for Manon; the two are separated and taken off.

ACT V

Des Grieux is waiting on the road to Le Havre, where Manon and other women are to be taken for deportation as prostitutes. Lescaut comes. They had hoped to hold up the convoy of deportees and rescue Manon, but the plan has gone awry. The soldiers approach with their charges. The sergeant says that one of the girls (Manon) is half-dead and Lescaut bribes him to let him take her away, promising to bring her back later.

Lescaut leaves her and des Grieux alone together. Des Grieux promises to contrive her rescue, but she is full of remorse. Her only consolation is a remembrance of their past happiness. Desperately ill, she has no strength left to escape; she dies, and with a cry des Grieux falls over her body.

*   *   *   *   *

In *Manon*, Massenet makes telling use of a number of recurring motives associated with his various characters, even though the work is made up of separate musical numbers. A feature of the score is the way in which, repeatedly, the orchestra takes on the role of commentator and itself utters the motives. This was enough to gain for the work the hostile label 'Wagnerian' from those who did not really appreciate Wagner. But, with the hindsight of today we might just as reasonably relate this trait to Puccini's method, particularly in the way the orchestra proclaims, for example, de Brétigny's characteristic theme at the end of Act II – for although de Brétigny is now off-stage, this is 'his' act: during it, he has won Manon. His theme is:

Manon is a girl in pursuit not of money or power but of pleasure. She harbours no good-will or ill-will or any moral feeling. Her music has a simple, light appeal; with complete

naturalness of idiom she tells des Grieux of her past, ending:
'And that is the story of Manon Lescaut!'

With this very phrase, at the end of the opera, she dies.

Des Grieux's music, gay or despairing, never loses its noble
character, and at first seems to be able to match Manon's own
capricious lightness.

But des Grieux, alas, is poor; poverty will diminish
pleasure; and pleasure-loving Manon accepts the rich de
Brétigny. She queens it at the Cours-la-Reine; this scene,
with a ballroom off-stage, introduces the musically picturesque style of the 18th century – a minuet first of all, and later
Manon's famous gavotte to the words 'Let us enjoy the days
of beauty':

The music of this scene is used to open the prelude (Massenet prefers this term to overture). The prelude also quotes
other themes in the work – notably two which we do not
hear again until the last act.

CLAUDE DEBUSSY

(1862–1918)

FOR part of his career, Debussy was a practising music critic as well as a composer, and what he wrote about other composers helps to define his own attitudes. Gluck he attacked as standing for 'Wagnerian formulas in embryo, which is unbearable'; Massenet and Gounod he defended, Bizet he exalted; Puccini and his Italian contemporaries he described as employing 'a film formula, whereby the characters fling themselves on one another and tear their melodies from each other's lips'; and one of Grieg's works was 'a pink bon-bon filled with snow'. Most significant was his love-and-hate affair with 'the arch-poisoner, Wagner'. He enormously admired Wagner's musical genius and his harmonic boldness, but totally rejected his symphonic method of composing operas in a texture woven out of leading-motives. In Debussy's view, the attempt to parallel the dramatic development with musical development is undramatic: 'Either the music gets out of breath in running after a character, or else the character sits down on a note to allow the music to catch up with him'.*

* These translations are by Oscar Thompson, from his book *Debussy, Man and Artist* (1937).

PELLÉAS ET MELISANDE

Libretto: Maurice Maeterlinck's play, slightly adapted by the composer

First performed: Paris, 1902

Five Acts

Cast in order of singing:

Golaud, grandson of Arkel	*baritone*
Mélisande	*soprano*
Geneviève, Arkel's daughter-in-law, mother of Golaud and Pelléas	*mezzo-soprano*
Arkel, King of Allemonde	*bass*
Pelléas, grandson of Arkel, half-brother to Golaud	*tenor*
Yniold, Golaud's son by his first marriage	*soprano* (*or boy treble*)
A shepherd	*baritone*
A doctor	*bass*

The scene is laid in the imaginary kingdom of Allemonde in medieval times

DEBUSSY and the Belgian dramatist Maurice Maeterlinck (1862–1949) were born in the same year. Maeterlinck's play *Pelléas et Mélisande* (1892) immediately commended itself to Debussy for an opera: he set the actual text of the play (very slightly cut and altered), not a conventional opera libretto worked up from it. This must be one of the few operas with singing parts for four generations: Yniold is son to Golaud, who is son to Geneviève, who is daughter-in-law to Arkel. One other play by Maeterlinck gave rise to an opera of some success: *Ariane et Barbe-Bleue* (Ariadne and Bluebeard, 1899), set in 1907 by Paul Dukas (1865–1935).

Debussy wrote no other operas. He found nowhere else the

inspiration which Maeterlinck had given him – the inspiration for a shadowy, legendary, understated tragic drama, in which the real and the symbolic intertwine, and in which the personages submit to fate. Ironically, Maeterlinck (after first having consented to the opera's being composed) publicly wished failure to the première: he had presumed that his wife would be chosen for the part of Mélisande, and she was not! The Scottish singer, Mary Garden, was.

The almost hypnotic, impressionistic appeal of Debussy's well-loved orchestral pieces – *The Afternoon of a Faun*, the *Nocturnes* – is felt too in this opera. There are no heroics, only the muted music suited to a remote kind of vision.

*   *   *   *   *

ACT I

In a forest, Mélisande is alone by a well. Golaud, who has been hunting in the forest and is now lost, chances upon her. He finds her trembling with fear and weeping: 'Do not touch me!' (Ne me touchez pas!), she says. It emerges that she has been hurt, though she will not tell him by whom. Visible at the bottom of the well is a golden crown that fell from her head while she was weeping. She wishes to stay in the forest alone, but he insists that she comes with him.

In a room in the royal castle, several months later, Geneviève is reading to her father-in-law King Arkel a letter from her son Golaud to her other son Pelléas, in which he tells his half-brother how he discovered Mélisande and eventually made her his wife. He has asked Pelléas to find out whether Arkel, who had intended him to make a different marriage, would forgive him and receive them. Arkel agrees to do so. Pelléas enters, asking his grandfather for permission to visit a dying friend but, as his own father is ill and his brother just returning, Arkel tells him to wait, and to light the lamp signifying that Golaud's ship has permission to land.

Later, Golaud and Mélisande are understood to have landed. In front of the castle, Geneviève is in discussion with Mélisande. Pelléas enters and talks with them. In the distance the sound of boatmen in the harbour can be heard, and

through the mist the ship which brought the newcomers can
be seen setting sail again. Geneviève goes, leaving Pelléas
to take Mélisande to the castle. In their brief moment alone
together the seeds of love between them are sown.

Act II

Pelléas and Mélisande are together by a well at a shaded spot
in a park. Mélisande longs to touch the water but cannot
reach. As she plays with the ring Golaud gave her she drops
it in the well; soon it is beyond their grasp and irretrievably
lost. What shall they tell Golaud? 'The truth!' (La vérité!)
says Pelléas.

Back in a room in the castle, Golaud is in bed. He was hurt
in a riding accident – at noon, just the moment the ring was
lost. By his bedside, Mélisande tries to make him comfortable.
Suddenly he sees that she is weeping: in response to his
kindly questions, she says she is unhappy in the gloomy surroundings of the castle and asks to be taken away. Golaud
takes her hand, and sees that the ring is missing. He is much
distressed and sends her out, in the dark, with Pelléas, to a
cave by the shore where she untruthfully says it slipped off.

Pelléas takes her down to the cave (so that she will at least
be able to describe it to Golaud). It is sinister and dark, and
Mélisande is frightened, especially when the light of the
moon discloses three aged paupers asleep. Pelléas leads her
off, determining to come back another time.

Act III

Mélisande is by herself at a window of one of the towers of
the castle, singing as she combs her long hair. Seeing her
from the path below, Pelléas is entranced by her beauty. At
his request she leans far out and he takes her hand; then her
hair tumbles down and envelops him, filling him with excitement. Doves fly around them. He refuses to let go of the long
soft tresses: 'I am binding them' (Je les noue, je les noue), he
sings. He finds they are caught in the branches of a tree; then
Golaud comes, and tells them to stop playing childishly so
late at night.

Golaud, alone with Pelléas, shows him the dank vaults of the castle and then leads him up to the terrace. There he tells Pelléas that he witnessed what happened the previous night and is disturbed by the relationship between Pelléas and Mélisande; he asks Pelléas to spend less time in her company, and mentions that she may soon become a mother.

In front of the castle, Golaud, plagued by jealous suspicions, asks his child Yniold what happens when Pelléas and Mélisande are together. The child's replies are innocent: they talk, he says, about a door, or a light, or how he (Yniold) will grow up into a big boy; once they kissed, when it was raining. There is nothing to anger Golaud, nothing to reassure him. A light goes on in Mélisande's room. Golaud holds Yniold up so that he can see in: Pelléas is there, he says, they are looking at one another, they are not close; but he begs to be put down, as this is hurting him. At length Golaud does so, and leads him off, deeply troubled.

ACT IV

In a room in the castle, Pelléas and Mélisande meet. He tells her that he has been with his ailing father, who is now rather stronger. His father has told him to go on a journey. They arrange to meet that evening by the well, and Pelléas goes out.

Arkel enters. He has noticed Mélisande's unhappiness in the gloomy surroundings and is anxious about her. Then Golaud comes in, with blood on his forehead. Speaking angrily to Mélisande, he asks for his sword. He comments on her large, beautiful eyes; Arkel sees in them only 'a great innocence'. But Golaud derides her 'innocence'. Becoming more and more angry and agitated, he eventually seizes her by her hair, pulls her to her knees and drags her across the room in a passionate, jealous rage. Arkel stops him: he suddenly feigns calmness, while Mélisande weeps pitifully: 'I am not happy!' (Je ne suis pas heureuse!).

By the well in the park, Yniold is playing. The bleating of sheep is heard as a shepherd and his flock pass nearby: the sheep are suddenly silent as the shepherd directs them away from their accustomed fold (they are to be slaughtered).

Yniold goes. Pelléas arrives, soliloquizing: he understands now that he and Mélisande are deeply in love and that he must go away as soon as possible, to live only on his fading memories of her. Mélisande arrives. First he and then she admit their love: 'Je t'aime' ... 'Je t'aime aussi'. It is dark and they can scarcely see one another. In the distance they hear the castle doors being barred and know that they are now certain to be discovered: 'All is lost, all is won!' (Tout est perdu, tout est sauvé!). They embrace. A moment later they hear and see Golaud, watching nearby; they keep calm, reconciled to the inevitable; as he comes they embrace, passionately, then again, still more passionately, for the last time. Golaud leaps at them, killing Pelléas, while Mélisande flees in terror.

ACT V

In a room in the castle, Mélisande is ill in bed, watched over by a doctor, Arkel and Golaud. She was wounded by Golaud, but the wound, the doctor says, is very slight, and not the cause of her illness. She has also given birth to a child. Golaud is repentant; he now believes that their embraces were not those of guilty lovers. She becomes conscious, but answers Arkel only vaguely. Golaud asks to be left alone with her. He begs for forgiveness, which she, not really comprehending, readily grants; then he asks whether her love with Pelléas was guilty, which she denies, but he presses her again and she returns to half-consciousness. Arkel comes in with the physician and talks to her, showing her the baby, which she is too weak to hold.

The servants silently assemble along the walls. Golaud again becomes impassioned and demands to be left alone with his dying wife. Arkel tries to calm him. The servants all fall to their knees as Mélisande's life ebbs away, and Arkel quietly observes her final tranquillity.

* * * * *

There are musical themes related to particular characters in *Pelléas et Mélisande*, of which we may instance the oboe

theme before the curtain rises, which is to be associated with
Mélisande (and last returns, also on the oboe, as she dies at
the very end of the opera):

But – here we quote from the most authoritative Wagner
scholar, Ernest Newman, in his *Opera Nights* (1943):

> It is characteristic of Debussy's entirely non-Wagnerian
> way of handling his motives that he should use the motive of
> Mélisande to accompany both her own words descriptive of
> Golaud, 'Oh, your hair is so grey' and Golaud's remark about
> herself, 'I am looking at your eyes. Do you never close your
> eyes?'. Wagner would have shuddered at the thought of em-
> ploying Mélisande's motive when it was a case of describing
> Golaud!

The declaration of love between Pelléas and Mélisande
(Act IV) is in a sense both the climax of the opera and the
ultimate expression of Debussy's method. At the opposite pole
from conventionally rapturous, expansive operatic declara-
tions of love we have Pelléas's low-toned confession: 'You
do not know that it's because ...' – and then he breaks off,
inconsequentially as lovers do, to utter the crucial words.
Mélisande follows him at the same level of pitch, an extraordinary effect:

Notice the orchestral part with its repetition and variation of
harmony. The placing of words in short, conversation-like
phrases (the antithesis of soaring Italian melody) also plays a
notable part in the dramatic expression, as in Mélisande's 'He
doesn't love me any more – I am not happy' in the previous
scene:

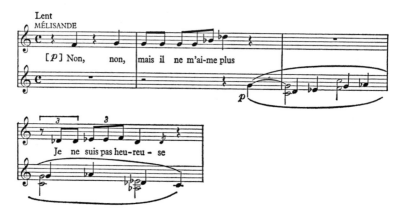

The harmonic language of the opera – especially sequences
of block chords outside the usual harmonic relationships –
owes something to Mussorgsky's *Boris Godunov*, a score of
which came into Debussy's hands in Paris about 1893.

VIII

BEDŘICH SMETANA

(1824–84)

D EBUSSY'S opera shows an element of positive revolt against
conventional notions of what opera should be. We turn
back now to an earlier phenomenon of musical revolt: the
desire of Czech and Russian composers to establish their own
national music, often *against* the conventions of Italian opera
and German symphony. Such revolutionary ideals in music
often went along in sympathy with revolutionary politics too
– as in the case of Smetana, now regarded as the founder of
a Czech national style in concert-hall and opera-house.

Sympathizing with Czech national feeling against the do-
minion of the Austrian Empire, Smetana found the atmosphere of Prague oppressive after the crushing of the abortive
revolution of 1848. He worked in Sweden from 1856 to 1861,
but returned when an easing of Austrian rule made it possible
for the Czechs to found in Prague a theatre for plays and
opera in their own language. Smetana's work became the
corner-stone of Czech opera and still remains so. But though
all his eight operas are cherished by his countrymen, only *The
Bartered Bride* entered the international repertory and remains there.

The operas of Antonín Dvořák (1841–1904) are also chiefly
the preserve of Czechoslovak theatres, though *Rusalka* (1901)
is occasionally heard elsewhere: the title-role is that of a
water-nymph.

THE BARTERED BRIDE

(Prodaná Nevěsta)

Libretto by Karel Sabina

First performed: Prague, 1866

Three Acts

Cast in order of singing:

Jeník, a peasant, son of Mícha by his first wife	*tenor*
Mařenka, daughter of Krušina and Ludmila	*soprano*
Kecal, a marriage broker	*bass*
Krušina, a peasant	*baritone*
Ludmila, his wife	*soprano*
Vašek, son of Mícha by his second wife	*tenor*
The Manager of a troupe of strolling players	*tenor*
Esmeralda, a dancer ⎫ members of the troupe ⎧	*soprano*
The Indian ⎭ ⎩	*tenor*
Háta, Mícha's second wife	*mezzo-soprano*
Mícha, a landlord	*bass*

Chorus of villagers, actors and children

The scene is laid in a Bohemian village, on the Patron Saint's day, in the first half of the 19th century

LIVELY rustic jollification, with catchy airs and invigorating dances – this, rather than any dramatic subtlety or opportunity for vocal fireworks, is provided by *The Bartered Bride*. We give this opera the title fixed by custom, but the Czech would be more literally rendered *The Sold Fiancée*.

* * * * *

ACT I

The exuberant overture sets the mood for the opening scene: a village with an inn and – for it is a festive day – a fair. Among the cheerful villagers only Mařenka is sad. Her sweetheart,

Jeník, asks why: because her parents are planning her marriage with a man she cannot love, she tells him—Vašek, the half-wit son of Mícha. Jeník, she feels, does not show sufficient concern; she asks him whether his mysterious past includes a love-affair. He reassures her, explaining that he was turned out after his father's second marriage: 'A cruel stepmother's nothing but a curse!' (Takž kletbou macecha zlá).*
They sing about the strength of their love and their confidence in the future.

They go off and Mařenka's parents, Krušina and Ludmila, enter with Kecal, a marriage broker, who is haranguing them about keeping to the bargain they have made. The husband, he says, is Micha's son, not the good-for-nothing one who disappeared, but Vašek: in the solo and trio which follow he assures them to their satisfaction that although the boy is a bit slow and odd he has every other virtue in abundance.

Mařenka enters. They tell her what they are planning, but Ludmila makes it clear that they will not insist on the marriage without Mařenka's consent. Mařenka objects that she has a lover to whom she has sworn fidelity. Confident of overcoming this trifling obstacle, Kecal determines to go off to the inn to have a word with her lover, Jeník, but is not entirely pleased when Krušina decides that Mařenka should at least meet Vašek.

The scene changes to the village inn, where young people dance and sing in a lively polka.

ACT II

At the inn, the young men are singing in praise of beer, while Jeník praises love; Kecal, watching them, praises only money. They dance a Furiant. Then Vašek enters—a ridiculous, stuttering figure. Mařenka arrives. She tells Vašek (who does not know her) that everyone pities him for having to marry such a disagreeable girl as Mařenka, especially as someone else is pining for him – implying it is herself. She runs off, with him in pursuit.

* English version by Joan Cross and Eric Crozier (Boosey & Hawkes).

Kecal approaches Jeník, promising to find him a rich wife and, in a duet, emphasizes the importance of money in marriage. Then he offers Jeník a hundred crowns to give up Mařenka. When the offer has trebled, Jeník agrees – on condition that Mařenka marries no one other than Mícha's eldest son. While Kecal goes to draw up the contract with this added clause, Jeník expresses his surprise that the broker could imagine that he would give her up so readily. Kecal returns with the contract, and with Krušina and many villagers as witnesses, Jeník signs. All are astonished and disgusted that he should have bartered his bride-to-be so readily.

ACT III

Vašek, alone on the village green, anxiously bewails his prospective fate as husband of the terrible Mařenka. A group of strolling players is about to perform and their manager calls out all the attractions. The 'Dance of the Show-people' (or 'of the Comedians') follows. Vašek is interested by the troupe, especially by Esmeralda, the Spanish dancer. The Indian in the troupe comes to the manager with news that the man who plays the dancing bear is drunk. Esmeralda, with hints of love, entices Vašek to take his place and she and the manager start showing him what he has to do.

Vašek's parents, Mícha and Háta, arrive with Kecal, who has the marriage contract. To their consternation, Vašek refuses to sign because of what he has heard about Mařenka. Mařenka, distraught at Jeník's apparent perfidy, enters with her parents, who, with Kecal and Vašek's parents in support, try to obtain her signature to the contract. Vašek, who had wandered off, is called back, and he recognizes Mařenka as the girl who spoke to him in the morning; he is now willing to sign, but Mařenka wants time to think it over. The four parents and Kecal agree to leave her alone for a few minutes. She sings, with bitter nostalgia, of her dreams of happiness with Jeník.

Jeník enters. Mařenka will not hear a word from him, cutting off contemptuously all his efforts to explain. In a lively duet he complains of her obstinacy, while she upbraids him.

Kecal arrives. Jeník mentions the clause in the contract about her marrying Mícha's son, gently assuring her that Mícha's son will always love her. Kecal heartily approves and Mařenka is still more disillusioned.

The villagers and the four parents return and ask Mařenka what she has decided: to annoy Jeník, she says, she will marry Vašek. All congratulate her, including Jeník himself. Háta and Mícha are disconcerted to see him – especially when Jeník greets Mícha as his father (the significance of the added clause now becomes clear). Kecal too is taken aback. Háta sneers at Jeník but Mařenka, free to choose and at last realizing what has happened, of course chooses Jeník, to Kecal's annoyance and Háta's fury. The villagers join in the laughter at Kecal's expense.

Suddenly there are cries of confusion, as a 'bear' appears. It is Vašek, to Háta's rage and embarrassment. She leads him off, while Ludmila, Krušina, Mícha and the villagers congratulate the united lovers.

*   *   *   *   *

Though the plot of *The Bartered Bride* hangs so perilously on one improbability (why does Jeník not *tell* Mařenka of his plan?), the opera lives by the racy cut of its melodies. They are closely related to those of the dance, even when not actually danced to on the stage. Smetana's gift was to find a great variety of exact musical characterizations, all within this melodic type.

Kecal the marriage-broker is the confident business-man, seemingly sharper than these village folk but really not so sharp as he thinks:

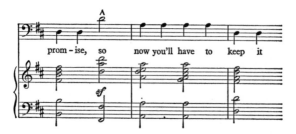

Note the *sforzando* slaps-on-the-back in the orchestra!

Vašek stutters nervously, opening his song like this – and again, note the orchestral accompaniment with its continuation of the stuttering (bar 5):

Though hero and heroine are allowed their music of real sentiment, even they are perhaps most memorably caught in the bickering duet of the last act. The tune is one which is naturally performed with a pulling-back of the rhythm at first and then a gradual resumption of tempo:

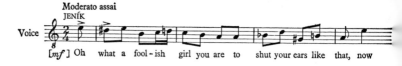

But to deduce that the score uses only a simple kind of music would be wrong. The cleverness of Smetana's art may be seen in the echoing of voices (not strictly in canon) in the lovers' Act I duet, and in the similar give-and-take in Kecal's and Jeník's matchmaking duet in Act II, which in the theatre is perhaps the most taking number in the whole score.

LEOŠ JANÁČEK
(1854–1928)

LIKE Smetana, Leoš Janáček is considered by his country-men an intensely national composer. At first his works made little international headway, but after the Second World War his operas became prominent in the theatres of German-speaking countries and three of them reached London at this time – *Katya Kabanova* and *The Cunning Little Vixen* (1924) at Sadler's Wells, and *Jenůfa* (1904) at Covent Garden. Of Janáček's other seven operas the two most important are the two last: *The Makropoulos Case* (1926) and *From the House of the Dead* (staged posthumously, 1930), of which the former reached Sadler's Wells in 1964.

Janáček set Czech words in a naturalistic idiom based on speech rhythms, as Mussorgsky had with Russian words. He was also influenced by Russian literature: *Katya Kabanova* is based on the play *The Storm* by Ostrovsky – a play to which Tchaikovsky wrote incidental music.

KATYA KABANOVA

Libretto by V. Cervinka after the play by Ostrovsky
First performed: Brno, 1921

Three Acts

Cast in order of singing:

Vanya Kudrash, teacher and chemist	*teno*
Glasha, a servant to the Kabanov family	*mezzo-sopran*
Savel Prokofievich Dikoy, a merchant	*bas*
Boris Grigorievich, his nephew	*teno*
Feklusha, a servant to the Kabanov family	*mezzo-sopran*
Marfa Ignatyevna Kabanova (known as Kabanikha), widow of a wealthy merchant	*contralt*
Tikhon Ivanovich Kabanov, her son	*teno*
Katerina (Katya) Kabanova, his wife	*sopran*
Varvara, adopted daughter of the Kabanov family	*mezzo-sopran*
Kuligin, a friend of Kudrash	*bariton*

Chorus of people

*The scene is laid in the town of Kalinov
on the Volga in the 1860s*

THE storm which rages through the small Russian town o
Kalinov echoes the storm in the mind of Katya – married t
a weak husband under the thumb of his cruel mother, an
guiltily in love with a man too weak to rescue her. The tor
tured mind of Katya is contrasted with the carefree youthful
ness of Varvara, the adopted daughter in the household o
Katya's mother-in-law; and their music contributes to
strange but compelling atmosphere in which the cruelties an
torments of small-town life find subtle operatic expression.

The Czech title of the opera is correctly written *Kát'*
Kabanová. But as this (and the other names in the Czec

core) are merely Czech spellings of the Russian names of the
original Russian play, we give here the usual English forms
or the original Russian spelling.

*   *   *   *   *

ACT I

By the Kabanov family house on the banks of the Volga, Kudrash sits watching the river, talking to the Kabanovs' servant
Glasha. They move aside as Dikoy and Boris enter; as usual,
Dikoy is rating his nephew. Dikoy leaves and Boris talks with
Kudrash, explaining that he has to live with his uncle in
order that he may eventually inherit a legacy. People are returning from church, among them Feklusha, another servant
of the Kabanovs, who talks to Glasha. Boris confides his unhappiness to Kudrash, and his eyes are fixed on Katya Kab-
nova, returning with her husband Tikhon from church.
Boris is, as he confesses, in love with her.

Tikhon is under the thumb of his mother, known as Kab-
nikha, who tells him he should go away at once on business.
She reprimands him for treating her with little affection since
his marriage, but he protests his love and respect of her, and
Katya does likewise. Kabanikha turns fiercely on Katya, who
goes into the house; she follows after warning her son to act
more sternly towards his wife. Varvara expresses to Tikhon
her pity for Katya.

The scene changes to a room in the Kabanov house, where
Katya is talking to Varvara about how sad she has become
lately and recalls her carefree younger days. Growing agitated, she mentions her guilty love for another man. Varvara
asks if she will meet the man while Tikhon is away, an idea
she at once rejects. Tikhon enters, followed by Glasha and
Feklusha. Katya begs him not to leave her, and when he says
he must go she begs him to take her with him. Despite her
repeated pleas, Tikhon is only irritated, and refuses. Desper-
tely, she asks him to make her swear not to speak to any
stranger.

Kabanikha interrupts, entering to say that all is ready for
his departure. She demands that Tikhon should tell his wife

how to behave in his absence; reluctantly and with embar
rassment, he does so, following his mother's instructions, t
Katya's deep humiliation. Before he leaves, they sit down fo
a moment together, following Russian custom. As he kisse
Katya goodbye, she embraces him passionately – to Kab
anikha's disgust.

ACT II

It is evening, and as Kabanikha, Katya and Varvara work a
their embroidery Kabanikha rebukes Katya for not showin
more obvious grief at her husband's departure. Kabanikh
leaves, and Varvara announces her intention of going out – sh
has obtained the key of the locked garden gate, and offers t
summon Boris to meet Katya. Katya, much agitated, rejec
the idea; but left alone (with Kabanikha's voice briefly hear
from outside) she decides that she will see him, only for
moment, and she goes. A moment later Kabanikha enter
with Dikoy, who is maudlin drunk; Kabanikha comforts him

Later that evening in the wooded garden behind the Kab
anov house, Kudrash is alone, singing a serenade and playin
his guitar as he waits for Varvara. Boris enters; a girl, he say
had come up to him and told him to come for an assignation
Kudrash warns him of the dangers of loving a marrie
woman. Soon Varvara approaches, singing a song by whic
her sweetheart will know her; joyously, Kudrash answers he
in song. Varvara tells Boris that Katya will come, and goes o
with Kudrash. Boris waits anxiously. Soon Katya arrives. Sh
is still tortured by her conscience, but eventually gives wa
to her emotions; they embrace and go off together, just a
Varvara and Kudrash return. Their loving voices are hear
in the distance, while Varvara and Kudrash talk, then sin
another happy song. It serves to call Katya back, for the tim
has come for the women to go in. Boris and Katya part word
lessly, too moved even to bid one another goodnight.

ACT III

It is a stormy afternoon and people are hurrying to shelte
in a large decrepit building near the river bank. Kudras

nd his friend Kuligin watch. Dikoy enters, everyone making
ray for him; Kudrash tries to persuade him of the value of
ghtning conductors, which he dismisses angrily, irritated by
.udrash's scientific and irreligious attitude to the elements.
. moment later Boris comes in, then Varvara, who anxiously
ells Boris that Katya, with her husband now returned, is almost deranged by her sense of guilt. The storm goes on and
Katya, Tikhon and Kabanikha come in. Boris conceals him-
elf. Katya's overwrought state is observed by the crowd and
y Dikoy, who comment on it and on her beauty. She notices
Boris, and can bear it no longer; she bursts out with a des-
erate confession of her guilty love, and rushes off.

At a deserted spot by the Volga, night is falling as Tikhon
nd Glasha, carrying a lantern, come searching for Katya.
Tikhon, though he still loves her, talks of the punishment she
eserves. As they move off, Varvara and Kudrash enter. Var-
ara is full of foreboding; she agrees to go away with him,
nd they depart. In the distance, Tikhon's and Glasha's voices
re heard calling Katya. Just then she enters, from the oppo-
ite direction; she only wishes now to see Boris once again.
Kuligin passes and mysterious, wordless voices are heard from
far. Katya speaks wildly, wishing half for death, half to see
Boris again. Then Boris enters. They embrace passionately,
nd talk of the future: Boris has been sent away by his uncle,
nd Katya will have to bear the taunts of her mother-in-law
nd the town. Boris goes. The distant voices are heard again.
Katya, utterly distraught, throws herself into the river. People
uickly gather – Kuligin, a passer-by, then Dikoy, Glasha,
Tikhon and Kabanikha. 'You killed my wife!' says Tikhon
itterly to his mother, who prevents him from diving in after
Katya. The body is pulled out of the river and Dikoy places
 on the bank, where Tikhon falls upon it. Kabanikha form-
lly thanks the people present for their kind assistance.

*　　　*　　　*　　　*　　　*

anáček's realistic setting of Czech words – realistic in the
ense that it flows in irregular patterns, like the prose of
rdinary speech – is complemented by his similarly 'irregular',

asymmetrical, and subtle treatment of recurring motives. I[n] the first scene as Boris begins to divulge to Kudrash his lov[e] for Katya a little theme steals in first high on the oboe, the[n] repeated by violins; then, when Katya herself enters with he[r] husband and family (orchestra without voices), the flute take[s] it over:

This symbolizes not only Boris's love for Katya but also he[r] for him, and recurs with that dual significance. Not the simi[-]lar phrase 'x' (and compare the previous example) at the poin[t] when, in the garden, she finally lets her passion express itse[lf] to Boris: her words ('Tvoje vule nade mnou vládne') sho[w] her anguish*:

The strongest contrast with this idiom is provided by th[e] songs (that is, musical material sung *as* interpolated song[s] given to the 'happy' pair of lovers in the garden scene. The[y] are in the spirit of Czech folksong and one (the first 'answer[-]ing'-duet) has a dance-like beat but an unexpected five-ba[r] rhythm:

* English version by Norman Tucker (Universal).

ALEXANDER BORODIN

(1833–87)

THE first Russian operas to become internationally famous were those of Mikhail Ivanovich Glinka (1804–57): *A Life for the Tsar* (1836, now performed in Russia under Glinka's intended title, 'Ivan Sussanin') and *Russlan and Ludmila* (1842). The nationalist-historical element in the first and Russian-legendary element in the second were prophetic of much that was to follow in Russian opera. So was the literary inspiration of Pushkin (in *Russlan and Ludmila*) and Glinka's use of musical elements drawn from Russian folk-song.

Borodin, like Mussorgsky and Rimsky-Korsakov (see below, pp. 349 and 365), was a member of the nationalist group of composers called 'The Five' or 'The Mighty Handful'. A professor of chemistry, he had a severely limited time available for music; but the fact that his only opera, *Prince Igor*, was left unfinished at his death appears partly due to other reasons. For nearly five years he left it almost untouched. It was completed after his death by his close associates, Rimsky-Korsakov and Alexander Glazunov (1865–1936): the overture was written out and orchestrated by Glazunov, to whom Borodin had often played it on the piano.

PRINCE IGOR

(Knyaz Igor)

Libretto by the composer

First performed: St. Petersburg, 1890

Prologue and four Acts

Cast in order of singing:

Igor, prince of Seversk	*baritone*
Prince Galitzky, his brother-in-law	*bass*
Skula ⎱ players of the gudok* and deserters from ⎰	*bass*
Yeroshka ⎰ Igor's army ⎱	*tenor*
Yaroslavna, Igor's second wife	*soprano*
A nurse in Yaroslavna's household	*soprano*
A Polovtsian maiden	*soprano*
Konchakovna, daughter of Khan Konchak	*mezzo-soprano*
Vladimir, Igor's son by his first marriage	*tenor*
Ovlur, a baptized Polovtsian soldier	*tenor*
Khan Konchak, a prince of the Polovtsi	*bass*

[The role of Khan Gzak is silent.]

Chorus of Russians and Polovtsi (soldiers, people, prisoners, etc.)

The scene is laid in Putivl (a town of the Seversk region) and in the camp of the Polovtsi, in 1185

Prince Igor sketches, in bold musical contours, a tale of war and peace, honour and dishonour. It makes dramatic and musical use of the picturesque-ness of the orient, sometimes for barbaric effect. Its story is set in the 12th century when Russia – at that time a loose federation of principalities – was under pressure from the Tatars. The Tatar (otherwise Mon-

* An old Russian bowed instrument with three strings.

ol) power, known as the 'Khanate of the Golden Horde',
became even stronger in the next century and actually estab-
ished sovereignty over Russia. The Polovtsi were one of these
Tatar peoples.

In the opera, Prince Igor, ruling at Putivl, leads the Rus-
ians; he falls prisoner to Konchak, one of the Khans (princes)
who rule the Polovtsi. The Russians are Christians (they were
converted about 990); the Polovtsi are pagan, but among
them is one, Ovlur, who has accepted Christianity and treach-
erously offers to help Igor escape.

It is an opera of spectacle, especially in the famous Polov-
sian Dances with chorus, which end the second act. Dramatically it displays noble enemies in opposition. The three leading
male characters – Igor, Konchak, Galitzky – are baritone,
bass and bass, which lends a distinctive vocal colour to the
score; and frequently the same singer doubles the two bass
roles.

*   *   *   *   *

PROLOGUE

Outside the cathedral in Putivl, Prince Igor is acclaimed as
he prepares to march to war against the Polovtsian Khans.
An eclipse of the sun takes place, which Galitzky (Igor's
brother-in-law) and others regard as a bad omen. Igor nevertheless sets out amid further acclaim. Two merry ne'er-do-
wells, Skula and Yeroshka, desert from Igor's army, preferring
to serve under Galitzky and avoid a foreign campaign. Igor
bids farewell to his sorrowing wife Yaroslavna; his son
Vladimir, who is to serve with his father, joins in. Igor appoints Galitzky to rule in his absence, then sets off on horseback with his army.

ACT I

In Galitzky's home his retainers are rejoicing, Yeroshka and
Skula among them. Now that Igor is away, Galitzky too rejoices. If only he were really the ruling prince, what a gay
reign would be his! A group of girls enters to complain that

one of their number has been abducted by Galitzky's men
He refuses to give her up, and leaves. Skula and Yeroshka
mock the petitioners, then embark on a drinking song with
chorus in Galitzky's honour. They and their fellows wish
Galitzky were their real ruler.

Meanwhile, in her home, Igor's wife Yaroslavna pines for
her husband. Introduced by a nurse, the girls who have vainly
implored Galitzky's justice now ask Yaroslavna's help. They
leave, and Galitzky enters: Yaroslavna argues with him
fiercely until he promises to free the abducted girl. He leaves

A group of noblemen enters with sad tidings for Yaro
slavna: her husband and his men are prisoners of the
Polovtsi. Moreover, the alarm bells sound even now and dis
tant fires are seen; the enemy is marching on Putivl.

ACT II

In the camp of the Polovtsi, at evening, young girls are singing (with solo) and dancing. Konchakovna, the daughter of
the Khan Konchak, is looking forward to seeing the man she
loves. She tells the girls to give food and drink to a group of
Russian prisoners-of-war who now enter. A patrol of Polovtsian soldiers, providing guards for the night, sings and departs – except Ovlur, a Christian convert among the Polovtsi.
He remains on guard, unobserved, when Vladimir (a prisoner
like his father) enters and calls for his beloved. It is Konchakovna. She enters: they declare their love for one another
and leave.

Igor himself appears, singing of his longing to be free.
Ovlur discloses himself and offers to help Igor escape; but
Igor, deeming such behaviour dishonourable, declines.

Konchak enters, treating his captive as an esteemed noble
guest, offering him treasure and slave-girls, and asking him
to stay and become his ally – or to go home, on condition of
not renewing the war. Igor declines the condition. Konchak
admires his honourable behaviour, and entertains his guest
with male and female dancers and singers (the Polovtsian
Dances).

ACT III

A march introduces a scene in the Polovtsian camp. The Polovtsi (basses) hail the arrival of the men of an allied army (tenors) under Khan Gzak. Konchak proclaims the success of the campaign. The victors leave for a feast, after which they will decide on the next military steps. The Russian prisoners, downcast, believe that only if Igor were free would a Russian force turn back their enemies.

The Polovtsian soldiers guarding the prisoners begin to sing and dance; they become drunk and fall down, asleep. Ovlur enters, and this time Igor (realizing his countrymen's dependence on him) accepts his help: he and his son will try to escape.

Konchakovna enters, seeking to persuade Vladimir to stay while his father urges their departure. Vladimir decides to leave with his father – but, as they try to make their escape, the love-sick Konchakovna raises the alarm. The Polovtsi, with Konchak following, rush in. Igor has escaped but Vladimir is recaptured. Konchak gives his orders: let Vladimir be free, and marry his daughter, but let the guards who permitted the escape be hanged. The crowd hails Konchak and the coming campaign.

ACT IV

Seated atop the city walls of Putivl, Yaroslavna laments the plight of her people and herself. A group of countryfolk appears, having fled before the oncoming Khans. But Yaroslavna sees a Russian prince approaching, ready to lead the defence of the city. She recognizes him: it is Igor. They embrace.

Yeroshka and Skula, tipsy and playing their gudoks, enter with a song about the happiness they have been enjoying while Igor has been a captive – only to behold him then, in conversation with his wife as he enters the citadel. They decide that it is not worth running away and instead start sounding the bells to announce Igor's return. The crowd assembles

joyfully. All acclaim Igor as he and his wife emerge in stat
from the citadel, ready to lead the people once more.

$$*\qquad*\qquad*\qquad*\qquad*$$

The celebrated overture contains some of the most stirrin
tunes of the opera. The rapid alternation of trumpets come
from the reunion of the triumphant Polovtsi and their allie
in Act III; and two bold tunes which come later are bot
taken from Igor's soliloquy in Act II. They are:

The 'oriental' element in the music, familiar in the concert
hall in the Polovtsian Dances, is also reflected in the musi
of Konchakovna. Her invocation to the absent Vladimir i
Act IV

uses one characteristic melodic interval (in this case from I
sharp to C natural) which also served Verdi as an orientalisn
in *Aida*.

MODEST MUSSORGSKY

(1839–81)

MUSSORGSKY was a Russian army officer and later an un-important civil servant. He did not study music sys-ematically and the composer's technique which he forged vas very much his own. But his willingness to tolerate a cer-ain 'roughness' of sound, without the gloss that might have •een brought by academic training, fitted his desire to repro-uce Russian speech-inflexions in his music and to use the folk-nusic idioms of the Russian people.

Mussorgsky's masterpiece is the opera *Boris Godunov*. Out f mistaken devotion, his friend Rimsky-Korsakov applied imself after Mussorgsky's death to 'correcting' what he con-eived to be crudities in the score of the opera; but Rimsky-Korsakov's version, though persisting by the sheer indolence f some singers and opera companies, is now recognized as alsifying Mussorgsky's conception.

Living a disorderly life, succumbing to drink, and dying arly, Mussorgsky left his other operas unfinished; they herefore had to come under someone else's hand if any were) be produced. *The Khovansky Affair* (in Russian, *Khovan-hchina*) was completed and characteristically retouched by Rimsky-Korsakov, and produced in 1886; a later completion, ruer to Mussorgsky, has been made by Shostakovich. *Soro-hintsy Fair*, left much less complete, has been finished a at least four different versions by different hands; *The Marriage*, also left very incomplete, was not performed until 931 in Moscow in a version finished by Mikhail Ippolitov-vanov (1859–1935).

BORIS GODUNOV

Libretto by the composer, after Pushkin

First performed: St Petersburg, 1874

Prologue and Four Acts

Cast in order of singing:

A police officer	*baritone*
Mityukha, one of the crowd in Moscow	*bass*
Shchelkalov, secretary of the state council	*baritone*
Prince Shuisky, a leader of the nobles	*tenor*
Boris Godunov, Tsar	*baritone*
Pimen, a monk and chronicler	*bass*
Grigori, afterwards known as Dmitri, the Pretender	*tenor*
Hostess of an inn	*mezzo-soprano*
Missail ⎱ vagabond monks	⎰ *tenor*
Varlaam ⎰	⎱ *bass*
An officer	*bass*
Xenia, Boris's daughter	*soprano*
Fyodor, Boris's son (a young child)	*mezzo-soprano*
Nurse to Boris's children	*contralto*
A boyar (nobleman) in waiting	*tenor*
Marina Mniszek, a Polish princess	*soprano*
Rangoni, her confessor, a Jesuit	*bass*
A simpleton	*tenor*
Lavitzky ⎱ Jesuits	⎰ *bass*
Chernikovsky ⎰	⎱ *bass*
Krushchov, an nobleman	*bass*

Chorus of Russian people, boyars, Poles, etc.

The scene is laid in Russia and Poland in 1598–1605

BORIS GODUNOV himself – a Tsar tormented not only by political intrigue but by his own conscience – is one of opera's most subtle and most commanding roles. Yet neither

Boris nor anyone else is allowed to dominate Mussorgsky's opera. We are shown a slice of history, and in history rulers come and go like other mortals. Historical fact is at the basis of Pushkin's chronicle-play (in twenty-four scenes) on which the opera is founded. Boris Godunov reigned as Tsar from 1598 to 1605. In 1604 a pretender arose who claimed to be Dmitri, the supposedly murdered son of a previous Tsar. He gained support among the Poles, intriguing with the Polish princess Marina Mniszek, and eventually usurped the throne for a brief period.

The opera is concerned with Boris's coronation, his guilty conscience, his relationship with his children, and his death; and with Dmitri (who is here depicted as a runaway monk, Grigori) and his relationship with Marina and his bid for the throne. Another major participant is the People – buffeted by political change, compelled to cheer when the police order it, breaking out in wild acts of rough justice, and producing the symbolic, pathetic figure of the Simpleton (or 'the Idiot', as he is sometimes called).

Originally Mussorgsky gave his opera no love interest and Marina did not appear. This original version (1868–9) had only seven scenes; the seventh showed the death of Boris, and the previous one was set outside St Basil's Cathedral in Moscow, introducing the Simpleton.

In this form the opera was rejected by the organization of the Imperial Theatres in St Petersburg. Mussorgsky thereupon expanded and revised his scheme. He rewrote the scene for Boris and his children; he put in a 'Polish act', bringing in Marina; he scrapped the scene outside St Basil's; and *after* the death of Boris he placed a new scene, set in a wood-clearing near Kromy, introducing the Simpleton here instead.

This revised version (1871–2) is regarded as the definitive one: the synopsis which follows corresponds to it. It was slightly cut by the composer in a vocal score published in 1874. There is a case for performing either this definitive version or the earlier, more tense version (without the love-interest). There is no case for performing the score as 'arranged' by Rimsky-Korsakov, that is, not only with Mussorgsky's harmonies and orchestration altered, but with the death of Boris *following* the scene near Kromy – a scene which, as we have noted, Mussorgsky expressly composed to come *after* Boris's death.

*   *   *   *   *

PROLOGUE

Outside the Novodevichy monastery in Moscow, the crowd in obedience to a policeman utters lamentations. Inside is Boris Godunov, who – as Shchelkalov, secretary of the State Council, now declares sadly – has declined the throne, despite the wishes of the nobles and clergy. A band of pilgrims arrives and enters the monastery. The police officer orders the crowd to appear at the Kremlin at dawn next day.

Next day the people are assembled in the courtyard of the Kremlin. Shuisky hails Boris, who has at last consented to become Tsar and now emerges, crowned. He speaks, revealing his troubled mind. The people hail him.

ACT I

In a monastery at Chudov, by night, an old monk, Pimen, is writing a chronicle of Russia. Dawn nears; the chanting of monks is heard. Grigori Otrepyev, a young monk sleeping in the cell, awakens. He asks and receives Pimen's blessing, then speaks of a dream that haunts him; he sees a crowd in Moscow pointing with scorn at him. Pimen speaks of how he himself saw, twelve years before, the body of the young Prince Dmitri, son of the late Tsar, who had been killed by order of the usurping Boris Godunov. Grigori (with cries of 'Boris, Boris!') is strongly impressed – and Pimen has mentioned that, were Dmitri still alive, he would be just of Grigori's age.

In a roadside inn, the hostess is singing to herself. Travellers arrive: two vagabond monks, Missail and Varlaam, followed by Grigori, who is now in peasant's clothes. The monks drink. Varlaam sings a racy song, 'By the walls of Kazan' (Kak vo gorode bilo vo Kazani),* about the military

* English version by M. D. Calvocoressi (O.U.P.).

exploits of Tsar Ivan. Grigori is restive: planning to pose as Dmitri and to claim the Russian throne, he wants first of all to cross the nearby frontier into Lithuania (part of the kingdom of Poland at this time).

Frontier guards knock, enter, and announce that they have a warrant for the arrest of one Grigori (short form, Grishka) Otrepyev. The illiterate guard hands the warrant to Grigori who reads out the description of the wanted man, but falsely, to make it correspond to Varlaam. Eventually Varlaam himself manages to read it out correctly, but in the nick of time Grigori escapes.

ACT II

In a room in the Kremlin, Boris's daughter, Xenia, is weeping for her dead fiancé. Her young brother Fyodor is engrossed by a mechanical clock. The old nurse tries to comfort Xenia with a song about a gnat. After another song (by the nurse and Fyodor) Boris suddenly enters. Xenia and the nurse leave; Fyodor with a globe proudly shows his father the Russian empire on it. As Fyodor withdraws Boris sings of the unhappiness he foresees and of how the thought of the murdered Dmitri haunts him: 'I stand supreme in power' (Dostig ya vishe vlasti).

A noise is heard outside. A boyar (nobleman) in waiting enters with news of a civil disturbance caused by Shuisky. Fyodor re-enters and tells his father how the noise outside was caused by a pet parrot misbehaving.

Shuisky enters, and Boris accuses him of plotting. Shuisky says a Pretender has arisen in Lithuania under the name of Dmitri – a name that shakes Boris, who seeks confirmation from Shuisky that the true Dmitri was in fact killed. Left alone, agitated, Boris imagines that the moving figures on the mechanical clock – which now begins to strike – are a vision of the murdered child.

ACT III

At Sandomir Castle in Poland, Princess Marina is being adorned by her attendants. But she does not care for the idle flattery of their song. She wants to hear of Poland's glory and hopes that Dmitri (with whom she has fallen in love) will make her empress in Moscow. Her confessor, the Jesuit Rangoni, tells her to lead Dmitri on and win his allegiance to the Roman Catholic Church. Marina curses Rangoni's artfulness, but gives way.

In the castle garden by moonlight the lovesick Grigori – or Dmitri, as he now calls himself – is awaiting Marina. Rangoni appears, addressing him as Tsarevich, and asking to be accepted as his spiritual guide. A polonaise is heard. Marina, who is entertaining guests, passes by with an old nobleman; the guests sing of Poland's coming triumph over the Russians.

Marina re-enters. Obedient to Rangoni, she pretends to spurn Dmitri's promises of love and demands assurance of a throne. They quarrel, then are reconciled; Rangoni, aside, is gleeful.

Act IV

The State Council of Boyars is meeting in the Moscow Kremlin. The secretary of the council, Shchelkalov, announces Boris's wish for support against the Pretender. They give it. Shuisky (whom the others suspect of rebellion) enters and reports that he secretly observed Boris trembling, declaring he saw the ghost of the murdered Dmitri, and calling 'Out, child!' (Chur, ditya!).

Boris himself, ill, lurches in and speaks those very words. He sits down. Shuisky, having asked permission, withdraws to bring in a monk who has sought audience. It is Pimen, who declares that he had become blind but, on revisiting the grave of the murdered Tsarevich Dmitri, was miraculously cured.

Boris falls. Knowing that death is near, he sends for his son and dismisses the boyars. Bells toll. He tells Fyodor to mistrust the boyars and to champion the people and the Russian Church. Distant voices are heard; the boyars re-enter, and Boris dies.

In a forest clearing near Kromy the rebellious crowd are baiting Krushchov, a captured boyar who is a supporter of

Boris. A simpleton enters and sings religious words. Urchins
mock him and tap the old pan he wears for a hat. Missail and
Varlaam (the vagabond monks) enter and lead the crowd in
praise of Dmitri; two Jesuits, Lavitzy and Chernikovsky, also
praise Dmitri – in Latin – but the crowd turn against them
and take them into the forest to hang them.

Heralded by a trumpet-call, Dmitiri enters on horseback.
The crowd hail him. Krushchov shakes off his bonds and
hails him too. Dmitri urges all: 'To Moscow!'. The voices
of the Jesuits, in prayer, are heard off-stage. All follow Dmitri
off, leaving only the simpleton singing of unhappy Russia.

*   *   *   *   *

Boris Godunov is remarkable for its reproduction of ordinary
speech-rhythms – the music thus being asymmetrical, with
frequent changes of time-signature. Mussorgsky also uses
actual folk-tunes, notably the following, which becomes the
crowd's salute to Boris on his coronation:

When in Act II the monk Pimen is writing his chronicle,
a most graphic musical figure 'describes' the slow moving of
the pen over parchment – first continuously, then intermittently as the work draws to an end and Pimen comments
on the approaching dawn. Later, as Pimen tells Grigori the
story of the murdered Dmitri, we hear:

The accompaniment figure in the last bar characterizes
Dmitri throughout – that is, the real murdered Dmitri and
also Grigori, as the Pretender. Other themes recur in the
opera, though less prominently. But one theme associated
with Boris recurs (in the bass of the accompaniment) at the
beginning of the Death Scene:

The unemphatic vocal line given to Boris is typical: the role
calls not for great vocal range or agility but for the ability to
bring out the dramatic intensity behind notes which look, on
paper, as ordinary as this.

PYOTR ILYICH TCHAIKOVSKY

(1840–93)

TCHAIKOVSKY wrote ten operas, three of them based on Pushkin's writings. Of these three, two have entered and remained in the world's repertory, and in Russia today are regarded as stable favourites. *Eugene Onegin* (1879) is the more lyrical; Tchaikovsky was utterly absorbed in the purely human passion of his heroine, Tatyana. *The Queen of Spades* (1890) is on a broader canvas, with stormier music as Fate buffets the characters and a ghost (real or imagined?) twists the hero's mind. While Mussorgsky, in his setting of Russian words, aims at a representation of the realism of speech, Tchaikovsky prefers a romantic idiom with formal numbers. In both *Eugene Onegin* and *The Queen of Spades* he included ballroom scenes with brilliant dance-music giving scope for the ballet.

EUGENE ONEGIN

Libretto by the composer and K. S. Shilovsky,
after Pushkin's narrative poem

First performed: Moscow, 1879

Three Acts

Cast in order of singing:

Tatyana ⎫ daughters of Mme Larina	⎧	*soprano*
Olga ⎭	⎨	*contralto*
Filipevna, their old nurse		*mezzo-soprano*
Mme Larina, a landowner		*mezzo-soprano*
Vladimir Lensky, engaged to Olga		*tenor*
Eugene Onegin, his friend		*baritone*
Tikhon Petrovich Buyanov, a captain		*bass*
Triquet, a French tutor		*tenor*
Zaretsky, a friend of Lensky		*bass*
Prince Gremin		*bass*

[The role of Guillot, a coachman, is silent.]

The scene is laid on a Russian country estate
near St Petersburg in the 1820s

FOR many, the most remarkable character of the opera is not
that of the title-role; it is the heroine, Tatyana, with her
romantic longings. Tchaikovsky himself almost fell in love
with his creation. The action is placed at a time when the
English romantic novel swept the literary taste of Europe.
'Oh, Grandison! ... Oh, Richardson!' sighs Tatyana's
mother, Mme Larina. *Sir Charles Grandison* is the title of
a novel (1753) by the English writer Samuel Richardson.

Tatyana (sometimes referred to by the pet forms Tanya
and Tanyusha), is also a novel-reader, and her literary,
romantic conception of love is contrasted with the matter-of-
fact approach of her sister Olga.

'Prince' in imperial Russia indicates the highest rank of aristocracy but *not* royalty. 'Larina' is the feminine form of the surname Larin.

*   *   *   *   *

ACT I

Mme Larina, assisted by Filipevna (her children's old nurse), is making jam on a portable stove in her garden. From inside the house a song is heard: Larina's two daughters, Tatyana and Olga, are singing a duet. The voices of Larina (reminiscing about her youth and marriage) and Filipevna are added and continue when the girls' song has ended.

The singing of peasants is heard. They approach and offer Larina a decorated sheaf as a symbol of the collected harvest. They sing and dance for her, then leave. Tatyana and Olga come out. Olga sings of her merry disposition. Larina bids Filipevna provide the peasants with refreshment. Tatyana looks sad – because of the tragic novel she is reading, she explains.

Filipevna announces the arrival of Lensky, Olga's betrothed; Onegin, a new neighbour whom they have not formally met, is with him and is presented. Larina and Filipevna leave the four young people together. Tatyana is romantically impressed by Onegin; Onegin, blasé, is mildly taken with Tatyana.

Lensky approaches Olga with loving words, and they walk away. Onegin asks Tatyana whether country life does not bore her; she replies that she daydreams. They stroll off. Lensky returns with Olga and declares his love for her ('Ya lyublyu vas'). Larina and Filipevna come out of the house again and beckon the others in. Filipevna comments to herself on Tatyana's bashful appearance: has she taken a fancy to this 'new gentleman'?

The scene changes to Tatyana's bedroom. She is in her nightdress, but does not feel sleepy and lets Filipevna tell her of her own strange marriage. Then she bids her go. Left alone, she writes a letter to Onegin, having difficulty in finding the right words. In it she confesses her love for him.

Dawn comes. Filipevna re-enters. Tatyana gives her the letter to send – and Filipevna pretends at first not to know for whom it is intended.

Next day, in a far corner of the Larins' garden, peasant girls sing as they gather berries, then move off. Tatyana enters, agitated, for Onegin is approaching: he speaks courteously but coldly to her of the letter she sent him, making it clear that he does not return her passion. She is mortified and silent. The peasant girls' chorus is heard again.

ACT II

At a ball at the Larins' to celebrate Tatyana's name-day, a waltz is danced amid conversation. Captain Buyanov, acting as host, is surrounded by girls; Onegin dances with Tatyana and overhears ill-natured gossip about himself. Bored, he determines on an idle revenge on Lensky for bringing him here. He takes Olga away from Lensky for a dance – 'Allow me!' (Proshu vas!)* – and flirts with her. The other guests' gay comments are resumed over the waltz. When it is ended, Lensky confronts Olga and Onegin angrily but they go off for another dance.

Triquet, the old French tutor, is brought forward and sings an old-fashioned song of compliments to Tatyana.

A cotillion begins. Onegin and Lensky, not dancing, quarrel: Lensky challenges Onegin to a duel. Larina protests at such an upset in her house. 'Yes, in your house!' (V vashem dome) says Lensky, bitterly recalling his former pleasure there; all the guests join in. Tempers rise; Lensky calls Onegin a seducer and Onegin hurls himself on Lensky. The pair leave separately, Lensky calling 'Goodbye for ever' (Proshchai navek) to Olga.

Early the next morning, by a river bank, Lensky is waiting with his second, Zaretsky, for Onegin to appear for the duel. Zaretsky withdraws, and Lensky, alone, laments the bygone golden days – 'Where have you disappeared?' (Kuda, kuda, kuda . . .) – and laments for Olga, whom he still loves.

* English version by Edward J. Dent (O.U.P.).

Onegin appears, lacking a 'gentleman' as second but bringing his coachman, Guillot, instead. The seconds retire to arrange the formalities. Lensky and Onegin sing (apart and aside from each other) of their new and perhaps ridiculous enmity. On three claps of Zaretsky's hands, both men fire. Lensky falls. 'Dead?' (Ubit?) asks Onegin. Zaretsky confirms it. Onegin is struck with horror.

ACT III

It is some years later. Onegin, after much travelling abroad, is at a ball in St Petersburg. A polonaise is danced. Onegin, aside, declares himself bored by the occasion; he is still pursued by the memory of Lensky's death.

The guests dance an écossaise, then comment as Prince Gremin enters. On his arm (to Onegin's astonishment) is Tatyana, who converses with others but notices Onegin. Gremin tells Onegin that Tatyana is his wife, and speaks of the great comfort she has brought him: 'The power of love is all-compelling' (Lyubvi vsye vosrasti pokorni). He presents Onegin to her; they acknowledge each other only as former neighbours in the country, but as Tatyana and her husband leave, Onegin feels powerfully drawn towards her.

Later, at her house, Tatyana is alone, holding a letter from Onegin. To herself she admits that her passion for him has reawakened. Onegin enters and kneels to her. She bids him rise, asking why he pursues her now. Although she attempts to be cold, Onegin seizes her hand and declares himself passionately; momentarily overcome, she allows herself to utter the words 'I love you' (Ya vas lyublyu).

But she will not leave her husband: bidding Onegin go, she leaves the room. Onegin, overcome with despair, quickly departs.

*   *   *   *   *

As Tatyana in the first scene tells how sympathetically she reacts to the lovers' tragedy in the novel she is reading, we hear in voice and orchestra a theme which has been foreshadowed in the overture:

In the following scene, when she is in her room, the theme is heard again from the orchestra; then, when left alone, Tatyana bursts out with a second theme – her purposeful as opposed to her dreamy side – as she prepares to write to Onegin:

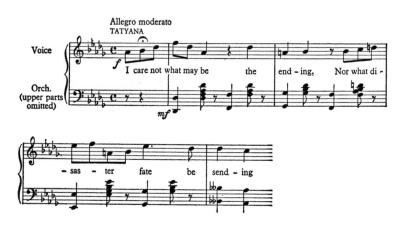

Later in this Letter Scene Tatyana asks, as she writes,
'Are you [Onegin] my guardian angel or a wily tempter?' –
to a third theme, heard a moment earlier in the orchestra:

Here are three of Tchaikovsky's most memorable themes,
all musically interrelated and all devoted to portraying his
beloved Tatyana. The music for Lensky, the last-act aria for
Gremin, the popular dance-music and the peasant choruses
are almost equally memorable. The duet for Lensky and
Onegin before their duel is a canon, an apt musical illustration of two men separated, not speaking to one another, yet
thinking along the same lines.

NIKOLAI RIMSKY-KORSAKOV
(1844–1908)

ALTHOUGH at first a naval officer, Rimsky-Korsakov developed a very full musical career – as conductor, teacher (his pupils included Stravinsky), promoter and editor of others' works, and a prolific composer. His fifteen operas are nearly all based on historical or legendary Russian material. As Tchaikovsky excelled in the operatic portrayal of emotions from within, so Rimsky-Korsakov excelled in the depiction of scenes from without – transforming, as it were, visions and colours into music, and making considerable play with eastern and other exotic elements.

His most important operas are *May Night* (1880), *The Snow Maiden* (1882), *Sadko* (1898), from which comes the so-called Hindu Song, really 'The Song of the Indian Merchant', *The Tale of Tsar Saltan* (1902), from which comes 'The Flight of the Bumble-Bee', *The Legend of the Invisible City of Kitezh* (1907) and *The Golden Cockerel* (1909).

THE GOLDEN COCKEREL

(Zolotoy Petushok)

Libretto by V. Belsky after a story by Pushkin
First performed: Moscow, 1909

Three Acts

Cast in order of singing:

The Astrologer	*tenor-altino*
King Dodon	*bass*
Prince Guidon, his elder son	*tenor*
General Polkan, in service to the king	*bass*
Prince Afron, the king's younger son	*baritone*
The Golden Cockerel	*soprano*
Amelfa, housekeeper to the king	*contralto*
The Queen of Shemakhan	*soprano*
Chorus of soldiers, courtiers, people, etc.	

The place and time of the action are left unstated

A FABLE, a fairy-tale, a thing of fantastic and sometimes garish music: superficially, *The Golden Cockerel* might seem to be no more than that. But the fantastic plumage conceals the barbs of satire. Indeed, the Tsarist censor at first forbade the production of *The Golden Cockerel*: its mocking exposure of stupid despotism perhaps struck too near home. It was not produced until the year after the composer's death.

The requirements for the cast include a 'tenor-altino', a type of voice which Rimsky-Korsakov said 'is rarely found' and which is not listed under that name in the chief British or Italian musical dictionaries. The current Soviet *Encyclopedic Musical Dictionary* (1959), however, appears to define it simply as a very high tenor. Rimsky-Korsakov's part rises to an E above the usual tenor 'top C', but his score also in-

cludes an alternative without quite such high notes in case
the part needs to be given to 'a lyric tenor with a good, strong
falsetto' as the next best thing.

* * * * *

Act I

In a brief prologue in front of the curtain, the Astrologer tells
the audience it is about to see a moral tale.

The curtain rises to show the ageing King Dodon with his
Council of State. He asks for advice on how to deal with the
foreign attack which threatens from all sides. His elder son,
Guidon, produces a brilliant idea: let the enemy invade the
surrounding country while the king and his army remain
secure in the central citadel and devise some way of repelling
them. The king and his courtiers applaud, and the king is
angry with General Polkan when he declares the plan in-
adequate.

The king's younger son, Afron, has an even better idea: dis-
band the army, then suddenly mobilize it again for a surprise
attack! Once again king and courtiers applaud – and once
again General Polkan doubts the plan and is abused and even
physically attacked. Well, what is to be done? Consult an
augury, perhaps – but then the courtiers begin to quarrel on
rival methods of foretelling the future. At the height of the
quarrel a mysterious Astrologer enters. To solve the difficulty,
he offers a golden cockerel who will crow to indicate an alarm
and point to the direction from which it comes.

The bird now crows ('Kiriki, kirikuku' in Russian) and
adds that the king may for the present sleep soundly. King
and courtiers hail the prodigy, and the king offers to do the
Astrologer any service he wishes. The Astrologer says he may
take advantage of this later, but not yet, and withdraws. The
king dismisses his Council, gets into a big bed, accepts delica-
cies from his housekeeper Amelfa, plays with a parrot, then
(lulled by the golden cockerel's repeated cry that all is safe)
goes to sleep, dreaming of an unknown beautiful woman.

Suddenly the cock crows to raise the alarm, which is taken
up all round. Polkan rushes in; then Dodon's sons, armed, go

off none too willingly to fight. A military march is heard from outside; but the atmosphere becomes calm again and the cock crows that the danger is averted.

Dodon tries to sleep again and, having remembered that he had a most pleasant dream but having forgotten what it was, asks Amelfa to make conjectures. At the third time she guesses rightly, and Dodon falls asleep again. Once more the cockerel sounds the alarm; Polkan dares to arouse the sleeping king; with difficulty he puts on his rusty armour and goes to mount a horse (making sure it is a docile one). Then, to the acclamation of his subjects, he rides away to fight.

ACT II

It is night. The battle has gone badly. The corpses of the king's two sons are seen; riderless horses stand motionless. Some surviving soldiers lament their state. King Dodon joins them, bewailing his sons and his army. General Polkan enters and tries to raise the soldiers' spirits; but they cannot attack the enemy because they do not even know where he is.

Suddenly the morning mists begin to disperse and a mysterious, luxurious tent is seen. In a ridiculous manner the soldiers fire a cannon at it. But it is unharmed, and the soldiers flee when it opens to reveal a beautiful woman. Accompanied by four slaves each bearing a musical instrument, she sings a hymn to the sun.

To Dodon's inquiries she reveals that she is the Queen of Shemakhan. She makes the men comfortable (the corpses are timidly taken away) but they are still uneasy in their minds. Polkan tries valiantly to make sociable conversation but the queen, carried away by the memory of a dream of love which she had the previous night, finds him gross and gets Dodon to send him away. She comes close to the embarrassed Dodon and sets out to conquer him with sensuous melody and sensuous description.

She makes Dodon sing in turn, which he does to a brief, ridiculous tune. Then she tearfully confesses her wish to find a man to dominate her. Dodon volunteers for the role and tells her 'Stop your weeping!' (Perestan plakat). She now insists that he shows his manliness by dancing. Extremely reluctant (in fact, consenting only when she threatens to take Polkan in his place), he dances while she instructs him, herself dancing with a tambourine in her hand. The dance music becomes more furious, and she laughs at Dodon, who falls down exhausted.

As soon as he recovers he offers her his heart and his kingdom, magnanimously offering also to have Polkan (whom the queen dislikes) beheaded. Dodon's chariot is brought in and the pair ride away – Dodon ecstatic, the queen's female slaves reflecting their mistress's attitude as they sing of this latest, ridiculous conquest of hers. Dodon's soldiers may be poor fighters, but now they sing 'Hurrah!' very well.

ACT III

Back in Dodon's city, with the golden cockerel still keeping watch, there is a general sense of foreboding, but Amelfa assures the people that Dodon is returning in triumph with a girl he has rescued. Trumpets sound his approach. First there enters the queen's procession, with giants, dwarfs and other grotesque participants. Then a chariot brings Dodon and the queen herself, to whom the crowd shouts 'Long life!' (Dolgo zhit tebya!).

Suddenly the Astrologer appears. The queen, seemingly disturbed, asks who he is. Dodon greets him warmly. The Astrologer reminds him of his promise of a gift and now asks, as this gift, the queen. Dodon remonstrates but the Astrologer persists, saying he wants to get married and refusing alternative gifts. Growing furious, Dodon hits him on the head with his sceptre and the Astrologer falls dead.

Dodon is troubled. The queen seems to make light of the affair, but when the reassured Dodon turns to embrace her she repulses him, telling him to vanish ('Propadi ti') and his stupid nation as well! Dodon starts to remonstrate gently, but the golden cockerel crows suddenly and attacks the king on his head with its beak. He too falls dead, amid a peal of thunder. Darkness descends. The laughter of the queen is heard. When the darkness lifts, both queen and cockerel have

disappeared; the people intone a long lament and throw themselves despairingly on the ground.

The story is over. The curtain falls. But in front of it
comes the Astrologer: only he and the queen were real
people, he says, and the rest were creatures of the imagination.

*   *   *   *   *

As in others of his operas, Rimsky-Korsakov here borrows
from Wagner the use of vividly descriptive leading-motives,
but rejects Wagner's symphonic, ever-developing texture in
favour of a more regular and symmetrical musical line.

The very opening of the orchestral introduction gives us
two of the most important motives, instantly recognizable
when they return in the opera itself. First we have the cockerel,
on a muted trumpet, followed by the Queen of Shemakhan in
a sensuous melody on the cellos:

This theme – which occurs in the opera not only when the
queen appears but, before that, when Dodon is in bed dreaming of love – leads to a prefiguring of the queen's 'Hymn to
the Sun' in Act II; then, with a complete change of mood,
a mysteriously tinkling sound with an off-beat tune for the
glockenspiel and harps introduces the Astrologer:

– and then the Astrologer himself comes to deliver the
prologue.

IX

GIACOMO PUCCINI

(1858–1924)

W E now resume the story of Italian opera. Verdi, in his middle years, reigned without substantial challenge. Almost the only opera by another Italian composer of that period to survive (just!) in the repertory of non-Italian countries is *La Gioconda* (1876) by Amilcare Ponchielli (1834–86), the teacher of both Puccini and Mascagni.

'Puccini looks to me more like the heir of Verdi than any of his rivals.' That was the verdict of a young London music critic called Bernard Shaw in 1894 – a verdict made, remarkably, on the evidence only of Puccini's first successful opera, *Manon Lescaut* (1893). Shaw pointed to Puccini's combination of a symphonic style (that is, a style of continuously developing music, like Wagner's) with a vein of traditional Italian melody.

Puccini thereafter turned out a chain of operatic successes unequalled since his day. He pursued and extended this symphonic method; he extended also his range of poignant and biting harmonies, learning from Debussy as well as Wagner. Dramatically he cared little for subtlety of character but much for the power of erotic or brutal impulses seen or suggested on the stage – impulses which are powerfully suggested in the high points of his music. Puccini's characteristic *genre* is thus what in English is called *melodrama* (it is amusing to recall that this word descends from the Italian *melodramma*, which simply means opera!). The comedy of *Gianni Schicchi* stands as an exception.

LA BOHÈME

(Bohemian Life)

Libretto by Giuseppe Giacosa and Luigi Illica, after the novel by Henry Mürger

First performed: Turin, 1896

Four Acts

Cast in order of singing:

Marcello, a painter	*baritone*
Rodolfo, a poet	*tenor*
Colline, a philosopher	*bass*
Schaunard, a musician	*baritone*
Benoit, their landlord	*bass*
Mimi	*soprano*
Parpignol, a toy seller	*tenor*
Musetta	*soprano*
Alcindoro, a counsellor of state	*bass*
A Customs official	*bass*
Sergeant	*bass*

Chorus of people, students, work-girls, shopkeepers, street vendors, soldiers, waiters children, etc.

The scene is laid in Paris about 1830

La Bohème, the tunes and the pathos of which have made it one of the most successful operas ever written, was Puccini's fourth opera. Preceding it were the unsuccessful *Le Villi* (The Wilis) and *Edgar*, produced in 1884 and 1889 respectively, and the successful *Manon Lescaut* (1893).

Mimi, the heroine of *La Bohème*, dies of consumption (i.e. in modern language, pulmonary tuberculosis) like the heroine of *La Traviata*. But whereas *La Traviata* is concerned with social taboos of love and marriage, *La Bohème* does not speak of marriage at all. The girls have Bohemian lovers and live with them in near-poverty or leave them for others who can provide more luxurious living – a point less clear in the opera than in its literary inspiration, Henry Mürger's prose work *Scènes de la Bohème* (1854). (A play on the subject was called *'Scènes de la vie de Bohème'*.) The period of Mürger's writings is retained in the opera, the libretto of which mentions Guizot, the French Prime Minister during the reign of Louis Philippe (1830–8). 'La Bohème' is defined in a French dictionary as: 'Bohemia; wild and disorderly people (*or* life), the loafing fraternity; vagrants, tramps'.

Following Italian custom, Puccini's librettists Italianized the original names 'Rodolphe' and 'Marcel' into Rodolfo and Marcello. The name 'Musetta' (meaning a bagpipe and indicating the girl's stridency and roughness, in contrast to the mildness and sweetness of Mimi) is an invention of the librettists, the character not having an exact counterpart in the French original.

*　　*　　*　　*　　*

ACT I

Marcello and Rodolfo, in the Parisian garret which they share with Colline and Schaunard, are doing their best to keep warm on a freezing Christmas Eve. With no fuel for their stove, they think of burning a chair, then Marcello's latest painting, but finally settle for the manuscript of the play Rodolfo has been writing. Act I is blazing when Colline enters. As the closing scene is reduced to ashes, Schaunard arrives, with attendants carrying food, wine and fuel, to the others' astonished delight, and flings some money on the floor. While he tells how he earned it – from an Englishman who wanted music lessons – they set the table; but Schaunard insists that they dine out.

As they are having a drink before leaving, the landlord, Benoit, comes in, asking for his rent: they offer him wine, then tease him about a woman they have seen him with, and finally hustle him out in mock disgust at such behaviour in a married man. Then, when the others go off to the Café

Momus, Rodolfo says that he will follow in five minutes – he has an article to finish.

He is making little progress. Suddenly there is a knock on the door. Mimi, a frail young girl who lives in a room above, is on the threshold, half fainting; her candle has blown out and she wants it re-lighted. Rodolfo helps her to a chair and gives her wine. She soon feels better and starts to go; but she loses her key and her candle again goes out. His conveniently goes out too and they are soon both in the dark, groping for the key, which Rodolfo finds and hides. Their hands meet; Rodolfo takes hers in his. 'Your tiny hand is frozen' (Che gelida manina),* he exclaims, and while warming it into life he introduces himself. Will she now tell him about herself, he asks? 'Yes. I'm always called Mimi' (Si. Mi chiamano Mimi), she begins; she tells him that she works in solitude, embroidering artificial flowers, but it is nature's flowers that delight her.

His friends call from the street below; he asks them to keep a place at the Café. In the duet 'Lovely maid in the moonlight' (O soave fanciulla) Rodolfo and Mimi find themselves falling in love. He agrees to take her with him to the Café (with a hint, too, of what he expects when they return), and their voices are heard as they go together down the staircase.

ACT II

In the square outside the Café Momus, in the Latin Quarter, there is a large crowd, with street vendors crying their wares, students, a mother calling her children; their noises mingle with those from the Café, where customers, some of them at tables outside, are calling to the waiters. Rodolfo and Mimi have arrived to join their friends. Schaunard is buying a horn, Marcello flirting with passing girls, Colline buying books and having some clothes repaired. They sit down for their meal at a table outside the Café, and Rodolfo introduces Mimi to his friends. Meanwhile, there is a further commotion in the

* English version by William Grist and Percy Pinkerton (Ricordi).

street, as the toy-seller Parpignol comes along, followed by children (calling Parpignol's name delightedly) and their mothers. The friends order their meal and talk gaily.

The vivacious Musetta, obviously known to the passers-by, enters. Formerly Marcello was her lover, but now she comes with an elderly admirer, Alcindoro, whom she treats like a tame dog. She spots the 'Bohemians', insists on taking the table next to them, and, to Alcindoro's embarrassment, she tries harder and harder to attract Marcello's attention, singing her Waltz Song: 'As through the street' (Quando me'n vo'). Marcello becomes more and more inflamed.

Eventually Musetta sends Alcindoro off on an errand, pretending one of her shoes is hurting, and she and Marcello embrace passionately. The waiter brings the bill, which the friends cannot pay. Now soldiers, with a band, approach: windows are flung open, and children pursued by their mothers come out into the street. In the general excitement the friends rush off, Marcello and Colline carrying the half-shod Musetta, leaving Alcindoro to pay both bills on his return. They sing Musetta's praises as the crowd sings those of the drum-major.

ACT III

Two months have elapsed. It is early morning at the Barrière d'Enfer, one of the gates of Paris, with street sweepers, a customs official (who opens the gate) and milkmaids and carters passing. Singing is heard from a nearby inn, with Musetta's voice prominent. Day is just dawning when Mimi arrives and asks a sergeant to point out the inn where a painter is working. He does so, and she asks there for Marcello. Soon he comes out, and tells her that he and Musetta have been living there for a month, he as a jobbing painter and she teaching singing. She asks if Rodolfo is there: on learning that he is, she refuses to enter and bursts into tears. They still love one another, she tells Marcello, but Rodolfo is fiercely jealous. He advises them to part, and she agrees that they must. Her persistent cough alarms him.

Rodolfo, who has been asleep, now comes out. As he talks

to Marcello, Mimi conceals herself. At first he says that h
wants to leave Mimi as she is such a coquette, but eventuall
he gives the true reason – her failing health, which is furthe
aggravated by their life together in his chilly room. Mimi ca
control her tears no longer, and Rodolfo hears her. They em
brace, then bid each other a sad farewell in the duet 'To th
home that she left' (Donde lieta uscì) – while in the back
ground Musetta and Marcello have a lively quarrel.

ACT IV

Marcello and Rodolfo have both left their girls and are bacl
sharing the garret. They are pretending to work. Each latel
happens to have seen the other's girl; on hearing the new
each pretends no longer to care. But memories of forme
happiness overwhelm them. Schaunard and Colline arrive
carrying food (four loaves and a herring) of which they mak
a mock-sumptuous meal. They then hold a mock dance, Ro
dolfo taking Marcello for his partner. Then Colline and
Schaunard fight a duel, with tongs and shovel.

Suddenly Musetta enters, highly agitated. She has found
Mimi, in utter exhaustion. They bring her in and prepare
bed for her; soon she feels rather better, but there is no foo
or drink in the house and it is clear that she is dying. Musett
takes off her earrings, to be sold to provide food and medic
attention, and she promises a muff, to warm Mimi's icy hands
She and Marcello leave. Colline sings a farewell to his ol
coat ('Vecchia zimarra'), intending to sell it to buy necessitie
for Mimi. He leaves with Schaunard.

The lovers, left alone, sing of their happy memories of thei
first meeting: 'Back to her nest comes the swallow in th
springtide' (Torna al nido la rondine). Mimi has a convulsiv
fit of coughing just as Schaunard, then Musetta and Marcello, return. Mimi delightedly takes the muff, sinking back
a moment later into unconsciousness. Musetta mutters
prayer.

As Colline returns with money for the doctor, who is al
ready on his way, Schaunard murmurs to Marcello that Mim
is dead. Rodolfo thinks she is resting peacefully: then he see

heir expressions and the truth dawns. He flings himself on he bed, sobbing over her lifeless body.

* * * * *

Your tiny hand is frozen' (Che gelida manina), which is one f the world's most famous operatic songs, starts with one ote nine times repeated – than which, in itself, nothing ould be less 'inspired'. Plainly it is not entirely in 'melody' n its purest sense that Puccini's power lies. In fact the suc- ess of *La Bohème* partly depends on a very strong, very dis- inctive harmonic style and on a structural development vhich interweaves various strands symphonically, sometimes vith Wagner-like concentration. This harmonic and this tructural trait combine in their effect: a theme that recurs s recognized by its well-defined harmonic background (and ometimes by characteristic orchestration) as well as by its tune'. Such recognition is, for most people, subconscious, but t is worth examining it in eighteen bars from the final pages f the vocal score. The failing Mimi is recalling her first neeting with Rodolfo.

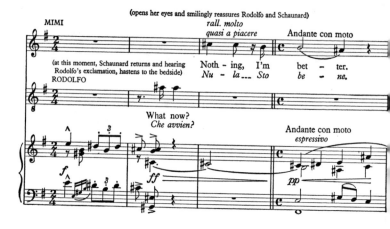

Note:
bar

1 single note which originally preceded Rodolfo's 'Your tiny hand is frozen'

2 Mimi begins to quote the same

7 Mimi ceases to quote and returns to her present conversation, but the orchestra goes on quoting

12 sudden change to the theme associated with Mimi's coughing and illness in Acts I and III

16 the return of Schaunard is signified by his own cheery theme, and

17 as Mimi tries to reassure Rodolfo and Schaunard that she has regained her old self, her old theme – 'I'm always called Mimi' (Mi chiamano Mimì) – returns in the orchestra. Significantly this theme has (and originally had) a one-note orchestral introduction, one of the signs of its kinship to 'Your tiny hand is frozen'.

TOSCA

Libretto by Giuseppe Giacosa and Luigi Illica, after the play by Victorien Sardou

First performed: Rome, 1900

Three Acts

Cast in order of singing:

Cesare Angelotti, leader of the proscribed Republican party	*bass*
A sacristan	*baritone*
Mario Cavaradossi, a painter	*tenor*
Floria Tosca, a famous singer	*soprano*
Baron Scarpia, chief of police	*baritone*
Spoletta, police agent	*tenor*
Sciarrone, a police officer	*baritone*

A gaoler   bas
A shepherd boy   boy's voice (or contralto)
   Chorus of choirboys, soldiers, police agents, ladies,
        nobles, citizens, artisans, etc.

The scene is laid in Rome, in June 1800

POLITICAL struggle and sexual struggle: it is a proven good
mixture for the stage, and the French playwright Victorien
Sardou (1831–1908) used it with great success in *La Tosca*
(1887). Moreover he was writing of a time and place (Rome,
1800) when religious and political attitudes were strongly
intertwined – which allowed him to add religious conflict to
his ingredients. Puccini's opera, based on the play, makes the
political and religious struggle less clear: not until the moment when Cavaradossi, about to face the firing-squad, refuses the services of a priest do we gather the force of his
conviction as a free-thinker, and we miss the point of Cavaradossi's doing a painting in a church (in the play, an intended
ruse to conceal his true political convictions).

   But the sexual battle – Scarpia torturing Cavaradossi in
earshot of Tosca so that she, who loves Cavaradossi, should
be willing to give herself to Scarpia to earn mercy for her
lover – is presented in Puccini's opera with great dramatic
violence and the maximum force of his musical language.
These three characters, each with their dramatic solos, are
memorably brought to theatrical life.

*   *   *   *   *

ACT I

In the church of Sant' Andrea della Valle, a painter's gear and
a large, covered picture are to be seen. Angelotti, an escaped
political prisoner, runs in, dishevelled and exhausted. He
glances round and, seeing an image of the Madonna, he looks
under it and eventually finds a key (left there for him by his
sister, the Marchesa Attavanti); with it he opens the door to
the Attavanti family chapel and goes within, closing the door
behind him.

A sacristan enters with some paint-brushes for Cavaradossi, he painter who has been at work. But Cavaradossi is not here to take them. The Angelus is rung, and the sacristan neels in prayer. Cavaradossi enters, uncovers his unfinished picture of the Magdalen and contemplates it; the sacristan is omewhat horrified by its resemblance to a lady whom he has een at worship in the church (in fact Angelotti's sister). Cavaradossi says that it is modelled on her. He starts painting, topping to contrast with the portrait a miniature of Tosca: Strange harmony of contrasts' (Recondita armonia).*

The sacristan soon departs and Angelotti, believing the hurch empty, comes out of the chapel. He sees Cavaradossi nd immediately recognizes him as a supporter of his own Republican party. Tosca's voice is heard outside, and Cavaradossi hurries Angelotti back into the chapel with the basket f food prepared for himself. He lets Tosca in. She momenarily suspects that he was not alone – perhaps with another voman – but is quickly reassured. She adorns the Madonna's image with flowers, then turns to him, suggesting an assignaion for the evening. The two sing tenderly of their love. As he is about to leave she sees his portrait of the Magdalen, recognizes its model, and is furiously jealous. He once more assures her that there is no cause for jealousy, and they again ing of their love.

After bidding Tosca an affectionate farewell, Cavaradossi ets Angelotti out of the chapel. He determines to hide Angelotti in his villa to help him escape from Scarpia, the evil chief f the Roman police. As Angelotti prepares to leave the church a cannon sounds – the sign that a prisoner's escape has been discovered – and the two hurry off.

The sacristan and a crowd of boys enter the church, excited at the news of Napoleon's defeat, which is to be celebrated by a cantata at the Palace with Tosca as soloist.

Suddenly they are interrupted (and terrified) by the arrival of the sinister Scarpia and his men. Scarpia tells his assistant, Spoletta, to search the building, while he himself questions the sacristan. They discover the Attavanti chapel unlocked;

* English version by W. Beatty-Kingston (Ricordi).

in it is a fan, bearing the Attavanti arms, and the empty food
basket. Then Scarpia recognizes the Marchesa Attavanti in
Cavaradossi's picture.

Tosca returns, disturbed to learn from the sacristan that
Cavaradossi has left. Scarpia speaks to her, showing her the
Marchesa's fan; he insinuatingly suggests to her that Cavara
dossi has gone to meet the Marchesa. Her jealousy is easily
aroused, and she goes off angrily to his villa, followed, on
Scarpia's instructions, by Spoletta.

The church is filling with people, and against the sound of
the organ and chanted prayer, with jubilant bells and cannon
shot in the background, Scarpia sings of his two objective
– the death of Angelotti and the possession of Tosca.

ACT II

'A good decoy is Tosca' (Tosca è buon falco), muses Scarpia
alone in his room in the Farnese Palace, at supper. He sum
mons Sciarrone, his henchman, and hands him a note for
Tosca. He sings of his plan to make Tosca his mistress
(actually, as he says, preferring force to more gentle methods)
and to hang both Angelotti and Cavaradossi.

Spoletta returns and tells how he and his assistants followed
Tosca to Cavaradossi's villa. They have brought back Cavara
dossi, but (to Scarpia's annoyance) they could not find Ange
lotti despite an extensive search. At this moment the cantata
is heard from the royal apartments below. Cavaradossi is
brought in, protesting. Scarpia starts questioning him about
Angelotti (they pause for an instant as Tosca's voice is heard
floating above the others) but he gives no information and, to
Spoletta's and Scarpia's irritation, only laughs when they
mention the searchers' vain efforts. Scarpia closes the win
dows so that the music cannot be heard, and resumes the
questioning more forcefully, but still to no result. Tosca enters
and embraces Cavaradossi, who whispers to her to keep silent.
Scarpia sends him into the torture chamber, with a judge to
take his deposition.

Left alone with Tosca, Scarpia tries unsuccessfully to ob
tain information from her about who was at the villa. He asks

Sciarrone if Cavaradossi has yet given way, but he has not. Then he horrifies Tosca by revealing that Cavaradossi is at that moment being tortured. She hears his groans and calls to him; Scarpia charges her to keep silent, pressing her to give way by threatening more excruciating tortures. The door is opened and now she can hear all her lover's groans. As Spoletta kneels in prayer, Cavaradossi cries out in intolerable pain and Tosca can stand no more: she tells Scarpia that Angelotti is hidden in the well in the garden of the villa. Terribly mauled, Cavaradossi is brought in. Tosca tries to comfort him, but when he realizes from a remark of Scarpia's that she has betrayed Angelotti he angrily repulses her. Then Sciarrone arrives to tell Scarpia that Napoleon has defeated the royal troops, to Cavaradossi's great delight: 'Victory!' (Vittoria!) he sings. Scarpia, infuriated, sends him away under guard.

Tosca begs Scarpia to spare him. He says he might and offers her wine. Pushing it contemptuously aside, she asks him realistically for his price: 'How much?' (Quanto?). His price is her body. She proudly refuses. Distant drums are heard as men march to the scaffold: she can choose whether or not Cavaradossi will be among them, he tells her. In her song 'Love and music' (Vissi d'arte) she indicates her helplessness and prays to heaven. Scarpia remains adamant.

Spoletta comes in to say that Angelotti took poison as he was captured. He asks for instructions for dealing with Cavaradossi; Scarpia looks at Tosca, who has no choice but to consent. In Tosca's hearing he orders only a mock execution for Cavaradossi, but secretly he conveys to Spoletta his real meaning – that Cavaradossi is, in fact, to be shot. Keeping up the deception, he writes and hands to Tosca a safe-conduct so that she and Cavaradossi can afterwards leave the country. Then he turns to her, 'Tosca, at last thou art mine' (Tosca, finalmente mia). But she has picked up a knife, and plunges it into his heart. Dying, he calls for help, unavailingly. 'And before *him* all Rome trembled!' (E avanti a lui remava tutta Roma!) remarks Tosca. She places a crucifix and candles by the body, and leaves with the safe-conduct.

ACT III

From a platform on the roof of Fort St. Angelo, where Cavaradossi is due for execution, a shepherd boy's voice is heard in
the distance as the new day dawns. Matin bells sound. A
group of soldiers arrives with Cavaradossi and a gaoler tells
him he has one hour to live. The gaoler allows him to write
his last letter to Tosca; as he does so he remembers the past:
'When the stars were brightly shining' (E lucevan le stelle).

Tosca arrives with the safe-conduct and shows it to Cavaradossi, who is sobbing with emotion. She tells him what took
place and warns him that, to keep up the appearances of the
mock-execution, he must fall down at the shot and not stand
up too soon, 'just like Tosca on the stage' (come la Tosca in
teatro). The firing-squad arrives and takes up its position.

She watches tensely. The shots ring out. He falls realistically and does not move. As the soldiers depart, she discovers
in horror that the execution was a real one. There is tumult
below. Spoletta and Sciarrone arrive, having found out that
Tosca has killed Scarpia. Tosca pushes Spoletta away as he
comes to arrest her. She springs up on the parapet and flings
herself to her death.

*   *   *   *   *

The opera is called *Tosca*, but it starts by proclaiming
'Scarpia!' – in three menacing chords:

The curtain at once rises on the entry of the escaped Angelotti. The same motive of three chords signals the arrival of
Scarpia at his first entrance (interrupting the jubilation of the

choristers); it occurs in his big soliloquy in Act II; altered
into a less positive succession of chords (ending with the
minor instead of the major) it accompanies his dying words
after Tosca has stabbed him; and it returns in its original
form, but subdued in power, when (in Act III) Tosca tells
Cavaradossi what has happened. There are other recurrences
too. Such recurrences and metamorphoses of motives is an
essential part of Puccini's operatic construction: some sixty
such motives have been detected in *Tosca*.

Cavaradossi has the first big lyric outpouring of the opera –
the celebrated 'Strange harmony of contrasts' (Recondita
armonia) – which Puccini, in the interests of dramatic continuity, 'accompanies' by the mutterings of the sacristan
against unbelievers like Cavaradossi himself. (Concert performances of the solo, and recorded versions, of course miss
this.) His aria near the end of the opera constitutes Cavaradossi's second great moment of self-revelation. His voice steals
in on one repeated note as though he is quietly thinking alone.
But the orchestra has already begun to play as a background
the tune which will come from Cavaradossi's voice a few
moments later ('When the stars were brightly shining'):

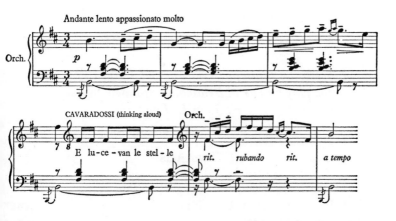

By the nature of opera we should expect Tosca to have a
climactic, sustained outburst at the point where her psychological tensions are highest – when Scarpia is bartering with

her for Cavaradossi's freedom – and instead she sings 'Love and music, these I have lived for' (Vissi d'arte). It is not an utterance of protest or resolution but of helplessness.

Indeed, it has been well said that Tosca is not really a tigress, even if some prima donnas like to play her so, but a 'little woman' like Mimi and Butterfly, forced to one deed of violence – like Butterfly, again.

MADAMA BUTTERFLY

*Libretto by Giuseppe Giacosa and Luigi Illica, after
the play by David Belasco, itself based on a story
by John L. Long*

First performed: Milan, 1904

Two Acts

Cast in order of singing:

Lieut. B. F. Pinkerton, U.S. Navy	*tenor*
Goro, a marriage broker	*tenor*
Suzuki, Madame Butterfly's servant	*mezzo-soprano*
Sharpless, American Consul	*baritone*
Madama Butterfly (Cho-cho-san)	*soprano*

The Imperial Commissioner   *bass*
The Official Registrar   *baritone*
The Bonze (priest), Butterfly's uncle   *bass*
Prince Yamadori   *tenor*
Mrs. Kate Pinkerton   *mezzo-soprano*
  Chorus of Butterfly's friends and relations, servants, sailors

The scene is laid in Nagasaki at the beginning of the
20th century

IN the summer of 1900 Puccini was in London and saw a
performance of a new, successful American one-act play –
Madame Butterfly, by David Belasco, adapted from a short
story by John Luther Long – and he immediately conceived
the idea of basing an opera on it. The hero-villain of the
play, a U.S. Navy lieutenant who deserts his trusting Japanese
wife, was surnamed Pinkerton. In the original story his ini-
tials were B.F. (for Benjamin Franklin), but for English
audiences he had become F. B., and in the libretto of the opera
his full name is mentioned as Sir (!) Francis Blummy Pinkerton. This, however, was in the first version of the opera (in
two acts with one interval) which was for various reasons a
complete failure when given in February 1904, and had only
a single performance. The successful revised version (Brescia,
May 1904), in which the second act is itself divided into two
parts, drops the incredible Sir Francis Blummy and restores
the B. F.
  Butterfly herself (on whom almost entirely, the opera rests)
is a most appealing figure, particularly because she is absolutely alone in her plight – her husband has deserted her, her
relatives have renounced her, the sympathetic Consul gives
her advice she cannot take, and her servant Suzuki cannot
grasp her noble single-mindedness. The poignancy of her
situation is added to – with a sentimentality which would
occasion giggles in the theatre today if the music were not
there to support it – by the appearance of her infant son,
Trouble, to whom she gives a Stars and Stripes as a plaything before she bandages his eyes and stabs herself. This

Trouble *is* a trouble, by the way: the child is supposed to be between two and three, a very difficult age to represent on the stage either by a dummy or otherwise. Butterfly has proudly given her son not a Japanese but an American name (*Dolore* in the Italian text). Butterfly's own Japanese name is represented in English as Cho-cho-san, in Italian as Cio-cio-san.

ACT I

The obsequious marriage-broker, Goro, is showing Pinkerton round the house he is buying as his matrimonial home in Japan. He is introduced to the three Japanese servants hired for him by Goro, including Suzuki, who compliments him. They depart and Goro watches for the arrival of Butterfly, Pinkerton's bride, her family and the others who will be at the wedding.

First to come is Sharpless, the American Consul. While Goro fetches refreshments, Sharpless admires the house and garden and the fine view of the harbour and ocean. Pinkerton expresses his easy-going attitude to life and to his forthcoming marriage, ending with 'America for ever!' (English words in the Italian original) while the orchestra blares out a phrase from 'The Star-Spangled Banner'. He sends Goro to fetch Butterfly and praises her charms, but makes Sharpless uneasy about his irresponsibility, especially when he drinks to a future 'real wife, from America' (una vera sposa americana).*

Butterfly and her friends are heard approaching. When Goro brings them in, she sings of coming to Pinkerton at the call of love, and on her instruction they all kneel ceremoniously before 'B. F. Pinkerton', as she names him. In conversation with Sharpless, she mentions that she comes of good family, is fifteen years old and has a mother but her father is dead. Now Goro announces the arrival of Butterfly's relations, including her mother, a cousin, an uncle (Yakuside) and an aunt. There is a great deal of chatter from the assembled friends, most of it inconsequential and slightly malicious, while servants provide food and drink. Sharpless warns Pinkerton not to trifle with Butterfly.

* English version by R. H. Elkin (Ricordi).

Soon Butterfly bids them all bow low before the two Americans. Rather embarrassed, Butterfly asks if he minds her bringing a few personal possessions, which she has in her baggy sleeves. (Among the most cherished is a knife sent to her father by the Mikado, Goro explains, with a message – which was obeyed.) She tells Pinkerton, out of her relatives' hearing, that the previous day she went to the Mission and embraced Christianity, to make her fit to be his wife.

The Imperial Commissioner, who has been in the background, comes forward, reads the marriage contract and hands it to Goro, who has it signed by Pinkerton, Butterfly and her relations. Congratulations are offered to the bride, first by her girl-friends and then by the Commissioner and the Official Registrar, who now depart. So does Sharpless, warning Pinkerton to be careful. The guests are beginning to drink a Japanese toast to the couple ('O Kami! O Kami!') when the old Bonze (a priest), Butterfly's uncle, arrives. He demands to know what Butterfly was doing at the Mission, accusing her of renouncing her religion and her relatives. The relatives are scandalized: they immediately refuse to have anything more to do with her, and Pinkerton orders them off. Their accusing voices die away in the distance.

From within, Suzuki is heard muttering her prayers. A moment later she emerges with her mistress's white nightgown; Butterfly retires to a corner and prepares herself. Alone, as evening falls, the couple sing a long, tender love duet.

ACT II (Part I)

It is three years later. Suzuki is praying, with a prayer-bell, asking the gods to stop Butterfly's weeping. Pinkerton has not returned since being recalled to America soon after the wedding, and they have hardly any money left. Butterfly, still believing he will come back, tries to persuade the more sceptical Suzuki; she looks forward to his return, imagining the scene: 'One fine day' (Un bel dì).

Goro arrives, with Sharpless. Butterfly (who insists on being called Madame Pinkerton) is excited to see them and makes them welcome, but her nervous, bubbling chatter prevents Sharpless from telling her news he has received in a letter from Pinkerton. She asks him at what time of year the robins nest in America – explaining that Pinkerton had promised to return at the robins' nesting time. She mentions that Goro has tried to persuade her to marry the rich Prince Yamadori – who enters at that moment to pay court to her. Goro explains to Sharpless that Butterfly could divorce Pinkerton for desertion under Japanese law, but she interposes by saying that she is an American citizen.

Alone with Butterfly, Sharpless starts to read the letter: her initial excitement changes to dismay when he hints that Pinkerton will not return. Sharpless is deeply touched when Butterfly produces her small son, Trouble, and says that she would rather kill herself than return to her old occupation of dancing to earn them enough to subsist on – 'That your mother should take you' (Che tua madre). Promising to tell Pinkerton of the child's existence, Sharpless leaves. A moment later Suzuki drags in Goro, who has been spreading tales that no one knows who is the child's father. Butterfly threatens him with a dagger, then pushes him away in disgust.

A cannon shot is heard, the sign that a ship is entering the harbour. Butterfly and Suzuki see that it is a man-o'-war, it is American, and its name is *Abraham Lincoln* – it is Pinkerton's ship! At last he is returning to her! She and Suzuki set about decorating the house with flowers, then Suzuki helps her to prepare herself, making up her face and slipping on her wedding garment. They make three holes in the screen for the two women and the child to watch for Pinkerton's coming. As night falls, distant humming voices are heard, and in the moonlight it can be seen that the child and Suzuki have fallen asleep; only Butterfly is awake, still patiently watching.

ACT II (Part II)

As the new day dawns, the voices of the sailors can be heard from the harbour. Butterfly is still watching. Suzuki wakes and sees that it is daylight; she insists that Butterfly goes upstairs, with the child, promising to call her when Pinkerton comes. A moment later there is a knock and Pinkerton enters with Sharpless. Hearing that Butterfly stayed up all night, and seeing the scattered flowers, Pinkerton is greatly troubled and cannot face her. Suzuki sees a woman outside in the garden and Sharpless tells her that it is Pinkerton's American wife, Kate. Sharpless asks Suzuki to tell Butterfly that Mrs. Pinkerton is willing to adopt the child. Suzuki, in anguish, remonstrates but then leaves, and Sharpless chides Pinkerton for his heartless behaviour. He is now remorseful: 'Farewell, O happy home!' (Addio, fiorito asil!).

Pinkerton goes out as Kate enters with Suzuki, promising to treat the child as if it were her own. Butterfly calls Suzuki from upstairs, then comes down, eagerly looking for Pinkerton. Seeing Sharpless and Kate, and Suzuki in tears, she guesses the situation, and Suzuki confirms her fears. She realizes that Kate is Pinkerton's wife and in response to their request she says she will hand over the child if Pinkerton will come in half an hour's time. Sharpless and Kate leave.

Suzuki tries to comfort the desolate Butterfly, but is sent away. Butterfly takes her father's knife from its case and reads its inscription: 'Death with honour is better than life with dishonour' (Con onor muore chi non può serbar vita con onore). In an effort to restrain her mistress, whose intention she has guessed, Suzuki pushes the child in. Butterfly smothers him with kisses, singing to him 'You! You! Beloved idol' (Tu! Tu! Piccolo iddio). She gives him an American flag and a doll to play with, binds his eyes gently, goes behind a screen and stabs herself. As Pinkerton arrives with Sharpless, she stumbles out, points to the child, and dies.

*　　*　　*　　*　　*

Puccini incorporated a number of Japanese melodies into his score. (For a full examination, see *Puccini: A Critical Biography*, by Mosco Carner.) We may quote one:

It occurs just at the moment when Butterfly, approaching from offstage with her girl friends, is seen for the first time:

'One fine day', Butterfly's own most famous aria, is additionally effective on the stage because it suggests 'acting within acting'. Puccini expressly says that Butterfly must 'act the scene [of Pinkerton's hoped-for return to her] as if it were actually taking place'; and the accompaniment is marked 'as if from a distance'. Note that in the accompaniment the melody is doubled at a lower octave and so becomes the bass-part as well, a typical Puccini device:

LA FANCIULLA DEL WEST

(The Girl of the Golden West)

*Libretto by Guelfo Civinini and Carlo Zangarini
after the play by David Belasco*

First performed: New York, 1910

Three Acts

Cast in order of singing:

Joe	⎫	*tenor*
Handsome	⎬ miners	*baritone*
Harry	⎭	*tenor*
Nick, bartender at the Polka tavern		*tenor*
Happy	⎫	*baritone*
Sid	⎬ miners	*baritone*
Trin	⎬	*tenor*
Sonora	⎭	*baritone*
Jim Larkens		*bass*
Jack Rance, Sheriff		*baritone*
Jake Wallace, a travelling ballad-singer		*baritone*
Ashby, agent for Wells Fargo		*bass*
Minnie, proprietress of the Polka tavern		*soprano*
Post-boy		*tenor*
Dick Johnson, alias Ramerrez, a bandit		*tenor*
Joe Castro, a half-caste		*bass*
Wowkle, Minnie's Red Indian servant		*mezzo-soprano*
Billy Jackrabbit, a Red Indian		*bass*

Chorus of men in the mining camp

*The scene is laid in a mining camp in California
during the gold-rush of 1849–50*

DAVID BELASCO'S play about the Californian gold-rush, *The Girl of the Golden West*, made a strong impression on Puc-

cini when he saw it in New York in 1907 – as Belasco's
Madame Butterfly had made on him in London. Although
the word 'golden' does not occur in the Italian title it is
customarily retained in English references to the opera.

Minnie in *The Girl of the Golden West* is a 'strong' heroine
– who takes out a pistol and defies a crowd of angry men. The
drama takes place in an exotic setting emphasized in the
Italian text by the use of English expressions such as 'Hello'
to convey atmosphere. The Wild West is still an unusual
enough setting for opera to have an appeal on its own, apart
from Puccini's typical strength of melody. Incidentally, the
refrain 'Dooda-dooda-day' is heard, but not to Stephen Foster's well-known tune; and the tune said by commentators to
be a folk-song 'The Old Dog Tray' (quoted on p. 397) is
not Foster's 'Old Dog Tray'. Puccini stipulates a horse on
the stage – thus gratifying an Italian operatic audience as well
as adding to the authenticity of his Wild West.

*   *   *   *   *

ACT I

It is evening, in the Polka; off-stage is a dance-hall. Voices
are heard from outside as Nick, the bartender, lights the
lamps. Joe, Handsome and Harry (miners) enter singing, followed later by Trin, Sonora and others. A game of cards
begins. Only Larkens is solitary and miserable; he is (as Nick
comments) homesick for 'that dear old place in Cornwall' (la
sua vecchia Cornovaglia).* Sonora and Trin both ask Nick
about Minnie, the owner of the tavern, and Nick tells each
separately that Minnie favours the questioner.

Jake Wallace, the travelling ballad-singer, approaches with
a song, 'What'll happen to my folk way back yonder?' (Che
faranno i vecchi miei), accompanying himself on the banjo.
The men, caught by the nostalgia of the song, join in. Larkens
bursts out sobbing; the men whip round for money to send
him back home. He leaves with it gratefully. The card-game

* English version by R. H. Elkin, revised by Tom Hammond
(Ricordi).

is resumed, and Sid is caught cheating. The men would hang him but Rance, as Sheriff, intervenes: 'Look here, you fellows' (Andiam, ragazzi). At his suggestion they pin his card on him to be worn in order to identify himself as a cheat. They kick him out.

Ashby, agent for the Wells Fargo company, enters and converses with Rance about Ramerrez, the bandit for whose capture his company has offered a reward. All the men drink to Minnie, whom Rance says is shortly to be the new Mrs. Rance – a boast which evokes a jealous outburst from Sonora, now drunk, who fires a pistol shot. Suddenly Minnie herself enters and quietens everyone. Joe, Sonora and Harry offer her presents, and Sonora pays his outstanding account with a bag of gold.

The men form an attentive group round Minnie as she starts 'school' with them, reading from the Psalms about the pure in heart. She also admonishes Billy Jackrabbit, the Red Indian who hangs round the camp, to marry Wowkle (of whose child he is the father).

The post-boy arrives and distributes mail. Ashby announces to Rance that he will shortly catch Ramerrez. Joe is saddened by news of his grandmother's death. Outside a stranger has arrived and has asked for water with his whisky – to the amazement of the hard drinkers present. Rance, left alone with Minnie, courts her (although he has a wife already). He tells her that once he valued only gold – 'When I left my little home' (Dalla mia casa son partito); but now he offers a thousand dollars for a kiss. Minnie repulses him: she seeks real love and recalls the love her mother knew – 'Back home in Soledad' (Laggiù nel Soledad).

Dick Johnson enters – the stranger who ordered water with his whisky. He and Minnie recognize each other from a past meeting and speak warmly together. Rance is angry, but Minnie persuades the others to accept Johnson, and Johnson leads her off to dance.

José Castro, a half-caste member of Ramerrez's gang, has been captured and is brought in. He pretends to be ready to betray Ramerrez's whereabouts – but in fact surreptitiously tells Johnson (who *is* Ramerrez) that his gang is near. The rest of the men, dragging Castro with them, leave. Minnie and Johnson, left together, feel the awakening of love between them; but a shrill whistle (the signal from his gang) makes Johnson depart. Before he goes he tells Minnie 'You've the face of an angel' (Avete un viso d'angelo) – a phrase which she repeats with a sigh, alone, as the curtain falls.

Act II

An hour later in Minnie's cabin, her maid Wowkle is singing as she rocks her baby. Billy comes in and promises to marry Wowkle. Minnie enters, orders supper for two and decks herself for Johnson, who arrives. She wonders why he came to the Polka – had he mistaken the path for the one leading to Nina Micheltorena, a loose-living girl living not far away? But soon Minnie loses herself in describing her enjoyment of the Wild West landscape: 'You can't imagine' (Oh, se sapeste).

Johnson passionately approaches Minnie, who, having dismissed Wowkle, yields to his kisses. He denies that Nina Micheltorena has been his mistress. Snow outside traps them within, and Minnie gives him permission to sleep in her room. A noise is heard outside – the other men, in pursuit of Ramerrez. Minnie hides Johnson and lets the men in: they disclose that Johnson is Ramerrez and that Nina, his former lover, has betrayed him. The men leave.

Minnie accuses Johnson of lying to her. He protests his love, and leaves. A shot rings out. Unable to control herself, Minnie opens the door and helps the wounded Johnson in. She confesses she still loves him and helps him up to the loft to hide. Rance comes in, pursues Minnie – 'I want you!' (Ti voglio) – but does not find Johnson until blood drips down from the loft, disclosing the hiding-place.

Minnie proposes a game of poker with Rance – if she wins, she and Johnson are free; if she loses, Rance can have both her and his prisoner. They play. Minnie cheats (unnoticed by Rance) and wins. Rance leaves, Minnie laughs and weeps.

Act III

Later, the hunt is on again for Johnson, alias Ramerrez. In a forest camp, Rance converses with Nick. An alarm is raised. Ashby is excited at the thought of catching his prey; Rance gesticulates with jealousy towards Minnie's cabin: 'Now, Minnie, weep in vain!' (Minnie, ora piangi tu). Eventually Johnson is captured (off-stage). The men exult: 'Dooda-dooda-day!'

Johnson is brought in. The men, led by Rance, prepare to hang him. He asks for a moment's grace, pleading 'Let her believe me far away in freedom' (Ch'ella mi credi libero).

Johnson's neck is in the noose when Minnie rushes in. With a pistol she defies the crowd. Then she appeals to the men individually by all that she has done to help them in the past – and finally she throws away her pistol. Sonora is the first to capitulate to her appeal. The others follow. While the men mourn her going – 'You'll never come again!' (Mai più ritornerai) – she leaves on Johnson's arm.

*   *   *   *   *

The travelling ballad-singer enters in Act I with this melody (heard in the distance first of all), to which words of home-sickness are attached:

There is dramatic point in the verse, because the emotion of homesickness is seen to be very strong in these 'forty-niners', and Minnie's role among them is really to supply 'home' amid their homelessness. When she pleads for her lover in the final scene it is her sisterly, homely services to the men that she bids them recall. And when they allow Johnson and her to go, and all sing a farewell to her, it is quite appropriately this tune that they repeat.

Minnie's first entrance, in which she performs the violent action of snatching Sonora's pistol before she sings a note, is accompanied in the orchestra by her characteristic theme:

In the hero's famous song in Act III there is a curious exotic touch, seemingly almost oriental in its melody and its harmonization: note how the melody is continued by the orchestra when the singer makes a brief break. We quote a part shortly after the aria begins, to the words 'She will wait for me to return and her days will go by...'

Such a style seemed suitable to Puccini in treating the oriental scenes of *Madama Butterfly* and (later) *Turandot*; here it serves to delineate what must have been, for Puccini, another 'orient' – equally remote and strange – located paradoxically in the Golden West.

IL TRITTICO
(The Triptych)

'The Triptych' (a three-panelled painting: in Italian, *Trit-tico*): this was how Puccini viewed the three one-act operas on which he began work in 1913. The three were to represent different aspects of life and together were to make up an evening's entertainment. They indeed shared a single evening at their first performance, but nowadays are rarely all performed together. This is partly because such an evening is very long (as Puccini himself came to recognize), and partly because the middle opera seems to many to fall below the other two in quality.

The first opera is an adaptation from a French play by Didier Gold, *La Houppelande* (The Cloak), the title literally translated by Puccini as *Il Tabarro*. It is a tense and terse drama, strongly in the 'realist' tradition.

Puccini adopted the Italian convention of Italianizing the French names, Louis becoming Luigi, and so on. The three nicknames used are also Italianized: Il Tinca (originally 'Le Goujon') means 'The Gudgeon', Il Talpa (originally 'La Taupe') means 'The Mole', La Frugola (originally 'La Furette') means 'The Rummager'.

Suor Angelica (Sister Angelica) has a cast only of women. It is a romantic opera, having as its climax a miracle shown on the stage. No 'realism' here! The opera is notable for a strongly drawn female villain, the Aunt, who (unless we count Suzuki in *Madama Butterfly*) is Puccini's only major characterization for a mezzo-soprano.

Gianni (short for Giovanni) Schicchi was an actual Florentine who is among the souls in purgatory mentioned in Dante's *Divine Comedy*: Puccini's *Gianni Schicchi* retains the name, the period and the background. This is a comic opera: and just as the normally 'tragic' Verdi excelled himself in the comedy of *Falstaff*, so Puccini shows a superb sureness (both

in the main character and in the total handling of the action
in the comic roguery of *Gianni Schicchi*.

* * * * *

IL TABARRO

(The Cloak)

Part I of 'The Triptych'

Libretto by Giuseppe Adami, after a play by Didier Gold

First performed: New York, 1918

One Act

Cast in order of singing:

Giorgetta, aged 25	soprano
Michele, her husband, a bargemaster, aged 50	baritone
Luigi, a bargeman, Giorgetta's lover, aged 20	tenor
Il Tinca, a bargeman, aged 50	bass
Il Talpa, a bargeman, aged 50	bass
A song-seller	tenor
La Frugola, Talpa's wife, a rag-picker, aged 50	mezzo-soprano
Two lovers	tenor and soprano

Chorus of bargemen and midinettes

The action takes place in a barge on the river Seine, in Paris

THE curtain rises before the music starts. The scene is set in a barge on the river Seine, with famous Parisian landmarks visible in the background and Parisian noises audible (including a motor-horn, written into the score). Giorgetta, doing various little jobs on the barge, talks with her husband Michele as he watches the sunset. Some bargemen can be heard from below, where they are emptying the hold; Giorgetta suggests a glass of wine to refresh them. Michele asks her for a kiss, but she is cold towards him, and he goes below.

Luigi, one of her husband's crew, comes aboard and Giorgetta goes to fetch wine and glasses, giving some to each of the bargemen, including Il Tinca and Il Talpa, who have been grumbling good-humouredly about the back-breaking work. An organ-grinder happens to come along and Giorgetta dances – at first with Il Tinca, rather stiffly, and then with Luigi, in a languid, yielding fashion. Michele returns: Luigi pays the organ-grinder and the men go back to work, while Michele and Giorgetta discuss plans for their departure and she chides him for his morose moods. While they talk, a song-seller on the shore is trying to find buyers for his ballads, and he sings one of his songs, to the accompaniment of a companion who plays a little harp. ' 'Tis the story of Mimi' (E la storia di Mimì),* he says, as the strings of the orchestra play a quotation from *La Bohème*. A group of midinettes, having bought the song, echo his singing.

La Frugola, Il Talpa's wife, arrives with a sack full of odds and ends. She talks to Giorgetta of her life and her cat. Michele asks Luigi to be present for a job the next day. Il Talpa and Il Tinca come up: La Frugola reprimands Il Tinca for his drinking, but he complains that drink is all he has to live for. Luigi angrily echoes his despair at the hard lot of the working man: 'What good is life?' (Per noi la vita). Il Tinca goes off.

La Frugola sings wistfully of her dream of happiness: 'Of a cottage sweet and homely' (Ho sognato una casetta). Giorgetta takes up the theme of longing: 'Do you know what my dream is?', she asks (E ben altro il mio sogno!). It is a nostalgic one for her early days in Belleville, a Paris suburb. Luigi lived there too; they recall it happily together. La Frugola and Il Talpa go off, singing of their dream cottage. Distant, impersonal voices are heard.

Giorgetta and Luigi are left alone. They are lovers, and he moves towards her, but she warns him to go as Michele will soon be back. They have exchanged only a few words of love when Michele comes: Luigi asks if he can be taken as far as Rouen, to seek work, but Michele says he would be better off in Paris and he agrees to stay. Michele goes into the cabin, and the lovers sing a passionate duet: 'You are right, love' (Hai ragione). Before he leaves, they arrange for him to return

* English version by Joseph Machlis (Ricordi).

later, when she shows a light to indicate that all is clear.

Michele comes up. They talk awhile, Michele desiring Giorgetta and reminding her of how in their happier days she used to nestle under his cloak, but she is cold and unresponsive – to his barely suppressed fury. She goes down to bed as Michele arranges the barge's lights. A pair of lovers passes by. A cornet sounds a military call from a barracks. Michele soliloquizes on his torment. He guesses that his wife is unfaithful and determines to wait, discover who her lover is, and kill him. He lights his pipe. Luigi, seeing a light, comes on to the barge. Michele watches him and lies in wait: suddenly he pounces and seizes him by the throat. As Michele strangles Luigi he forces him to confess repeatedly that he is Giorgetta's lover.

Giorgetta comes up from below as Luigi dies. Michele quickly wraps the body in his cloak. She is in a nervous mood; she apologizes for her earlier heartlessness and wants to come close to him. 'Where? Under my cloak?' (Dove? Nel mio tabarro?), he asks. As she comes closer, he rises, and undoes the cloak so that Luigi's body rolls out: then he seizes her and pushes her against her lover's face.

*   *   *   *   *

Here realism in the plot – in the sense of sordidness – is combined with musical realism (the sound of a motor-horn, the imitation of a cat). The whole opera preserves a hard intensity of mood; to the characterization of the participants Puccini adds what seems a characterization to the scene itself, in impressionist musical terms influenced by Debussy. The opening is hypnotic, and its 'wavy' motion surely represents the onward yet unchanging course of the Seine in Paris:

The first two bars are given to strings only with one flute, one clarinet, and a bass clarinet – one of the many remarkable touches of instrumentation in this work, which calls for four trombones instead of the usual three. It is this opening theme which the unseen impersonal voices sing later (before Luigi and Giorgetta's love-duet). The construction of the whole work is thematic, in Puccini's habitual way, and Michele's two references to his cloak (*tabarro*) – in his plea for Giorgetta's love and his final gesture of disgust towards her – have the same theme in different guises.

SUOR ANGELICA

(Sister Angelica)

Part II of 'The Triptych'

Libretto by Giovacchino Forzano
First performed: New York, 1918

One Act

Cast in order of singing:

Sister Angelica, a nun	*soprano*
The Monitor (La Suora Zelatrice)	*mezzo-soprano*
A Lay Sister (La Conversa)	*soprano*
The Mistress of the Novices (La Maestra della Novizie)	*mezzo-soprano*
A Lay Sister (La Conversa)	*mezzo-soprano*
Sister Osmina	*soprano*
Sister Genovieffa	*soprano*
Three other nuns	*two sopranos, mezzo-soprano*
Sister Dolcina	*soprano*

The Nursing Sister (La Suora Infermeria)   *mezzo-soprano*
The Alms Sisters (Le Cercatrici)   *two soprano.*
The Abbess (La Badessa)   *mezzo-soprano*
The Princess, Angelica's aunt (La Zia
   Principessa)   *mezzo-soprano*
Chorus of nuns and angels

The scene is laid in a convent, at the end of the
17th century

THE scene shows the cloister of a convent, with a garden, and the door of a chapel, through which the voices of nuns at prayer can be heard. Two lay sisters, then the young Sister Angelica, go into the chapel. Her voice is clearly audible from within. When the service ends the sisters come out of the chapel, two by two, bowing to the Abbess.

After the Monitor has reprimanded three nuns for minor offences (the Mistress of the Novices explaining this to her charges), Sister Genovieffa draws the sisters' attention to the rays of the setting sun, which will soon make the font glow as if the water is golden. This happens just three evenings in the year. The sisters resolve to sprinkle some 'golden water' on the tomb of one of their number who has lately died. In the course of a conversation about worldly desires, Genovieffa admits that, as a former shepherdess, she longs to see and hold a lamb. Genovieffa asks Angelica if she desires anything. No, she replies ('Io no, sorella, no'): but all are aware that this is not the truth and that she is constantly sad at having heard no word from her family in her seven years in the convent.

The nursing sister comes in, agitated: one of the sisters has been stung by wasps. She asks Angelica, who understands curative potions, for help, and Angelica gives her a herbal mixture. Then two alms sisters arrive with provisions, which the others unload with pleasure from a donkey. One of the alms sisters mentions that a very grand carriage is drawn up before the entrance. Angelica, flustered, asks her ('Ah! ditemi, sorella') to describe the carriage, but she cannot. The sisters watch her with kindly pity: as the visitors' bell rings they assemble, excited, each one wondering if the visitor is for herself. Genovieffa tells Angelica, who is praying for help, that all hope it is for her. The Abbess enters and summons Angelica. The others go off towards the cemetery, with golden water': their prayers can be heard while the Abbess tells Angelica that her aunt, the Princess, has come.

The Abbess goes and the stern figure of the Princess enters. Angelica is much moved, and goes to embrace her aunt. But the Princess coldly stares straight ahead, only offering Angelica her hand to kiss and beginning to recite Angelica's history: 'The Prince Gualtiero, your father ...'.* She tells Angelica she has come to obtain her signature to a document, in which she renounces all claims to the money left by her parents in favour of her younger sister, who is to be married. Angelica looks to her aunt for some sign of pity or kindness, but the Princess is inexorably harsh, only reminding her of the disgrace she brought upon the family and the eternal penance due from her. Angelica says she is repentant, but nothing can make her forget her son – the son she has seen only once. She asks her aunt for news of him. The old woman is at first silent, then – when Angelica's demand is repeated with increasing emotion – she explains: two years ago he was taken ill, and died. Angelica falls to the ground, sobbing.

It is now becoming dark. Without words a sister brings an oil-lamp, the Abbess a pen and ink, and Angelica signs the document; the Princess takes it and moves towards Angelica, who shrinks away; then she leaves, glancing back at her niece.

Angelica is once more alone. As the sisters light the lanterns on the tombstones in the cemetery, she bursts into tears, and sings of her child: 'Dying thus without a mother's blessing!' ('Senza mamma, o bimbo, tu sei morto). Genovieffa and the other sisters come in and comfort her. Angelica, now in a state of mystical ecstasy, tells them that heavenly grace has descended on her, and that she knows what she must do. They all give thanks to God and the Virgin and move off to their cells.

* English version by Herbert Withers (Ricordi).

Angelica comes from her cell. Alone, she mixes a poisonous potion from some flowers, using water from the font. Then she sings of the peace her draught will bring; she bids the sisters farewell, and in a state of exaltation she drinks. Now her serenity fades, and she returns to reality: in anguish she cries 'Ah! lost for ever!' (Ah, son dannata!), and she prays for forgiveness for her terrible sin.

Distant voices, of angels, are heard. Suddenly the chapel is miraculously suffused with light. The church doors open: the Blessed Virgin appears; in front of her is a child, clad in white, whom she pushes towards Angelica. Angelica raises her arms to the child, who steps towards her, as the voices sing 'Salve, Maria!'. She falls to the ground and dies, and the miraculous vision fades.

*   *   *   *   *

The moments before the second-act curtain of *Tosca*, in which the heroine performs with tremendous effect her dumb-show action with candles and crucifix to orchestral accompaniment, are paralleled in *Suor Angelica*. Here a much longer dumb-show action involving four people (Angelica, another nun, Angelica's aunt, and the Abbess) takes places and lasts for several minutes (more than forty bars of music): the action is minutely described in the score. The resulting tension is immediately released in Angelica's aria, the climax of Puccini's portrayal of his heroine (the published English translation, 'Dying thus without a mother's blessing', does not render the sentimental language of the original, which is nearer to 'Darling baby died without his Mummy'):

lab – bra, sen – za ba – ci mie – i,

Note the modal touch in melody and harmony (the flat seventh, that is the G natural in the tonality of A – characteristic of Puccini's idiom in this opera, where he plainly hints at old church music. The modal touch is also used – but for its oriental associations, with quite different effect – in *Madama Butterfly* and *Turandot*.

GIANNI SCHICCHI

Part III of 'The Triptych'

Libretto by Giovacchino Forzano

First performed: New York, 1918

One Act

Cast in order of singing:

Zita, Buoso Donati's cousin, aged 60	*mezzo-soprano*
Simone, Buoso's cousin, aged 70	*bass*
Rinuccio, Zita's nephew, aged 24	*tenor*
Marco, Simone's son, aged 45	*baritone*
Ciesca, Marco's wife, aged 38	*soprano*
Gherardo, Buoso's nephew, aged 40	*tenor*
Nella, Gherardo's wife, aged 34	*soprano*
Betto of Signa, Buoso's impoverished brother-in-law, of uncertain age	*bass*
Lauretta, Gianni Schicchi's daughter, aged 21	*soprano*

Gherardino, Gherardo and Nella's son, aged 7   *contralto*
     (*or boy's voice*)
Gianni Schicchi, aged 50   *baritone*
Spinelloccio, a Bolognese physician   *bass*
Ser Amantio di Nicolao, a notary   *bass*
Pinellino, a cobbler   *baritone*
Guccio, a dyer   *tenor*

The scene is laid in Florence, in 1299

THE relatives of Buoso Donati are assembled in prayer and tears around the bed where he has just died. 'Poor old Buoso!' (Povero Buoso)* – this and similar laments go up from Buoso's cousin Zita, with her nephew Rinuccio; another cousin, Simone, with his son Marco and his wife Ciesca; Buoso's nephew Gherardo, with his wife Nella and their seven-year old son, Gherardino; and Betto, Buoso's brother-in-law. The small boy, bored, is being a nuisance, and all silence him from time to time.

Betto whispers that rumours are afoot in Signa where he lives, that Buoso has left all his money to a monastery instead of to the family. Simone, as the senior relative, declares that they are lost if the will is already in the lawyers' hands, but if it were hidden in the room ... – whereupon a frenzied search begins, ending when Rinuccio finds the will in a cupboard. Before they open it, he asks whether, if they are all now rich, he could marry Lauretta, Gianni Schicchi's daughter. Zita, as his aunt, reluctantly consents. While they are opening the will (with difficulty, for Betto has pocketed the scissors), Rinuccio sends the small boy to fetch Gianni Schicchi and Lauretta. As they light more candles in his honour, they all mutter 'Poor old Buoso' again, and each hopes for the prize possessions – the house, the mills at Signa and the mule.

They all gather round and read the document, their mouths moving but saying nothing aloud, with mounting horror and dismay. 'So it was true then!' (Dunque era vero!), exclaims Simone, promptly extinguishing the candles. They all join

* English version by Percy Pitt (Ricordi).

in an outburst of hate directed at the fortunate monks. How
the monks will laugh at the Donatis, they exclaim, their mock
laughter changing almost to tears. They begin to think of
ways of getting round the will, but to no avail. The only
person to help, says Rinuccio, is Gianni Schicchi – and he's
coming, says Gherardino, rushing in. First Zita, then the
others object to the outsider, especially as he is not a Florentine, but Rinuccio talks them round: in his song 'Our Florence like a tree is firmly planted' (Firenze è come un albero
fiorito), he points out that Florence has traditionally derived
her strength from newcomers.

Schicchi enters with Lauretta. As Rinuccio and Lauretta
snatch a lovers' greeting, Schicchi sees the sad faces and at
first thinks Buoso must be recovering; then he realizes that he
is dead, and thinks what good actors they are; and finally the
truth is explained to him. Zita says she will not let her nephew
marry Lauretta, who has no dowry. A lively quartet ensues,
Zita and Schicchi quarrelling vigorously while the lovers beg
not to be parted. All join in the argument. Schicchi, offended,
tries to take Lauretta away. Rinuccio, however, asks his help
in circumventing the will; but he refuses, only giving way
when Lauretta adds her plea in order that she and Rinuccio
may marry: 'Oh my beloved daddy' (O mio babbino caro).

Schicchi takes the will and studies it. At first he says that
nothing can be done (the lovers lament); then an idea dawns.
He sends Lauretta out to feed the birds, and discloses his
scheme. After making sure that no-one else knows Buoso has
died, he tells them to take out the body and remake the bed.
Then there is a knock at the door. It is the doctor, Spinelloccio
(who speaks with a nasal voice and in a Bolognese accent –
Bologna is the site of a famous faculty of medicine). Hurriedly
they darken the room, and Schicchi hides behind the bed-
curtains. They admit Spinelloccio and tell him Buoso is resting. With an imitation of Buoso's voice convincing enough to
startle the relatives, Schicchi asks the doctor to come back in
the evening, as he feels very sleepy. Spinelloccio goes.

Schicchi comes out and explains his plan. He himself will
pose as the dying Buoso while a notary takes down his last will

and testament. Zita sends Rinuccio off for the notary and the delighted relatives embrace one another. But they are less affectionate when it comes to dividing the spoils. Five parts of the estate are claimed by the four men and Zita: but violent quarrels break out over the three prize items, starting when Simone claims them on grounds of seniority.

The tolling of a funeral bell interrupts the uproar: they are terrified that Buoso's death might have been discovered. (Here Lauretta comes in for a moment – the birds are sated – but Schicchi dispatches her again.) Soon Gherardo brings welcome news that someone else has died, and they breathe again, with a very happy 'Resquiescat in pace'! Schicchi dresses himself in Buoso's night attire, with a kerchief and night-cap; first Zita, then Simone, Betto, Nella and Ciesca in turn offer him bribes to leave them the three controversial items. 'So be it!' (Sta bene!) he answers each one, and each one is satisfied. The three women stand back and admire him in his disguise, singing him a mock lullaby. As he gets into bed, he warns them all of the legal punishment for falsifying a will – the loss of a hand and exile: 'Farewell, dear Florence' (Addio, Firenze), he sings, and makes them join in, glancing through the window at the familiar landmarks of the town.

There is a knock, and the notary, Amantio, enters with two of Buoso's friends, Pinellino and Guccio, to act as witnesses. Pinellino expresses his sorrow at seeing Buoso in such a state. Amantio reads the opening rigmarole in Latin, to which Schicchi is careful to add a sentence revoking all previous wills, to the relatives' admiration. First he decides on an economical funeral; then five lire to the monks – rather a little, Amantio suggests, which Schicchi counters by saying that when people leave large sums of money to the Church they are suspected of having come by it dishonestly. Then he goes on to the five items as arranged, with profuse thanks from each beneficiary. Now for the mule – he leaves it 'to my devoted friend Gianni Schicchi' (al mio devoto amico Gianni Schicchi). (The lawyer writes, repeating the words in Latin.) The relatives jump up in surprise: Simone protests but is quickly silenced by Schicchi, while the others mutter. Then the house goes – to Gianni Schicchi. There are loud protests this time, quelled by Schicchi singing his 'Farewell, dear Florence' and flapping an empty sleeve of his nightshirt – an eloquent warning! Finally, the mills at Signa: again to Gianni Schicchi, but between every few words comes a phrase of 'Farewell, dear Florence'. The notary and witnesses depart sadly, bidding the relatives to bear up.

A riot breaks out the moment they have gone – 'Scoundrel, robber!' (Ladro, ladro!) – as all the relatives set about Schicchi, who defends himself with a stick. Then they do their best to ransack the house, while Schicchi orders them off 'his' property. As their angry voices fade away into the distance, Rinuccio opens the balcony window from outside, where he and Lauretta are embracing and singing of their love. Schicchi, who has been chasing the rapacious relatives, comes back and sees them, smiles, and turns to the audience. (Now he speaks, not sings.) Who could think of a better use for the money? For this escapade he has been sent to perdition, and so be it: but, with Dante's permission, if the audience have enjoyed themselves, may he be allowed to plead 'extenuating circumstances'?

*   *   *   *   *

The sweetmeat in the score belongs not to the title-role but to Lauretta: it is 'Oh my beloved daddy':

Andante ingenuo
LAURETTA
Voice
Oh! mio bab - bi - no ca - ro, mi pia - ce, bel - lo, bel - lo;

Note that she naturally uses the colloquial form 'babbino', not 'padre' – 'daddy', not 'father', though many singers of the English version try to 'refine' it.

But the title-role is the commanding one, with two extraordinary theatrical strokes in it: first, when Schicchi (impersonating Buoso) recites the final and vital clauses of 'his' will in a half-spoken, impersonated voice but intersperses it by

recalling his warning to the relatives ('Farewell, dear Flor
ence') in a normal singing voice; second, when he turns at th
very end to the audience and (speaking, not singing) plead
that, if his action was criminal, at least there were extenuat
ing circumstances. (The published English version says 'No
Guilty'. This is both false to the original and nonsense in itself.

TURANDOT

Libretto by Giuseppe Adami and Renato Simoni,
after the play by Carlo Gozzi
First performed: Milan, 1926

Three Acts

Cast in order of singing:

A mandarin	bas.
Liu, a slave girl	sopran
The Unknown Prince (Calaf)	tenor
Timur, Calaf's father, a dethroned king	bass
The Prince of Persia	tenor
Ping, the Grand Chancellor	baritone
Pong, the General Purveyor	tenor
Pang, the Chief Cook	tenor
Three of Turandot's handmaidens	three sopranos
The Emperor Altoum	tenor
Princess Turandot	soprano

[The role of the executioner is silent.]
Chorus of soldiers, attendants, children,
priests, mandarins and people

The scene is laid in Peking, in legendary times

IN *Turandot* Puccini returned to an oriental scene (as in *Mad-*
ame Butterfly) and to a strongly stressed connection between
sex and cruelty (as in *Tosca*). In fact, on any normal consideration, the story is perhaps the most repulsive that any opera

udience is regularly called on to enjoy. Richard Strauss's
Salome is at least killed for her perversion, but the love-
triumph of Turandot and Calaf is a triumph based on the
acceptance of the torture and death of Liu, the only character
of the story who shows any positive action for good.

Moreover, there are several incidental touches in Puccini's
opera (not in Gozzi's original play of 1762, Turandotte)
which specially emphasize horror and cruelty – among them
the personal appearance of the Executioner and the procession
taking the previous rejected suitor to the scaffold. But it is not
difficult in the theatre to let moral scruple be overpowered by
the force of Puccini's resplendent score.

Puccini died in November 1924: he had not completed the
love-duet and the ensuing final scene, though he had left
sketches for them. On Toscanini's advice the completion was
entrusted after his death to Franco Alfano (1876–1954), a
composer whose style had been influenced by Puccini and
who had once himself meditated an opera on the same subject. This completion, using Puccini's sketches, has been
found by musicologists to show a distinct break with Puccini's
style; it is fair to say that few ordinary opera-goers, even
seasoned ones, experience this in the theatre.

*   *   *   *   *

ACT I

By the walls of Peking, a mandarin reads out a decree to the
assembled crowd. In accordance with the law, he proclaims,
the Princess Turandot will only marry if a prince of royal
blood comes forward who can solve her three riddles: failure
to solve them means death; and death awaits the Prince of
Persia, who has just failed. The crowd is crying for his blood.
Guards push back the people who rush towards the Palace,
calling the name of the executioner, Pu-Tin-Pao.

In the crush an old man has fallen. Liu, the slave-girl who
is his devoted companion, calls for help and a man, the Unknown Prince, runs up. He recognizes the old man, Timur, as
his father, and Timur greets his son. (Both are fugitives from

a usurper of the throne in their own country, and have to remain unknown.) While the bloodthirsty shouts of the crowd continue in the background, Timur tells his son how he has been cared for by Liu; and she explains her devotion – it was because the Prince himself once smiled at her.

Preparations for the execution proceed, with the sharpening of the blade. The crowd continue their savage chanting. Their mood changes as darkness descends and they wait for the moon to appear, but again they call for Pu-Tin-Pao. Voices of children are heard. Then the procession appears: the people, seeing the pale young Prince of Persia, now beg for pity for him (with the Unknown Prince adding his voice). Turandot appears on the balcony; all the people fall on their faces except the executioner and the two princes. She makes a decisive gesture – the death sentence. She utters no sound.

The Unknown Prince is dazzled by his brief glimpse of her beauty. As the procession passes, with priests, the Prince determines to remain, despite the pleas of Timur and Liu. From a distance, the Prince of Persia's voice is heard, in one final call, 'Turandot'; then there is a scream from the crowd as he is executed. The Prince resolves to try to win her himself and goes to strike the ceremonial gong as a signal.

Ping, Pang and Pong, three of Turandot's ministers, clad in grotesque masks, intercept him and try to dissuade him. Ping says that Turandot is just a woman, like any other – it isn't worth the risk, and he is sure to fail, like all her previous suitors. Their chatter is disturbed by Turandot's handmaidens, who demand quiet as she is resting. But the ministers soon resume their stream of words. Shadows of Turandot's dead suitors flit by. The Prince eventually shakes off the three 'masks', but his father again tries to draw him away, and finally Liu tries – 'Oh! I entreat thee' (Signore, ascolta)* – saying that she and Timur must die if the Prince persists. He is much moved – 'Oh, weep no more, Liu' (Non piangere, Liù) – but remains resolute, though all five repeatedly beg him to give way, supported by hidden voices warning him of certain death. At the climax he calls Turandot's name three

* English version by R. H. Elkin (Ricordi).

times, and sounds three strokes on the gong, committing himself finally as a suitor – for her hand or for death.

Act II

In a pavilion, Ping, Pang and Pong are ready to make arrangements for a wedding or a funeral, as may be required. At some length, they muse on the happy days before Turandot's bloody reign, Ping recalling his house on the Lake of Homan, Pang his forests at Tsiang, Pong his garden at Kiu. They think once again of Turandot's innumerable beheaded suitors; if only they could have the pleasure of preparing a nuptial couch instead of an execution! Sounds from the palace and the assembling crowd recall them to their duties.

The scene changes to the square before the palace, where the crowds gather for the asking of the fateful riddles. At the head of an imposing staircase the aged Emperor Altoum appears, on a huge throne, and the people prostrate themselves. In a weary, trembling voice, he too tries to dissuade the Prince, but again without avail. A mandarin, as before, proclaims the decree, and the voices of children are heard calling to Turandot. She enters, clad in gold. In her song 'Within this palace' (In questa reggia) she explains the reason for her savage edict – it is in revenge of an event a thousand thousand years ago, when a princess was carried off and cruelly ravished by a barbarian. She menacingly advises him to withdraw, but he determinedly refuses.

She poses the first riddle: he quickly answers 'Hope' (La speranza). The wise men open their scrolls and check; it is right. He takes longer over the second, but again answers correctly: 'Blood' (Il sangue). The crowd's suspense mounts. To the third riddle – 'What is the ice which gives you fire' (Gelo che ti da foco) – he hesitates yet more, but then answers: 'Turandot'. To universal delight, he has triumphed: the Emperor and people declare that the oath is binding and Turandot must give way.

She protests wildly, asking whether he wants her by force. He does not, he replies; and he gives her an opportunity of escape – if she can discover his name by morning he is prepared to die. The Emperor prays that the Prince will be his son by morning. As the court rises, the people prostrate themselves and sing in his praise.

ACT III

From the garden of the palace, heralds can be heard in the distance proclaiming Turandot's decree that 'None shall sleep tonight' (Nessun dorma); the Prince's name must be discovered, on pain of death. The Prince takes up the words in an aria in which the off-stage voices join. Ping, Pang and Pong approach, trying to persuade him (pushing forward a bevy of beautiful girls and coffers of gold and jewels) to accept an alternative to Turandot and abandon his suit which is bringing such terror to Peking. The people add their voices, but despite threats of torture he stands firm.

Suddenly, soldiers drag in Timur and Liu, who had earlier been seen with the Prince: 'Here is the name' (Eccolo il nome), they exclaim. The Prince declares they know nothing, but the people ignore him. Turandot is summoned. Ping offers to wring the name out of them; then Liu steps forward, declaring that she alone, not the old man, knows it. The people clamour to have her tortured. Ping repeatedly demands the name, but despite cruel tortures she will not answer. Tied up, the Prince cannot intervene.

Turandot asks Liu how she can endure: through her love, she answers. The tortures are renewed and the executioner appears. Then Liu says she will speak. In her song 'Thou who with ice art girdled' (Tu che di gel sei cinta) she predicts Turandot's eventual capitulation to the Prince – and her own (Liu's) death. As she finishes she seizes a dagger, stabs herself, and falls, dying, at the Prince's feet, the name still undisclosed. Timur, helpless without her, holds her hand: 'Liu, so good! Liu, so gentle!' (Liù, bontà! Liù, dolcezza!). The crowd, now repentant, ask her spirit to pardon them.

[At this point Puccini's music ends.]

All depart, except the Prince and Turandot. He chides her for her hardness, and tears the veil from her. She at first repulses him, protesting that she is sacred and he must not profane her; but he seizes her and kisses her passionately. As women's voices are heard in the distance, she begins to melt. Children's voices sing a hymn to the morning. Deeply ashamed that he has triumphed over her, Turandot sheds her first tears. She asks him to leave her now, victorious, his name still unknown. But he tells her his name – Calaf, son of Timur; she may kill him if she wishes.

The brief final scene takes place before the palace, where crowds are paying homage to the Emperor. Turandot brings in Calaf, telling her father that she knows the name of the stranger: 'His name is love' (Il suo nome è Amor). The people sing jubilantly.

*   *   *   *   *

Turandot is objectively the richest (that is, the biggest and most complex in sound) of Puccini's scores. Its harmony is more advanced than that of any of his previous works. As well as a very large orchestra in the pit (including tuned gongs and other unusual percussion) there is an off-stage band of brass, two alto saxophones, percussion and organ. The two saxophones double the melody sung by the children in the first act ('Over the hills, far away, doth the stork sing her lay'):

This is one of several authentic Chinese tunes incorporated in the score: in its melody and in Puccini's striking harmonization (plus the effect of children's voices) it denotes serenity.

It is thus directly contrasted with the violent, 'tortured' chromatic themes like the one which thunders out in the first two bars of the opera and which portrays Turandot's cruelty:

An extraordinary battle of keys takes place in the Riddle Scene (Act II). We translate literally:

Turandot: The riddles are three, death is one!

Prince: No, no! the riddles are three, one is life.

The theme proclaimed by Turandot is 'trumped' by the Prince who sings it in a higher key; then when Turandot tries to 'trump' him with a higher key still, he keeps up with her, as it were matching force with force.

nig - mi so - no tre, la mor - te è u - na!

nig - mi so - no tre, la mor - te è u - na!

Liu is one of Puccini's most touching characters – her torture, her aria 'Thou who with ice art girdled' (Tu che di gel
sei cinta), her heroic suicide and then her funeral procession
constitute the big moment of compassion in the opera. But the
dominating tune in the work remains the Prince's: it is 'None
shall sleep tonight!' (Nessun dorma) with words which continue: 'Within my heart my secret lies, and what my name is
none shall know'.

Ma il mio mis - te - ro è chiu - sa in me,

il no - me mio nes - sun sa - prà! No, no, sul - la tua boc - [ca]

The sonorous richness is increased by a variation of the harmony later. Alfano, in completing the work, was acting entirely in accord with Puccini's own principles in 'plugging' it – *with* the enriched harmony – in the final pages.

RUGGIERO LEONCAVALLO

(1858–1919)

THE exploration of low life (as in *La Bohème*) and of the extremes of emotional agony (as in *Tosca*) are marks of
'realistic' opera. The Italian word *verismo*, sometimes encountered in English contexts, simply denotes realism in its
theatrical and literary sense. The soprano-tenor-baritone plot
of *Tosca* was curiously foreshadowed four years earlier in
Andrea Chénier (1896) by Umberto Giordano (1864–1948).

Theatrical realism attracted another of Puccini's contemporaries, Ermanno Wolf-Ferrari (1876–1948), in *I gioielli
della Madonna* (1911; the Jewels of the Madonna); but Wolf-
Ferrari also composed two longer-lasting comedies in a
mock-formal vein which looks back to the 18th century – *I
quatro rusteghi* (1906; known in Britain in Dent's translation as 'School for Fathers') and *Il segreto di Susanna* (1909;
Susanna's Secret).

Among Italian composers, one who made a more radical
approach to musical composition was Ferruccio Busoni
(1866–1924) who wrote four operas, with librettos (in German) by himself: *Die Brautwahl* (The Bride-Choosing;
1912), *Arlecchino* (1917), *Turandot* (1917) and *Doctor Faust*
(unfinished, completed by Philipp Jarnach and performed in
1925). The last is the most highly regarded, but intellectual
regard rather than theatrical success has been Busoni's lot.

Celebrated in the realist tradition of Italian opera are
'*Cav* and *Pag*' – to use the colloquial English names for the
two works which form an almost invariable double bill. *Cavalleria Rusticana* by Pietro Mascagni and *Pagliacci* by Ruggiero
Leoncavallo are treated here in reverse order, since Leoncavallo was slightly the elder composer. Leoncavallo wrote
an unsuccessful *La Bohème* at the same time as Puccini's, but
Pagliacci is his only well-known piece.

PAGLIACCI

(Clowns)

Libretto by the Composer

First performed: Milan, 1892

Two Acts

Cast in order of singing:

Tonio (in the play, Taddeo, a clown)	*baritone*
Canio (in the play, Pagliaccio)	*tenor*
A villager	*baritone*
Beppe (in the play, Arlecchino)	*tenor*
A villager	*tenor*
Nedda, Canio's wife (in the play, Colombina)	*soprano*
Silvio, a villager	*baritone*

Chorus of villagers and peasants

The scene is laid near Montalto, in Calabria
1865–70

A PLAY within a play: the device is an ancient one (Shakespeare has made it familiar to us). The comic scene enacted for a village audience by a group of strolling players becomes a tragic drama of real life.

Additionally, the composer (who was his own librettist) introduces a prologue spoken by one of the actors in costume but supposedly giving a message direct from the author. This is, of course, also an ancient theatrical device, and its effect of providing a frame (and thus an effect of theatrical 'remoteness') for the subsequent action is similar to the mid-20th-century use of a prologue or epilogue (as in Britten's *The Rape of Lucretia* and Stravinsky's *The Rake's Progress*). In its own period it was particularly bold, and it is still very telling.

The title of the work is just *Pagliacci* (Clowns). The usual introductory *I* (The) is unauthentic. In the standard English version the familiar English harlequinade-names of Punchinello, Harlequin and Columbine replace Pagliaccio, Arlecchino and Colombina.

*   *   *   *   *

ACT I

The orchestral introduction is interrupted by the singer who is about to play the role of Tonio. He pushes his head between the curtains and then steps forward, telling the audience that he is the Prologue. He announces that the drama they are to witness, though represented by actors, is nevertheless about real human beings with ordinary feelings. The curtain rises.

On the afternoon of the Feast of the Assumption, a troupe of travelling actors has arrived, and villagers, in festive mood, come to greet them. Canio, leader of the troupe, steps down from the wagon and thanks the villagers for their welcome, announcing that a performance will take place at eleven o'clock that evening in the improvised theatre. Canio's wife, Nedda, begins to alight from the wagon and Tonio – a hunchback, vainly in love with her – moves to help her; but Canio angrily pushes him aside and lifts her down himself. The people laugh at Tonio, who mutters that he will avenge his humiliation.

A villager invites Canio and his colleagues to come to the tavern. Beppe says he will come too, but Tonio declines. Another villager jocularly remarks that Tonio is staying so as to make love to Nedda. Canio solemnly warns that although such a situation might be funny on the stage, in real life it would not: 'Such a game' (Un tal gioco).* Nedda hears and is anxious, but Canio assures the villagers that he does not really suspect her. Bagpipes are heard, then bells: as evening descends, the villagers go off, imitating the clang of the bells and singing of love.

Alone, Nedda sings nervously of her husband's suspicions,

* English version by Frederic E. Weatherly (Ascherberg, Hopwood & Crew).

then, carried away by the sound of the birds, she breaks into happy song: 'High aloft they cry' (Stridono lassù). As she finishes, Tonio appears. She mocks heartlessly at the hunchbacked clown and his declaration of love; eventually he can bear no more and tries to force a kiss from her, but she has picked up a donkey-whip and strikes him across the face. In pain and humiliation, he goes off, swearing revenge.

A moment later Silvio, a villager who is Nedda's real lover, appears. He pleads with Nedda to fly with him, but she begs him not to tempt her. Eventually she gives way. During their long duet Tonio enters, unseen but not unseeing. He fetches Canio, too late to see the departing Silvio but just in time to hear her words: 'Tonight and for ever I am thine' (A stanotte e per sempre tua sarò). Tonio tells Nedda that it was he who brought Canio back. Canio demands to know her lover's name, which she refuses to give. In his fury he almost stabs her, but Beppe intervenes, calms him and leads Nedda off, while Tonio promises to watch for the man. Beppe returns for a moment, telling Canio to dress for the performance and Tonio to beat his drum to attract the crowds. Left alone, Canio faces the fact that despite his private tragedy he has still to be the clown and amuse his public: 'On with the motley' (Vesti la giubba).

ACT II

Later that evening the crowd begins to assemble for the performance, Tonio calling on them to 'Walk up! Walk up!' (Avanti, avanti). Beppe helps to sort out the seating, and in the general confusion Nedda and Silvio manage to exchange a few words. The people are beginning to get impatient when the bell rings and the curtain rises on the play.

To a mock 18th-century minuet, Colombina (Nedda) is seen on her own. Her husband, Pagliaccio, is away, she says, and the clown Taddeo is at market, so all is safe. Soon the serenade of Arlecchino (Beppe) is heard. But before he can enter Taddeo (Tonio) comes in and makes a grotesque declaration of love, in the course of which Arlecchino enters by the window. Arlecchino throws out Taddeo, who promises to keep watch for them. They sing a little love duet (in gavotte rhythm) over their supper, but are interrupted by a warning from Taddeo – Pagliaccio (Canio) is approaching. Arlecchino leaves, and as Pagliaccio enters he hears Colombina say 'To-night, and for ever I am thine' (the very words Canio had heard Nedda use earlier in reality).

At this point Canio, unnerved, hesitantly tries to go on with the play, and in his role of Pagliaccio accuses Colombina of having a lover; she says that her visitor was only Taddeo, whom she brings in, and Taddeo assures Pagliaccio with a meaningful sneer that his wife is true to him. Now Canio can stand no more; he forgets the play and fiercely demands to know her lover's name. She tries to laugh it off, calling him Pagliaccio. 'No! Pagliaccio no more!' (Nò! Pagliaccio non son!) he bursts out in fury.

The audience (but not Silvio) suppose this is really splen-did, true-to-life acting, and call 'bravo'. Nedda for a moment replies in her own nature, but when once more he demands her lover's name she tries to resume the play. Thinking she is mocking him, he threatens to kill her. The audience begin to get agitated as they realize that the actors are no longer acting. During their angry, impassioned dialogue Silvio tries to rush forward; then Beppe, restrained by Tonio, tries to make a move. Canio stabs Nedda; she calls to Silvio for help, and as he rushes to her aid Canio stabs him too. Turning to the audience, he says: 'The comedy is ended!' (La commedia è finita!).

*   *   *   *   *

The notion of a play within a play, which is the fundamental dramatic point of the opera, also provides the two strongest and best-known musical excerpts – the baritone's prologue and the tenor's 'On with the motley' (Vesti la giubba). The one, in fact, melodically anticipates the other. The prologue's final line 'Ring up the curtain!' takes the baritone to a splen-didly effective high G – not in the score (where the note is D) but in all performances.

The inner play features the traditional characters of the

harlequinade, and the point is musically made by the old-fashioned, artificial style of music. This, for instance, is Arlecchino's serenade to Colombina, with pizzicato strings imitating a serenader's guitar:

PIETRO MASCAGNI
(1863–1945)

ONE work made Mascagni famous, the one-act *Cavalleria Rusticana*: and, very remarkably, it was his *first* opera. He wrote fourteen more, none as successful – though *Friend Fritz* (L'Amico Fritz; 1891), *Iris* (1898, set in Japan), and one or two others are occasionally still given.

CAVALLERIA RUSTICANA

(Rustic Chivalry)

*Libretto by Giovanni Targioni-Tozzetti and Guido Menasci,
after a play by Giovanni Verga*

First performed: Rome, 1890

One Act

Cast in order of singing:

Turiddu, a peasant	*tenor*
Santuzza, a peasant girl	*soprano*
Mamma Lucia, Turiddu's mother, keeper of an inn	*contralto*
Alfio, a carrier	*baritone*
Lola, Alfio's wife	*mezzo-soprano*

Chorus of villagers

The scene is laid in a Sicilian village

Two bold theatrical touches distinguish the score of *Cavalleria* Rusticana. Within the overture, which is based on tunes to be heard in the opera itself, a serenade is sung behind the curtain – supposedly the secret serenade sung by Turiddu to his illicit love, Lola. It is as though we are not just hearing an overture but are sensing, through the closed curtains, the life going on in the Sicilian village which is soon to be visually revealed. (In fact, Lola makes her first entrance with a song that seems like a recollection of this.)

Then, later in the opera, an intermezzo is played *with the curtain up*: our eyes concentrate on the empty stage, stimulated by the orchestra to recall what we have seen.

The meaning of the title is really 'The Rustic Code of Honour': the opera shows this code operating in a working village community, as earlier operas had shown the operation of codes of honour in aristocratic society. The climax is violent, with a duel off-stage; the soprano, tenor, and baritone express in powerful solos the fierce pride from which the violence results; and a strong choral part emphasizes the collective strength of village life.

*   *   *   *   *

Early on the morning of Easter Day, the church bells are ringing and people are entering church. Their songs in praise of spring are heard. Santuzza, heart-broken at being deserted by her lover, Turiddu, comes to his mother's inn to ask if he is there. He is away buying wine, says his mother, Lucia, but Santuzza says he was seen in the village the previous night.

Alfio the carrier enters with his horses, singing gaily, and the square fills with people, who echo his song before they move off or enter the church. He asks Lucia for wine: she replies that she has none – Turiddu has gone to get some. He is surprised, since he saw him near his own cottage that morning. Lucia is about to exclaim but Santuzza quickly silences her. Alfio leaves. The sound of the organ and prayers are heard from the church, echoed by the people in the square, led by Santuzza and Lucia in the Resurrection hymn.

Left alone as all the others enter the church, Lucia asks Santuzza why she silenced her earlier. Santuzza explains – 'Mother, you know the story' (Voi lo sapete) – that Turiddu had been engaged to Lola before he went away to war; then Lola had married Alfio, and Santuzza became Turiddu's lover; but now the jealous Lola, although married, has drawn Turridu's affection away from Santuzza.

Lucia goes into the church and Turiddu enters. Santuzza reproaches him for his conduct with Lola: at first he denies it, then tells her that no amount of pleading will move him. Lola approaches, singing 'O gentle flower of love' (Fior di giaggiolo),* converses with them briefly, mocking at Santuzza, and passes into the church, inviting Turiddu to follow. He is on the point of following but Santuzza begs him to hear

---

* English version by Frederic E. Weatherly (Ascherberg, Hopwood & Crew).

her (Turiddu, ascolta!). She passionately begs him to return to her (No, no, Turiddu), but he says that all is over between them. As he goes off into the church he throws her to the ground in fury.

Alfio enters and the jilted Santuzza tells him of his wife's infidelity with Turiddu. He swears to avenge his honour in blood, and both depart.

The stage is empty (nearly all the villagers are in the church) as the Intermezzo is played. Then, the service over, the people come out of church and happily head for their homes. Turiddu asks Lola to join the group outside his mother's inn, and he sings a gay Brindisi (drinking song), 'See the merry wine' (Viva il vino). Then Alfio arrives. He insultingly declines the glass which Turiddu fills for him. The women, sensing sinister happenings, lead Lola off. Alfio and Turiddu exchange a few words, then Turiddu bites Alfio's ear, the traditional Sicilian manner of accepting a challenge to a duel. Turiddu tells Alfio not to blame Lola for what has happened, and he expresses his fear for Santuzza should he be killed.

As the others go off, Lucia enters. Turiddu asks her for her blessing and charges her to look after Santuzza if he fails to return. Terrified, she guesses what is happening and calls after him desperately as he goes. Santuzza enters and the two women embrace. An agitated crowd gathers. In the distance a woman's voice is heard saying that Turiddu has been killed. Santuzza, Lucia and the assembled crowd scream, and the two women fall to the ground.

*   *   *   *   *

Cavalleria Rusticana is a story of love stolen and avenged, but there is no love-song in it after the serenade behind the curtain (before the opera starts) and no love-duet at all. The big duet expresses Santuzza's love for Turiddu, it is true, but on Turiddu's part it expresses his indifference towards her. Its striking melody (to the words 'Stay, stay, Turiddu') partly depends for its impact on a strong descending bass:

It is noteworthy that the opera's other memorable vocal line, part of the Easter Hymn ('O rejoice that the Lord has arisen'), has very much the same heavy support in a trudging bass, and also has the characteristically insistent triplet movement for a background:

X

ENGELBERT HUMPERDINCK

(1854–1921)

WAGNER influenced operatic composers everywhere – composers as dissimilar as Puccini, Dvořák and Sullivan. On German and Austrian composers his influence was, naturally, direct. Of these, Humperdinck was Wagner's professed disciple, and worked with him at Bayreuth on the production of *Parsifal*. *Hänsel und Gretel*, the first of Humperdinck's own six operas, was the only one to enjoy lasting success.

HÄNSEL UND GRETEL

(Hansel and Gretel)

Libretto by Adelheid Wette, after the Brothers Grimm
First performed: Weimar, 1893

Three Acts

Cast in order of singing:

Gretel	*soprano*
Hänsel	*mezzo-soprano*
Gertrud, their mother	*mezzo-soprano*
Peter, their father, a broom-maker	*baritone*
The Sandman (Sleep-fairy)	*soprano*
The Dew Fairy	*soprano*
The Witch	*mezzo-soprano*

Chorus of children

ADELHEID WETTE, the composer's sister, modified a familiar fairy-tale of the Brothers Grimm to make the libretto of *Hansel and Gretel*. (The boy's name is really Hänsel; but the form and pronunciation 'Hansel' has become standard in English performances.) Never before had an opera for children won such an international success. The two child roles need to be impersonated by women, however: it was left for Benjamin Britten to write successful operas with children singing leading roles – in *The Little Sweep* (the core of *Let's Make an Opera!*), *The Turn of the Screw* and *Noye's Fludde* (see page 474).

There is thus a marked preponderance of women's voices in the original score. But a recent German production has successfully used a tenor as a comically grotesque witch, and the part of the Sandman might well be given to a baritone instead of a soprano. In any form the opera retains a great charm, simple on the surface but with a good deal of musical subtlety beneath.

*　　*　　*　　*　　*

ACT I

Hänsel and Gretel are seen in a small, impoverished-looking broom-maker's hut. Gretel is knitting, Hänsel is making brooms; both are hungry and their parents are away. They try hard to keep cheerful, Gretel taking the lead. Eventually they dance, more and more energetically, until they tumble on to the floor. At that moment their mother comes in. She is annoyed to find them playing when they should have been hard at work. In her anger she knocks down and breaks a jug, full of milk which was to have served as the supper. So she despatches them to the Ilsenstein woods with a basket, telling them to bring it back full of strawberries instead.

Alone, she sits down, exhausted, wondering how to provide food for her starving family. Soon the father comes in, in gay mood, having had a successful day's business and a few drinks on the way home. At first she is irritated, but irritation changes to delight when he unpacks a large basket of food. He asks about the children: she tells him that they were misbehaving, and about the milk jug (over which they can now laugh) and that she sent them to the Ilsenstein woods. He is horror-struck, for in the woods, he tells her, there is a fearsome witch who rides on brooms (he illustrates with one of his besoms) and cooks and eats little children. They both rush off to bring Hänsel and Gretel back.

ACT II

In the forest, the two children are singing quietly as Gretel makes a garland and a nosegay of roses and Hänsel fills the basket with strawberries. They hear a cuckoo, and in imitation of the pirate bird they steal a few strawberries from the basket. Quickly they finish the whole lot, then realize that they must refill the basket and that it is getting too dark to see clearly. They begin to get a little afraid at the strange shapes in the twilight, and they call for help – to be answered only by echoes and by the cuckoo, now mysterious. Their fear grows as it becomes misty.

Then suddenly the mist partly rises, to disclose the Sand-man, who calms them with his song and settles them down to sleep. They say their prayers, 'When at night I go to sleep' (Abends will ich schlafen gehn).* As sleep finally overcomes them, a bright light breaks through the darkness and the mist and fourteen angels, in shining white, come down a ladder and group themselves round the children in a 'Dream Pan-tomime'.

ACT III

The Dew Fairy comes to arouse the sleeping children. Gretel wakes first, then calls Hänsel. They talk of the dream of angels, which they both had. As the distant mist lifts, they excitedly see that they are near a gingerbread house. Natur-ally, they go towards it, not without a little trepidation at first on Gretel's part, and as they reach it they begin to eat bits of it. A voice from inside asks who is eating the house: 'Nibble, nibble, mousekin!' (Knusper, knusper, Knäuschen!). But they ignore it. Suddenly the witch comes out, throwing a rope round Hänsel's neck, and draws them towards her. She promises them quantities of delicious food. Hänsel tries to escape, but she invokes a spell to bind them to the spot.

The witch takes Hänsel to a kennel and shuts him in, leav-ing Gretel while she fetches food for him; he needs fattening, but Gretel does not! Then the witch sends Gretel indoors to set the table (having first broken the spell that kept her motionless). Hänsel, pretending to sleep, overhears the witch planning to push Gretel into the oven so as to cook her and eat her. In her excitement the witch goes for a quick ride on a broomstick, singing 'So hop, hop, hop, gallop, lop lop!'. She goes back to Hänsel, inspects him, finds him still rather lean and calls Gretel to bring him more food. While the witch feeds him, Gretel pronounces over him the spell of disenchant-ment – 'Hocus, pocus, elderbush' (Hokus, pokus, Holder-busch) – which she had earlier heard the witch use.

* English version by Constance Bache (Schott).

Then the witch tells Gretel to peep into the oven to see if the gingerbread is ready. Hänsel, now able to move, slips out of the kennel and warns Gretel to be careful. She pretends not to understand how to look into the oven, and asks the witch to demonstrate; as she does so, they push her in and bang the door closed. In relief, the two sing a gay waltz: 'Hurrah! Now sing the witch is dead' (Juchhei! Nun ist die Hexe tot).

The children go back into the house to eat their fill. The oven starts crackling and explodes, and suddenly they find they are surrounded by a troop of motionless children, who a moment earlier had been cakes. When Gretel touches them, they are able to open their eyes, and when Hänsel pronounces the formula for breaking the spell they jump up and thank Hänsel and Gretel for saving them and restoring them to life. Then Hänsel and Gretel's parents appear, and the family are happily reunited. Two children bring out the witch – now baked into a cake – and all join in thanks to God.

*   *   *   *   *

Hänsel und Gretel is usually said to be Wagnerian, and so it is in the way that motives recur throughout. But, unlike Wagner, Humperdinck preserves a structure of clearly separated numbers and uses tunes which are complete in themselves (often appropriately like those of nursery rhymes) rather than fragments of Wagner's 'endless melody'.

In the opening scene, when Hänsel interrupts his playing with Gretel to mention how hungry he is, Gretel replies by recalling the words of comfort their father always speaks: 'When past bearing is our grief, God alone will send relief':

Then Hänsel and Gretel start their dance with tapping of feet
and clicking of fingers:

The first half of the example on p. 437 becomes the first line of
the children's prayer before they go to sleep in the wood in
the second act. And when, almost at the end of the opera, the
relieved father greets the children, what he sings develops into
a cunningly transformed version of the dance-tune above:

and after this he recalls his habitual words of comfort which
are repeated by the assembled company.

The episode when, in the wood, the children become
frightened by the dark and are answered only by echoes and
by the cuckoo (formerly a friendly sound, now a mysterious
one) is evidence of a truly poetic imagination at work in the
theatre. The witch herself – whose ride on a broomstick is
orchestrally depicted in a prelude to Act II – is not too horri-
fically portrayed.

RICHARD STRAUSS

(1864–1949)

Following Wagner, Richard Strauss embraced a method of composing with recurrent thematic motives and with an opulent orchestral texture which can often stand independently on its own. But Strauss made his operas faster and more concentrated in action. *Salome* and *Elektra* (1909) each play in one continuous scene. *Der Rosenkavalier*, a realistic comedy, takes up three long acts but crams them full of detail: and in place of Wagner's characteristically slow-paced delivery we have fast dialogue-in-music. Moreover, Strauss – not for nothing a contemporary of Zola, Ibsen and Wilde – made deliberate use of plots intended to deliver a shock in the theatre. They duly shocked – and succeeded.

Before these three operas (his most famous) Strauss wrote *Guntram* and *Dearth of Fire* (Feuersnot). Afterwards followed *Ariadne on Naxos* (see p. 454); *The Woman without a Shadow* (Die Frau ohne Schatten; 1919); *Intermezzo* (1924); *The Egyptian Helen* (Die Aegyptische Helena, 1928); *Arabella* (1933); *The Silent Woman* (Die schweigsame Frau; 1935); *Peace Day* (Friedenstag; 1938); *Daphne* (1938); *The Love of Danae* (Die Liebe der Danae, completed 1940 but not produced till 1952); and *Capriccio* (1942).

SALOME

Libretto by Hedwig Lachmann from Oscar Wilde's play
First performed: Dresden, 1905

One Act

Cast in order of singing:

Narraboth, captain of the royal guard	*tenor*
Page to Herodias	*contralto*
Two soldiers	*two basses*
John the Baptist (Jokanaan)	*baritone*
A Cappadocian	*bass*
Salome, daughter of Herodias (by Herodias's former marriage to the brother of Herod, now killed by Herod's command)	*soprano*
A slave	*soprano* or *tenor*
Herod, the Tetrarch	*tenor*
Herodias, his wife	*mezzo-soprano*
Five Jews	*four tenors, bass*
Two Nazarenes	*tenor, bass*
[The role of the executioner is silent.]	

The scene is laid in Palestine in biblical times

RICHARD STRAUSS put all his power of musical descriptiveness into *Salome*; we are invited to feel the neurotic sexuality of the heroine as both alluring and repulsive. The opera is based on Oscar Wilde's play *Salome* (1894), written in French. Wilde made Salome infatuated with John the Baptist, and King Herod infatuated with Salome (his step-daughter) — two additions to the New Testament narrative. The play, literally translated into German and slightly cut, forms the libretto for Richard Strauss's one-act opera. Salome herself is supposed to be only in her teens, an impression which sopranos with the necessary stamina for the part do not find it easy to convey. Many, but not all, singers of the role use a stand-in for the Dance of the Seven Veils.

In the German pronunciation of 'Salome', the accent falls on the first syllable.

* * * * *

ON a terrace outside the banqueting hall of Herod's palace, Narraboth, captain of the guard, is with a page and two soldiers (who are guarding the cistern in which John the Baptist is imprisoned). Narraboth, looking into the hall, expresses his admiration of Salome; the page warns him of the danger of looking at her thus. John's voice is heard from the cistern in impassioned prophecy of one 'who will follow me' ('Nach mir wird Einer kommen'). The soldiers and a Cappadocian converse.

Soon Salome comes out of the banqueting hall: she is irritated by the Romans, Egyptians and Jews at Herod's feast and by Herod's lascivious glances at her. Hearing the prophet's voice, she is curious to see him; she knows that he has persistently reviled her mother. A slave comes to recall her to the feast, but she dismisses him. Her curiosity is further stimulated when she learns that John is a young man. Obeying Herod's order, the soldiers refuse to let her speak with him, but Narraboth, in response to her promises to look favourably on him, eventually orders them to let the prophet out.

As he comes forth, repulsive in appearance after his imprisonment, he fiercely denounces the evil acts of Herod and especially Herodias. Salome is both fascinated and repelled. He shows no interest in her and merely tries to send her away, but this only inflames her fascination, which soon turns into lust. She expresses luridly her compulsive desire to touch his body, then his hair, then to kiss his mouth: he refuses, to her frustration and fury. Narraboth vainly tries to restrain her, and, when Salome continues to express her desire to kiss John, Narraboth stabs himself and falls to the ground between them.

Telling Salome that she is accursed, John the Baptist descends into the cistern again. Herod and Herodias, with attendants, enter. Herod is seeking Salome, to Herodias's annoyance; he comes upon Narraboth's body and orders it to be taken away. Then he invites Salome to share with him wine, then fruit and eventually his throne. But she is cold towards him. John the Baptist's voice is heard again, to Herodias's discomfiture; but Herod is afraid of the prophet and refuses to have him silenced or to hand him over to the Jews. Among a group of Jews present a dispute breaks out, in which two Nazarenes (talking of the coming of the Messiah), and eventually Herod, join. John's denunciation of 'the daughter of Babylon' (Tochter Babylons) is taken by Herodias as an attack on her.

Now Herod asks Salome to dance for him. She is at first unwilling, and Herodias orders her not to dance. But the desperate Herod promises her anything she desires; she makes him swear it, and then, despite her mother's protests, she dances the Dance of the Seven Veils. At the end of it, the inflamed Herod asks her what she desires. She asks for the head of John the Baptist ('den Kopf des Jokanaan') on a silver charger.

Herod, aghast, at first refuses. He thinks this is the doing of Herodias (who is delighted) but Salome assures him it is not. He does all he can to dissuade her from her request, promising her fabulous jewels or anything else she wants, but she steadfastly insists on holding him to his oath and having John's head. Eventually Herod gives way, full of foreboding. Herodias takes the ring of death from his finger, giving it to a soldier; he passes it to the executioner, who descends into the cistern.

Salome waits tensely to hear John's cry, but there is none. She imagines that the executioner is afraid and has not killed John, and she tells the page to go to summon soldiers. But then the huge black arm of the executioner appears from the cistern; in his hand is a silver shield, with John's head upon it. Hungrily she kisses its lips, gloating in the triumph of her lust. Herod, repelled and full of fear, decides to go indoors. The lights are put out. Before going in, Herod turns and sees

Salome, in the light of the moon, still gloating, her passion sated. He orders the soldiers to kill her ('Man töte dieses Weib!') and they crush her beneath their shields.

* * * * *

An impressive contrast is created musically between the lascivious, spiritually corrupt atmosphere which embraces Herod, Herodias and Salome, and the uprightness of John the Baptist with his certainty of prophecy. The characteristic themes of the former group are nervous, angular and shifting in key; but when John first speaks, prophesying that One will follow him who is stronger than he ('I am not worthy to loosen the laces of his shoes'), the orchestra too conveys the feeling of utter firmness, the voice joining in:

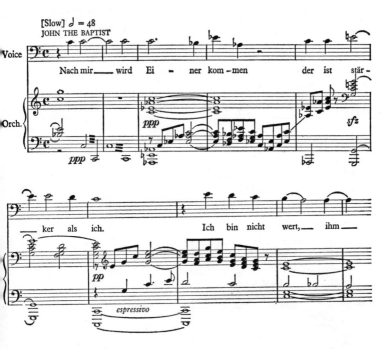

The rising figure marked '*espressivo*' stands as a 'prophecy motive' throughout the work.

When John is brought out of his cistern Salome remarks of

him: 'He's horrible' (note the expressiveness of the *pianis-simo*!):

The little musical motive here tossed between voice and orchestra, expressing Salome's fascination with John (turning from horror to sexual desire), is one of the motives later used in the Dance of the Seven Veils and then again when Salome demands her reward ('I want you to bring me now, on a silver charger ...'):

But what does she want on the silver charger? The suspense is intensified when Herod interrupts with delight, saying how charming is the choice of such a container to hold the promised gift. Only when he has finished does Salome shatter him by naming her choice – and there again, just preceding the words 'John's head' (den kopf des Jokanaan) the little motive seen in the last two examples recurs.

DER ROSENKAVALIER

(The Knight of the Rose)
Libretto by Hugo von Hofmannsthal
First performed: Dresden, 1911

Three Acts

Cast in order of singing:

Octavian, Count Rofrano, a young gentleman of noble family	*mezzo-soprano*
The Feldmarschallin, Princess von Werdenberg	*soprano*
Baron Ochs auf Lerchenau, the Feldmarschallin's kinsman	*bass*
Major-Domo to the Feldmarschallin	*tenor*
Four footmen to the Feldmarschallin	*two tenors, two basses*
Three poor orphans	*soprano, mezzo-soprano, contralto*
Milliner	*soprano*
Animal-seller	*tenor*
Valzacchi, an Italian intriguer	*tenor*
Italian tenor	*tenor*
Attorney to the Feldmarschallin	*bass*
Annina, Valzacchi's companion	*contralto*
Herr von Faninal, a nouveau-riche, recently ennobled	*baritone*
Marianne Leitmetzerin, duenna to Sophie	*soprano*
Major-domo to Faninal	*tenor*
Sophie, Faninal's daughter	*soprano*
Landlord of an inn	*tenor*
Four waiters	*tenor, three basses*

Four children   *sopranos*
Commissioner of Police   *bass*
        Chorus of servants, people, musicians, etc.

The scene is laid in Vienna in the early years of the reign of
Empress Maria Theresa (mid-18th century)

'A COMEDY for music' – such is the original description of the
libretto which Hugo von Hofmannsthal wrote for Richard
Strauss. There is comedy here indeed but also (especially in
the young lovers' music and the final trio) a melting pathos
which represents Strauss's late-flowering romantic art at its
best.

In *Der Rosenkavalier* we encounter a youth who retains a
boy's voice (and so is impersonated by a female singer) and
who is called on by the plot to dress up as a girl. This double
operatic transvestism was classically brought off by Mozart
with the subsidiary role of Cherubino in *The Marriage of
Figaro* – but Strauss goes further, applying it to one of the
main characters, so that the sole love-interest of the work
involves no male singer at all. Strauss later wrote another
famous breeches-part in the role of the Composer in the second
version of *Ariadne on Naxos* (see page 454).

The breeches-part in *Der Rosenkavalier* is that of Octavian,
who is chosen in the plot to be a 'Rosenkavalier' – that is, the
bearer of a ceremonial silver rose from a nobleman to his betrothed. Octavian is at this stage in love with a woman older
than himself, the Feldmarschallin.

Older, but not *so* much older. We may gather that Octavian (who is 17) was not her first lover nor will be her last.
'Feldmarschallin' (abbreviated to Marschallin) means 'wife of
the Field-Marshal', following the custom in German whereby
a woman uses a female form of her husband's title. The feminine ending '-in' was also formerly applied to surnames: the
duenna is thus referred to as 'Leitmetzerin', though her true
surname is Leitmetzer.

*   *   *   *   *

ACT I

The morning sun streams into the Feldmarschallin's bed-room. Octavian is still kneeling beside her bed, embracing her and pouring out endearments. (She calls him by the French nickname, Quinquin; he calls her Marie-Thérèse or Bichette.) Tinkling bells are heard, and Octavian hides as breakfast is brought for the Feldmarschallin by Mahomet, her negro page-boy. In tender mood, they share it. They hear a man approaching and Octavian hides again. For a moment they think it is her husband, returned from the hunt, but in fact it is her kinsman Baron Ochs, who enters with a footman. Octavian emerges from hiding, disguised in a chambermaid's clothes, and the lecherous Ochs is much taken with 'her'. He has come to tell the Feldmarschallin that he is planning to marry the daughter of the wealthy Herr von Faninal and to ask her advice on the choice of a man to act as his 'Rosenkavalier', bearing the ceremonial silver rose to his betrothed.

The Major-Domo enters and tells the Feldmarschallin that various people are waiting to see her. Meanwhile, Ochs flirts outrageously with 'Mariandel', really Octavian in disguise. The Feldmarschallin mildly takes him to task, but he tries hard to justify the eternal pursuit, boasting coarsely of his prowess and experience. The Feldmarschallin offers the ser-vices of her kinsman, Octavian, as the Rosenkavalier, showing Ochs a medallion of him; he comments on the resemblance to 'Mariandel'.

The morning's callers are now admitted. First, three poor, high-born girl orphans, ushered in by their mother, present their petition; then a milliner offers her hats and an animal-seller his apes and parrots; then an Italian intriguer, Valzacchi, offers a scandal sheet. The orphans bow themselves out, thanking the Feldmarschallin for her generosity. Her hair-dresser enters and starts work on her hair, while a flautist comes in and plays, followed by an Italian tenor who sings an aria ('Di rigori armato'). All this time the Baron has been confer-ring with the attorney about his marriage contract: their voices are now heard, with the Baron in irritable mood, and continue while the flautist plays again and the tenor sings another verse. The bustling scene comes to an end as the Feldmarschallin waves them all off. Valzacchi and his companion Annina, however, take the opportunity to ingratiate themselves with Ochs, who asks them to find out all about 'Mariandel' for him. Ochs leaves the silver rose, brought by his servants, in the Feldmarschallin's care.

Left alone, the Feldmarschallin thinks of how the days are passing and how she must eventually be referred to as 'the old Princess' (die alte Fürstin). Octavian returns, in his own clothes, and finds her in pensive mood. She tries to explain to the passionate youth that their love can only be ephemeral. In answer to his protests, she says he must leave her now, and perhaps see her later. Reluctantly but obediently he goes. Suddenly realizing that she has dismissed him without a farewell or a last kiss, she starts up violently: she summons four footmen to call him back, but they report that he went too fast to be caught. The negro page-boy is summoned, to take the silver rose to Octavian.

ACT II

Faninal is just leaving his house, about to bring Ochs to meet his daughter for the first time. Sophie's duenna, Marianne Leitmetzer, tells him that his fine new carriage is awaiting him and the Major-Domo hurries him off – etiquette demands that the bride's father must not be present when the Rosenkavalier arrives as the bridegroom's messenger. Sophie prays for protection from the sin of pride, interrupted by Marianne's commentary from the window.

Calls of 'Rofrano' are heard and Marianne tells Sophie that the Rosenkavalier has arrived. His resplendent entry follows: he is clad all in white and silver, followed by his servants, in white and green, some with plumes and swords. As he advances with the silver rose, he and Sophie are each taken aback by the other's grace. He presents the rose to her and the two talk for a few breathless moments.

The servants withdraw and the two, with Marianne nearby, sit down to converse. They are strongly attracted – youth to

youth. Then Faninal brings in Ochs. His coarsely condescend-
ing behaviour distresses Sophie (whom Marianne tries to comfort) and infuriates Octavian. Soon Ochs asks Sophie to sit on
his knee and he behaves with gross familiarity. The fawning
Faninal is delighted to have both a Lerchenau and a Rofrano
in his house but his daughter is sickened by the Baron's manner: she tears herself angrily away as he becomes more and
more importunate. But Ochs is untroubled, reminding her
gaily of an old song in waltz time, 'With me, with me' (Mit
mir). Meanwhile, the attorney and his clerk have arrived, and
Faninal shows Ochs into an ante-room with them to draw up
the contract.

Sophie and Octavian turn to one another, she begging him
for help. Then there is a commotion among the servants
(Ochs's ill-mannered men are chasing Faninal's maids); the
Major-domo comes for help and Marianne goes off. Alone,
Sophie and Octavian are free to express their mutual feelings
and sing a tender duet, culminating in a declaration of their
love.

Suddenly they are seized from behind by Valzacchi and
Annina, who call Ochs. He enters, confronts the young couple
and asks Sophie for an explanation ('Eh bien, Mam'zelle?').
She will not answer; but, after sarcastic remarks from Ochs,
Octavian tells him that Sophie will not marry him. Ochs,
brushing aside the protests, starts to lead her off; Octavian,
enraged, challenges him. Still Ochs takes no notice, so Octavian insults him vigorously. Ochs whistles for his servants, but
Octavian draws and for a moment they fight. Octavian's sword
scratches Ochs's arm, whereupon his servants rush on Octavian and Ochs yells 'Murder! Murder!' (Mörder! Mörder!).

Now confusion reigns. Servants bustle round, tending
Ochs's scratch; Sophie, Annina and Marianne express their
varying concern. Faninal comes in and takes command, ordering someone to fetch a surgeon, apologizing profusely to Ochs
and raging at Octavian and Sophie. He orders Octavian out
and, in response to Sophie's downright refusal to marry Ochs,
says he will force her to take him or she will go to a convent.
Marianne takes her to her room. With more apologies to Ochs,

Faninal rushes off.

Ochs, left alone with his servants and the doctor – and some wine – gradually recovers his humour, even beginning to waltz. His humour is further improved when Annina (now in Octavian's pay) comes with a letter from 'Mariandel', suggesting an assignation. He agrees with delight and sends Annina away – but without her expected tip.

ACT III

In a private room at an inn, the scene is prepared in dumb show during the orchestral introduction for Ochs's encounter with 'Mariandel' – in which Octavian plans to trap and expose Ochs. Octavian (ready in female clothes for his role), Valzacchi and Annina hide various assistants behind trapdoors opening into the room. When eventually all is ready, Octavian leaves the room. Dance music is heard in the distance and Ochs arrives, leading 'Mariandel'. Valzacchi greets Ochs with silent feigned respect, pointing out a bed in a recess. The landlord and waiters ask obsequiously if everything is all right, and answer a few of Ochs's queries before he sends them and Valzacchi off.

Now the tête-à-tête begins, 'Mariandel' speaking in raw, peasant fashion. Ochs offers 'Mariandel' wine, which she declines ('Nein, nein, nein, nein! i trink kein Wein'); she runs off as if afraid – into the recess, where she sees the bed and feigns great wonder at who sleeps there. They sit down and Ochs is about to kiss her when he notices, with discomfiture, the striking resemblance to Octavian. A moment later a head appears through a trapdoor, to Ochs's alarm.

A servant brings in the supper (the distant music becomes clearer when the door opens). 'Mariandel', to Ochs's perturbation, is rather melancholy in mood, but giving him an occasional languid glance. Soon the faces start appearing in mysterious places at an alarming rate, unseen, apparently, by 'Mariandel', but terrifying to Ochs, who rings the bell. Annina, in disguise, suddenly rushes in, pretending to claim Ochs as her husband, and followed by the landlord and three waiters. He protests vigorously, but the landlord and waiters are scandalized, especially when four children come in, calling 'Papa, Papa, Papa!'.

The Police Commissioner enters, and is suspicious of Ochs. Who, he wishes to know, is the girl? Ochs says that she is his fiancée, Sophie von Faninal. At this moment Faninal himself arrives. He identifies Ochs but is furious at the suggestion that the girl is his daughter.

Hunting around the room for his wig, which he had discarded earlier, Ochs runs into the children, who resume their cries. Sophie, whom Faninal has sent for, enters. Faninal, humiliated, faints and is carried out to the next room, with Sophie and the landlord following, and the police remove everyone except Ochs, 'Mariandel', Annina and the children.

Ochs now asks to be allowed to escort 'Mariandel' home, but she refuses to go with him. She whispers a few words to the Commissioner, then disappears into the recess. Female clothes are thrown out, one by one, to Ochs's fury. The landlord announces the Feldmarschallin, who has been summoned to Ochs's aid by one of his servants.

Octavian emerges in his proper clothes. Sophie, who has re-entered, angrily passes on to Ochs her father's instruction that he must never come near the Faninal house again. The Feldmarschallin advises Ochs to depart and assures the police officers that they can go, as what has happened was merely a prank. She asks Octavian to explain the position to Ochs, who now sees why the resemblance between Octavian and 'Mariandel' was so strong – and begins to understand rather more about the relationship between Octavian and the Feldmarschallin. Since he now realizes that the evening's events were a masquerade, Ochs hopes to resume his plans of marriage; but the Feldmarschallin says decisively that he must forget them.

The concealed trap-door-manipulators now emerge, Annina removes her disguise and Valzacchi leads out his accomplices – all to Ochs's astonishment. They remind him ironically of what has passed. The musicians, the coachmen, the 'boots', the waiters and the landlord start pestering him and he is only too glad to get out.

Only the Feldmarschallin, Sophie and Octavian remain. The two women each understand the claim of the other on Octavian. But the Feldmarschallin is strong enough to wipe away her tears and approach Sophie kindly. Sophie, abashed, curtseys. Octavian is deeply moved by the Feldmarschallin's goodness but the Feldmarschallin cuts short his thanks with the words 'I know nothing ... nothing' (ich weiss nix, gar nix).

Now, standing apart from the lovers, the Feldmarschallin expresses the poignancy of her situation: 'I made a vow ...' (Hab mir's gelobt): it is the beginning of a long trio for her and the lovers. The Feldmarschallin leaves; the lovers fall into each other's arms with the words ' 'Tis a dream' (Ist ein traum). The Feldmarschallin re-enters, now with Faninal, who leads her away again. The lovers end their song, embrace, and go. The room is left empty.

But Sophie has dropped her handkerchief. Who comes to fetch it? It is Mahomet, the Feldmarschallin's page-boy. With tripping footsteps he runs out again and the opera is over.

*   *   *   *   *

Before the curtain rises the orchestra 'tells' us of the night of love of the Feldmarschallin and Octavian. The very opening gives us two themes, representing the boy's youthful ardour (*a*) and the full, sensual passion of the mature woman (*b*):

The unconcealed eroticism of the whole plot goes with an equally unconcealed eroticism in the music. This is linked to another major element of sensuous appeal: the use of Viennese waltz-tunes. Here the spirit of Johann Strauss was taken by his namesake to enliven (with triumphant anachronism) a scene set in Vienna a hundred years before Johann Strauss's day. There are several of these waltzes in *Der Rosenkavalier*, which have been made into various suites for concert-hall use.

The most famous is what might be called Ochs's theme-song: he first sings it when trying to fondle Sophie in Faninal's house. We give its orchestral version:

Before this, Octavian has presented the silver rose to the accompaniment of a strange chord-sequence in an orchestration that itself sounds 'silvery' (flutes, harps, solo violins, celesta). We quote it (*a* below) not at its first appearance but as Strauss brings it back – with an utter simplicity of telling effect – when the young lovers are finally each other's, and are singing their duet just before the end of the opera. Sophie's words may be translated: 'It is a dream, it cannot be true that we two are together'.

ARIADNE AUF NAXOS

(Ariadne on Naxos)

Libretto by Hugo von Hofmannsthal

Original version first performed: Stuttgart, 1912
Revised version first performed: Vienna, 1916

Revised version: Prologue and One Act

Cast in order of singing:

The Major-domo	*speaking part*
The Music Master	*baritone*
A lackey	*bass*
An officer	*tenor*
The Composer	*soprano*
The Tenor (later Bacchus)	*tenor*
A wig maker	*bass*
Zerbinetta, an actress	*soprano*
The Dancing Master	*tenor*
The Prima Donna (later Ariadne)	*soprano*
Naiad ⎫	*soprano*
Dryad ⎬ three nymphs	*contralto*
Echo ⎭	*soprano*
Harlequin ⎫	*baritone*
Brighella ⎬ characters in the harlequinade	*tenor*
Truffaldino ⎪	*bass*
Scaramuccio ⎭	*tenor*

The scene is laid in Vienna in the early 18th century

IN *Ariadne on Naxos* we see a curious marriage between Strauss's fondness (like Wagner's) for mythological or other ancient stories and his leaning to realistic comedy. *Ariadne on Naxos* was at first designed as a one-act opera, to be performed as the divertissement in a condensed version of Molière's comedy *Le Bourgeois Gentilhomme* (for which Strauss also provided incidental music). In this form it was not particularly successful; moreover, the difficulty of providing separate companies of actors and singers made it prohibitive for most theatres. So Strauss and his librettist wrote a musical prologue to replace the play. The original 'opera' was retained, in slightly revised form; but now, instead of being offered as M. Jourdain's entertainment for his dinner guests, it is offered by a Viennese *nouveau riche* to his.

It is in the revised form – to which the following synopsis adheres – that the work is generally given today. The prologue introduces the supposed artists who are to perform the entertainment for the wealthy patron's guests; it also introduces the particularly sympathetic character of the Composer himself (a soprano role, representing a youth). To fit in with its 18th-century conception and inspiration, *Ariadne* is scored for a far smaller orchestra than Strauss's other operas. In it the charm of a mock old-fashioned harlequinade is set beside a virtuoso handling of three types of soprano: coloratura (Zerbinetta), lyric (Composer) and dramatic (Ariadne).

* * * * *

PROLOGUE

Backstage in the private theatre of a Viennese mansion, the Music Master agitatedly approaches the Major-domo, complaining that the serious opera (*Ariadne on Naxos*) by his pupil the Composer, to be given that evening, will be spoilt if followed, as is proposed, by a comic opera or harlequinade. The Major-domo tells him that the plans will not be changed, and that the opera will need to be shortened; he goes off, and the Music Master follows.

A lackey brings in an officer, who goes into the room where Zerbinetta, the actress of the harlequinade, is dressing. The Composer enters, anxious about rehearsing his opera. He is irritated when the lackey goes off and leaves him; but then a melody occurs to him and he tries to write it down. One of the dressing-room doors suddenly flies open and the Tenor angrily ejects a wig-maker; then Zerbinetta comes out of her room with the officer, and is joined by the Dancing Master; and then the Prima Donna comes out of hers, with the Music Master. The Music Master tells the Composer, who has noticed – and been attracted by – Zerbinetta, of the plans for the evening. The Composer is outraged at the demands made on him, but recovers as another 'inspiration' comes to him. Zerbinetta, her troupe around her, talks with the Dancing Master, and finishes her make-up; meanwhile, the Prima Donna makes slighting remarks about the comedians.

The Major-domo returns and creates further consternation by announcing that, on his master's orders, the two entertainments are to be given simultaneously. The Composer is horrified, but the Dancing Master and the Music Master agree that a compromise must be managed. Both the Prima Donna and the Tenor demand that any necessary cuts shall be in the other's part – on which both are reassured (separately) by the Music Master.

The story of Ariadne is explained to Zerbinetta, who, not believing in a woman who truly longs for death when deserted by a lover, treats it somewhat cynically when telling it to her troupe. The Composer, idealistically, tries to explain it to Zerbinetta, and as they talk he is strongly drawn to her. She goes off; then the Prima Donna returns and, to the Music Master, renews her protests at having to appear alongside a comic troupe. The Composer, seeing the harlequinade players, is once more aghast at the pollution of his art, and rushes off in despair.

OPERA

On a stage within the stage, the scene is set for the opera of *Ariadne* – a seashore, with a cave, and wings made from rocks and trees. The three nymphs (Naiad, Dryad and Echo) are commenting on Ariadne's sadness, while she reclines on the shore asleep. She awakes, recalling her love for Theseus: 'How beauteous once' (Ein schönes war).* From the wings, Harle-

* English version by Alfred Kalisch (Boosey & Hawkes).

quin, Zerbinetta and the other comedians comment; Ariadne continues as if she has not heard them. Soon the comedians, uncomprehending, give up; Ariadne, rising, sings to herself of the happy prospect of death: 'There is a land' (Es gibt ein Reich).

The comedians return, to try to enliven Ariadne with singing and dancing: 'This lady is too much inclined' (Die Dame gibt mit trübem Sinn'). Zerbinetta enters, sends them away and approaches Ariadne: 'Most gracious sovereign lady' (Grossmächtige Prinzessin). She tries to talk to her as woman to woman; Ariadne pointedly ignores her and retires into the cave, but Zerbinetta continues at some length her attempt to console her, relating the story of her own love-life.

Harlequin enters and attempts to make love to Zerbinetta. She resists him coquettishly. The other three enter, also in pursuit of her, while she dances around them; soon she and Harlequin, who has remained in the background, go off together, to the annoyance of the others.

As they go, the three nymphs return, commenting on what they have just seen – a young god approaching the island. It is Bacchus. He enters, singing of his escape from the enchantress Circe (which the nymphs had recalled). Ariadne comes from the cave happily: she believes her visitor to be Hermes, the messenger of death, and welcomes him.

The nymphs go off, leaving Bacchus and Ariadne together. He is entranced by her beauty; as they sing together, their feelings warm into love. He eventually kisses her and she believes she is dying. She revives, and with a sense of wonderment they move off together into the cave. As their loving voices are heard, the nymphs comment, and Zerbinetta enters to remark characteristically on the inevitability of the outcome.

*   *   *   *   *

Ariadne is an opera full of contrasts. Most of Strauss's operas are much concerned with the essential nature of Woman: here two different feminine types (or different aspects of femininity) are powerfully contrasted by musical means. This is how the 'faithful-unto-death' Ariadne recalls her happiness with Theseus:

Compare this with the music allocated to the fickle, light-hearted Zerbinetta – in perhaps the most brilliant and intensely difficult coloratura aria in the entire repertory – as she sings of her past love affairs. She then breaks into a cheerful rondo ('Like a god each one did I welcome'):

Note the more 'serious' transformation of Zerbinetta's rondo theme as, in the opera's closing pages, she applies the same idea to Ariadne ('When a new god comes to woo us, Captive are we, helpless, dumb'):

The other marked contrast is between what one might call the 'satellites' of the two women. Ariadne's are the three nymphs, whose trios are like those of Wagner's Rhinemaidens, but lighter, more translucent, in texture (Echo, by the way, is often an echo in fact as well as name). Zerbinetta's – the four men of the harlequinade – are on quite another level: indulging in all kinds of frivolous antics and singing in lively, dancing rhythms.

XI

ALBAN BERG

(1885–1935)

THE distance between the first performances of Richard
Strauss's *Ariadne auf Naxos* and Alban Berg's *Wozzeck*
is a mere twelve years – but these twelve years include those
of the First World War, and for most music-lovers the gap
between the two works is the gap separating 'old' from 'modern' music. Of all the pioneers and innovators of modernism
in music, the most influential has proved to be the Viennese,
Arnold Schoenberg (1874–1951), of whom Berg was a disciple.

Schoenberg himself composed four operatic works: *Erwartung* (Expectation), composed in 1909 though not performed
until 1924; *Die glückliche Hand* (The Lucky Hand), composed 1910–13; *Von Heute auf Morgen* (From Today till
Tomorrow), 1930; and *Moses and Aaron*, which was only
partially completed. Of the first three, all short, *Erwartung* is
the best known: it is for one character only. The full-length
Moses and Aaron was (despite its incomplete nature) brought
to the stage in 1957 and has aroused great interest.

But the first major operatic success of the 'Schoenberg
school' was won by Berg's *Wozzeck*. It is, with the exception
of an orchestral interlude, atonal (keyless) – but not twelve-
note, i.e., not in the system of order which Schoenberg
evolved within atonality to replace the lost order of key. Berg's
later opera, *Lulu* (unfinished, performed in 1937 after the
composer's death), *is* written in the twelve-note technique.
The title-role of *Lulu* is that of a woman who incarnates sexual
pleasure and, after becoming the wife and mistress of several
men, ends up as one of Jack the Ripper's victims in London.

WOZZECK

Libretto by the composer, after Georg Büchner

First performed: Berlin, 1925

Three Acts

Cast in order of singing:

The Captain	*tenor*
Wozzeck, a soldier, batman to the Captain	*baritone*
Andres, another soldier, his friend	*tenor*
Marie, a woman living with Wozzeck	*soprano*
Margret, Marie's neighbour	*contralto*
The Doctor	*bass*
The Drum-Major	*tenor*
Two apprentices	*baritone (or tenor) and bass*
An idiot	*tenor*
Marie's and Wozzeck's child	*treble*

Chorus of soldiers, apprentices, servants and children

The scene is laid in a German town in the early 19th century

IN its depiction of the agony of the unbalanced, persecuted individual at the hands of unfeeling society *Wozzeck* seems so modern that it is hard to realize that it is based on a play written before Victoria came to the throne. This play was *Woyzeck* (that was the original spelling), left unfinished by its German author, Georg Buchner, who died in 1837 at the age of 23.

Wozzeck is a simple soldier, distinguished neither by intelligence nor any other special gift: an anti-hero, in fact. Yet he wins our sympathy – ill-treated as he is by his superiors, deceived by the woman with whom he lives. Even this woman, however, has her glimpse of redemption. Theirs is a pathos which they themselves cannot express articulately, but it is a pathos which becomes intensely moving in the theatre. Berg's

music (orchestral as well as vocal) seems to convey the fears
and fantasies of Wozzeck's mind as well as the frustrations of
his material existence.

ACT I

Scene 1. The Captain is being shaved by the agitated, nervous
Wozzeck, his batman. He teases Wozzeck, reproaching him
for having a child out of wedlock. Wozzeck attempts to justify
himself: 'We poor people' (Wir arme Leut)* 'cannot afford
the morality of the rich'.
Scene 2. Wozzeck and his friend Andres are cutting wood in
a field. Andres is singing gaily while Wozzeck, confused in his
mind, believes the place to be haunted and sees strange visions.
Scene 3. Marie is minding her small child and talking through
the window of her room with a neighbour, Margret. As a
military band passes by, Marie waves to the Drum-Major.
Margret comments on Marie's friendliness with men and the
two quarrel. Marie sings her child a lullaby: 'Maiden, what
song shall you sing?' (Mädel, was fangst Du jetzt an?). The
child falls asleep. Soon there is a knock at the window. Wozzeck, still agitated, looks in, talks for a moment with Marie,
and rushes off again. Soon after, the distressed Marie breaks
out in anguish and goes out.
Scene 4. In his study, the Doctor talks to Wozzeck, who has
consented for a small extra wage to be subjected to the Doctor's medical experiments. The Doctor hectors him, then lis-
tens to Wozzeck's descriptions of his strange world – he hopes
to become famous through the medical discoveries arising
from his studies of Wozzeck.
Scene 5. Outside her house, Marie talks with the handsome,
bearded Drum-Major and admires his physique. He is strongly
attracted by her and tries to embrace her: at first she resists,
then, with a shrug, she leads him indoors.

ACT II

Scene 1. In her room, Marie is impatiently trying to get her
child to sleep, intermittently admiring herself (wearing a pair

* English version by Eric Blackall and Vida Harford (Universal).

of gold ear-rings) in a broken mirror. Wozzeck enters and is suspicious on seeing the ear-rings. He looks at the sleeping child, gives Marie some money which he has received from the Captain and the Doctor, and goes off, leaving her in remorse over her infidelity.

Scene 2. In the street, the Captain catches up with the Doctor, who is in a hurry; the Doctor makes the Captain uneasy by talking about disease and death. They stop Wozzeck as he passes and, with allusions to soldiers wearing beards, tease him cruelly about the Drum-Major. He goes off distracted, soon followed by the Captain and the Doctor.

Scene 3. In front of her house again, Marie greets Wozzeck. He questions her and reproaches her angrily for her behaviour with the Drum-Major. Before she goes off, she says "Better a knife-blade in my heart than lay a hand on me' (Lieber ein Messer in den Leib, als eine Hand auf mich).

Scene 4. Soldiers, girls and apprentices are drinking and dancing in a tavern to the music of a band. Two drunken apprentices sing of brandy. Wozzeck enters and is enraged to see Marie and the Drum-Major among the dancers; he is about to rush at them when the dance ends and the soldiers and apprentices, led by Andres, sing a hunting song: 'A hunter from the south' (Ein Jäger aus der Pfalz). Andres and Wozzeck talk for a moment, then one of the drunken apprentices climbs on to a table and delivers a rambling sermon. An idiot approaches Wozzeck and talks to him of blood; the thought of blood preys on Wozzeck's mind as the dancing is resumed.

Scene 5. Soldiers are asleep in the barrack room. Wozzeck, still tortured by thoughts of the dance-hall, talks to the half-sleeping Andres. The Drum-Major, drunk, enters noisily, boasting of his possession of a woman and hinting at her identity. He torments Wozzeck and offers him brandy: in reply Wozzeck merely whistles. Angrily, the Drum-Major seizes him and they fight, the Drum-Major completing his humiliation by pushing him to the floor and beating his face.

The Drum-Major goes and the disturbed soldiers settle themselves again, Wozzeck sitting on his bed and staring before him.

ACT III

Scene 1. Marie, alone with her child in her room, reads her Bible by candlelight. She is in penitent mood and prays for mercy.

Scene 2. At dusk, Wozzeck and Marie are walking by a pool. She is nervous and wishes to go home, but he insists on their sitting down. He recalls their first meeting and kisses her; then he draws his knife and cuts her throat.

Scene 3. Apprentices and girls are dancing a polka in a tavern. Wozzeck watches them. He sings raucously and calls Margret over, starting to make love to her. Then he asks her to sing, which she does, accompanied by an out-of-tune piano: 'To Swabia' (In's Schwabenland). She notices a dark red stain on his right hand. He says that he had cut his arm; but the crowd gathers round him and he rushes off.

Scene 4. Back by the pool, Wozzeck is searching for the knife with which he killed Marie. He comes upon her corpse. Finding the knife, he throws it in the pool; and as the blood-red moon shows through the clouds, wades in after it as if to wash off his own blood. He drowns. Arriving at that moment, the Captain and the Doctor pause, thinking that they heard something. Then the Captain, disturbed by the uncanny atmosphere, drags the Doctor off.

Scene 5. In front of Marie's house, a crowd of children, among them Marie's, is playing. News comes of the discovery of Marie's body and they hurry off to see it, one of them telling Marie's child that his mother is dead. He goes on riding his hobby horse for a while, then, finding himself alone, runs off after the others.

*   *   *   *   *

'We poor people': the basic dramatic motive of the opera is musically characterized by Wozzeck in the opening scene.

As distinct from ordinary notation, parts of the opera employ a device called 'Speech-song' (*Sprechgesang*) which Schoenberg devised. In it the singer does not sustain the pitch of the note indicated but just touches it: the effect is something of a compromise between speech and song. This is only one of the ways in which Berg develops a peculiarly intense expression for the words, away from the older conventions of what is beautiful and regular in music.

On occasion Berg comes close to a 'popular' musical style (lullaby, military march, hunting song) but deliberately distorts the kind of melody we should expect. Thus Marie, singing to her child in Act I ('Maiden, what song shall you sing?'), has the following melody:

Here is the typical rocking of the traditional lullaby, and indeed a typical lullaby melody – except for the violent distortion induced by the out-of-key notes in the phrases marked 'x'.

A similar kind of 'distorted reality' is achieved by the tavern orchestra in Act II and the out-of-tune piano in Act III. But it is not only in the unusual instruments required here that Berg's use of the orchestra is original and impressive. Notable are the orchestral *crescendo* on the single note B, after Marie's murder – an overwhelming effect in the theatre – and the interlude between the two final scenes of the opera. It is this interlude (not atonal, but in the key of D minor) which seems to sum up Wozzeck's tragedy and to speak directly from composer to audience. The chorus is also sometimes used orchestrally – that is, for its power of sheer tone-colour and atmosphere, notably in the 'snoring' heard when Wozzeck returns to his barrack-room in Act II.

The scenes are composed by Berg in what are usually considered instrumental forms – fugue, variations, etc. – though it is the dramatic, not the formal, development which we sense in the theatre.

IGOR STRAVINSKY

(born 1882)

BORN a Russian, afterwards taking French and then American nationality, Igor Stravinsky has had a musical career of extraordinary variety and extraordinary success. In the 1950s he began writing serial and then strict twelve-note music – to which he had been attracted by the work not of Schoenberg but of Schoenberg's disciple, Anton Webern (1883–1945). But Stravinsky's operas date from before this 'conversion'.

The Nightingale (words in Russian by the composer and S. N. Mitusov, but first produced in France, and in French, in 1914) has been less widely heard than *Oedipus Rex* (1927) and *The Rake's Progress* (1951). The last of these has an English text by W. H. Auden and Chester Kallman, based on Hogarth's pictures: there is a back-to-Mozart, back-to-Bellini stylization about the music, at the end of which (as in *Don Giovanni*) the characters turn to the audience and warn them to draw a moral lesson from the tale.

Oedipus Rex is chosen for detailed comment here because its break with tradition is particularly striking (and was even more so in the 1920s). Stravinsky's only other opera is the half-hour comedy *Mavra* (Russian text by Boris Kochno, first given in 1922 in French); *The Soldier's Tale* (1918) uses speech, dance and instrumental music but no singing, and is not an opera.

OEDIPUS REX

(King Oedipus)

Libretto by Jean Cocteau (after Sophocles),
translated into Latin by J. Daniélou

First performed: Paris, 1927

Two Acts

Cast in order of singing:

Oedipus, King of Thebes	*tenor*
Creon, Jocasta's brother	*bass-baritone*
Tiresias, a seer	*bass*
Jocasta, Oedipus's wife	*mezzo-soprano*
A messenger	*bass-baritone*
A shepherd	*tenor*

[A narrator also takes part, telling the story as it proceeds. Points at which he intervenes are indicated in the synopsis.]
Chorus of men of Thebes

The scene is laid in Thebes in classical times

SIGNIFICANTLY, Stravinsky set a version of Sophocles' *Oedipus Rex* not in the author's own Greek nor the composer's own Russian nor in the language of modern France (where the work was to be staged) but in Latin – a language which Stravinsky described as 'a medium not dead, but turned to stone, and so monumentalized as to have become immune from all risks of vulgarization'. The libretto was therefore written in French (by Cocteau) and translated into Latin. A narrator is required to interrupt the action by telling the story in the audience's own language.

The work is described as an 'opera-oratorio', and the novelty of the form was doubtless a deliberate challenge to tradition and especially to the idea that opera should be realistic.

The characters of *Oedipus Rex* are costumed, but (according to the original scheme) restricted in their movements: Oedipus, Creon and Jocasta use masks and move only their arms and heads.

It is fitting to this conception that the music, too, should seem severe and monumental. But such is the skill of the music – not only in itself but in the way its variety of mood and pace reflect the drama – that the piece comes over in the theatre with impressive power.

ACT I

[Narration]

King Oedipus is begged by the people of Thebes to save them from the plague, which is destroying the city. He promises to do so, saying that he has sent Creon, his wife's brother, to ask the oracle of Apollo what is to be done. Creon appears and is greeted by the people.

[Narration]

Creon tells Oedipus and the people the god's answer: the Thebans must discover the murderer of the previous king, Laius; he must be driven out of the city, for it is he who is causing the city's misery. Oedipus boasts to the people that he will find the guilty man.

[Narration]

The chorus pray that Oedipus will succeed. They greet the seer Tiresias, whom Oedipus decides to consult; but Tiresias declines to speak, asking not to be compelled to do so. Oedipus, made suspicious by his silence, accuses him of being the murderer himself. In indignation, Tiresias resolves to speak, and he tells Oedipus what the god has said: 'The king's murderer is a king' (Regis est rex peremptor). Oedipus, believing Tiresias to be in league with Creon in a plot against himself, turns angrily on him. Then the queen, Jocasta, appears, to be greeted by the people in a jubilant chorus.

ACT II

[Narration]

The chorus repeat their greeting to Jocasta. She rebukes the princes for quarrelling in the plague-ridden city. She tells Oedipus not to trust oracles ('Ne probentur oracula'): she knows that they can lie – for they predicted that her son would kill her husband, the previous king, whereas he was in fact murdered by a thief at a meeting of three roads (the chorus echo the word 'trivium').

Oedipus becomes uneasy: he remembers killing an old man once at a meeting of three roads. (He believes, however, that he is the son of the Corinthian king, Polybus; he had left Corinth as it was predicted that he would kill his father and marry his mother.) In a long duet, Jocasta tries to lead him away, but he is bent on discovering the truth and sends for the shepherd who witnessed his crime.

[Narration]

The chorus announce the arrival of a messenger, who bears news of the death of Polybus. He relates that Polybus was not Oedipus's true father; he, the messenger, had brought Oedipus, exposed on a mountainside in his infancy, to Polybus. The truth seems clear, but the people still hope that some miraculous explanation will come to light. The shepherd then comes forward and tells how the infant son of Laius and Jocasta had been abandoned in this way on a mountainside.

Jocasta has departed; Oedipus, not comprehending the truth, at first believes she does not wish to hear of his humble ancestry. But at last he realizes the terrible facts: he is the son of Jocasta, and has murdered his true father, Laius, and married his mother. He leaves.

[Narration]

The messenger returns with news of the death of Jocasta: 'Dead is the sacred head of Jocasta' (Divum Jocastae caput mortuum). The people tell of how Jocasta hanged herself and of how Oedipus cut her down, then put out his eyes with her brooch. He reappears to their horror; but when they see their

king's blind mutilated face their horror turns to pity as they
bid him farewell.

* * * * *

Though the music is both hard in texture and apparently
rigid in shape (which is what we mean by the 'monumental'
aspect of Stravinsky's work in this vein) it is nevertheless varied
not only between characters but even within their utterances.
Oedipus, at the beginning, is vain and self-confident: his
promise to deliver his people ('Ego vos liberabo') is uttered
with flaunting coloratura. But when he discovers the terrible
truth about himself, he is reduced to:

These words ('Light has come!') bear their own terrible
irony: in a few minutes we shall hear that Oedipus has put out
his eyes.

Jocasta's earlier utterance in distrust of oracles shows
Stravinsky's characteristic rough-riding over the natural
rhythms of language to create musical and dramatic tension:

BENJAMIN BRITTEN

(born 1913)

FROM Stravinsky we pass to one of the many composers who has gained considerably from his work as a harmonic innovator: Benjamin Britten, the leading British composer of today. But Stravinsky's highly individual approach to the theatre contributed nothing to *Peter Grimes*, with which Britten began his conquering operatic career in 1945. The astonishing thing about Britten as an opera composer is, indeed, the degree to which he is self-made – with a great versatility of musical resources, with natural debts to some composers but chains to none, and showing very little connection with previous English opera.

At this point we may look over what might be justly called the pre-Britten century in English opera. Its two considerable international successes were *The Bohemian Girl* (1843) by Michael William Balfe (1808–70) and *The Mikado* (1881) by Arthur Sullivan (1842–1900). But Sullivan failed with his one serious opera, *Ivanhoe* (1891), and of the composers coming after him only a few wrote works to which much interest attaches today, even in Britain. It is perhaps not invidious to pick out *A Village Romeo and Juliet* (originally in German, 1907) by Frederick Delius (1862–1934), *The Boatswain's Mate* (1916) by Ethel Smyth (1858–1934) and *Sāvitri* (1916), on an Indian legend, by Gustav Holst (1874–1934).

Ralph Vaughan Williams (1872–1958), like his teacher, Charles Villiers Stanford (1852–1924), wrote operas persistently but not very successfully: perhaps the best is *Riders to the Sea* (1937). Another Stanford pupil, Arthur Benjamin (1893–1960) showed a surer theatrical flair in *Prima Donna* (composed 1934, performed 1949) and *A Tale of Two Cities* (radio 1953, staged 1957). Composers who are older than

Britten, but who began their operatic career after he did, include William Walton (born 1902) with *Troilus and Cressida* (1954); Michael Tippett (born 1905) with *The Midsummer Marriage* (1955) and *King Priam* (1962); and Lennox Berkeley (born 1903) whose most successful work is *A Dinner Engagement* (1954).

Britten's own operas may be divided into three categories. Full-scale operas for large theatres: *Peter Grimes* (1945), *Billy Budd* (1951) and *Gloriana* (1953). 'Chamber' operas (i.e. using chamber orchestra): *The Rape of Lucretia* (1946), *Albert Herring* (1947), *The Turn of the Screw* (1953), and *A Midsummer Night's Dream* (1960, later re-scored for full orchestra); also his very free arrangement of *The Beggar's Opera* (1948; see also p. 23). Dramatic works not primarily intended for the opera-house at all: *Let's Make an Opera* (1949; for children; incorporates *The Little Sweep*); *Noye's Fludde* (1958; for church performance with audience-participation); and a triptych of 'parables for church performance', *Curlew River* (1964, based on a Japanese Nōh-play), *The Burning Fiery Furnace* (1966) and *The Prodigal Son* (1968), all three presented as if enacted by medieval monks, with small instrumental ensemble.

PETER GRIMES

Libretto by Montague Slater, after George Crabbe
First performed: London, 1945

Prologue and Three Acts

Cast in order of singing:

Hobson, a carrier and village constable	*bass*
Swallow, a lawyer and coroner of the Borough	*bass*
Peter Grimes, a fisherman	*tenor*
Mrs Sedley, a rentier widow of an East India Company's factor	*mezzo-soprano*
Ellen Orford, a widow, schoolmistress of the Borough	*soprano*

Auntie, landlady of the Boar Inn	*contralto*
Bob Boles, a fisherman and Methodist	*tenor*
Balstrode, a retired merchant skipper	*baritone*
The two nieces, 'main attractions' of the Boar	*sopranos*
Ned Keene, apothecary and quack	*baritone*
The Rev. Horace Adams, the Rector	*tenor*

[The part of John, Grimes's new apprentice, is silent.]
Chorus of townspeople and fisherfolk

*The scene is laid in the Borough, a small fishing
town on the East Coast of England about 1830*

LIKE *Wozzeck*, *Peter Grimes* has a persecuted misfit for its
protagonist – a characteristically 20th-century post-Freudian
operatic choice, we may think. Thus, beyond the multiplicity
of individual tensions, the opera presents a conflict between the
lone fisherman and the community in which he works. The
moral scales are not, as usual in opera, tilted conveniently in
the hero's favour. When the villagers recoil from Grimes's
cruelty, we do so too; but such is the illumination afforded by
the music that we sympathize with him as well. We feel (to
quote the libretto itself) 'the pity and the truth'.

'The Borough', the setting for this opera (and for Crabbe's
poem of 1810 on which it is based), is a thinly disguised form
of Aldeburgh, the Suffolk fishing village where Britten has
made his home. 'I am native, rooted here,' declares Grimes,
and we may perhaps imagine the composer – born not far
away, at Lowestoft – speaking through him.

PROLOGUE

The villagers are assembled in the Borough's Moot Hall for an
inquest on Peter Grimes's apprentice, who has died at sea.
Hobson calls Peter Grimes, who is questioned by Swallow,
acting as coroner. Grimes explains the circumstances of the
death and of his return with the boy's body (there is a brief
intervention from Mrs Sedley, one of the leading gossips, and
the mutterings of the villagers are heard, silenced by Hobson).
Swallow advises Grimes to manage without a boy apprentice

in future and returns a verdict that death was due to accidental circumstances. Grimes, suspected of treating the boy brutally, asks to be confronted by his accusers, but Hobson clears the court and Grimes is left alone with the schoolmistress, Ellen Orford, who gently tries to console him.

ACT I

As dawn rises, the Borough's men and women set to work preparing the nets. A fisherman calls to Auntie, landlady of the Boar, who beckons some of them to the inn despite the protestations of Bob Boles, a Methodist. The retired skipper, Balstrode, comments on the approach of a storm. The Rector and Mrs Sedley pass, greeted by Auntie's two nieces, to whom the apothecary Keene calls out jocularly. Swallow, too, passes by.

From a distance, Grimes's voice is heard asking for help. At first nobody moves, but then Keene and Balstrode haul at the capstan for him while Boles talks to Auntie of Grimes's sinfulness. Keene tells Grimes that he has obtained an apprentice for him, and asks Hobson to fetch the boy in his cart. Hobson at first refuses, to the approval of the people assembled, but when Ellen Orford offers to look after the boy on the journey he agrees, and they depart. After asking Keene for a supply of the laudanum to which she is addicted, Mrs Sedley goes off.

Balstrode draws attention to the gathering storm, and he, Keene, Auntie, the nieces, Boles and the chorus sing of its approach and the rising of the tide. The fisher-folk fasten their boats and go into the Boar for shelter, leaving Balstrode and Grimes alone. Balstrode advises Grimes to leave the Borough, but despite the malice of the people Grimes finds the ties too strong. As the winds become fiercer, he describes to Balstrode the scene of the boy's death, and goes on to tell of his dreams of becoming wealthy, marrying Ellen and winning the Borough's respect. Balstrode leaves Grimes as the storm breaks.

The scene changes to the interior of the Boar. Mrs Sedley is there, waiting for Keene. Balstrode, then Boles and other fishermen arrive, struggling with the door in the fierce wind as they enter. The nieces come down, frightened, from their bedroom. More people enter with news of the storm's ravages. Boles, unaccustomed to drink, becomes tipsy; he behaves importunately to one of the nieces and is dealt with by Balstrode.

Keene and others come in (Keene mentioning a landslide on the cliff near Grimes's hut), soon followed by Grimes. Mrs Sedley faints, and the others mutter 'Talk of the devil', in a general unease. To the puzzlement of the others, Grimes philosophizes: 'Now the Great Bear and Pleiades where earth moves are drawing up the clouds of human grief.' To break the tension Balstrode calls for a song. Keene obliges, and soon all are singing a round, 'Old Joe has gone fishing'. Its liveliness is shattered when Ellen, Hobson and the new apprentice enter, soaked and storm-beaten. Auntie tries to make them warm and comfortable, but Grimes is in a hurry to be off. Ellen hands the boy over and, to the disapproval of all but her, Grimes takes him off into the howling storm.

ACT II

It is Sunday morning. Villagers are moving towards the church as the bell sounds, and Ellen comes in with the boy. She decides to stay on the beach rather than go to church, and sits knitting and talking to the boy as the voices of the congregation and the Rector are heard from the church. She suddenly sees that the boy's clothing is torn and that his neck is bruised. The suspicion that Grimes is ill-treating the boy is not lost on Mrs Sedley, who is passing.

Grimes enters excitedly. He has seen a large shoal and wants the apprentice to come, despite Ellen's reminder that it is the boy's day of rest. She reproaches Grimes, wondering whether they were right to plan a future together. Grimes cannot suppress his fury: he strikes her and goes off with the boy, seen by Auntie, Keene and Boles. Keene observes that 'Grimes is at his exercise', and as the people leave the church (among them Balstrode, who tries to calm the angry Boles and Mrs Sedley) they join in the angry buzz of conversation about Grimes 'at his exercise'. Swallow, the Rector and others join in. Eventually Boles starts haranguing the crowd against the apprentice system, against Grimes and against Ellen ('She helped him in his cruel games').

Ellen explains that she and Grimes planned to care for the boy's welfare but the crowd is in a jeering and angry mood, and Auntie leads Ellen off. The Rector proposes a deputation of the village men to Grimes's hut, to find out the truth about Grimes's suspected cruelties once and for all. Led by Hobson, beating his drum, and watched by the women, they go off. Ellen, Auntie and the nieces ponder upon the bitterness of woman's lot.

The scene changes to Grimes's hut. Grimes enters, pushing the boy before him; he throws the boy's sea clothes to him and shouts at the sobbing lad to prepare himself quickly. Seeing the sea seething with fish, he again dreams of a less troubled future with Ellen, then recalls the last apprentice. Sounds of the approaching procession are heard; realizing that the villagers are coming, he thinks the boy has been talking and becomes angry, telling him to hurry and get ready to go down by the cliff. Grimes warns his apprentice to take care. The boy goes first: he slips and, screaming, falls down the cliff to his death. Grimes goes out.

The villagers, led by the Rector, Swallow and Keene, enter the hut. They are surprised to find it empty and well-kept; Swallow says that there seems no cause for alarm, and that they should no longer interfere. They all go, except Balstrode, who looks around the hut, sees the precipice outside, and follows the route Grimes took down the cliff.

ACT III

From the beach, in the evening, the distant sound of a Barn Dance is heard from the Moot Hall. Swallow comes out of the hall, tipsily bantering with the two nieces. Keene follows a little later and is accosted by Mrs Sedley: she tells him that Grimes and his apprentice have not been seen for two days and she feels sure Grimes has killed the boy. He takes little notice and soon eludes her. The Rector and others come out of the Moot Hall – the time has arrived for the older people to leave the festivities and go home to bed.

Mrs Sedley broods on the situation, concealing herself when

Ellen and Balstrode pass by. They are talking of Grimes: his boat is in but they have not seen him, though they have found the boy's embroidered jersey by the sea. They go off, full of foreboding, hoping they can help Grimes.

As they disappear, Mrs Sedley runs off to the Boar, asking for Swallow. Auntie tries to send her away but Swallow hears the commotion and comes out. Mrs Sedley tells him that Grimes is back and he promptly orders Hobson, as village constable, to organize a search for him. The people, angry and suspicious, assemble, crying 'Peter Grimes! Peter Grimes!'

Some hours later, Grimes enters, weary and half-demented. There is a thick fog: in the distance the cries of the villagers are still audible. Grimes's thoughts are a jumble as he recalls the fate of the apprentices (he repeats the Coroner's verdict of 'Accidental circumstances!') and other events which have driven him to his present crisis. The voices grow nearer. Ellen and Balstrode arrive. She wants to lead Grimes home, but Balstrode tells him [spoken] to take his boat out to sea and sink it. He helps Grimes to put out, then leads Ellen away.

For a moment the beach is deserted. Then, as another day dawns, the people come out to start their work. Swallow reports to some fishermen that a boat has been seen sinking out at sea beyond the reach of help. The other villagers come out too. They sing of the inexorable tides, for the life of the Borough in joy and sorrow is governed by the sea.

*   *   *   *   *

Peter Grimes derives its characteristic and powerful musical shape from Britten's use of orchestral interludes which not only indicate the passage of time but serve as comment and convey atmosphere. The sequence is: Court-room – *Interlude 1 (Dawn)* – Beach – *Interlude 2 (Storm)* – Inn – *Interlude 3 (Sunday morning)* – Beach – *Interlude 4 (Procession to hut)* – Hut – *Interlude 5 (Moonlight)* – Beach at night – *Interlude 6 (Peter's disturbed mind)* – Beach, just before dawn. The titles we have given to Interludes 4 and 6 are our own; those of the others are Britten's own, not from the opera itself but from the suite called 'Four Sea Interludes' (in the order 1–3–5–2) published for orchestra alone.

There is, however, no overture, and almost as soon as the curtain rises Britten begins to differentiate Grimes from his fellow villagers. Swallow reads out the formula for taking the oath ('I swear by Almighty God', etc.) punctuated by heavy staccato brass discords; Grimes not only alters the rhythm but also sings it more slowly, refusing to rattle it off emptily, and is accompanied by sustained strings.

Peter's only friend in the court-room is Ellen Orford; they are finally left alone together and at the end of their duet, singing unaccompanied and in unison, they sing a phrase marked by a distinctive upward leap which is a kind of motive representing Peter's striving for a happier life and also representing the compassion Ellen offers:

The chorus in the role of 'the people' plays a major part in the opera, at two points joining in with the soloists in big, cumulative set-pieces: the round 'Old Joe has gone fishing' (Act I) and the derisive 'Grimes is at his exercise!' – first heard as:

Note the 'chiming-in' of the second voice as if gossip were spreading. This musical phrase is actually sung first of all to different words by Grimes himself ('God have mercy upon me') and is afterwards carried over into the Passacaglia which joins Interlude 4 as the men are marching towards Grimes's hut: it may be called a 'persecution' theme.

The chorus also utters the menacing cries of 'Peter Grimes! Peter Grimes!' which are still heard, off-stage, in the final scene as Grimes recalls the past – and, musically, recalls the previous music of the opera. We give the passage where he quotes his own philosophizing (from Act I, in the inn) and then quotes the round that was also sung in the inn; in between comes the distant shout of the chorus and the dull yet alarming note of the foghorn (played in the opera-house by an off-stage tuba):

Ellen is denied the tragic farewell aria which an earlier type of opera might have given her; instead the other villagers (soloists and chorus) remind us that fishermen's work goes on though this man or that boy be lost. The final bars recall the first orchestral interlude – dawn recalls dawn.

EPILOGUE: THE MODERN SCENE

THAT Britten has written some operatic works which are not for the opera-house at all is symptomatic of the suspicion with which many composers of different countries have viewed the old-fashioned operatic form and the conservatively-inclined managements and audiences of established opera houses. Opera has become in the 20th century, as it was not in Mozart's or Verdi's day, a kind of 'classic' theatre, with interest concentrated on the modes of performance of a little-changing standard repertory. There is a case for saying that the Broadway musical has inherited the theatrical aliveness, and the audiences eager for novelty, which once belonged to opera.

It is significant that most successful of Italian-born composers since Puccini, Gian-Carlo Menotti (born 1918), has established himself mainly through 'theatre' rather than 'opera' channels – and, moreover, lives in America and writes his own librettos in English. In *The Consul* (1950) he brought Puccini up to date (the opening scene, with a fugitive dashing in, exactly parallels *Tosca*); in *Amahl and the Night Visitors* (1951) he wrote the first opera for television. The successfully horrific one-act opera *The Medium* (1946) was, remarkably, later filmed with the composer as film director. In 1963 he brought out *The Last Savage*; more recent works include *Help, help, the Globolinks!* (1968).

In Italy itself, considerable esteem is given to the veteran Ildebrando Pizzetti (born 1880), whose works include an operatic version (1958) of T. S. Eliot's *Murder in the Cathedral*. But the modern Italian opera which has won most notice elsewhere is *The Prisoner* (Il Prigioniero; 1950), in one act, by Luigi Dallapiccola (born 1904). Its story of 'torture by hope', particularly relevant to the crisis of human freedom in the 20th century, is treated with an un-sensational, oratorio-like seriousness. His *Odysseus* was produced in 1968.

Among German composers Paul Hindemith (1895–1963)

retained a traditionalist approach to opera, as in *Mathis the Painter* (Mathis der Maler; 1938) and his setting of Thornton Wilder's play *The Long Christmas Dinner* (1961). But Kurt Weill (1900–1950) recoiled from the grandiosity and romanticism of opera in favour of a simpler, more drect, more popular approach. The flavour of the modern song-hit is strong in his two most notable collaborations with the playwright Bertolt Brecht, *The Rise and Fall of the City of Mahagonny* (Aufstieg und Fall der Stadt Mahagonny; 1930) and *The Threepenny Opera* (Die Dreigroschenoper; 1928), both savagely satirical of modern capitalist society. The later uses a modernized version of the plot, though not of the music, of *The Beggar's Opera* (see page 23).

Equally radical in his approach to the musical theatre is another German composer Carl Orff (born 1895. Leaving aside those of his stage works which are really cantatas mimed by dancers, we may note especially *The Clever Girl* (Die Kluge; 1943) with its deliberately simple tunes, repetitive rhythms, and artless, fairy-tale atmosphere, and *Antigone* (1949), a German setting of Sophocles's play which gives complete sovereignty to the words, the voices mainly reciting on one or two notes and the orchestra mainly punctuating – but with impressive musical effect.

Of today's younger German composers the most notable is Hans Werner Henze (born 1926) with a succession of works – *Boulevard Solitude* (1952), a modernization of the story of Manon; *King Stag* (König Hirsch; 1956); *The Prince of Homburg* (Der Prinz von Homburg; 1960); *Elegy for Young Lovers* (1961), with an English libretto by W. H. Auden and Chester Kallman; *The Young Lord* (Der Junge Lord, 1965), and *The Bassarids* (1968), also with Auden and Kallman. Among his prominent German contemporaries are Bernd Alois Zimmermann (b. 1918) especially for *The Soldiers* (Die Soldaten; 1965) and Giselher Klebe (b. 1925), whose works include *Figaro Seeks a Divorce* (Figaro lässt sich scheiden; 1963).

In France, Maurice Ravel (1875–1937) shared the addiction of his contemporary, Debussy, and of other French composers to Spanish themes. He wrote a one-act comedy

L'heure espagnole (1911; an ambiguous title, probably best translated 'Spanish Time') in which clock-chimes enter the score as a naturalistic element. A similar naturalism shows in the cries of various creatures in *The Child and the Spells* (L'enfant et les sortilèges; 1925): but here any grotesqueness is subordinated to a deep human tenderness not always evident in Ravel.

Among other Frenchmen Francis Poulenc (1899–1963) explored two extremes – tragic, Mussorgsky-influenced chronicle opera in 1957 in *The Carmelites* (to use the title under which *Dialogues des Carmélites* has been given in Britain) and near-operetta ten years before in his comic treatment of myth, *The Breasts of Tiresias* (Les Mamelles de Tirésias). The operas of Darius Milhaud (born 1892) are sometimes revived. Some success has been won by *Joan of Arc at the Stake* (Jeanne d'arc au Bûcher; 1938) by Arthur Honegger (1852–1955), a semi-opera in which the heroine does not sing.

Manuel de Falla (1876–1946), the most notable of Spanish composers, employed a device of deliberate artificiality in *Master Peter's Puppet Show* (El Retablo de Maese Pedro, 1923), based on an episode from *Don Quixote*: there is an inner play, enacted by puppets, commented on by the other characters (who may themselves be bigger puppets, or live actors). The artificiality is admirably set off by the stylized music, which includes a part for harpsichord.

Russia, since the 1917 Revolution, has pursued an artistic path of its own, with composers subjected to varying degrees of political pressure. Dmitri Shostakovich (born 1906) wrote an opera called *Lady Macbeth of the Mtsensk District* which met with a 'scandalous' success for its supposed modernity in 1935 and with a 'scandalous' suppression by Communist fiat in 1936. Under the new title of *Katerina Ismailova* (the name of the heroine) it reappeared in a revised version in 1963. Other Soviet operas which have won a following in Russia include *The Decembrists* (1953) by Yuri Shaporin (b. 1887) and *The Taming of the Shrew* (1957; after Shakespeare) by Vissarion Shebalin (1902–63).

But it was with the return to Russia of Sergei Prokofiev

(1891–1953) in the mid-1930s that the Soviet regime began to enjoy the presence of the only major operatic composer it has yet known. Of his operas in Soviet patriotic mould, most acclaim has gone to Prokofiev's version of Tolstoy's *War and Peace* (final version first performed posthumously, 1955). An admirable comic spirit is evident in *Betrothal in the Monastery* (1946), also known as *The Duenna*, after the play by Sheridan on which it is based. Before his voluntary exile from Russia, Prokofiev completed *The Gambler* in 1916, but it was not performed until 1928. He worked on *The Fiery Angel* (responding intensely to its story of medieval passions) from 1919 to 1927, but it did not reach the stage until 1955. More immediate success was won by *Love for Three Oranges* (produced at Chicago in 1921), couched in a deliberately fable-like, artificial vein of detached comedy.

In Hungary, Béla Bartók (1881–1945) wrote, for only two characters, his *Bluebeard's Castle* (1918): its mixture of scenic demands and symbolic meaning make it difficult to stage, but it has both pathos and a sense of theatrical climax.

In America, no native-born composer has approached Menotti's success. But a certain notoriety was won by *Four Saints in Three Acts* (1934) by Virgil Thomson (b.1896) in which a non-logical text by Gertrude Stein was set to artfully artless music for an all-Negro cast. It quite a different way George Gershwin (1898–1937) used Negro singers (and Negro and jazz idioms) for his *Porgy and Bess* (1938), which has become an 'American classic'; it might have qualified for higher status had its music been as apt in dramatic shape as in melodic power. A brand of 'folky' operas by more conventionally trained composers – we may instance *Ballad of Baby Doe* (1956) by Douglas Moore (b. 1893) – has proved unexportable. The most notable of today's younger American composers of opera are probably Carlisle Floyd (b. 1926) whose work includes *Wuthering Heights* (1958) and Jack Beeson (b. 1921) with *Lizzie Borden* (1965).

That versatile composer-conductor-commentator, Leonard Bernstein (b.1918) brought out his *Candide* (1956) as a musical, though it is near-operatic in resource. Its commercial failure seemed to indicate that it was too light for opera-goers, too heavy (and too detached in spirit) for those who flocked to the same composer's *West Side Story*. Readers may draw their own moral.

Postcript, 1969. Is opera a museum art? Is it still relevant in contemporary society? Questions like these are being asked, if not wherever opera is performed, at least wherever young composers forgather. There is widespread impatience with a form so stylized and whose appeal is directed at an audience of so restricted a social grouping. The composer and conductor Pierre Boulez, has gone so far as to say that opera houses should be 'blown up' (in an article first published in Germany, reprinted in *Opera* magazine, June 1968).

Yet many young composers continue to feel drawn towards the form, and we may note some of the remarkable crop of recent operas by British composers, nearly all of the younger-than-Britten generation. Those by Malcolm Williamson (born 1931 in Australia) include *Our Man in Havana* (1963), *The Violins of Saint-Jacques* (1966) and two for children, *The Happy Prince* (1965) and *Julius Caesar Jones* (1966); those of Richard Rodney Bennett (born 1936) include *The Mines of Sulphur* (1965) and *A Penny for a Song* (1967). Nicholas Maw (born 1935), after composing *One Man Show* (1964) became the first British composer to have a new work commissioned by the Glyndebourne Festival (*The Rising of the Moon*); Alexander Goehr (born in Germany, 1932) wrote his *Arden Must Die* (1967) to a commission from the Hamburg State Opera (in German, as 'Arden muss sterben'), and in 1968 the Aldeburgh Festival (where so many of Britten's operas had originated) produced *Punch and Judy* by Harrison Birtwistle (born 1934). *Hamlet* by Humphrey Searle (born 1915) and *Full Circle* by Robin Orr were both produced in 1968, respectively by the Hamburg State Opera and by Scottish Opera.

In Sweden – where, in 1959, *Aniara* by Karl-Birger Blomdahl (1916–68) had brought the modernity of a space-navigation plot and a partly electronic score into opera – a challenge

to the conventional theatrical 'spacing' of opera was successfully issued by Lars Johan Werle (b. 1926). In his *Dreaming
About Thérèse* (Drömmen om Thérèse) of 1964, the audience
encircles the stage and the orchestral players (who change
positions during the course of the work) encircle the audience.

BIBLIOGRAPHY

E DWARD J. DENT'S *Opera* (Penguin Books; revised edition 1949) is a brilliant one-man survey of the whole subject which has now inevitably become out of date. For the general reader, nothing has replaced it. *The World of Opera* by Wallace Brockway and Herbert Weinstock (Methuen, 1963) is a lively American account which quotes many other authorities and which pursues the history of opera into the 1960s, though not always quite dependably.

To the analysis of individual operas Ernest Newman brought his unique blend of musical, literary and historical skill in *Opera Nights* (1943), *Wagner Nights* (1949) and *More Opera Nights* (1955), all published by Putnam. The most comprehensive single volume of this nature in English is Kobbé's *Complete Opera Book*, revised and edited by the Earl of Harewood (Putnam, 1954).

Of books about the composers treated in detail in the present volume, those listed below are recommended to the general readers as the best available in English at the beginning of 1969. All are published in London except as stated. The dates mentioned, which are those of the most recent editions of each book, are of some importance: in several cases the newer edition incorporates considerable emendations relating to fact or critical opinion.

Printed librettos and paper-backed booklets on individual operas (including those issued with gramophone records) are not listed here, but often provide useful background information. So do the introductions to certain modern editions of the scores themselves.

PURCELL
   Franklin B. Zimmermann, *Henry Purcell*. Macmillan, 1967

Robert Etheridge Moore, *Henry Purcell and the Restoration Theatre*. Heinemann, 1961

HANDEL

Gerald Abraham (ed.), *Handel: a symposium*. O.U.P., 1954
Otto Erich Deutsch, *Handel: A Documentary Biography*. Black, 1955
Stanley Sadie, *Handel*. Calder, 1962

GLUCK

Martin Cooper, *Gluck*. Chatto & Windus, 1935
Alfred Einstein, *Gluck* (tr. Eric Blom). Dent, 1936
Patricia Howard, *Gluck and the Rebirth of Modern Opera*. Barrie & Rockliff, 1963

MOZART

Edward J. Dent, *Mozart's Operas*. O.U.P., 1947
Eric Blom, *Mozart*. Dent, 1952
Stanley Sadie, *Mozart*. Calder, 1964

BEETHOVEN

Marion M. Scott, *Beethoven*. Dent, 1934
Romain Rolland, *Beethoven the Creator* (tr. Ernest Newman). Gollancz, 1929

WEBER

John Warrack, *Carl Maria von Weber*. Hamilton, 1968

ROSSINI

Stendhal (Henri Beyle) *Life of Rossini* (tr. Richard N. Coe). Calder, 1956
Francis Toye, *Rossini: a study in tragi-comedy*. Barker, 1959

DONIZETTI

William Ashbrook, *Donizetti*. Cassell 1965

VERDI

Spike Huges, *Famous Verdi Operas*. Hale 1968
Vincent Sheean, *Orpheus at Eighty*. Cassell, 1959
Francis Toye, *Verdi: his life and works*. Gollancz, 1962
Frank Walker, *The Man Verdi*. Dent, 1962

WAGNER

Robert L. Jacobs, *Wagner*. Dent, 1935
Ernest Newman, *Wagner Nights*. Putnam, 1949

Ernest Newman, *The Life of Richard Wagner* [4 vols].
  Cassell, 1933–47
BELLINI
  Leslie Orrey *Bellini*. Dent 1969
  Robert Donington, *Wagner's 'Ring' and its Symbols*. Faber,
  1963
BERLIOZ
  David Cairns (Ed. and tr.), *The Memoirs of Hector Berlioz*.
  Gollancz, 1969.
  J. H. Elliot, *Berlioz*. Dent, 1938
  Jacques Barzun, *Berlioz and the Romantic Century*. Gol-
  lancz, 1957
GOUNOD
  Norman Demuth, *Introduction to the Music of Gounod*.
  Dobson, 1950
OFFENBACH
  S. Kracauer, *Offenbach and the Paris of his Time*. Con-
  stable, 1937
BIZET
  Winton Dean, *Bizet*. Dent. 1948
  Mina Curtiss, *Bizet and his World*. Secker & Warburg, 1959
MASSENET
  Henry T. Finck, *Massenet and his Operas*. Lane, 1910
DEBUSSY
  Edward Lockspeiser, *Debussy*. Dent, 1951
SMETANA
  Miloslav Maly, *Smetana*. Orbis, Prague, 1956
JANÁČEK
  Hans Holländer, *Leoš Janáček: his life and works* (tr. Paul
  Hamburger). Calder, 1963
BORODIN
  Serge Dianin, *Borodin* (tr. Robert Lord). O.U.P., 1963
MUSSORGSKY
  M. D. Calvocoressi, *Modest Mussorgsky: his life and works*.
  Rockliff, 1956
RIMSKY-KORSAKOV
  N. A. Rimsky-Korsakov, *My Musical Life* (tr. J. A. Joffe).
  Knopf, New York, 1942

TCHAIKOVSKY

   Gerald Abraham (ed.), *Tchaikovsky: a symposium.* Drummond, 1945

   Herbert Weinstock, *Tchaikovsky.* Cassell, 1946

PUCCINI

   Mosco Carner, *Puccini: a critical biography.* Duckworth, 1958

   Spike Hughes, *Famous Puccini Operas.* Hale, 1959

RICHARD STRAUSS

   Norman Del Mar, *Richard Strauss: a critical commentary on his life and work.* Barrie & Rockliff vol. 1, 1963, vol. 2, 1969

   William S. Mann, *Richard Strauss: a critical study of the operas.* Cassell, 1964

BERG

   Hans F. Redlich, *Alban Berg: the man and his music.* Calder, 1957

STRAVINSKY

   Roman Vlad, *Stravinsky* (tr. F. & A. Fuller). O.U.P. (2nd ed.), 1962

   Eric Walter White, *Stravinsky: The Composer and his Works.* Faber, 1967

BRITTEN

   Eric Walter White, *Benjamin Britten: a sketch of his life and works.* Boosey & Hawkes, 1954

   A. Gishford (ed.), *Tribute to Benjamin Britten on his Fiftieth Birthday.* Faber & Faber, 1963

   Patricia Howard, *The Operas of Benjamin Britten.* Barrie & Rockliff, 1969